myPerspectives®

AMERICAN LITERATURE

SAVVAS
LEARNING COMPANY

ISBN-13: 978-1-418-37125-8
ISBN-10:   1-418-37125-4

1   21

Welcome!

*my*Perspectives™ *English Language Arts* is a student-centered learning environment where you will analyze text, cite evidence, and respond critically about your learning. You will take ownership of your learning through goal-setting, reflection, independent text selection, and activities that allow you to collaborate with your peers.

Each unit of study includes selections of different genres—including multimedia—all related to a relevant and meaningful Essential Question. As you read, you will engage in activities that inspire thoughtful discussion and debate with your peers allowing you to formulate, and defend, your own perspectives.

*my*Perspectives *ELA* offers a variety of ways to interact directly with the text. You can annotate by writing in your print consumable, or you can annotate in your digital Student Edition. In addition, exciting technology allows you to access multimedia directly from your mobile device and communicate using an online discussion board!

We hope you enjoy using *my*Perspectives *ELA* as you develop the skills required to be successful throughout college and career.

Authors' Perspectives

*my*Perspectives is informed by a team of respected experts whose experiences working with students and study of instructional best practices have positively impacted education. From the evolving role of the teacher to how students learn in a digital age, our authors bring new ideas, innovations, and strategies that transform teaching and learning in today's competitive and interconnected world.

" The teaching of English needs to focus on engaging a new generation of learners. How do we get them excited about reading and writing? How do we help them to envision themselves as readers and writers? And, how can we make the teaching of English more culturally, socially, and technologically relevant? Throughout the curriculum, we've created spaces that enhance youth voice and participation and that connect the teaching of literature and writing to technological transformations of the digital age."

Ernest Morrell, Ph.D.

is the Macy professor of English Education at Teachers College, Columbia University, a class of 2014 Fellow of the American Educational Research Association, and the Past-President of the National Council of Teachers of English (NCTE). He is also the Director of Teachers College's Institute for Urban and Minority Education (IUME). He is an award-winning author and in his spare time he coaches youth sports and writes poems and plays. Dr. Morrell has influenced the development of *my*Perspectives in Assessment, Writing & Research, Student Engagement, and Collaborative Learning.

Elfrieda Hiebert, Ph.D.

is President and CEO of TextProject, a nonprofit that provides resources to support higher reading levels. She is also a research associate at the University of California, Santa Cruz. Dr. Hiebert has worked in the field of early reading acquisition for 45 years, first as a teacher's aide and teacher of primary-level students in California and, subsequently, as a teacher and researcher. Her research addresses how fluency, vocabulary, and knowledge can be fostered through appropriate texts. Dr. Hiebert has influenced the development of *my*Perspectives in Vocabulary, Text Complexity, and Assessment.

" The signature of complex text is challenging vocabulary. In the systems of vocabulary, it's important to provide ways to show how concepts can be made more transparent to students. We provide lessons and activities that develop a strong vocabulary and concept foundation—a foundation that permits students to comprehend increasingly more complex text."

Kelly Gallagher, M.Ed.

teaches at Magnolia High School in Anaheim, California, where he is in his thirty-first year. He is the former co-director of the South Basin Writing Project at California State University, Long Beach. Mr. Gallagher has influenced the development of *my*Perspectives in Writing, Close Reading, and the Role of Teachers.

" The *my*Perspectives classroom is dynamic. The teacher inspires, models, instructs, facilitates, and advises students as they evolve and grow. When teachers guide students through meaningful learning tasks and then pass them ownership of their own learning, students become engaged and work harder. This is how we make a difference in student achievement—by putting students at the center of their learning and giving them the opportunities to choose, explore, collaborate, and work independently."

" It's critical to give students the opportunity to read a wide range of highly engaging texts and to immerse themselves in exploring powerful ideas and how these ideas are expressed. In *my*Perspectives, we focus on building up students' awareness of how academic language works, which is especially important for English language learners."

Jim Cummins, Ph.D.

is a Professor Emeritus in the Department of Curriculum, Teaching and Learning of the University of Toronto. His research focuses on literacy development in multilingual school contexts as well as on the potential roles of technology in promoting language and literacy development. In recent years, he has been working actively with teachers to identify ways of increasing the literacy engagement of learners in multilingual school contexts. Dr. Cummins has influenced the development of *my*Perspectives in English Language Learner and English Language Development support.

UNIT (1) Writing Freedom

Words That Shaped a Nation

UNIT INTRODUCTION

UNIT ACTIVITY AND VIDEO 2

LAUNCH TEXT: ARGUMENT MODEL
Totally Free? 6

 WHOLE-CLASS LEARNING

HISTORICAL PERSPECTIVES
Focus Period: 1750–1800
A New Nation 12

ANCHOR TEXT: FOUNDATIONAL DOCUMENT
Declaration of Independence
Thomas Jefferson. 18
  ⊙ MEDIA CONNECTION: President John F. Kennedy
  reads the Declaration of Independence

ANCHOR TEXT: FOUNDATIONAL DOCUMENTS
Preamble to the Constitution
Gouverneur Morris
Bill of Rights
James Madison 31

ANCHOR TEXT: SPEECH
Speech in the Convention
Benjamin Franklin. 42
  ⊙ MEDIA CONNECTION: The U.S. Constitution

MEDIA: IMAGE GALLERY
The American Revolution:
Visual Propaganda 53

───────────────────────────

⊙ PERFORMANCE TASK
  WRITING FOCUS
  Write an Argument 60

SMALL-GROUP LEARNING

EXPOSITORY NONFICTION
from America's Constitution:
A Biography
Akhil Reed Amar. 73

MEDIA: GRAPHIC NOVEL
from The United States Constitution:
A Graphic Adaptation
Jonathan Hennessey and Aaron
McConnell 83

AUTOBIOGRAPHY
from The Interesting Narrative of
the Life of Olaudah Equiano
Olaudah Equiano. 93

LETTER | BIOGRAPHY
Letter to John Adams
Abigail Adams 104

from Dear Abigail: The Intimate
Lives and Revolutionary Ideas
of Abigail Adams and Her
Two Remarkable Sisters
Diane Jacobs .107

SPEECH
Gettysburg Address
Abraham Lincoln 120

───────────────────────────

⊙ PERFORMANCE TASK
  SPEAKING AND LISTENING FOCUS
  Present an Argument 126

 COMPARE

INDEPENDENT LEARNING

ESSAY

from Democracy Is Not a Spectator Sport
Arthur Blaustein with Helen Matatov

SPEECH

Reflections on the Bicentennial of
the United States Constitution
Thurgood Marshall

POETRY COLLECTION

Speech to the Young
Speech to the Progress-Toward
Gwendolyn Brooks

The Fish *Elizabeth Bishop*

SHORT STORY

The Pedestrian *Ray Bradbury*

POLITICAL DOCUMENT

from the Iroquois Constitution
Dekanawidah, translated by Arthur C. Parker

ARGUMENT

from Common Sense
Thomas Paine

These selections can be accessed via the
Interactive Student Edition.

 PERFORMANCE-BASED
ASSESSMENT PREP

Review Evidence for an Argument . . . 133

 PERFORMANCE-BASED
ASSESSMENT

Argument:
Essay and Video Commentary 134

UNIT REFLECTION

Reflect on the Unit 137

DIGITAL
PERSPECTIVES

• Unit Introduction Videos
• Media Selections/Media Enrichment
• Modeling Videos
• Selection Audio Recordings

Additional digital resources can be found in:

• Interactive Student Edition
• *my*Perspectives+

UNIT INTRODUCTION

UNIT ACTIVITY AND VIDEO 138

LAUNCH TEXT: NARRATIVE MODEL
from Up From Slavery
Booker T. Washington 142

 ## WHOLE-CLASS LEARNING

HISTORICAL PERSPECTIVES
Focus Period: 1800–1870
An American Identity. 148

ANCHOR TEXT: ESSAY | POETRY COLLECTION
*from the Preface to the 1855 Edition of Leaves
of Grass* | *from* Song of Myself | I Hear America
Singing | On the Beach at Night Alone | America
Walt Whitman 154

COMPARE

ANCHOR TEXT: POETRY COLLECTION
The Soul selects her own Society – | The Soul
unto itself | Fame is a fickle food | They shut
me up in Prose – | There is a solitude of
space | I heard a Fly buzz – when I died – | I'm
Nobody! Who are you? *Emily Dickinson* . .172

MEDIA: RADIO BROADCAST
from Emily Dickinson
from Great Lives
BBC Radio 4 187

 PERFORMANCE TASK
WRITING FOCUS
Write a Personal Narrative 192

SMALL-GROUP LEARNING

PHILOSOPHICAL WRITING
from Nature |
from Self-Reliance
Ralph Waldo Emerson 205

PHILOSOPHICAL WRITING
from Walden |
from Civil Disobedience
Henry David Thoreau 215

MEDIA: PUBLIC DOCUMENTS
Innovators and Their Inventions 231

POETRY
The Love Song of J. Alfred Prufrock
T. S. Eliot 238

SHORT STORY
A Wagner Matinée
Willa Cather. 249

PERFORMANCE TASK
SPEAKING AND LISTENING FOCUS
Present a Personal Narrative 262

 INDEPENDENT LEARNING

 PERFORMANCE-BASED ASSESSMENT

NEWS ARTICLE

Sweet Land of . . . Conformity?
Claude Fischer

LITERARY CRITICISM

Reckless Genius
Galway Kinnell

SHORT STORY

Hamadi
Naomi Shihab Nye

SHORT STORY

Young Goodman Brown
Nathaniel Hawthorne

Narrative: Personal Narrative and
Storytelling Session 270

UNIT REFLECTION

Reflect on the Unit 273

These selections can be accessed via the Interactive Student Edition.

PERFORMANCE-BASED
ASSESSMENT PREP

Review Evidence for a Personal
Narrative. 269

DIGITAL
PERSPECTIVES

- Unit Introduction Videos
- Media Selections/Media Enrichments
- Modeling Videos
- Selection Audio Recordings

Additional digital resources can be found in:

- Interactive Student Edition
- *my*Perspectives+

UNIT ③ Power, Protest, and Change

A Spirit of Reform

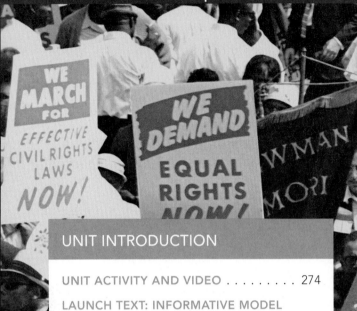

UNIT INTRODUCTION

UNIT ACTIVITY AND VIDEO 274

LAUNCH TEXT: INFORMATIVE MODEL
The Zigzag Road to Rights 278

WHOLE-CLASS LEARNING

HISTORICAL PERSPECTIVES
Focus Period: 1850–1890
Civil War and Social Change 284

ANCHOR TEXT: SPEECH
from What to the Slave
Is the Fourth of July?
Frederick Douglass 289

ANCHOR TEXT: SPEECH
Second Inaugural Address
Abraham Lincoln 301

MEDIA: IMAGE GALLERY
Perspectives on Lincoln 311

PERFORMANCE TASK

WRITING FOCUS
Write an Informative Essay 318

SMALL-GROUP LEARNING

SPEECH
Ain't I a Woman?
Sojourner Truth 331

COMPARE

PUBLIC DOCUMENT
Declaration of Sentiments
Elizabeth Cady Stanton 339

MEDIA: PODCAST
Giving Women the Vote
Sandra Sleight-Brennan 347

SHORT STORY
The Story of an Hour
Kate Chopin 353

LEGAL OPINION
Brown v. Board of Education:
Opinion of the Court
Earl Warren 361

PERFORMANCE TASKS

SPEAKING AND LISTENING FOCUS
Hold a Panel Discussion 372

RESEARCH FOCUS
Research Presentation 374

 INDEPENDENT LEARNING

POETRY COLLECTION 1

I, Too | The Negro Speaks of Rivers |
Refugee in America | Dream Variations
Langston Hughes

POETRY COLLECTION 2

Douglass *Paul Laurence Dunbar*
The Fifth Fact *Sarah Browning*
Who Burns for the Perfection of Paper
Martín Espada

HISTORY

from The Warmth of Other Suns
Isabel Wilkerson

ESSAY

What a Factory Can Teach a Housewife
Ida Tarbell

PERSUASIVE ESSAY

from Books as Bombs *Louis Menand*

MEDIA: PODCAST

A Balance Between Nature and Nurture
Gloria Steinem

These selections can be accessed via the
Interactive Student Edition.

 PERFORMANCE-BASED
ASSESSMENT PREP

Review Evidence for an
Informative Essay 387

 PERFORMANCE-BASED
ASSESSMENT

Informational Text:
Essay and Podcast 388

UNIT REFLECTION

Reflect on the Unit 391

DIGITAL ⌖
PERSPECTIVES

- Unit Introduction Videos
- Media Selections/Media Enrichment
- Modeling Videos
- Selection Audio Recordings

Additional digital resources can be found in:

- Interactive Student Edition
- *my*Perspectives+

UNIT (4) Grit and Grandeur

The Importance of Place

UNIT INTRODUCTION

UNIT ACTIVITY AND VIDEO 392

LAUNCH TEXT: EXPLANATORY MODEL
Planning Your Trip to Gold Country . . . 396

WHOLE-CLASS LEARNING

HISTORICAL PERSPECTIVES
Focus Period: 1880–1920
Bright Horizons, Challenging Realities . . 402

ANCHOR TEXT: MEMOIR
from Life on the Mississippi
Mark Twain 408
 ▶ MEDIA CONNECTION: Mark Twain and
Tom Sawyer

ANCHOR TEXT: SHORT STORY
The Notorious Jumping Frog
of Calaveras County
Mark Twain 419

ANCHOR TEXT: SHORT STORY
A White Heron
Sarah Orne Jewett 433

COMPARE

PERFORMANCE TASK
WRITING FOCUS
Write an Explanatory Essay 450

SMALL-GROUP LEARNING

LITERARY CRITICISM
A Literature of Place
Barry Lopez 463

MEDIA: FINE ART GALLERY
American Regional Art 473

COMPARE

AUTOBIOGRAPHY
from Dust Tracks on a Road
Zora Neale Hurston 481

POETRY COLLECTION 1
Chicago | Wilderness
Carl Sandburg 494
 🔊 MEDIA CONNECTION: Carl Sandburg
Reads "Wilderness"

MEDIA: PHOTO GALLERY
Sandburg's Chicago 503

COMPARE

POETRY COLLECTION 2
In the Longhouse, Oneida Museum
Roberta Hill 512
Cloudy Day
Jimmy Santiago Baca 514

MEMOIR
Introduction *from* The Way to Rainy
Mountain *N. Scott Momaday* 520

COMPARE

PERFORMANCE TASK
SPEAKING AND LISTENING FOCUS
Give an Explanatory Talk 532

INDEPENDENT LEARNING

SHORT STORY
The Rockpile
James Baldwin

POETRY
The Latin Deli: An Ars Poetica
Judith Ortiz Cofer

ESSAY
Untying the Knot
Annie Dillard

POETRY COLLECTION 3
The Wood-Pile | Birches
Robert Frost

These selections can be accessed via the Interactive Student Edition.

 PERFORMANCE-BASED ASSESSMENT PREP

Review Evidence for
an Explanatory Essay 539

 PERFORMANCE-BASED ASSESSMENT

Explanatory Text:
Essay and Oral Presentation 540

UNIT REFLECTION

Reflect on the Unit 543

DIGITAL ⌖ PERSPECTIVES

- Unit Introduction Videos
- Media Selections/Media Enrichment
- Modeling Videos
- Selection Audio Recordings

Additional digital resources can be found in:

- Interactive Student Edition
- *my*Perspectives+

UNIT INTRODUCTION

UNIT ACTIVITY AND VIDEO 544

LAUNCH TEXT: ARGUMENT MODEL
Is It Foolish to Fear?. 548

WHOLE-CLASS LEARNING

HISTORICAL PERSPECTIVES
Focus Period: 1920–1960
Times of Trouble 554

ANCHOR TEXT: DRAMA
The Crucible
Arthur Miller
Act I. 562
Act II 601
Act III. 629
Act IV. 661

MEDIA: AUDIO PERFORMANCE
The Crucible
L.A. Theatre Works 686

COMPARE

PERFORMANCE TASK
WRITING FOCUS
Write an Argument. 692

SMALL-GROUP LEARNING

AUTOBIOGRAPHY
from Farewell to Manzanar
*Jeanne Wakatsuki Houston
and James D. Houston* 705

MEDIA: VIDEO
Interview With George Takei
Archive of American Television 717

COMPARE

SHORT STORY
Antojos
Julia Alvarez. 723

PERFORMANCE TASK
SPEAKING AND LISTENING FOCUS
Present an Argument 738

(👤) INDEPENDENT LEARNING

MAGAZINE WRITING

What You Don't Know Can Kill You

Jason Daley

POETRY

Runagate Runagate

Robert Hayden

POETRY COLLECTION

1-800-FEAR

Jody Gladding

Bears at Raspberry Time

Hayden Carruth

For Black Women Who Are Afraid

Toi Derricotte

ESSAY

What Are You So Afraid Of?

Akiko Busch

These selections can be accessed via the Interactive Student Edition.

(✓) PERFORMANCE-BASED ASSESSMENT PREP

Review Evidence for an Argument . . .745

(✓) PERFORMANCE-BASED ASSESSMENT

Argument:
Essay and Speech. 746

UNIT REFLECTION

Reflect on the Unit 749

DIGITAL ⬀ PERSPECTIVES

- Unit Introduction Videos
- Media Selections/Media Enrichment
- Modeling Videos
- Selection Audio Recordings

Additional digital resources can be found in:

- Interactive Student Edition
- *my*Perspectives+

UNIT **6** Ordinary Lives, Extraordinary Tales

The American Short Story

UNIT INTRODUCTION

UNIT ACTIVITY AND VIDEO 750

LAUNCH TEXT: NARRATIVE MODEL

Old Man at the Bridge
Ernest Hemingway 754

 ## WHOLE-CLASS LEARNING

HISTORICAL PERSPECTIVES

Focus Period: 1950–Present
A Fast-Changing Society 760

ANCHOR TEXT: SHORT STORY

Everyday Use
Alice Walker 765

 MEDIA CONNECTION: Alice Walker's
"Everyday Use"

ANCHOR TEXT: SHORT STORY

Everything Stuck to Him
Raymond Carver 781

ANCHOR TEXT: SHORT STORY

The Leap
Louise Erdrich 795

 PERFORMANCE TASK

WRITING FOCUS
Write a Narrative 808

 ## SMALL-GROUP LEARNING

LITERARY HISTORY

A Brief History of the Short Story
D. F. McCourt 821

COMPARE

SHORT STORY

An Occurrence at
Owl Creek Bridge
Ambrose Bierce 829

SHORT STORY

The Jilting of Granny Weatherall
Katherine Anne Porter 843

PERFORMANCE TASK

SPEAKING AND LISTENING FOCUS
Present a Narrative 858

INDEPENDENT LEARNING

SHORT STORY
The Tell-Tale Heart
Edgar Allan Poe

SHORT STORY
The Man to Send Rain Clouds
Leslie Marmon Silko

SHORT STORY
Ambush
Tim O'Brien

SHORT STORY
Housepainting
Lan Samantha Chang

These selections can be accessed via the Interactive Student Edition.

 PERFORMANCE-BASED
ASSESSMENT PREP
Review Notes for a Narrative 865

 PERFORMANCE-BASED
ASSESSMENT

Narrative: Short Story and
Storytelling Session 866

UNIT REFLECTION

Reflect on the Unit 869

DIGITAL
PERSPECTIVES

- Unit Introduction Videos
- Media Selections/Media Enrichment
- Modeling Videos
- Selection Audio Recordings

Additional digital resources can be found in:
- Interactive Student Edition
- *my*Perspectives+

Standards Overview

The following English Language Arts standards will prepare you to succeed in college and your future career. The College and Career Readiness Anchor Standards define what you need to achieve by the end of high school, and the grade-specific Standards define what you need to know by the end of your current grade level.

The following provides an overview of the Standards.

Standards for Reading

College and Career Readiness Anchor Standards for Reading
Key Ideas and Details
1. Read closely to determine what the text says explicitly and to make logical inferences from it; cite specific textual evidence when writing or speaking to support conclusions drawn from the text.
2. Determine central ideas or themes of a text and analyze their development; summarize the key supporting details and ideas.
3. Analyze how and why individuals, events, and ideas develop and interact over the course of a text.
Craft and Structure
4. Interpret words and phrases as they are used in a text, including determining technical, connotative, and figurative meanings, and analyze how specific word choices shape meaning or tone.
5. Analyze the structure of texts, including how specific sentences, paragraphs, and larger portions of the text (e.g., a section, chapter, scene, or stanza) relate to each other and the whole.
6. Assess how point of view or purpose shapes the content and style of a text.
Integration of Knowledge and Ideas
7. Integrate and evaluate content presented in diverse formats and media, including visually and quantitatively, as well as in words.
8. Delineate and evaluate the argument and specific claims in a text, including the validity of the reasoning as well as the relevance and sufficiency of the evidence.
9. Analyze how two or more texts address similar themes or topics in order to build knowledge or to compare the approaches the authors take.
Range of Reading and Level of Text Complexity
10. Read and comprehend complex literary and informational texts independently and proficiently.

Grade 11 Reading Standards for Literature

Standard

Key Ideas and Details

Cite strong and thorough textual evidence to support analysis of what the text says explicitly as well as inferences drawn from the text, including determining where the text leaves matters uncertain.

Determine two or more themes or central ideas of a text and analyze their development over the course of the text, including how they interact and build on one another to produce a complex account; provide an objective summary of the text.

Analyze the impact of the author's choices regarding how to develop and relate elements of a story or drama (e.g., where a story is set, how the action is ordered, how the characters are introduced and developed).

Craft and Structure

Determine the meaning of words and phrases as they are used in the text, including figurative and connotative meanings; analyze the impact of specific word choices on meaning and tone, including words with multiple meanings or language that is particularly fresh, engaging, or beautiful. (Include Shakespeare as well as other authors.)

Analyze how an author's choices concerning how to structure specific parts of a text (e.g., the choice of where to begin or end a story, the choice to provide a comedic or tragic resolution) contribute to its overall structure and meaning as well as its aesthetic impact.

Analyze a case in which grasping a point of view requires distinguishing what is directly stated in a text from what is really meant (e.g., satire, sarcasm, irony, or understatement).

Integration of Knowledge and Ideas

Analyze multiple interpretations of a story, drama, or poem (e.g., recorded or live production of a play or recorded novel or poetry), evaluating how each version interprets the source text. (Include at least one play by Shakespeare and one play by an American dramatist.)

Demonstrate knowledge of eighteenth-, nineteenth- and early-twentieth-century foundational works of American literature, including how two or more texts from the same period treat similar themes or topics.

Range of Reading and Level of Text Complexity

By the end of grade 11, read and comprehend literature, including stories, dramas, and poems, in the grades 11–CCR text complexity band proficiently, with scaffolding as needed at the high end of the range.

Standards Overview

Grade 11 Reading Standards for Informational Text

Standard

Key Ideas and Details

Cite strong and thorough textual evidence to support analysis of what the text says explicitly as well as inferences drawn from the text, including determining where the text leaves matters uncertain.

Determine two or more central ideas of a text and analyze their development over the course of the text, including how they interact and build on one another to provide a complex analysis; provide an objective summary of the text.

Analyze a complex set of ideas or sequence of events and explain how specific individuals, ideas, or events interact and develop over the course of the text.

Craft and Structure

Determine the meaning of words and phrases as they are used in a text, including figurative, connotative, and technical meanings; analyze how an author uses and refines the meaning of a key term or terms over the course of a text (e.g., how Madison defines *faction* in *Federalist* No. 10).

Analyze and evaluate the effectiveness of the structure an author uses in his or her exposition or argument, including whether the structure makes points clear, convincing, and engaging.

Determine an author's point of view or purpose in a text in which the rhetoric is particularly effective, analyzing how style and content contribute to the power, persuasiveness or beauty of the text.

Integration of Knowledge and Ideas

Integrate and evaluate multiple sources of information presented in different media or formats (e.g., visually, quantitatively) as well as in words in order to address a question or solve a problem.

Delineate and evaluate the reasoning in seminal U.S. texts, including the application of constitutional principles and use of legal reasoning (e.g., in U.S. Supreme Court majority opinions and dissents) and the premises, purposes, and arguments in works of public advocacy (e.g., *The Federalist*, presidential addresses).

Analyze seventeenth-, eighteenth-, and nineteenth-century foundational U.S. documents of historical and literary significance (including The Declaration of Independence, the Preamble to the Constitution, the Bill of Rights, and Lincoln's Second Inaugural Address) for their themes, purposes, and rhetorical features.

Range of Reading and Level of Text Complexity

By the end of grade 11, read and comprehend literary nonfiction in the grades 11–CCR text complexity band proficiently, with scaffolding as needed at the high end of the range.

Standards for Writing

College and Career Readiness Anchor Standards for Writing

Text Types and Purposes

1. Write arguments to support claims in an analysis of substantive topics or texts, using valid reasoning and relevant and sufficient evidence.

2. Write informative/explanatory texts to examine and convey complex ideas and information clearly and accurately through the effective selection, organization, and analysis of content.

3. Write narratives to develop real or imagined experiences or events using effective technique, well-chosen details, and well-structured event sequences.

Production and Distribution of Writing

4. Produce clear and coherent writing in which the development, organization, and style are appropriate to task, purpose, and audience.

5. Develop and strengthen writing as needed by planning, revising, editing, rewriting, or trying a new approach.

6. Use technology, including the Internet, to produce and publish writing and to interact and collaborate with others.

Research to Build and Present Knowledge

7. Conduct short as well as more sustained research projects based on focused questions, demonstrating understanding of the subject under investigation.

8. Gather relevant information from multiple print and digital sources, assess the credibility and accuracy of each source, and integrate the information while avoiding plagiarism.

9. Draw evidence from literary or informational texts to support analysis, reflection, and research.

Range of Writing

10. Write routinely over extended time frames (time for research, reflection, and revision) and shorter time frames (a single sitting or a day or two) for a range of tasks, purposes, and audiences.

Grade 11 Writing Standards

Standard

Text Types and Purposes

Write arguments to support claims in an analysis of substantive topics or texts, using valid reasoning and relevant and sufficient evidence.

Introduce precise, knowledgeable claim(s), establish the significance of the claim(s), distinguish the claim(s) from alternate or opposing claims, and create an organization that logically sequences claim(s), counterclaims, reasons, and evidence.

Standards Overview

Grade 11 Writing Standards
Standard
Text Types and Purposes (continued)
Develop claim(s) and counterclaims fairly and thoroughly, supplying the most relevant evidence for each while pointing out the strengths and limitations of both in a manner that anticipates the audience's knowledge level, concerns, values, and possible biases.
Use words, phrases, and clauses as well as varied syntax to link the major sections of the text, create cohesion, and clarify the relationships between claim(s) and reasons, between reasons and evidence, and between claim(s) and counterclaims.
Establish and maintain a formal style and objective tone while attending to the norms and conventions of the discipline in which they are writing.
Provide a concluding statement or section that follows from and supports the argument presented.
Write informative/explanatory texts to examine and convey complex ideas, concepts, and information clearly and accurately through the effective selection, organization, and analysis of content.
Introduce a topic; organize complex ideas, concepts, and information so that each new element builds on that which precedes it to create a unified whole; include formatting (e.g., headings), graphics (e.g., figures, tables), and multimedia when useful to aiding comprehension.
Develop the topic thoroughly by selecting the most significant and relevant facts, extended definitions, concrete details, quotations, or other information and examples appropriate to the audience's knowledge of the topic.
Use appropriate and varied transitions and syntax to link the major sections of the text, create cohesion, and clarify the relationships among complex ideas and concepts.
Use precise language, domain-specific vocabulary, and techniques such as metaphor, simile, and analogy to manage the complexity of the topic.
Establish and maintain a formal style and objective tone while attending to the norms and conventions of the discipline in which they are writing.
Provide a concluding statement or section that follows from and supports the information or explanation presented (e.g., articulating implications or the significance of the topic).
Write narratives to develop real or imagined experiences or events using effective technique, well-chosen details, and well-structured event sequences.
Engage and orient the reader by setting out a problem, situation, or observation and its significance, establishing one or multiple point(s) of view, and introducing a narrator and/or characters; create a smooth progression of experiences or events.
Use narrative techniques, such as dialogue, pacing, description, reflection, and multiple plot lines, to develop experiences, events, and/or characters.

Grade 11 Writing Standards

Standard

Text Types and Purposes (continued)

Use a variety of techniques to sequence events so that they build on one another to create a coherent whole and build toward a particular tone and outcome (e.g., a sense of mystery, suspense, growth, or resolution).

Use precise words and phrases, telling details, and sensory language to convey a vivid picture of the experiences, events, setting, and/or characters.

Provide a conclusion that follows from and reflects on what is experienced, observed, or resolved over the course of the narrative.

Production and Distribution of Writing

Produce clear and coherent writing in which the development, organization, and style are appropriate to task, purpose, and audience. (Grade-specific expectations for writing types are defined in standards 1–3 above.)

Develop and strengthen writing as needed by planning, revising, editing, rewriting, or trying a new approach, focusing on addressing what is most significant for a specific purpose and audience. (Editing for conventions should demonstrate command of Language standards 1–3 up to and including grades 11–12)

Use technology, including the Internet, to produce, publish, and update individual or shared writing products in response to ongoing feedback, including new arguments or information.

Research to Build and Present Knowledge

Conduct short as well as more sustained research projects to answer a question (including a self-generated question) or solve a problem; narrow or broaden the inquiry when appropriate; synthesize multiple sources on the subject, demonstrating understanding of the subject under investigation.

Gather relevant information from multiple authoritative print and digital sources, using advanced searches effectively; assess the strengths and limitations of each source in terms of the task, purpose, and audience; integrate information into the text selectively to maintain the flow of ideas, avoiding plagiarism and overreliance on any one source and following a standard format for citation.

Draw evidence from literary or informational texts to support analysis, reflection, and research.

Apply *grades 11–12 Reading standards* to literature (e.g., "Demonstrate knowledge of eighteenth-, nineteenth- and early-twentieth-century foundational works of American literature, including how two or more texts from the same period treat similar themes or topics").

Apply *grades 11–12 Reading standards* to literary nonfiction (e.g., "Delineate and evaluate the reasoning in seminal U.S. texts, including the application of constitutional principles and use of legal reasoning [e.g., in U.S. Supreme Court Case majority opinions and dissents] and the premises, purposes, and arguments in works of public advocacy [e.g., *The Federalist*, presidential addresses]").

Range of Writing

Write routinely over extended time frames (time for research, reflection, and revision) and shorter time frames (a single sitting or a day or two) for a range of tasks, purposes, and audiences.

Standards Overview

Standards for Speaking and Listening

Comprehension and Collaboration

1. Prepare for and participate effectively in a range of conversations and collaborations with diverse partners, building on others' ideas and expressing their own clearly and persuasively.

2. Integrate and evaluate information presented in diverse media and formats, including visually, quantitatively, and orally.

3. Evaluate a speaker's point of view, reasoning, and use of evidence and rhetoric.

Presentation of Knowledge and Ideas

4. Present information, findings, and supporting evidence such that listeners can follow the line of reasoning and the organization, development, and style are appropriate to task, purpose, and audience.

5. Make strategic use of digital media and visual displays of data to express information and enhance understanding of presentations.

6. Adapt speech to a variety of contexts and communicative tasks, demonstrating command of formal English when indicated or appropriate.

Grade 11 Standards for Speaking and Listening

Standard

Comprehension and Collaboration

Initiate and participate effectively in a range of collaborative discussions (one-on-one, in groups, and teacher-led) with diverse partners on *grades 11–12 topics, texts, and issues*, building on others' ideas and expressing their own clearly and persuasively.

Come to discussions prepared, having read and researched material under study; explicitly draw on that preparation by referring to evidence from texts and other research on the topic or issue to stimulate a thoughtful, well-reasoned exchange of ideas.

Work with peers to promote civil, democratic discussions and decision-making, set clear goals and deadlines, and establish individual roles as needed.

Propel conversations by posing and responding to questions that probe reasoning and evidence; ensure a hearing for a full range of positions on a topic or issue; clarify, verify, or challenge ideas and conclusions; and promote divergent and creative perspectives.

Respond thoughtfully to diverse perspectives; synthesize comments, claims, and evidence made on all sides of an issue; resolve contradictions when possible; and determine what additional information or research is required to deepen the investigation or complete the task.

Integrate multiple sources of information presented in diverse formats and media (e.g., visually, quantitatively, orally) in order to make informed decisions and solve problems, evaluating the credibility and accuracy of each source and noting any discrepancies among the data.

Evaluate a speaker's point of view, reasoning, and use of evidence and rhetoric, assessing the stance, premises, links among ideas, word choice, points of emphasis, and tone used.

Presentation of Knowledge and Ideas

Present information, findings, and supporting evidence, conveying a clear and distinct perspective, such that listeners can follow the line of reasoning, alternative or opposing perspectives are addressed, and the organization, development, substance, and style are appropriate to purpose, audience, and a range of formal and informal tasks.

Make strategic use of digital media (e.g., textual, graphical, audio, visual, and interactive elements) in presentations to enhance understanding of findings, reasoning, and evidence and to add interest.

Adapt speech to a variety of contexts and tasks, demonstrating a command of formal English when indicated or appropriate. (See grades 11–12 Language standards 1 and 3 for specific expectations.)

Standards Overview

Standards for Language

College and Career Readiness Anchor Standards for Language
Conventions of Standard English
1. Demonstrate command of the conventions of standard English grammar and usage when writing or speaking.
2. Demonstrate command of the conventions of standard English capitalization, punctuation, and spelling when writing.
Knowledge of Language
3. Apply knowledge of language to understand how language functions in different contexts, to make effective choices for meaning or style, and to comprehend more fully when reading or listening.
Vocabulary Acquisition and Use
4. Determine or clarify the meaning of unknown and multiple-meaning words and phrases by using context clues, analyzing meaningful word parts, and consulting general and specialized reference materials, as appropriate.
5. Demonstrate understanding of figurative language, word relationships, and nuances in word meanings.
6. Acquire and use accurately a range of general academic and domain-specific words and phrases sufficient for reading, writing, speaking, and listening at the college and career readiness level; demonstrate independence in gathering vocabulary knowledge when considering a word or phrase important to comprehension or expression.

Grade 11 Standards for Language
Standard
Conventions of Standard English
Demonstrate command of the conventions of standard English grammar and usage when writing or speaking.
Apply the understanding that usage is a matter of convention, can change over time, and is sometimes contested.
Resolve issues of complex or contested usage, consulting references (e.g., *Merriam-Webster's Dictionary of English Usage*, *Garner's Modern American Usage*) as needed.
Demonstrate command of the conventions of standard English capitalization, punctuation, and spelling when writing.
Observe hyphenation conventions.
Spell correctly.

Grade 11 Standards for Language

Standard

Knowledge of Language

Apply knowledge of language to understand how language functions in different contexts, to make effective choices for meaning or style, and to comprehend more fully when reading or listening.

Vary syntax for effect, consulting references (e.g., Tufte's *Artful Sentences*) for guidance as needed; apply an understanding of syntax to the study of complex texts when reading.

Vocabulary Acquisition and Use

Determine or clarify the meaning of unknown and multiple-meaning words and phrases based on *grades 11–12 reading and content*, choosing flexibly from a range of strategies.

Use context (e.g., the overall meaning of a sentence, paragraph, or text; a word's position or function in a sentence) as a clue to the meaning of a word or phrase.

Identify and correctly use patterns of word changes that indicate different meanings or parts of speech (e.g., *conceive, conception, conceivable*).

Consult general and specialized reference materials (e.g., dictionaries, glossaries, thesauruses), both print and digital, to find the pronunciation of a word or determine or clarify its precise meaning, its part of speech, its etymology, or its standard usage.

Verify the preliminary determination of the meaning of a word or phrase (e.g., by checking the inferred meaning in context or in a dictionary).

Demonstrate understanding of figurative language, word relationships, and nuances in word meanings.

Interpret figures of speech (e.g., hyperbole, paradox) in context and analyze their role in the text.

Analyze nuances in the meaning of words with similar denotations.

Acquire and use accurately general academic and domain-specific words and phrases, sufficient for reading, writing, speaking, and listening at the college and career readiness level; demonstrate independence in gathering vocabulary knowledge when considering a word or phrase important to comprehension or expression.

Writing Freedom

Words That Shaped a Nation

Boston Tea Party

💬 Discuss It In what ways is the concept of "no taxation without representation" central to America's identity as a nation?

Write your response before sharing your ideas.

UNIT 1

ESSENTIAL QUESTION:

What is the meaning of freedom?

LAUNCH TEXT
ARGUMENT MODEL
Totally Free?

 WHOLE-CLASS LEARNING

HISTORICAL PERSPECTIVES

Focus Period: 1750–1800
A New Nation

ANCHOR TEXT: FOUNDATIONAL DOCUMENT

Declaration of Independence
Thomas Jefferson

▶ MEDIA CONNECTION:
  John F. Kennedy Reads the Declaration of Independence

ANCHOR TEXT: FOUNDATIONAL DOCUMENTS

Preamble to the Constitution
Gouverneur Morris

Bill of Rights
James Madison

ANCHOR TEXT: SPEECH

Speech in the Convention
Benjamin Franklin

▶ MEDIA CONNECTION:
  The U. S. Constitution

MEDIA: IMAGE GALLERY

The American Revolution: Visual Propaganda

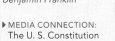

PERFORMANCE TASK

WRITING FOCUS:
Write an Argument

 SMALL-GROUP LEARNING

COMPARE

EXPOSITORY NONFICTION

from **America's Constitution: A Biography**
Akhil Reed Amar

GRAPHIC NOVEL

from **The United States Constitution: A Graphic Adaptation**
Jonathan Hennessey and Aaron McConnell

AUTOBIOGRAPHY

from **The Interesting Narrative of the Life of Olaudah Equiano**
Olaudah Equiano

LETTER | BIOGRAPHY

Letter to John Adams
Abigail Adams

from **Dear Abigail: The Intimate Lives and Revolutionary Ideas of Abigail Adams and Her Two Remarkable Sisters**
Diane Jacobs

SPEECH

Gettysburg Address
Abraham Lincoln

PERFORMANCE TASK

SPEAKING AND LISTENING FOCUS:
Present an Argument

 INDEPENDENT LEARNING

ESSAY

from **Democracy Is Not a Spectator Sport**
Arthur Blaustein with Helen Matatov

SPEECH

Reflections on the Bicentennial of the United States Constitution
Thurgood Marshall

POETRY

Speech to the Young Speech to the Progress-Toward
Gwendolyn Brooks

The Fish
Elizabeth Bishop

SHORT STORY

The Pedestrian
Ray Bradbury

POLITICAL DOCUMENT

from the **Iroquois Constitution**
Dekanawidah, translated by Arthur C. Parker

ARGUMENT

from **Common Sense**
Thomas Paine

PERFORMANCE-BASED ASSESSMENT PREP

Review Evidence for an Argument

PERFORMANCE-BASED ASSESSMENT

Argument: Essay and Video Commentary

PROMPT:

What are the most effective tools for establishing and preserving freedom?

Unit Goals

Throughout this unit, you will deepen your perspective of American freedoms by reading, writing, speaking, listening, and presenting. These goals will help you succeed on the Unit Performance-Based Assessment.

Rate how well you meet these goals right now. You will revisit your ratings later when you reflect on your growth during this unit.

SCALE	1 NOT AT ALL WELL	2 NOT VERY WELL	3 SOMEWHAT WELL	4 VERY WELL	5 EXTREMELY WELL

READING GOALS	1	2	3	4	5
• Read a variety of texts to gain the knowledge and insight needed to write about American freedoms.					
• Expand your knowledge and use of academic and concept vocabulary.					

WRITING AND RESEARCH GOALS	1	2	3	4	5
• Write an argument that has a clear structure and that draws evidence from texts and original research to support a claim.					
• Conduct research projects of various lengths to explore a topic and clarify meaning.					

LANGUAGE GOALS	1	2	3	4	5
• Note differences in language style over time and in various contexts.					
• Establish a writing "voice."					
• Correctly use parallelism and verb tenses to convey meaning and enrich your writing and presentations.					

SPEAKING AND LISTENING GOALS	1	2	3	4	5
• Collaborate with your team to build on the ideas of others, develop consensus, and communicate.					
• Integrate audio, visuals, and text to present information.					

⠿ STANDARDS

Language
Acquire and use accurately general academic and domain-specific words and phrases, sufficient for reading, writing, speaking, and listening at the college and career readiness level; demonstrate independence in gathering vocabulary knowledge when considering a word or phrase important to comprehension or expression.

Academic Vocabulary: Argument

Understanding and using academic terms can help you to read, write, and speak with precision and clarity. Here are five academic words that will be useful to you in this unit as you analyze and write arguments.

Complete the chart.

1. Review each word, its root, and the mentor sentences.

2. Use the information and your own knowledge to predict the meaning of each word.

3. For each word, list at least two related words.

4. Refer to a dictionary or other resources if needed.

TIP

FOLLOW THROUGH

Study the words in this chart, and mark them or their forms wherever they appear in the unit.

WORD	MENTOR SENTENCES	PREDICT MEANING	RELATED WORDS
confirm ROOT: **-firm-** "strong"; "steadfast"	**1.** We could *confirm* the bird's species by its unusual song. **2.** Please *confirm* your position on this topic; right now, I am unsure where you stand.		confirmation; unconfirmed
demonstrate ROOT: **-mon-** "show"; "point out"	**1.** In today's art class, Justin will *demonstrate* his use of pastels. **2.** Like humans, some apes use facial expressions to *demonstrate* feelings.		
supplement ROOT: **-ple-** "fill"	**1.** Some people *supplement* their diet with a daily multivitamin. **2.** Camila will *supplement* her income by taking a second, part-time job.		
establish ROOT: **-sta-** "stand"	**1.** That observant witness was able to *establish* the suspect's alibi. **2.** Max reports that he is second in his class, but his grades *establish* that he is actually first.		
conviction ROOT: **-vict-/-vinc-** "conquer"	**1.** A speaker is far more effective if she speaks with confidence and *conviction*. **2.** During the debate, the candidate's *conviction* about the rightness of his policies seemed to weaken.		

LAUNCH TEXT | ARGUMENT MODEL

This selection is an example of an **argument,** a type of writing in which the author presents a claim and organizes evidence and reasons to support that claim. This is the type of writing you will develop in the Performance-Based Assessment at the end of the unit.

As you read, look closely at the writer's argument, including the consideration of various viewpoints. Mark facts and examples that provide strong evidence to support the main claim.

Totally Free?

NOTES

1   If you ask a dozen high school students to define *freedom*, odds are that ten of them will answer, "Freedom means that I can do anything I want." For many people, freedom is an absolute. It implies the right to think, speak, or act however one wishes. Because we live in a civil society, however, we need to consider other people's rights as we exercise our own freedoms. A better world would combine essential human freedoms with the understanding that my freedoms should not conflict with your right to lead a safe and happy life.

2   Suppose that those ten high school students had the total freedom they describe. They might drive a car without a license, because they were free to do so. They might even drive *your* car, because total freedom means that they can have anything they want and do anything they like. They would be free to attend school or not, to run screaming down the hallways if they chose, or even to treat other people cruelly without fear of reprisal. Total freedom could result in lawless mayhem.

3   Despite their desperate desire to be free from England's rule, our nation's early leaders carefully defined freedoms in the Bill of Rights. They did not say, "Everyone is free to do as he or she chooses." They said, "Congress shall make no law respecting an establishment of religion, or prohibiting the free exercise thereof; or abridging the freedom of speech, or of the press; or the right of the people peaceably to assemble, and to petition the Government for a redress

NOTES

of grievances." They established a delicate line between the rights of individuals and the power of the government.

4　　In his 1941 State of the Union address, President Franklin Roosevelt identified four key freedoms as being basic human rights: freedom of speech and expression, freedom of worship, freedom from want, and freedom from fear. Those are not freedoms that one finds in a dictatorship. Nor are they freedoms that we grant to each other without the oversight and protection of government institutions. With the government's help, and the writing of laws, my freedom from want does not allow me to steal your food, and your freedom of speech does not let you publish lies about me. We are free, but only up to the point at which our freedoms clash.

5　　Is it even possible to be "totally free"? A person living "off the grid," far away from civilization, might achieve that kind of liberation. Such a person could live as he or she pleased without ever imposing on the freedoms of others.

6　　Most of us, however, live in a community. We are bound by laws that both restrict and protect us. If we live in a dictatorship, we may be more restricted and less protected. If we live in a democracy, we may be more protected and less restricted. Human history is a balancing act between the desire for individual freedom and the need to protect everyone's freedoms.

7　　*Freedom* implies a lack of restraint, but we are all better off if our freedoms are preserved and protected. At the same time, as members of a society, we must be sure that our freedoms do not conflict. "Life, liberty, and the pursuit of happiness" are powerful goals, but we must never allow one person's liberty to impose on another's happiness. ❧

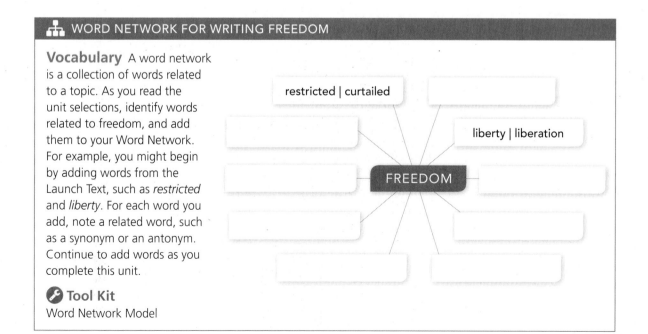

🔧 WORD NETWORK FOR WRITING FREEDOM

Vocabulary A word network is a collection of words related to a topic. As you read the unit selections, identify words related to freedom, and add them to your Word Network. For example, you might begin by adding words from the Launch Text, such as *restricted* and *liberty*. For each word you add, note a related word, such as a synonym or an antonym. Continue to add words as you complete this unit.

restricted | curtailed

liberty | liberation

FREEDOM

🔧 Tool Kit
Word Network Model

Summary

Write a summary of "Totally Free?" Remember that a **summary** is a concise, complete, and accurate overview of a text. It should not include a statement of your opinion or an analysis.

Launch Activity

Define and Explain Roll a six-sided die, and use your result to perform one of these tasks.

1. Write a definition of the word *freedom*.

2. Describe a historical example of freedom.

3. Describe a current example of freedom.

4. Explain why freedom is important to you.

5. Explain why freedom is important to a society.

6. Explain how freedom might be protected or preserved.

Find other classmates who performed the same task. Share your responses, and consider how best to convey your thinking to the rest of the class. For example, you may combine your answers, or you may revise them to write a new answer. Then, share your work with the class.

QuickWrite

Consider class discussions, the video, and the Launch Text as you think about the prompt. Record your first thoughts here.

PROMPT: **What are the most effective tools for establishing and preserving freedom?**

EVIDENCE LOG FOR WRITING FREEDOM

Review your QuickWrite. Summarize your initial position in one sentence to record in your Evidence Log. Then, record evidence from "Totally Free?" that supports your position.

After each selection, you will continue to use your Evidence Log to record the evidence you gather and the connections you make. The graphic shows what your Evidence Log looks like.

Tool Kit
Evidence Log Model

Title of Text: _____   Date: _____

CONNECTION TO PROMPT	TEXT EVIDENCE/DETAILS	ADDITIONAL NOTES/IDEAS

How does this text change or add to my thinking?   Date: _____

ESSENTIAL QUESTION:

What is the meaning of freedom?

As you read these selections, work with your whole class to explore the meaning of freedom.

From Text to Topic For Thomas Jefferson and the other founders, freedom meant breaking away from Great Britain and establishing a nation based on democratic principles and individual liberties. Convincing the colonial majority of that idea would take persuasive words and images. For James Madison and Benjamin Franklin, after independence, freedom needed to be codified in a constitution—again, not an easy task. Issues relating to independence gripped Americans in the mid-eighteenth century. As you read, consider what the selections show about the meaning of American freedom during the country's formative years, and how they continue to shape our ideas about freedom today.

Whole-Class Learning Strategies

Throughout your life, in school, in your community, and in your career, you will continue to learn and work in large-group environments.

Review these strategies and the actions you can take to practice them as you work with your whole class. Add ideas of your own for each step. Get ready to use these strategies during Whole-Class Learning.

STRATEGY	ACTION PLAN
Listen actively	• Eliminate distractions. For example, put your cellphone away. • Jot down brief notes on main ideas and points of confusion. •
Clarify by asking questions	• If you're confused, other people probably are, too. Ask a question to help your whole class. • Ask follow-up questions as needed—for example, if you do not understand the clarification or if you want to make an additional connection. •
Monitor understanding	• Notice what information you already know and be ready to build on it. • Ask for help if you are struggling. •
Interact and share ideas	• Share your ideas and answer questions, even if you are unsure. • Build on the ideas of others by adding details or making a connection. •

CONTENTS

HISTORICAL PERSPECTIVES

Focus Period: 1750–1800
A New Nation

The second half of the eighteenth century was a dramatic period of deep social engagement, as Americans wrestled with the possibility of independence—and the challenges of governing the country that resulted from it.

ANCHOR TEXT: FOUNDATIONAL DOCUMENT

Declaration of Independence

Thomas Jefferson

When is a colony justified in seeking freedom from the country that governs it?

▸ MEDIA CONNECTION: John F. Kennedy Reads the Declaration of Independence

ANCHOR TEXT: FOUNDATIONAL DOCUMENTS

Preamble to the Constitution   *Gouverneur Morris*

Bill of Rights   *James Madison*

Why do Americans need a governing document, and what rights should it guarantee?

ANCHOR TEXT: SPEECH

Speech in the Convention

Benjamin Franklin

How do you persuade people to support a document with which they do not completely agree?

▸ MEDIA CONNECTION: The U. S. Constitution

MEDIA: IMAGE GALLERY

The American Revolution: Visual Propaganda

A picture is worth a thousand words—especially when it comes to propaganda.

PERFORMANCE TASK

WRITING FOCUS
Write an Argument
The Whole-Class readings were born during a time when conflicts between Great Britain and its American colonies were about to change history. After reading, you will write an argument about the continuing relevance of these foundational documents.

A New Nation

Voices of the Period

"Courage, then, my countrymen; our contest is not only whether we ourselves shall be free, but whether there shall be left to mankind an asylum on earth for civil and religious liberty."

—Samuel Adams,
advocate for colonial rights and
signer of the Declaration of Independence

"The Enemy have now landed on Long Island, and the hour is fast approaching, on which the Honor and Success of this army, and the safety of our bleeding Country depend. Remember officers and Soldiers, that you are Freemen, fighting for the blessings of Liberty—that slavery will be your portion, and that of your posterity, if you do not acquit yourselves like men."

—George Washington,
then- Commander-in-Chief
of the Continental Army

"Accordingly he signed the manumission that day; so that, before night, I who had been a slave in the morning, trembling at the will of another, . . . became my own master, and completely free. I thought this was the happiest day I had ever experienced. . . . "

—Olaudah Equiano,
abolitionist and formerly
enslaved African

History of the Period

Founded on Freedom The quest for freedom drove the establishment of the colonies. The Pilgrims and Puritans settled Massachusetts so that they could practice their religion freely. The Quakers, who settled Pennsylvania, and the Catholics, who settled Maryland, also brought their religious convictions with them as they fled from England's restrictions.

An "American" Society By the mid-eighteenth century, the thirteen disparate colonies had created a new society. Each colony was fiercely independent, but together they viewed themselves as different from societies across the Atlantic. "American" society generally valued equality and opportunity. It was much more homogenous than what was commonplace in Europe, without either nobility or a class of paupers who had no chance of bettering their lives. (Enslaved African Americans were the notable exception. Indentured servants also had limits on their freedom.) Furthermore, most of the colonial governments had two-house legislatures, elected by voters. The colonial governments may not have been fully democratic by modern standards, but colonists had—and expected—far more rights and freedoms than their counterparts in England did.

Tightening Controls By the mid-1700s, most Americans took pride in being in charge of their colonial governments, so the demands that Great Britain began to make after winning the French

TIMELINE

1754: The Albany Congress discusses Benjamin Franklin's Plan of Union for the Colonies.

1755: England Samuel Johnson's *Dictionary of the English Language* is published.

1765: The British Parliament taxes the Colonies with the Stamp Act.

1768: British troops occupy rebellious Boston.

1700

Integration of Knowledge and Ideas

Notebook How was each of the causes resolved as a result of the American Revolution? Which effect do you think may have been most on the minds of the Americans when they rebelled? Which may have been least?

Causes and Effects of the American Revolution

CAUSES

- Britain imposes taxes without providing for colonial representation in Parliament.
- Britain issues the Intolerable Acts to punish the American "rebels."
- A growing number of colonial leaders see themselves more as American than as British.

The American Revolution

EFFECTS

- The thirteen British colonies become the independent United States of America.
- The United States becomes an example for other peoples seeking freedom and self-government.
- American trade becomes free of British restrictions.
- Westward expansion becomes possible, extending to the Mississippi River.

and Indian War (known in Britain as the Seven Years' War) led inevitably to trouble. Colonists who were eager to move west were stymied by the Proclamation of 1763, which forbade settlement beyond the Appalachian Mountains. Furthermore, the taxes that Britain imposed to pay the cost of securing victory grew more and more onerous to the colonists. Quickly, "no taxation without representation" became a colonial rallying cry.

In response, England tightened its grip. In 1774, Parliament cracked down on American freedoms even more, with laws that the colonists called the Intolerable Acts. Then, in April 1775, the conflict turned from words and laws to bullets and deaths when the first shots were fired at Lexington and Concord in Massachusetts, the hotbed of rebellion.

Declaring Independence Six months before patriots and redcoats clashed in Massachusetts, colonial delegates had gathered to consider their complaints at the First Continental Congress. A few weeks after the events at Lexington and Concord, the Second Continental Congress convened in Philadelphia. By June, the colonies were on the road to a real break from Britain.

1770: Colonists and British soldiers clash in the Boston Massacre.

1774: Colonial representatives meet for the First Continental Congress.

1776: The Second Continental Congress adopts the Declaration of Independence.

1773: Parliament's Tea Act prompts the Boston Tea Party.

1775: The American Revolution begins.

1776

When the delegates officially declared the colonies' independence, they made freedom a central factor in their rationale. It is "self-evident," they stated, that all people have "unalienable rights, that among these are life, liberty, and the pursuit of happiness." In concluding, they pronounced the colonies to be "free and independent states."

Breaking the Bonds The new United States battled for independence for the next seven years. The British had a clear goal: to keep the rebellious colonies within the British Empire. The Americans were more divided, however. Although probably no more than 20 percent of the American people were loyal to Great Britain, many others were uncertain about this radical venture of independence. Undeterred, the patriots fought on.

The colonies had a population of about 2.5 million and no standing military forces. By contrast, Great Britain boasted a population of about 7.5 million as well as the world's most powerful army and navy. However, the colonists were fighting on home territory, whereas the British were 3,000 miles away from home and lacked easy access to supplies.

Then, in 1778, France entered the war on the side of the Americans. It was French aid that enabled the Americans to win the decisive battle at Yorktown. Tradition says that as the British surrendered, their band played "The World Turn'd Upside Down," a fitting tune for what had happened. The new nation that had demanded and won its independence would be unique in the world of its day: a self-governing democracy. In 1783, the Treaty of Paris officially brought the American Revolution to an end.

Defining Freedoms Having fought for freedom, the new nation had to structure a government that would preserve it. The Articles of Confederation, approved in 1777 and formally ratified in 1781, confirmed the union of the thirteen states as one nation. However, the agreement largely left each state free to function on its own—an arrangement that created an often dysfunctional union. Correcting the problems led to a complete re-creation of the governmental structure and triggered the writing of the Constitution of the United States.

Not satisfied with the guarantees of freedom embedded in the Constitution, however, many leaders urged the creation of what became the Bill of Rights. These first ten amendments to the Constitution focus on guarantees of individual liberties, including freedom of speech, freedom of the press, and the right to legal counsel and trial by jury.

These rights did not extend to all Americans, however. For all of the focus on freedom and individual rights in the founding of the United States, enslaved African Americans—about 20 percent of the population—were left out of this discussion. In addition, even though property requirements were abolished for male voters in the new nation, 125 years would pass before suffrage was extended to American women.

A Motivating Force Freedom has been a defining goal throughout American history. The literature in this unit explores how freedom has shaped the United States, and how authors of both the past and present have applied visions of freedom to an ever-changing world.

TIMELINE

1777: The thirteen original states adopt the Articles of Confederation.

1777

1781: American forces defeat the British at Yorktown.

1783: The Treaty of Paris ends the American Revolution.

1787: Delegates meet in Philadelphia to create a new constitution.

1788: The United States Constitution is ratified.

Literature Selections

Literature of the Focus Period Several of the selections in this unit were written during the focus period and pertain to the establishment of a free United States and the rights granted to some, but not all, of its people:

> Declaration of Independence, Thomas Jefferson
>
> Preamble to the Constitution, Gouverneur Morris
>
> Bill of Rights, James Madison
>
> Speech in the Convention, Benjamin Franklin
>
> from *The Interesting Narrative of the Life of Olaudah Equiano*, Olaudah Equiano
>
> Letter to John Adams, Abigail Adams
>
> from *Common Sense*, Thomas Paine

Connections Across Time A consideration of the importance of freedom both preceded and continued past the focus period. Indeed, it has influenced writers and commentators in many times and places.

> from *America's Constitution: A Biography*, Akhil Reed Amar
>
> from *Dear Abigail: The Intimate Lives and Revolutionary Ideas of Abigail Adams and Her Two Remarkable Sisters*, Diane Jacobs
>
> Gettysburg Address, Abraham Lincoln
>
> from *Democracy Is Not a Spectator Sport*, Arthur Blaustein with Helen Matatov
>
> Reflections on the Bicentennial of the United States Constitution, Thurgood Marshall
>
> "Speech to the Young | Speech to the Progress-Toward," Gwendolyn Brooks
>
> "The Fish," Elizabeth Bishop
>
> "The Pedestrian," Ray Bradbury
>
> from the Iroquois Constitution, Dekanawidah, translated by Arthur C. Parker

1789: George Washington is elected the first President of the United States.

1789: France The French Revolution begins.

1791: Ten amendments— the Bill of Rights—are added to the Constitution.

1796: John Adams is elected the second U.S. president.

1800: Thomas Jefferson is elected the third U.S. president.

1800

Declaration of Independence

Concept Vocabulary

You will encounter the following words as you read the Declaration of Independence. Before reading, note how familiar you are with each word. Then, rank the words in order from most familiar (1) to least familiar (6).

WORD	YOUR RANKING
unalienable	
constrains	
tyranny	
assent	
acquiesce	
rectitude	

After completing the first read, come back to the concept vocabulary and review your rankings. Mark changes to your original rankings as needed.

First Read NONFICTION

Apply these strategies as you conduct your first read. You will have an opportunity to complete the close-read notes after your first read.

🔧 **Tool Kit**
First-Read Guide and Model Annotation

NOTICE the general ideas of the text. *What* is it about? *Who* is involved?

ANNOTATE by marking vocabulary and key passages you want to revisit.

First Read

CONNECT ideas within the selection to what you already know and what you have already read.

RESPOND by completing the Comprehension Check and by writing a brief summary of the selection.

⬚ STANDARDS
Reading Informational Text
By the end of grade 11, read and comprehend literary nonfiction in the grades 11–CCR text complexity band proficiently, with scaffolding as needed at the high end of the range.

About the Author

Thomas Jefferson (1743–1826)

Author of the Declaration of Independence

When you look at all of Thomas Jefferson's achievements, it seems almost nothing was beyond his reach. Not only did he help our nation win its independence and serve as its third president, but he also founded the University of Virginia, helped establish the public school system, designed his own home, invented a type of elevator for sending food from floor to floor, and created the decimal system for American money. He was a skilled violinist, an art enthusiast, and a brilliant writer.

Revolutionary Leader Born into a wealthy Virginia family, Jefferson attended the College of William and Mary and went on to earn a law degree. While serving in the Virginia House of Burgesses, he became an outspoken defender of American rights. When conflict between the colonists and the British erupted into revolution, Jefferson emerged as a leader in the effort to win independence.

Valued Statesman When the war ended, Jefferson served as the American minister to France for several years. He then served as the nation's first secretary of state and second vice president before becoming president in 1801.

Building the Nation While in office, Jefferson negotiated with France to buy a tract of land extending from the southern coast of Louisiana north into what is now Canada. This vast expanse of land included all of present-day Arkansas, Missouri, Iowa, Oklahoma, Kansas, and Nebraska. It also included most of North and South Dakota, northeastern New Mexico, northern

Texas, and portions of Minnesota, Colorado, Montana, and Wyoming. This enormous real-estate deal became known as the Louisiana Purchase, and it was one of the defining achievements of Jefferson's presidency. In a single treaty, Jefferson added more than 800,000 uncharted square miles to the holdings of the nation, effectively doubling its size.

The Lewis and Clark Expedition Jefferson had long wanted to pursue exploration of the Pacific Northwest. The completion of the Louisiana Purchase strengthened his resolve. He convinced Congress to allocate $2,500 to fund an expedition, writing:

> *The river Missouri, and Indians inhabiting it, are not as well known as rendered desirable by their connection with the Mississippi, and consequently with us. . . . An intelligent officer, with ten or twelve chosen men . . . might explore the whole line, even to the Western Ocean. . . .*

The "intelligent officer" he had in mind was his secretary, Captain Meriwether Lewis (1774–1809). Captain William Clark became co-leader of the group, which became known as the Corps of Discovery. Between 1804 and 1806, the team completed an 8,000-mile trek from St. Louis to the source of the Missouri River, across the Rocky Mountains to the Pacific coast, and back to Missouri.

A Patriotic Departure On the morning of July 4, 1826, the fiftieth anniversary of the Declaration of Independence, Jefferson died at the age of 83. John Adams, Jefferson's fellow contributor to the Declaration of Independence, died several hours later, after his longtime friend. Adams's last words were "Thomas Jefferson still survives."

Declaration of Independence

Thomas Jefferson

BACKGROUND

The Continental Congress was formed in 1774 by the American colonies to coordinate resistance to British laws considered by most colonists to be unfair. In the summer of 1776, after about a year of war against Britain, representatives met to consider an official break with Britain.

IN CONGRESS, July 4, 1776.

1 *The unanimous declaration of the thirteen united states of America,*

2 When in the course of human events, it becomes necessary for one people to dissolve the political bands which have connected them with another, and to assume among the powers of the earth, the separate and equal station to which the laws of nature and of nature's God entitle them, a decent respect to the opinions of mankind requires that they should declare the causes which impel them to the separation.

3 We hold these truths to be self-evident: that all men are created equal; that they are endowed by their creator with certain **unalienable** rights, that among these are life, liberty and the pursuit of happiness; that to secure these rights, governments are instituted among men, deriving their just powers from the consent

NOTES

unalienable (uhn AYL yuh nuh buhl) *adj.* impossible to take away or give up

of the governed; that whenever any form of government becomes destructive of these ends, it is the right of the people to alter or to abolish it, and to institute new government, laying its foundation on such principles and organizing its powers in such form, as to them shall seem most likely to effect their safety and happiness. Prudence, indeed, will dictate that governments long established should not be changed for light and transient causes; and accordingly all experience hath shown, that mankind are more disposed to suffer, while evils are sufferable, than to right themselves by abolishing the forms to which they are accustomed. But when a long train of abuses and usurpations,[1] pursuing invariably the same object evinces a design to reduce them under absolute despotism, it is their right, it is their duty, to throw off such government, and to provide new guards for their future security. Such has been the patient sufferance of these colonies; and such is now the necessity which **constrains** them to alter their former systems of government. The history of the present King of Great Britain is a history of repeated injuries and usurpations,[1] all having in direct object the establishment of an absolute **tyranny** over these states. To prove this, let facts be submitted to a candid world.

4   He has refused his **assent** to laws the most wholesome and necessary for the public good.

5   He has forbidden his governors to pass laws of immediate and pressing importance, unless suspended in their operation till his assent should be obtained; and when so suspended, he has utterly neglected to attend to them.

6   He has refused to pass other laws for the accommodation of large districts of people, unless those people would relinquish the right of representation in the legislature, a right inestimable to them and formidable to tyrants only.

7   He has called together legislative bodies at places unusual, uncomfortable, and distant from the depository of their public records, for the sole purpose of fatiguing them into compliance with his measures.

8   He has dissolved representative houses repeatedly, for opposing with manly firmness his invasions on the rights of the people.

9   He has refused for a long time, after such dissolutions, to cause others to be elected, whereby the legislative powers, incapable of annihilation, have returned to the people at large for their exercise, the state remaining in the mean time exposed to all the dangers of invasion from without, and convulsions within.

10   He has endeavored to prevent the population of these states; for that purpose obstructing the laws for naturalization of foreigners, refusing to pass others to encourage their migrations hither, and raising the conditions of new appropriations of lands.

NOTES

CLOSE READ

ANNOTATE: Mark words in the last two sentences of paragraph 3 that seem especially strong or extreme.

QUESTION: Why would Jefferson employ such strong language?

CONCLUDE: What effect might this language have had on the American colonists? The British officials?

constrains (kuhn STRAYNZ) *v.* requires or forces

tyranny (TIHR uh nee) *n.* oppressive power

assent (uh SEHNT) *n.* approval or agreement

---

1. **usurpations** (yoo zuhr PAY shuhnz) *n.* unlawful or violent seizures of power or possessions.

Declaration of Independence **19**

11   He has obstructed the administration of justice, by refusing his assent to laws for establishing judiciary powers.

12   He has made judges dependent on his will alone, for the tenure of their offices, and the amount and payment of their salaries.

13   He has erected a multitude of new offices, and sent hither swarms of officers to harass our people, and eat out their substance.

14   He has kept among us in times of peace standing armies without the consent of our legislatures.

15   He has affected to render the military independent of, and superior to, the civil power.

16   He has combined with others to subject us to a jurisdiction foreign to our constitution, and unacknowledged by our laws; giving his assent to their acts of pretended legislation:

17   For quartering[2] large bodies of armed troops among us:

18   For protecting them, by a mock trial, from punishment for any murders which they should commit on the inhabitants of these states:

19   For cutting off our trade with all parts of the world:

20   For imposing taxes on us without our consent:

21   For depriving us in many cases, of the benefits of trial by jury:

22   For transporting us beyond seas to be tried for pretended offenses:

23   For abolishing the free system of English laws in a neighboring province, establishing therein an arbitrary government, and enlarging its boundaries so as to render it at once an example and fit instrument for introducing the same absolute rule into these colonies:

24   For taking away our charters, abolishing our most valuable laws, and altering fundamentally the forms of our governments:

25   For suspending our own legislatures, and declaring themselves invested with power to legislate for us in all cases whatsoever.

26   He has abdicated government here, by declaring us out of his protection and waging war against us.

27   He has plundered our seas, ravaged our coasts, burned our towns, and destroyed the lives of our people.

28   He is at this time transporting large armies of foreign mercenaries to complete the works of death, desolation and tyranny, already begun with circumstances of cruelty and perfidy scarcely paralleled in the most barbarous ages, and totally unworthy the head of a civilized nation.

29   He has constrained our fellow citizens taken captive on the high seas to bear arms against their country, to become the executioners of their friends and brethren, or to fall themselves by their hands.

30   He has excited domestic insurrections amongst us, and has endeavored to bring on the inhabitants of our frontiers, the merciless Indian savages, whose known rule of warfare, is an undistinguished destruction of all ages, sexes, and conditions.

31   In every stage of these oppressions we have petitioned for redress in the most humble terms: Our repeated petitions have been

CLOSE READ

ANNOTATE: Mark the verbs in paragraph 27 that describe what the king has done to the colonists.

QUESTION: Why do you think Jefferson chose these verbs?

CONCLUDE: What is the effect of this language?

2. **quartering** v. housing.

answered only by repeated injury. A prince whose character is thus marked by every act which may define a tyrant, is unfit to be the ruler of a free people.

32   Nor have we been wanting in attentions to our British brethren. We have warned them from time to time of attempts by their legislature to extend an unwarrantable jurisdiction over us. We have reminded them of the circumstances of our emigration and settlement here. We have appealed to their native justice and magnanimity, and we have conjured them by the ties of our common kindred to disavow these usurpations, which, would inevitably interrupt our connections and correspondence. They too have been deaf to the voice of justice and of consanguinity.[3] We must, therefore, **acquiesce** in the necessity, which denounces our separation, and hold them, as we hold the rest of mankind, enemies in war, in peace friends.

33   We, therefore, the representatives of the United States of America, in General Congress assembled appealing to the Supreme Judge of the world for the **rectitude** of our intentions, do in the name and by authority of the good people of these colonies, solemnly publish and declare that these united colonies are and of right ought to be free and independent states; that they are absolved from all allegiance to the British Crown, and that all political connection between them and the state of Great Britain is and ought to be totally dissolved; and that as free and independent states, they have full power to levy war,

NOTES

acquiesce (ak wee EHS) *v.* accept something reluctantly but without protest

rectitude (REHK tuh tood) *n.* morally correct behavior or thinking; uprightness

---

3. **consanguinity** (kon sang GWIHN uh tee) *n.* blood relationship.

Image of the final, signed version of the Declaration of Independence

conclude peace, contract alliances, establish commerce, and to do all other acts and things which independent states may of right do. And for the support of this declaration, with a firm reliance on the protection of divine providence, we mutually pledge to each other our lives, our fortunes and our sacred honor.

The 56 signatures on the Declaration appear in the positions indicated:

Column 1

Georgia:
Button Gwinnett
Lyman Hall
George Walton

Column 2

North Carolina:
William Hooper
Joseph Hewes
John Penn

South Carolina:
Edward Rutledge
Thomas Heyward, Jr.
Thomas Lynch, Jr.
Arthur Middleton

Column 3

Massachusetts:
John Hancock

Maryland:
Samuel Chase
William Paca
Thomas Stone
Charles Carroll
  of Carrollton

Virginia:
George Wythe
Richard Henry Lee
Thomas Jefferson
Benjamin Harrison
Thomas Nelson, Jr.
Francis Lightfoot Lee
Carter Braxton

Column 4

Pennsylvania:
Robert Morris
Benjamin Rush
Benjamin Franklin
John Morton
George Clymer
James Smith
George Taylor
James Wilson
George Ross

Delaware:
Caesar Rodney
George Read
Thomas McKean

Column 5

New York:
William Floyd
Philip Livingston
Francis Lewis
Lewis Morris

New Jersey:
Richard Stockton
John Witherspoon
Francis Hopkinson
John Hart
Abraham Clark

Column 6

New Hampshire:
Josiah Bartlett
William Whipple

Massachusetts:
Samuel Adams
John Adams
Robert Treat Paine
Elbridge Gerry

Rhode Island:
Stephen Hopkins
William Ellery

Connecticut:
Roger Sherman
Samuel Huntington
William Williams
Oliver Wolcott

New Hampshire:
Matthew Thornton

John F. Kennedy Reads the Declaration
of Independence

💬 **Discuss It** In 1957, then-Senator John F. Kennedy read the Declaration of Independence as part of an Independence Day radio broadcast. What do you think the reading would have meant to radio listeners?

Write your response before sharing your ideas.

Comprehension Check

Complete the following items after you finish your first read.

1. What does Jefferson state directly as the reason this declaration had to be written?

2. According to Jefferson, what is a people's duty when their government is abusive?

3. What new relationship between Great Britain and the United States is announced in this document?

4. 📓 **Notebook** Write a summary of the Declaration of Independence to confirm your understanding of the text.

RESEARCH

Research to Clarify Choose at least one unfamiliar detail from the text. Briefly research that detail. In what way does the information you learned shed light on an aspect of the document?

Research to Explore Conduct research to find out how some signers of the Declaration of Independence expressed their convictions about the document.

DECLARATION OF INDEPENDENCE

Close Read the Text

1. This model, from paragraph 2 of the text, shows two sample annotations, along with questions and conclusions. Close read the passage, and find another detail to annotate. Then, write a question and your conclusion.

> **ANNOTATE:** This is very grand language, referring to all of human history.
>
> **QUESTION:** Why does Jefferson present this argument in the context of the entirety of human history?
>
> **CONCLUDE:** Jefferson is saying that the severing of political ties between nations is of momentous importance.

ANNOTATE: These words seem to be gentle.

QUESTION: Why might Jefferson have chosen such language?

CONCLUDE: Perhaps he wanted to make his argument sound reasoned and logical, and not angry.

> When in the course of human events, it becomes necessary for one people to dissolve the political bands which have connected them with another, . . . a decent respect to the opinions of mankind requires that they should declare the causes which impel them to the separation.

2. For more practice, go back into the text and complete the close-read notes.

3. Revisit a section of the text you found important during your first read. **Annotate** what you notice. Ask yourself **questions** such as "Why did the author make this choice?" What can you **conclude**?

🔧 Tool Kit
Close-Read Guide and Model Annotation

Analyze the Text

CITE TEXTUAL EVIDENCE to support your answers.

📓 Notebook Respond to these questions.

1. **Make Inferences** Why does Jefferson begin with points about human rights before discussing the colonists' specific grievances?

2. (a) **Interpret** What does Jefferson mean by saying that people do not change governments for "light reasons"? (b) **Speculate** Why might people be more inclined to put up with a government that is less than satisfactory rather than change it?

3. (a) **Generalize** According to Jefferson, what has been the king's attitude toward the laws of the colonies? (b) **Analyze** Why is that attitude an important factor in the decision to declare independence?

4. **Historical Perspectives** The signers of the Declaration of Independence knew that their announcement could mean war with powerful, well-equipped Britain. In your opinion, why isn't that idea more prominent in the document?

5. **Essential Question: *What is the meaning of freedom?*** What have you learned about American freedoms from reading this text? How does Jefferson connect the meaning of freedom to the idea of human rights?

▤ STANDARDS
Reading Informational Text
• Cite strong and thorough textual evidence to support analysis of what the text says explicitly as well as inferences drawn from the text, including determining where the text leaves matters uncertain.
• Delineate and evaluate the reasoning in seminal U.S. texts, including the application of constitutional principles and use of legal reasoning and the premises, purposes, and arguments in works of public advocacy.
• Analyze seventeenth-, eighteenth-, and nineteenth-century foundational U.S. documents of historical and literary significance for their themes, purposes, and rhetorical features.

Analyze Craft and Structure

Author's Purpose: Argumentation An **argument** is writing that is meant to get readers to think in a certain way or take a particular action. In an effective argument, the writer presents reasons and supports them with convincing evidence. He or she also uses a variety of **persuasive appeals**, or ways of framing ideas for specific effect:

- **Appeals to Emotion:** ideas or language that attempts to influence readers' feelings; appeals to emotion may include **charged language**— strong words with powerful connotations—as well as references to the divine, references to concepts like justice or fairness, and stories or anecdotes.

- **Appeals to Logic:** ideas or language that connects to readers' rationality or reason; appeals to logic emphasize relationships between evidence, such as facts, and consequences or outcomes.

- **Appeals to Authority:** ideas or language that suggests the writer has special expertise or demonstrates character in a way that merits readers' attention on the subject.

Practice

CITE TEXTUAL EVIDENCE
to support your answers.

📓 Notebook Respond to these questions.

1. (a) What appeal to emotion does Jefferson use in paragraph 1?
   (b) Why is this an important technique for him to use as he begins his argument?

2. (a) Mark examples of appeals to emotion in this excerpt from paragraph 2.

   > But when a long train of abuses and usurpations, pursuing invariably the same object, evinces a design to reduce them under absolute despotism, it is their right, it is their duty, to throw off such government, and to provide new guards for their future security. Such has been the patient sufferance of these colonies; and such is now the necessity which constrains them to alter their former systems of government. The history of the present king of Great Britain is a history of repeated injuries and usurpations, all having in direct object the establishment of an absolute tyranny over these states.

   (b) How does the description of Great Britain and its king constitute charged language? Explain, citing specific words.

3. (a) Which kind of appeal is represented by Jefferson's organized list of grievances? (b) How does the evidence he provides add to his argument?

4. Jefferson wrote this document during the Age of Reason, an era characterized by logic and scientific methodology. How does the Declaration of Independence reflect Jefferson's faith in reason?

DECLARATION OF INDEPENDENCE

Concept Vocabulary

unalienable	tyranny	acquiesce
constrains	assent	rectitude

Why These Words? These concept vocabulary words convey ideas about power and rights. For example, Jefferson refers to life, liberty, and the pursuit of happiness as *unalienable* rights. He states that the king's actions established absolute *tyranny* over the colonies.

1. How does the concept vocabulary help readers grasp the issues leading to the Declaration of Independence?

2. What other words in the selection connect to these concepts?

Practice

🔲 **Notebook** **Complete these activities.**

1. Use each concept vocabulary word in a sentence that demonstrates your understanding of the word's meaning.

2. In two of your sentences, replace the concept vocabulary word with a synonym. What is the effect? For example, which sentence is stronger? Which one makes the sentence seem more positive or more negative?

Word Study

Latin Root: *-rect-* The Latin root *-rect-* means "right" or "straight." It is the basis for many English words, including such mathematical terms as *rectangular* (having right angles) and *rectilinear* (formed by straight lines).

1. Write a definition of *rectitude* that demonstrates your understanding of its Latin root.

2. Use a print or online college-level dictionary to find the meanings of *rectify* as the word relates to chemistry and as it relates to electronics.

🔗 WORD NETWORK

Add words related to freedom from the text to your Word Network.

☰ STANDARDS

Language
• Apply the understanding that usage is a matter of convention, can change over time, and is sometimes contested.
• Resolve issues of complex or contested usage, consulting references as needed.
• Vary syntax for effect, consulting references for guidance as needed; apply an understanding of syntax to the study of complex texts when reading.
• Identify and correctly use patterns of word changes that indicate different meanings or parts of speech.
• Consult general and specialized reference materials, find the pronunciation of a word or determine or clarify its precise meaning, its part of speech, its etymology, or its standard usage.

Conventions and Style

Changes in Syntax and Usage Language changes over time. During the eighteenth century, when Jefferson wrote the Declaration of Independence, English spelling was almost identical to that of today's English. However, there are elements of Jefferson's style—the style of his era—that may seem old-fashioned to today's readers.

- **Syntax:** the structure of sentences. Some of Jefferson's sentences are very long by today's standards; in fact, the second paragraph of the Declaration is a lengthy single sentence.

- **Usage:** the way in which a word or phrase is used. Jefferson uses some words that would rarely be used—and might even be contested—today. For example, the word *consanguinity* in paragraph 32 is a term that few modern writers would use.

- **Formality:** the level of familiarity with which writers address the reader. While there are still ceremonial and public forums that require formal language, American culture is more casual now than it was in the eighteenth century. Both the purpose of the document and the style of the era are reflected in the Declaration's high level of formality.

Read It

1. Reread paragraphs 1–2 of the Declaration of Independence. Identify four words or phrases that represent an earlier style of English.

2. Locate Jefferson's use of *conjured* in paragraph 32. What does the word mean to Jefferson in this context? What does the word often mean today? Use an etymological dictionary or other source to explain how the two meanings are connected by word origin and word history.

3. **Connect to Style** What qualities of eighteenth-century style do you find in paragraphs 28–29? Consider syntax, usage, and level of formality.

Write It

📝 Notebook Rewrite this excerpt from the Declaration of Independence. Use modern English usage and syntax to express the same meaning. Then, compare the two versions and take note of ways in which each version would likely appeal to different audiences.

> He has refused his assent to laws, the most wholesome and necessary for the public good.
>
> He has forbidden his governors to pass laws of immediate and pressing importance, unless suspended in their operation till his assent should be obtained; and when so suspended, he has utterly neglected to attend to them.

DECLARATION OF INDEPENDENCE

Writing to Sources

The Declaration of Independence represents the position of one side in a conflict. There were numerous other colonial writings, including speeches, pamphlets, and essays, that centered on the same conflict. Together, these multiple writings are a record of the ongoing debate over the colonies' relationship with Britain. Today, debates over public issues often take place in the media—in newspaper articles and editorials.

Assignment

An editorial is a brief argumentative essay that appears in a newspaper or on a news site and expresses a position on an issue. Write an **editorial** for a local or school newspaper in which you argue your side of an issue that affects your school or community. Use modern syntax and usage, but apply some of Jefferson's persuasive techniques. For example, present a list of reasons just as Jefferson does in the Declaration of Independence.

Your editorial should include:

- a clear statement of your claim, or position
- a list of reasons that support and clarify your claim
- appeals to emotion, logic, and—if warranted—authority
- a concluding statement that follows from the argument

Vocabulary and Conventions Connection Consider including several of the concept vocabulary words. Also, remember to use appropriate word choices, grammar, syntax, and a style that makes your ideas clear.

unalienable	tyranny	acquiesce
constrains	assent	rectitude

- -

Reflect on Your Writing

After you have drafted your editorial, answer the following questions.

1. How did writing your editorial help you understand Jefferson's writing process?

2. Which of the reasons that you listed do you think offers the strongest evidence in support of your argument?

3. **Why These Words?** The words you choose can greatly increase the effect of your writing. Which words helped you create a clear and memorable argument?

STANDARDS

Writing
Write arguments to support claims in an analysis of substantive topics or texts, using valid reasoning and relevant and sufficient evidence.

Speaking and Listening
Propel conversations by posing and responding to questions that probe reasoning and evidence; ensure a hearing for a full range of positions on a topic or issue; clarify, verify, or challenge ideas and conclusions; and promote divergent and creative perspectives.

Speaking and Listening

Assignment

You may have listened to the 1957 recording of Senator John F. Kennedy reading the Declaration of Independence. Listen to that recording again and think about his presentation. Then, participate in a **class discussion** about these questions:

- Would you find it meaningful to hear a modern politician of your choice reading this historical document today? Why or why not?
- Would it be just as meaningful to hear the document read by a classmate or a neighbor? Explain.

1. **Think About the Question** Before the discussion, consider the meaning of the Declaration of Independence.

   - Does Kennedy's reading enhance your understanding of the document?
   - Which aspects of the Declaration would a modern politician most likely consider important?

2. **Prepare Your Contribution** Make some notes for the discussion.

   - Which modern politician would you choose as a reader? Why?
   - In what ways would a reading from a classmate or a neighbor be more or less meaningful?

3. **Discuss the Questions** Keep these principles in mind.

   - Speak clearly so that your listeners can follow what you are saying.
   - Respond respectfully to the opinions of others.
   - Be prepared to answer questions that your teacher or classmates ask about your positions.

4. **Listen and Evaluate** As your classmates speak, listen attentively. Decide whether you agree or disagree with their ideas, and why. Contribute your responses with care, and support them with specific examples. In addition, take brief notes that will help as you complete a presentation evaluation guide.

PRESENTATION EVALUATION GUIDE

Rate each statement on a scale of 1 (not demonstrated) to 5 (demonstrated).

- [ ] Classmates made meaningful contributions to the discussion.
- [ ] All of the details in the assignment were discussed.
- [ ] Each person spoke clearly and in an appropriate tone of voice.
- [ ] Speakers supported their positions with specific examples.

✒ EVIDENCE LOG

Before moving on to a new selection, go to your Evidence Log and record what you learned from the Declaration of Independence.

About the Authors

Gouverneur Morris (1752–1816), a distinguished scholar, represented Pennsylvania at the Constitutional Convention. He made some 173 speeches during the proceedings of the Convention, many of them in opposition to slavery. His work on the Preamble to the Constitution earned him the title "Penman of the Constitution."

James Madison (1751–1836) grew up in Virginia and later served in the state's legislature. The youngest member of the Continental Congress, he was skilled at working with delegates who held opposing views. He is often called "Father of the Constitution" for his role in drafting that document and the Bill of Rights, which followed it. Madison later served in the United States's fourth president.

🔧 **Tool Kit**
First-Read Guide and Model Annotation

▤ **STANDARDS**
Reading Informational Text
By the end of grade 11, read and comprehend literary nonfiction in the grades 11–CCR text complexity band proficiently, with scaffolding as needed at the high end of the range.

Preamble to the Constitution
Bill of Rights

Concept Vocabulary

You will encounter the following words as you read the Preamble to the Constitution and the Bill of Rights. Before reading, note how familiar you are with each word. Then, rank the words in order from most familiar (1) to least familiar (6).

WORD	YOUR RANKING
exercise	
abridging	
petition	
redress	
infringed	
prescribed	

After completing the first read, come back to the concept vocabulary and review your ratings. Mark changes to your original rankings as needed.

First Read NONFICTION

Apply these strategies as you conduct your first read. You will have an opportunity to complete the close-read notes after your first read.

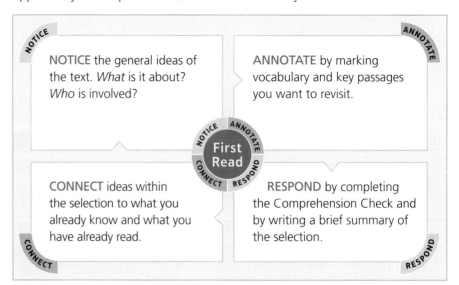

NOTICE the general ideas of the text. *What* is it about? *Who* is involved?

ANNOTATE by marking vocabulary and key passages you want to revisit.

CONNECT ideas within the selection to what you already know and what you have already read.

RESPOND by completing the Comprehension Check and by writing a brief summary of the selection.

Preamble to the Constitution

Gouverneur Morris

Bill of Rights

James Madison

BACKGROUND

After the Framers approved the Constitution, several of them called for the addition of more protections for individual liberties. James Madison wrote up a list of amendments. Congress passed them, and the states ratified ten of them. These ten amendments are now known as the Bill of Rights.

Preamble to the United States Constitution

1 We the people of the United States, in order to form a more perfect union, establish justice, insure domestic tranquility, provide for the common defense, promote the general welfare, and secure the blessings of liberty to ourselves and our posterity, do ordain and establish this Constitution for the United States of America.

❈ ❈ ❈

Bill of Rights
Preamble

2 Congress of the United States begun and held at the City of New York, on Wednesday the fourth of March, one thousand seven hundred and eighty-nine.

3   THE Conventions of a number of the States, having at the time of their adopting the Constitution, expressed a desire, in order to prevent misconstruction or abuse of its powers, that further declaratory and restrictive clauses should be added: And as extending the ground of public confidence in the Government, will best ensure the beneficent ends of its institution.

4   RESOLVED by the Senate and House of Representatives of the United States of America, in Congress assembled, two thirds of both Houses concurring, that the following Articles be proposed to the Legislatures of the several States, as amendments to the Constitution of the United States, all, or any of which Articles, when ratified by three fourths of the said Legislatures, to be valid to all intents and purposes, as part of the said Constitution; viz.[1]

---

1. **viz** *abbr.* that is; namely.

NOTES

CLOSE READ
ANNOTATE: Mark the nouns in paragraph 1, which is the Preamble to the Constitution.

QUESTION: Why does the author list this particular series of nouns?

CONCLUDE: What do these nouns establish as the purpose of this document?

Copyright © SAVVAS Learning Company LLC. All Rights Reserved.

5   ARTICLES in addition to, and Amendment of the Constitution of the United States of America, proposed by Congress, and ratified by the Legislatures of the several States, pursuant to the fifth Article of the original Constitution.

Amendment I

6 Congress shall make no law respecting an establishment of religion, or prohibiting the free **exercise** thereof; or **abridging** the freedom of speech, or of the press; or the right of the people peaceably to assemble, and to **petition** the Government for a **redress** of grievances.

Amendment II

7 A well regulated militia, being necessary to the security of a free State, the right of the people to keep and bear arms, shall not be **infringed**.

Amendment III

8 No soldier shall, in time of peace be quartered in any house, without the consent of the owner, nor in time of war, but in a manner to be **prescribed** by law.

Amendment IV

9 The right of the people to be secure in their persons, houses, papers, and effects, against unreasonable searches and seizures, shall not be violated, and no warrants shall issue, but upon probable cause, supported by oath or affirmation, and particularly describing the place to be searched, and the persons or things to be seized.

Amendment V

10 No person shall be held to answer for a capital,[2] or otherwise infamous crime, unless on a presentment or indictment of a Grand Jury, except in cases arising in the land or naval forces, or in the militia, when in actual service in time of war or public danger; nor shall any person be subject for the same offence to be twice put in jeopardy of life or limb; nor shall be compelled in any criminal case to be a witness against himself, nor be deprived of life, liberty, or property, without due process of law; nor shall private property be taken for public use, without just compensation.

Amendment VI

11 In all criminal prosecutions, the accused shall enjoy the right to a speedy and public trial, by an impartial jury of the State and district wherein the crime shall have been committed, which district shall have been previously ascertained by law, and to be informed of the nature and cause of the accusation; to be confronted with the witnesses against him; to have compulsory process for obtaining witnesses in his favor, and to have the Assistance of Counsel[3] for his defense.

exercise (EHK suhr syz) *n.* implementation; state of putting something into action

abridging (uh BRIHJ ihng) *adj.* limiting

petition (puh TIHSH uhn) *v.* formally request; seek help from

redress (rih DREHS) *n.* correction; setting right of some wrong

infringed (ihn FRIHNJD) *v.* violated

prescribed (prih SKRYBD) *v.* stated in writing; set down as a rule

CLOSE READ

ANNOTATE: Mark the adjectives that appear in Amendment VI.

QUESTION: Why are the few adjectives used in this section important?

CONCLUDE: What effect might this language have on someone accused of a crime?

---

2. **capital** *adj.* punishable by execution.
3. **Counsel** *n.* lawyer or group of lawyers giving advice about legal matters and representing clients in court.

Amendment VII

12 In suits[4] at common law, where the value in controversy shall exceed twenty dollars, the right of trial by jury shall be preserved, and no fact tried by a jury, shall be otherwise re-examined in any Court of the United States, than according to the rules of the common law.

Amendment VIII

13 Excessive bail[5] shall not be required, nor excessive fines imposed, nor cruel and unusual punishments inflicted.

Amendment IX

14 The enumeration in the Constitution, of certain rights, shall not be construed to deny or disparage others retained by the people.

Amendment X

15 The powers not delegated to the United States by the Constitution, nor prohibited by it to the States, are reserved to the States respectively, or to the people. 🔊

---

4. **suits** *n.* lawsuits, or legal actions brought by one party against another.
5. **bail** *n.* property or money given to the court to ensure that an arrested person released from custody will return at a certain time.

NOTES

Comprehension Check

Complete the following items after you finish your first read.

1. According to its Preamble, who is responsible for establishing the Constitution?

2. What laws are forbidden in Amendment I of the Bill of Rights?

3. Which amendments cover legal proceedings?

4. 🗒 **Notebook** Write a summary of the Preamble to the Constitution and a summary of the Bill of Rights to confirm your understanding of the texts.

- -

RESEARCH

Research to Clarify Choose at least one unfamiliar detail from these texts. Briefly research that detail. In what way does the information you learned shed light on an aspect of these documents?

PREAMBLE TO THE
CONSTITUTION | BILL OF RIGHTS

Close Read the Text

1. This model—Amendment III of the Bill of Rights—shows two sample annotations, along with questions and conclusions. Close read the passage, and find another detail to annotate. Then, write a question and your conclusion.

ANNOTATE: These parallel phrases speak to both peace and wartime situations.

QUESTION: What do these details say about early American attitudes toward the military?

CONCLUDE: They suggest that early Americans wanted to limit military power unless it was needed.

ANNOTATE: The paragraph presents contrasting ideas—"consent of the owner" and "prescribed by law."

QUESTION: What balance of power do these terms suggest?

CONCLUDE: In peacetime, personal choice overrides government concerns; the opposite may be true during wartime.

> No soldier, shall in time of peace be quartered in any house, without the consent of the owner, nor in time of war, but in a manner to be prescribed by law.

Tool Kit
Close-Read Guide and
Model Annotation

2. For more practice, go back into the text and complete the close-read notes.

3. Revisit a section of the text you found important during your first read. **Annotate** what you notice. Ask yourself **questions** such as "Why did the author make this choice?" What can you **conclude**?

Analyze the Text

CITE TEXTUAL EVIDENCE
to support your answers.

Notebook Respond to these questions.

1. **Analyze** How can you tell from the Preamble that the Constitution is meant to do more than merely resolve the country's issues at that time?

2. **Connect** How does Amendment II of the Bill of Rights reinforce Amendment I?

3. (a) **Paraphrase** When you **paraphrase**, you restate a text in your own words. Paraphrase Amendment VIII. (b) **Analyze** How does this amendment relate to the theme of freedom? Explain.

4. **Historical Perspectives** Which Americans were not granted the freedoms and rights set forth in the Constitution and the Bill of Rights?

5. **Essential Question: *What is the meaning of freedom?*** What have you learned about American freedoms by reading these documents?

STANDARDS
Reading Informational Text
• Analyze and evaluate the effectiveness of the structure an author uses in his or her exposition or argument, including whether the structure makes points clear, convincing, and engaging.
• Analyze seventeenth-, eighteenth-, and nineteenth-century foundational U.S. documents of historical and literary significance for their themes, purposes, and rhetorical features.

Analyze Craft and Structure

Author's Choices: Structure Both the Constitution and the Bill of Rights are **resolutions**, or legal foundational statements that explain a set of decisions approved by a governing body. Likewise, both begin with a **preamble**, a statement that explains who is issuing the document and for what purpose. The text that follows the Preamble to the Bill of Rights illustrates a simple structure called **enumeration**, in which the major ideas (the first ten amendments) are listed in numerical order. Each of the amendments follows a regular structure, beginning with a **heading**, or label.

Practice

CITE TEXTUAL EVIDENCE
to support your answers.

Answer these questions.

1. What does the preamble to the Bill of Rights tell readers about the reasons the document was created?

2. Why is "RESOLVED" used to begin the second paragraph of the Preamble?

3. Explain why enumeration is an effective organizational pattern for the Bill of Rights.

4. (a) In the chart, record the major idea of each amendment listed—specifically, what rights or related set of rights does each amendment protect? (b) How is Amendment IX different from the other amendments? Explain.

AMENDMENT	MAJOR IDEA
II	
III	
IV	
VI	
VII	
X	

Concept Vocabulary

exercise	petition	infringed
abridging	redress	prescribed

Why These Words? These concept vocabulary words suggest legal limitations or remedies. For example, the Bill of Rights was written to ensure that nothing *infringed* upon citizens' rights. The document outlines basic rights but does not explain certain points in detail—for example, exactly what *redress* will be available when a wrong is committed. Both *infringed* and *redress* refer to legal matters.

1. How does the concept vocabulary allow the writers to present ideas with both formality and precision?

2. What other words in these documents connect to the concept of legal limitations or remedies?

Practice

🖥 **Notebook** **Complete these activities.**

1. Use each concept vocabulary word in a sentence that demonstrates your understanding of the word's meaning.

2. Replace each concept word with a synonym. Use a thesaurus, if you wish. Then, consider which word best expresses your meaning. Which is the clearer, more precise word?

Word Study

Multiple-Meaning Words The concept vocabulary word *exercise* has more than one meaning. As a noun, *exercise* can refer to physical exertion that maintains or improves health. It also can refer to an activity that tests or displays a particular skill. As a verb, it can refer to the action of physical training or the action of implementing one's right to do something.

1. Write four sentences using the word *exercise*. Each sentence should demonstrate one of the four meanings of the word noted above.

2. The concept words *abridging*, *petition*, and *prescribed* are also multiple-meaning words. For each word, write its meaning as it is used in the Bill of Rights. Then, write a second meaning for each word. Use a college-level dictionary to verify your work.

🔗 WORD NETWORK

Add words related to freedom from the text to your Word Network.

≣ STANDARDS

Language
• Apply the understanding that usage is a matter of convention, can change over time, and is sometimes contested.
• Determine or clarify the meaning of unknown and multiple-meaning words and phrases based on *grades 11–12 reading and content*, choosing flexibly from a range of strategies.
• Consult general and specialized reference materials, both print and digital, to find the pronunciation of a word or determine or clarify its precise meaning, its part of speech, its etymology, or its standard usage.

Conventions and Style

Punctuation for Enumeration Listing, or enumeration, is an important characteristic of the style used in these documents. When enumerating ideas, place a comma between each item in the series. The choice to use the **serial comma** in a list of three or more enumerated items is a matter of style. If it is used, the serial comma is placed immediately before the coordinating conjunction (usually *and, or,* or *nor*). In addition, enumerated text must demonstrate **parallel structure.** For instance, if two items in the list are prepositional phrases, then the remaining items should also be prepositional phrases.

TYPE OF ITEM	EXAMPLE OF PARALLEL STRUCTURE
single words	*nor be deprived of life, liberty, or property* (*nouns, from Amendment V*)
phrases	*in order to form a more perfect union, [to] establish justice, [to] insure domestic tranquility, [to] provide for the common defense, [to] promote the general welfare, and [to] secure the blessings of liberty to ourselves and our posterity* (*infinitive phrases, from the Preamble to the Constitution*)
clauses	*Excessive bail shall not be required, nor [shall] excessive fines [be] imposed, nor [shall] cruel and unusual punishments [be] inflicted* (*independent clauses, from Amendment VIII*)

Read It

1. Add commas to each sentence about these documents. Then, identify what type of item has been enumerated in each sentence.

   a. The Preamble to the Constitution secures "the blessings of liberty" to the American people to their descendants and to every generation.
   b. These brief historic and comprehensive amendments shape many aspects of American life.
   c. Today, Americans can read the text of the Bill of Rights online they can purchase printed copies or they can see one of the original documents on display.

2. **Notebook Connect to Style** Reread the Preamble to the Constitution. Explain how enumeration helps Madison convey a great deal of information in a compact space.

Write It

Notebook Use enumeration to revise and expand upon these sentences. Use commas to make the enumeration clear.

> **EXAMPLE**
> **Original Sentence:** Amendment VI identifies rights of defendants.
> **Sentence with Enumeration:** According to Amendment VI, defendants **will have a speedy and public trial, will face witnesses,** and **will be represented by a lawyer.**

1. James Madison included several freedoms in Amendment I.
2. Today, the Bill of Rights does many things for Americans.

TIP

CLARIFICATION
Serial commas can increase the clarity of your writing. Consider this sentence without a serial comma: "The actress plays Marina, a mermaid and a comedian." Did the actress play one person, Marina, who is a mermaid and a comedian? Or did she play three separate characters? Use of the serial comma eliminates this ambiguity.

PREAMBLE TO THE
CONSTITUTION | BILL OF RIGHTS

Writing to Sources

The Preamble to the Constitution and the Bill of Rights are examples of informative writing. Like other kinds of informative writing, they were written primarily to convey facts. The facts are organized and presented in a way that best suits the writer's purpose and the audience's needs.

Assignment

An extended definition is an informative text—usually one or two paragraphs—that explains a key concept. Choose and reread one amendment from the Bill of Rights. Then, write an **extended definition** of a key word or concept presented in that amendment. Your extended definition should explain both the dictionary meaning of the word or concept and any shades of meaning reflected in the amendment. Use at least two of these techniques to clarify your information and engage readers.

- Compare and contrast the word or concept with more familiar words or concepts.
- Discuss what the word or concept does *not* mean.
- Identify meanings that people often assign to the word or concept.
- Provide examples of ways in which the word or concept is used today.
- Share a personal experience that helped you understand the word or concept.

Vocabulary and Conventions Connection Consider including several of the concept vocabulary words. Also, remember to use commas correctly if you include enumeration.

exercise	petition	infringed
abridging	redress	prescribed

- -

Reflect on Your Writing

After you have drafted your extended definition, answer these questions.

1. Which techniques did you use to develop your extended definition?

2. In what ways did those techniques strengthen your writing?

3. **Why These Words?** The words you choose make a difference in your writing. Which words made your text more powerful or precise?

STANDARDS

Writing
Develop the topic thoroughly by selecting the most significant and relevant facts, extended definitions, concrete details, quotations, or other information and examples appropriate to the audience's knowledge of the topic.

Speaking and Listening
Present information, findings, and supporting evidence, conveying a clear and distinct perspective such that listeners can follow the line of reasoning, alternative or opposing perspectives are addressed, and the organization, development, substance, and style are appropriate to purpose, audience, and a range of formal and informal tasks.

Speaking and Listening

Assignment

Write and deliver a **speech** about the Bill of Rights, in which you explain how the document as a whole, or a particular amendment, applies to your life. If you wish, work as a class to share these speeches as part of a lecture series called "It's My Right!"

1. **Write the Speech** Think about the Bill of Rights. How does it relate to your life? Which amendments are especially significant to you? Why?

   - Have you had any experiences involving freedom of religion, freedom of speech, or freedom of the press? If so, think about the protections offered by Amendment I.

   - How do you expect the Bill of Rights to affect your life in the future?

   - Draft your speech, using facts and examples to illustrate your personal response to the document.

2. **Deliver the Speech** To prepare to deliver your speech, review your text and practice presenting it. Mark the words you will emphasize, points at which to pause or stop for effect, and so on.

   - As you deliver the speech, make eye contact with your audience. Don't stare; rather, look at audience members for a few seconds to make sure they understand your message.

   - Use appropriate volume so everyone can hear you, even in the back rows. Carry yourself proudly, and hold your head up so that your voice carries.

   - Avoid rushing. Remember that your audience has not heard your speech before. Give them time to absorb your words and meaning.

3. **Evaluate Your Presentation** After your speech, use the evaluation guide to assess how well you presented your ideas. Did you fulfill the assignment by showing how the Bill of Rights applies to your life? Were your ideas logical, clear, and appropriate to your audience and subject? Use your self-evaluation to establish several goals for your next oral presentation.

PRESENTATION EVALUATION GUIDE

Rate each statement on a scale of 1 (not demonstrated) to 5 (demonstrated).

- [ ] I conveyed a personal understanding of the Bill of Rights.

- [ ] I held the audience's attention.

- [ ] I used appropriate eye contact to convey meaning and sufficient volume to be heard.

- [ ] I did not rush and pronounced words correctly and clearly.

EVIDENCE LOG

Before moving on to a new selection, go to your Evidence Log and record what you learned from the Preamble to the Constitution and from the Bill of Rights.

Speech in the Convention

Concept Vocabulary

You will encounter the following words as you read the speech Benjamin Franklin gave at the Constitutional Convention in 1787. Before reading, note how familiar you are with each word. Then, rank the words in order from most familiar (1) to least familiar (6).

WORD	YOUR RANKING
infallibility	
despotism	
corrupted	
prejudices	
salutary	
integrity	

After completing the first read, come back to the concept vocabulary and review your rankings. Mark changes to your original rankings as needed.

First Read NONFICTION

Apply these strategies as you conduct your first read. You will have an opportunity to complete the close-read notes after your first read.

Tool Kit
First-Read Guide and
Model Annotation

NOTICE the general ideas of the text. *What* is it about? *Who* is involved?

ANNOTATE by marking vocabulary and key passages you want to revisit.

CONNECT ideas within the selection to what you already know and what you have already read.

RESPOND by completing the Comprehension Check and by writing a brief summary of the selection.

First Read

STANDARDS
Reading Informational Text
By the end of grade 11, read and comprehend literary nonfiction in the grades 11–CCR text complexity band proficiently, with scaffolding as needed at the high end of the range.

About the Author

Benjamin Franklin

From his teen years until his retirement at age forty-two, Benjamin Franklin (1706–1790) worked as a printer. He got his start as an apprentice to his brother James Franklin, a Boston printer. By the time he was sixteen, Ben was not only printing, but writing parts of his brother's newspaper. Using the name "Silence Dogood," he wrote letters satirizing daily life and politics in Boston. When he was seventeen, Franklin moved to Philadelphia to open his own print shop. This move gave birth to one of his most enduring contributions to American culture, *Poor Richard's Almanack*. This annual publication, which was published from 1732 to 1752, contained information, observations, and advice and was a colonial bestseller.

The "Write" Reputation Just as he had signed "Silence Dogood" to the letters he wrote for his brother's paper, Franklin created a fictitious author/editor for the *Almanack*. The chatty Richard Saunders, or Poor Richard, first appeared as a dull and foolish astronomer. However, over the years his character developed, becoming more thoughtful, pious, and funny.

Like most almanacs, *Poor Richard's Almanack* contained practical information about the calendar, the sun and moon, and the weather. It also featured a wealth of homespun sayings and observations, or aphorisms, many of which are still quoted today. It was these aphorisms that made the *Almanack* so popular. Franklin included an aphorism at the top or bottom of most of the Almanack's pages. The wit and brevity of these sayings allowed him to weave in many moral messages, while also entertaining his readers.

Inventor and Scientist When Franklin was forty-two, he retired from the printing business to devote himself to science. He proved to be as successful a scientist as he had been a printer. Over the course of his life, Franklin was responsible for inventing the lightning rod, bifocals, and a new type of stove. He confirmed the laws of electricity, charted the Gulf Stream, and contributed to the scientific understanding of earthquakes and ocean currents. In spite of all these achievements, Franklin is best remembered for his career in politics.

Statesman and Diplomat Franklin played an important role in drafting the Declaration of Independence, enlisting French support during the Revolutionary War, negotiating a peace treaty with Britain, and drafting the United States Constitution. In his later years, he was the United States ambassador to England and then to France. Even before George Washington earned the title, Franklin was considered to be "the father of his country."

American Success Story Perhaps it is no surprise that a person of Franklin's accomplishments, longevity, and historic importance would write the story of his life. Franklin's *The Autobiography* remains a classic of the genre as well as a prototype for the American success story. Franklin wrote the first section of the work in 1771, when he was sixty-five years old. At the urging of friends, he wrote three more sections—the last shortly before his death—but succeeded in bringing the account of his life only to the year 1759. Though never completed, his autobiography, filled with his opinions and advice, provides not only a record of his achievements, but also an understanding of his extraordinary character.

Speech
in the
Convention

Benjamin Franklin

BACKGROUND

After the American Revolution, each of the newly independent states created its own constitution. While Congress was able to pass limited laws, it had no power to tax the states or regulate issues, such as trade, that were affected by state boundaries. These problems led to the Constitutional Convention in 1787. Representatives from twelve states met to approve a national constitution. The argument was lively and often contentious. At the age of eighty-one, Benjamin Franklin—representing Pennsylvania—brought his diplomatic skills to the debate.

Mr. President,

1   I confess, that I do not entirely approve of this Constitution at present; but, Sir, I am not sure I shall never approve it; for, having lived long, I have experienced many instances of being obliged, by better information or fuller consideration, to change my opinions even on important subjects, which I once thought right, but found to be otherwise. It is therefore that, the older I grow, the more apt I am to doubt my own judgment of others. Most men, indeed, as well as most sects in religion, think themselves in possession of all truth, and that wherever others differ from them, it is so far error. . . . Though many private persons think almost as highly of their own **infallibility** as of that of their sect, few express it so naturally as a certain French lady, who, in a little dispute with her sister, said, "But I meet with nobody but myself that is *always* in the right." "*Je ne trouve que moi qui aie toujours raison.*"

2   In these sentiments, Sir, I agree to this Constitution, with all its faults,—if they are such; because I think a general government necessary for us, and there is no form of government but what may be a blessing to the people, if well administered; and I believe, farther, that this is likely to be well administered for a course of years, and can only end in **despotism**, as other forms have done before it, when the people shall become so **corrupted** as to need despotic government, being incapable of any other. I doubt, too, whether any other convention we can obtain, may be able to make a better constitution; for, when you assemble a number of men, to have the advantage of their joint wisdom, you inevitably assemble with those men all their **prejudices**, their passions, their errors of opinion, their local interests, and their selfish views. From such an assembly can a *perfect* production be expected? It therefore astonishes me, Sir, to find this system approaching so near to perfection as it does; and I think it will astonish our enemies, who are waiting with confidence to hear, that our councils are confounded like those of the builders of Babel, and that our states are on the point of separation, only to meet hereafter for the purpose of cutting one another's throats. Thus I consent, Sir, to this Constitution, because I expect no better, and because I am not sure that it is not the best. The opinions I have had

NOTES

infallibility (ihn fal uh BIHL uh tee) *n.* inability to be in error

CLOSE READ

ANNOTATE: Franklin refers humorously to "a certain French lady." Mark her words and their English translation in paragraph 1.

QUESTION: Why does Franklin choose to illustrate his point in this way?

CONCLUDE: What is the effect of this quotation?

despotism (DEHS puh tihz uhm) *n.* absolute rule; tyranny

corrupted (kuh RUHPT ihd) *adj.* dishonest

prejudices (PREHJ uh dihs ihz) *n.* unfavorable opinions or feelings formed beforehand or without factual support

salutary (SAL yuh tehr ee)
adj. beneficial; promoting a positive purpose

integrity (ihn TEHG ruh tee) *n.* virtue; commitment to moral or ethical principles

of its *errors* I sacrifice to the public good. I have never whispered a syllable of them abroad. Within these walls they were born, and here they shall die. If every one of us, in returning to our constituents, were to report the objections he has had to it, and endeavor to gain partisans in support of them, we might prevent its being generally received, and thereby lose all the **salutary** effects and great advantages resulting naturally in our favor among foreign nations, as well as among ourselves, from our real or apparent unanimity. Much of the strength and efficiency of any government, in procuring and securing happiness to the people, depends on *opinion*, on the general opinion of the goodness of that government, as well as of the wisdom and **integrity** of its governors. I hope, therefore, for our own sakes, as a part of the people, and for the sake of our posterity, that we shall act heartily and unanimously in recommending this Constitution, wherever our influence may extend, and turn our future thoughts and endeavors to the means of having it *well administered*.

3   On the whole, Sir, I cannot help expressing a wish, that every member of the convention who may still have objections to it, would with me on this occasion doubt a little of his own infallibility, and, to make manifest our *unanimity*, put his name to this instrument. ❧

MEDIA CONNECTION

The U. S. Constitution

💬 **Discuss It** How does this video help you understand the challenges that Franklin faced in persuading the delegates to approve the Constitution?

Write your response before sharing your ideas.

Comprehension Check

Complete the following items after you finish your first read.

1. What does Franklin admit has caused him to change his mind in the past?

2. Why does Franklin believe that any constitution the Convention approves will be an imperfect document?

3. Why does Franklin want the delegates to keep their divided opinions to themselves once the Constitution is approved?

4. Whose "opinion" does Franklin believe is key to a government's strength and efficiency?

5. 📓 **Notebook** Write a summary of Franklin's speech to confirm your understanding of the text.

RESEARCH

Research to Clarify Choose at least one unfamiliar detail from the text. Briefly research that detail. In what way does the information you learned shed light on an aspect of the speech?

Research to Explore Conduct research on an aspect of the text you find interesting. For example, you might research why Franklin was one of the most popular authors and public figures of his time.

SPEECH IN THE CONVENTION

Close Read the Text

1. This model, from paragraph 1 of the speech, shows two sample annotations, along with questions and conclusions. Close read the passage, and find another detail to annotate. Then, write a question and your conclusion.

ANNOTATE: The word "confess" is a startling beginning to a speech.

QUESTION: Why does Franklin say this?

CONCLUDE: By confessing to his own struggle, Franklin shows that compromise is not a sign of weakness.

> I confess, that I do not entirely approve of this Constitution at present; but, Sir, I am not sure I shall never approve it; for, having lived long, I have experienced many instances of being obliged, by better information or fuller consideration, to change my opinions. . . .

ANNOTATE: Franklin reminds listeners of his old age.

QUESTION: Why does he make this point?

CONCLUDE: He is reminding them of his age and experience—he has authority his listeners lack.

Tool Kit
Close-Read Guide and Model Annotation

2. For more practice, go back into the text and complete the close-read notes.

3. Revisit a section of the text you found important during your first read. Read this section closely, and **annotate** what you notice. Ask yourself **questions** such as "Why did the author make this choice?" What can you **conclude**?

Analyze the Text

CITE TEXTUAL EVIDENCE to support your answers.

Notebook Respond to these questions.

1. **Draw Conclusions** Franklin addresses his remarks to "Mr. President"—George Washington, who led the proceedings. How can you tell that his remarks do not concern Washington alone?

2. (a) Early in the speech, what does Franklin admit that he sometimes doubts? (b) **Connect** How does this admission relate to his overall argument?

3. An **allusion** is a passing or unexplained reference to something from history or culture. (a) **Interpret** In paragraph 2, what is the purpose of Franklin's allusion to the builders of Babel? (b) **Criticize** Do you consider this allusion to be effective? Explain.

4. **Historical Perspectives** In what ways does Franklin fear the delegates may undermine the Constitution even after they sign it? Explain.

5. **Essential Question:** *What is the meaning of freedom?* What have you learned about the nature of freedom by reading this speech?

STANDARDS
Reading Informational Text
• Cite strong and thorough textual evidence to support analysis of what the text says explicitly as well as inferences drawn from the text, including determining where the text leaves matters uncertain.
• Determine an author's point of view or purpose in a text in which the rhetoric is particularly effective, analyzing how style and content contribute to the power, persuasiveness or beauty of the text.

Analyze Craft and Structure

Author's Purpose: Rhetoric Franklin's speech was successful: The Constitution was approved and sent to the states for ratification. Franklin's text provides examples of several **rhetorical devices**, or ways of using language for effect, that appeal to an audience and produce a successful oratory.

- **Paradox** is a statement or idea that seems contradictory but actually presents a truth. For example, in Shakespeare's *Hamlet*, the statement "I must be cruel to be kind" seems illogical. On reflection, however, it demonstrates a deeper truth: Sometimes, one must face a painful reality in order to rise above or learn from it.
- **Concession** is the acknowledgment of an opponent's arguments.
- **Rhetorical questions** are questions asked for effect—to make a point, or introduce a topic. The speaker does not expect the audience to answer, because the answer is obvious.

While not strictly an example of a rhetorical device, a speaker's **tone,** or attitude toward the subject and audience, can also sway listeners. Phrasing and word choice combine to convey tone, which may be ironic, serious, humorous, friendly, distant, cynical, earnest, and so on.

Practice

CITE TEXTUAL EVIDENCE to support your answers.

📓 **Notebook** **Complete these activities.**

1. Use the chart to identify examples from Franklin's speech of each rhetorical device noted. Explain how each device serves to strengthen Franklin's argument or influence his audience.

RHETORICAL DEVICE	EFFECT
paradox:	
concession:	
rhetorical question:	

2. (a) Choose the set of adjectives that best describes the tone of the first paragraph of this speech.

- [ ] slyly humorous and self-deprecating
- [ ] deeply earnest, concerned, and frustrated
- [ ] serious, witty, and informal

(b) Explain your choice, citing specific words and phrases that support your answer.

3. During his long political career, Franklin had extensive experience as a diplomat. In what ways does this speech reflect a diplomatic approach to conflict? Explain.

SPEECH IN THE CONVENTION

Concept Vocabulary

infallibility	corrupted	salutary
despotism	prejudices	integrity

Why These Words? These concept vocabulary words are used to describe human vices and virtues, especially when it comes to the power governments can wield over citizens. Franklin believes any government can be *corrupted*, and that those in positions of leadership should have *integrity*.

1. How does the concept vocabulary suggest human goals—and the human failings that make the achievement of those goals difficult?

2. What other words in the speech connect to this concept?

WORD NETWORK

Add words related to freedom from the text to your Word Network.

Practice

📓 **Notebook** Respond to these questions.

1. Why might it be difficult to deal with people who never doubt their own *infallibility*?

2. What are two negative effects that might result from a government ruled by *despotism*?

3. What safeguards could a constitution include to minimize the chance that a government will be *corrupted*?

4. Name two ways in which *prejudices* can affect human behavior.

5. What *salutary* effects can result from cooperation?

6. Would you vote for a candidate who displayed *integrity*? Why or why not?

Word Study

Latin Suffix: -ity The suffix *-ity* means "state or quality of." When this suffix is added to an adjective, the resulting word is a noun. For example, in the word *infallibility,* the suffix is added to the adjective *infallible,* which means "incapable of failing." The resulting noun means "the state of being incapable of failing."

1. Find and define two other words near the end of Franklin's speech that end with the suffix *-ity*. Check your definitions in a print or digital college-level dictionary.

2. Identify and define two other words that end with the suffix *-ity*. Use a dictionary to verify your definitions.

STANDARDS

Language
• Demonstrate command of the conventions of standard English capitalization, punctuation, and spelling when writing.
• Vary syntax for effect, consulting references for guidance as needed; apply an understanding of syntax to the study of complex texts when reading.
• Consult general and specialized reference materials, both print and digital, to find the pronunciation of a word or determine or clarify its precise meaning, its part of speech, its etymology, or its standard usage.

Conventions and Style

Syntax and Rhetoric **Parallelism** is the use of similar grammatical forms or patterns to express similar ideas. Effective use of parallelism adds rhythm and balance to writing and strengthens connections among ideas. Faulty parallelism presents equal ideas in a distracting and potentially confusing mix of grammatical forms.

EXAMPLE

Nonparallel: Franklin **was supportive of** the Constitution, **went to express** his feelings, and **was writing** emphatically about the document.

Parallel: Franklin **supported** the Constitution, **expressed** his feelings to others, and **wrote** emphatically about the document.

The parallel sentence states three similar ideas as phrases that begin with an action verb in the simple past tense.

Read It

1. Underline the parallel elements in these sentences.

   a. The sensible, brilliant, and influential James Wilson was among the delegates from Pennsylvania.

   b. Franklin was too weak to deliver the speech himself—but was the weakness due to his unremitting pain, his unceasing work for compromise, or his exhaustion after days of argument?

   c. Wilson read the speech, which came at a critical moment in the proceedings, addressed the need for compromise, and swayed several delegates.

2. **Connect to Style** Reread paragraph 2 of Franklin's speech. Identify two examples of parallelism. Explain the ideas the parallel items express.

Write It

 Notebook Rewrite each sentence so that it uses parallelism. Be sure to place commas to separate the ideas or details.

EXAMPLE

Incorrect: *Fueled by love for liberty, eager to form an effective government,* and *with personal determination,* several political leaders founded the Society for Political Inquiries in 1787.

Correct: *Fueled by love for liberty, eagerness to form an effective government,* and *personal determination,* several political leaders founded the Society for Political Inquiries in 1787.

---

1. The society's members considered issues of government, wrote essays on political topics, and there were discussions about how governments can serve people.

2. At the Constitutional Convention, throughout the fight for state ratification, and when Washington was president, this group continued to function.

TIP

USAGE

When you use correlative conjunctions (which appear in pairs) to achieve parallelism, make sure that the words are in the correct order.

Incorrect: Franklin **not only** wanted unanimity **but also** civility.

Correct: Franklin wanted **not only** unanimity **but also** civility.

SPEECH IN THE CONVENTION

Writing to Sources

When you evaluate a text—whether you do so in writing, in discussions with other readers, or just in your own thinking process—you consider what an author sought to achieve in a piece of writing and whether he or she was successful.

Assignment

Franklin's speech in the Convention has been called a masterpiece. Do you agree? Write an **evaluation** of the speech. Consider Franklin's goal and the techniques he used to accomplish it. Be sure to include these elements in your evaluation:

- an introduction that includes a statement of your position
- at least one reference to Franklin's goal
- valid reasoning, supported by textual evidence that clearly relates to each point
- specific references to the ideas Franklin conveyed and to his use of rhetorical devices
- original rhetorical devices that help you make your points
- a conclusion that reasserts your opinion in a memorable way

Vocabulary and Conventions Connection Consider including several of the concept vocabulary words in your evaluation. Also, remember to use parallelism to emphasize related ideas and create rhythm in your writing.

infallibility	corrupted	salutary
despotism	prejudices	integrity

- -

Reflect on Your Writing

After you have drafted your evaluation, answer the following questions.

1. What evidence did you provide in your evaluation?

2. What rhetorical devices did you use in your evaluation?

3. Why These Words? The words you choose make a difference in your writing. Which words helped you express your ideas?

STANDARDS

Writing
• Write arguments to support claims in an analysis of substantive topics or texts, using valid reasoning and relevant and sufficient evidence.
• Provide a concluding statement or section that follows from and supports the argument presented.

Speaking and Listening
• Evaluate a speaker's point of view, reasoning, and use of evidence and rhetoric, assessing the stance, premises, links among ideas, word choice, points of emphasis, and tone used.
• Make strategic use of digital media in presentations to enhance understanding of findings, reasoning, and evidence and to add interest.

Speaking and Listening

Assignment

As a class, prepare to make a **video recording** of a dramatic delivery of Franklin's speech. Follow these steps to complete the assignment.

1. **Discuss the Speech** Use a class discussion to clarify your thoughts about the speech. Be prepared to share notes you made while reading the text as you and your classmates respond to these questions.

   - What is Franklin's opinion of the Constitution in its draft form?
   - How does he use concession and paradox as he argues his position?
   - What is his tone? How does Franklin's tone appeal to his audience and help persuade them of the validity of his opinion?
   - What are some of the ways in which Franklin's tone could be expressed in a dramatic reading?

2. **Practice and Present** Work together to decide who will read various parts of the speech. Have classmates take a few minutes to practice their parts individually, using Franklin's punctuation to help with phrasing and checking the pronunciation of challenging words. Next, practice together so that the reading moves smoothly from one speaker to the next. Then, present the speech as your teacher makes a video recording. Remember these points:

   - Be quiet and attentive while others are presenting their parts.
   - Use the tone and emphasis that you think Franklin might have used if he had delivered the speech himself.
   - Use appropriate gestures to convey key points.

3. **Evaluate the Video** Schedule sufficient time to watch the video. Allow about ten minutes for the follow-up discussion. Then, use the evaluation guide to analyze what you saw and heard. Encourage everyone to contribute. If possible, add the video to the class website or digital portfolio.

EVALUATION GUIDE

Rate each statement on a scale of 1 (not demonstrated) to 5 (demonstrated). Be prepared to defend your rating, using examples.

- [ ] Speakers clearly conveyed the text's meaning.
- [ ] Speakers held the audience's attention.
- [ ] Speakers used the tone and emphasis that Franklin likely intended when he wrote the speech.
- [ ] Speakers used appropriate gestures and body language.

✐ EVIDENCE LOG

Before moving on to a new selection, go to your Evidence Log and record what you learned from Franklin's speech in the Convention.

About Visual Propaganda

Whether printed on posters or in newspapers, sewn into the design of a flag, broadcast in television commercials, or presented in other forms, **visual propaganda** uses striking images (and sometimes simple slogans) to convey a persuasive message, especially during times of turmoil, such as war. One of the earliest examples can be seen in Mesopotamian carvings announcing a military victory in 2250 B.C. The Bayeux Tapestry provided woven visual propaganda about the Norman Conquest in A.D.1066. Visual propaganda was especially critical during the Russian Revolution in 1917, and during World War I, when the political poster was created to rouse patriotic fervor.

The American Revolution: Visual Propaganda

Media Vocabulary

These words or concepts will be useful to you as you analyze, discuss, and write about visual propaganda.

propaganda: information, ideas, or rumors spread widely and deliberately to help or harm a person, group, movement, cause, or nation	• Creators of propaganda attempt to persuade people by presenting images and words that strongly suggest a particular *slant*, or viewpoint. • Propaganda encourages people to react emotionally rather than logically—for example, to vote a certain way out of fear or to oppose a cause out of anger.
appeal: the ability to attract and engage an audience's mind or emotions	• A logical appeal (called *logos*) influences reason. • An emotional appeal (called *pathos*) targets or manipulates people's feelings. • Propaganda depends much more heavily upon pathos than upon logos.
symbolism: the use of images or objects to represent ideas or qualities	• Symbolism uses images and objects that many people associate with certain concepts, such as a flag to represent a country, a rose to represent love, or the color red to represent danger. • In propaganda, symbolism appears primarily in visuals because it provides a quick way to convey meaning. • An image or object can have more than one symbolic meaning. The meaning can vary from one culture to another.

First Review MEDIA: ART AND PHOTOGRAPHY

Apply these strategies as you conduct your first review.

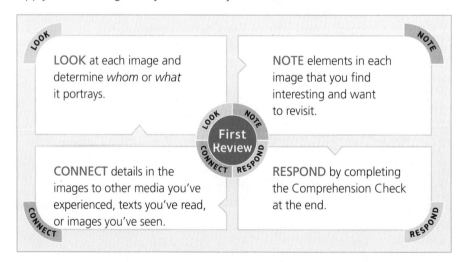

LOOK at each image and determine *whom* or *what* it portrays.

NOTE elements in each image that you find interesting and want to revisit.

First Review

CONNECT details in the images to other media you've experienced, texts you've read, or images you've seen.

RESPOND by completing the Comprehension Check at the end.

STANDARDS

Reading Informational Text
By the end of grade 11, read and comprehend literary nonfiction in the grades 11–CCR text complexity band proficiently, with scaffolding as needed at the high end of the range.

The American Revolution:
Visual Propaganda

BACKGROUND

The practice of persuading people with paintings, drawings, and other kinds of images has a long history in the United States, dating back to the colonial period. The images that follow are examples of visual propaganda published by both the colonists and the British in support of their respective causes.

IMAGE 1: Join or Die This political cartoon was published by Benjamin Franklin in 1754. The segments of the snake are labeled with the initials of American colonies. The purpose of the cartoon was to urge the colonies to unite against the French in the French and Indian War. During the American Revolution, it took on new meaning as a symbol of colonial protest against Great Britain.

NOTES

The BLOODY MASSACRE perpetrated in King — Street BOSTON on March 5th 1770 by a party of the 29th REGT.

Engrav'd Printed & Sold by PAUL REVERE BOSTON

Unhappy Boston! see thy Sons deplore,
Thy hallow'd Walks besmear'd with guiltless Gore:
While faithless P——n and his savage Bands,
With murd'rous Rancour stretch their bloody Hands,
Like fierce Barbarians grinning o'er their Prey,
Approve the Carnage and enjoy the Day.

If scalding drops from Rage from Anguish Wrung
If speechless Sorrows lab'ring for a Tongue,
Or if a weeping World can ought appease
The plaintive Ghosts of Victims such as these:
The Patriot's copious Tears for each are shed.
A glorious Tribute which embalms the Dead

But know Fate summons to that awful Goal.
Where Justice strips the Murd'rer of his Soul:
Should venal C—ts the scandal of the Land.
Snatch the relentless Villain from her Hand,
Keen Execrations on this Plate inscrib'd.
Shall reach a Judge who never can be brib'd.

The unhappy Sufferers were Mess'rs Sam'l Gray Sam'l Maverick, Jam's Caldwell, Crispus Attucks & Pat'k Carr
Killed. Six wounded; two of them (Christ'r Monk & John Clark) Mortally

IMAGE 2: The Boston Massacre

Paul Revere engraved this image in 1770 after the Boston Massacre, in which several colonists were shot to death by British soldiers. Revere's depiction does not show the events exactly as they happened. For example, the Americans had been rioting against the British authorities when the shots were fired. Also, the British did not have a clear firing line. Rather, they had been surrounded and were struggling with the crowd.

NOTES

IMAGE 3: The Bostonians in Distress This print was published in a London newspaper during the British blockade of Boston in 1774. In the image, colonists feed caged Bostonians as the British navy continues to keep Boston Harbor closed. The image may have amused the British—but it may have provoked very different feelings among Americans who saw it.

NOTES

DONT TREAD ON ME

IMAGE 4: The Gadsden Flag Colonist Christopher Gadsden created this flag during the American Revolution. Referencing Franklin's "Join or Die" cartoon, the flag is expressly directed at the English, showing a whole snake ready to strike.

Poor old England endeavoring to reclaim his wicked american Children.

IMAGE 5: Poor Old England The caption for this cartoon reads, "Poor Old England, Endeavoring to Reclaim His Wicked American Children." The scene represents efforts by King George III to harness and control the colonists, who show no signs of either respecting or submitting to the king's wishes. This cartoon was published in London in 1777, fourteen months after the signing of the Declaration of Independence.

Comprehension Check

Use the chart to note details about each image. Identify the main people and/or objects in the image and the activity depicted. Use the captions where helpful. In the final column, express your idea about the overall purpose of the image as a piece of propaganda.

IMAGE	PEOPLE AND/OR OBJECTS	ACTIVITY IN THE IMAGE	PURPOSE OF THE IMAGE
IMAGE 1			
IMAGE 2			
IMAGE 3			
IMAGE 4			
IMAGE 5			

JOIN, or DIE.

THE AMERICAN REVOLUTION:
VISUAL PROPAGANDA

Close Review

Revisit the images and your first-review notes. Write down any new observations that seem important. What **questions** do you have? What can you **conclude**?

- -

Analyze the Media

CITE TEXTUAL EVIDENCE
to support your answers.

📓 **Notebook** Respond to these questions.

1. (a) In Image 1, what does the snake represent? (b) **Connect** How does that representation shed light on the meaning of Image 4?

2. (a) **Compare and Contrast** From the colonial point of view, how do Images 2 and 3 have a similar slant? (b) **Analyze** Which details in the two images suggest that slant? Explain.

3. **Historical Perspectives** What do these images suggest about the colonists' growing sense of an American versus a British sense of identity? Explain.

4. **Essential Question:** *What is the meaning of freedom?* What have you learned about American freedoms from analyzing these images?

LANGUAGE DEVELOPMENT

Media Vocabulary

Use these words as you discuss and write about the images.

propaganda	appeal	symbolism

1. Which image most clearly presents the British as aggressors in the conflict with the colonies? Explain your choice, citing details from the image.

2. Which image most clearly expresses the colonists' resolve in their fight against Britain? Explain your choice, citing details from the image.

3. (a) In what ways does Image 2 distort facts in order to present a story that is favorable to one side? (b) What does this image suggest about propaganda as a source of reliable information? Explain.

📋 STANDARDS

Reading Informational Text
• Analyze and evaluate the effectiveness of the structure an author uses in his or her exposition or argument, including whether the structure makes points clear, convincing, and engaging.
• Integrate and evaluate multiple sources of information presented in different media or formats as well as in words in order to address a question or solve a problem.

Speaking and Listening

Assignment

With a partner, create an imaginary candidate who is campaigning for a major office, and develop a **political infomercial,** or extended, informative advertisement. Design and write the script for a presentation, including images that take a particular slant. Include a campaign slogan and a logo. As you work, take into account aspects of propaganda, appeal, and symbolism. Record and present the infomercial to the class.

1. Plan the Project To help you prepare your infomercial, consider these questions.

- What ideas does the candidate represent? What is his or her stance on issues such as education, the economy, and national defense?

- What facts from real life will you include? Which sources will you research for that information? Which visuals will best present that information in a way that helps the candidate's cause?

- How will you display your ideas and images? For example, you might create a video, use presentation software, or project on a whiteboard.

2. Consider Image Choices As you select or create images, consider the appeal that each one will have. For example, decide whether it adds emotional impact, symbolism, information, or serves another purpose.

ELEMENT	PURPOSE

3. Prepare the Script Once you have a final set of images and ideas, decide how you will weave them together to create your infomercial.

- Decide on the order of presentation. Add transitions to link related ideas.

- Create a pacing guide to determine the amount of time you will spend on each image.

- Choose which partner will narrate, and allow time to practice.

4. Present and Discuss Record the infomercial and share it with the class. After all of the infomercials have been presented, discuss how the types of techniques and images students used compare to that of American Revolutionary War propaganda.

TIP

PROCESS
Make sure that you and your partner agree to and understand the slant that your infomercial will present. Doing so will help you choose images and decide what to say about them.

EVIDENCE LOG

Before moving on to a new selection, go to your Evidence Log and record what you learned from "The American Revolution: Visual Propaganda."

STANDARDS
Speaking and Listening
Make strategic use of digital media in presentations to enhance understanding of findings, reasoning, and evidence and to add interest.

WRITING TO SOURCES

- DECLARATION OF INDEPENDENCE

- PREAMBLE TO THE CONSTITUTION

- BILL OF RIGHTS

- SPEECH IN THE CONVENTION

- THE AMERICAN REVOLUTION: VISUAL PROPAGANDA

 **Tool Kit**
Student Model of an Argument

ACADEMIC VOCABULARY

As you craft your argument, consider using some of the academic vocabulary you learned in the beginning of the unit.

confirm
demonstrate
supplement
establish
conviction

Write an Argument

You have just read a variety of documents from the early years of our nation. Each text reveals, in its own way, the principles that guided the nation's founders and other Americans of that era.

Assignment

Write a brief **argumentative essay** in which you address this question:

> Which statement do you find most compelling for Americans today: the Preamble to the Constitution or the first sentence of paragraph three of the Declaration of Independence?

Begin by choosing a position and stating a claim. Then, use specific details from the texts, historical examples, and your observations of our society today to support your claim. Make sure that your reasons link directly to your claim.

Elements of an Argument

In an **argument** a writer articulates a position, viewpoint, belief, or stand on an issue. Well-written arguments may convince readers to change their minds about an issue or to take a certain action.

An effective argument contains these elements:

- a precise claim
- consideration of counterclaims, or opposing positions, and a discussion of their strengths and weaknesses
- logical organization that makes clear connections among claim, counterclaims, reasons, and evidence
- word choices that are appropriate for a given audience
- clear reasoning and well-chosen evidence
- a concluding statement or section that logically completes the argument
- formal and objective language and tone
- error-free grammar, including correct and consistent use of verbs

Model Argument For a model of a well-crafted argument see the Launch Text, "Totally Free?" Review the Launch Text for examples of the elements of an effective argument. You will look more closely at these elements as you prepare to write your own argument.

☰ STANDARDS

Writing
• Write arguments to support claims in an analysis of substantive topics or texts, using valid reasoning and relevant and sufficient evidence.
• Write routinely over extended time frames and shorter time frames for a range of tasks, purposes, and audiences.

Prewriting / Planning

Break Down the Prompt Reading the prompt carefully and thoroughly can assist you in your planning. Complete these sentences to ensure that you understand the task that you are being asked to accomplish.

1. I am supposed to write a(n) _____.

2. In my own words, the question I must answer is _____.

3. My writing must include _____

   and _____.

4. I need to use examples from _____ as evidence and

   connect my ideas to _____.

Develop a Claim Start by deciding on a basic response to the question in the prompt. Then, develop your response into a claim. Use the sentence frame below to do so. Then, as you gather details and clarify your ideas, adjust your claim to reflect your new thinking.

I believe that _____

_____

because _____

_____

Gather Evidence The assignment asks you to use a variety of evidence, including examples from history, to support your position. In what sorts of resources might you find the types of historical information you need? Write some possibilities here.

_____ _____ _____

_____ _____ _____

_____ _____ _____

Always confirm your evidence by using more than one source.

Connect Across Texts The prompt asks you to connect your ideas to the texts you have read. The Launch Text shows you two means of doing this:

- You may **paraphrase**, or restate ideas in your own words. The Launch Text presents a paraphrase in the discussion of Roosevelt's "Four Freedoms" speech (his 1941 State of the Union address).

- You may also use **direct quotations**, as happens when the Launch Text quotes from the Declaration of Independence.

✐ EVIDENCE LOG

Review your Evidence Log and identify key details you may want to cite in your argument.

≡ STANDARDS

Writing
- Introduce precise, knowledgeable claim(s), establish the significance of the claim(s), distinguish the claim(s) from alternate or opposing claims, and create an organization that logically sequences claim(s), counterclaims, reasons, and evidence.
- Develop claim(s) and counterclaims fairly and thoroughly, supplying the most relevant evidence for each while pointing out the strengths and limitations of both in a manner that anticipates the audience's knowledge level, concerns, values, and possible biases.

ENRICHING WRITING WITH RESEARCH

Using Research A strong argument is always based on sound evidence and thoughtful, logical support. You may find support for your ideas in online or library resources.

Read It

This excerpt from the Launch Text provides an example of the use of researched evidence. After doing some reading, the writer decided to use Franklin D. Roosevelt's "Four Freedoms" speech to support the contention that freedoms should not clash.

> The writer located a specific speech from American history to support the claim that we need to consider other people's rights and needs as we exercise our own freedoms.

LAUNCH TEXT EXCERPT

In his 1941 State of the Union address, President Franklin Roosevelt identified four key freedoms as being basic human rights: freedom of speech and expression, freedom of worship, freedom from want, and freedom from fear. Those are not freedoms that one finds in a dictatorship. Nor are they freedoms that we grant to each other without the oversight and protection of government institutions. With the government's help, and the writing of laws, my freedom from want does not allow me to steal your food, and your freedom of speech does not let you publish lies about me. We are free, but only up to the point at which our freedoms clash.

Using a Search Engine As you develop an argument, you may not have specific examples and reasons in mind. You may need to use a search engine wisely to develop your argument's support. The writer of the Launch Text may have used a path like this.

> To narrow the search, the writer used a phrase rather than just the word *freedom*.

Search: Freedom in American History

Result: A website on different meanings of freedom over time in America

Action: Skim article to locate interesting and relevant examples.
1. Civil War: A new birth of freedom
2. World War II: The Four Freedoms
3. Cold War: The Free World

Search: The Four Freedoms

Result: An article about the "Four Freedoms" speech from the FDR Presidential Library

> Notice how one search led to a second, more specific search, and so on until the writer found the best possible support for the claim.

Actions: Skim article to learn about the Four Freedoms.
    Decide whether they apply to the original argument—and, if so, how.

Write It

Review the facts and evidence that you have gathered. Use this flowchart to organize your materials.

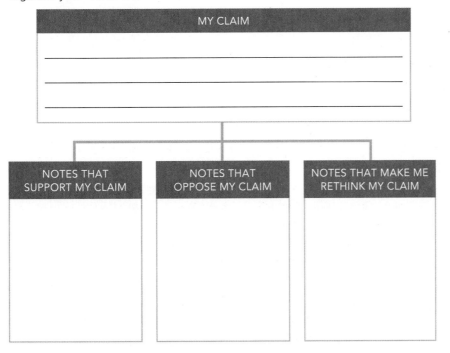

MY CLAIM

NOTES THAT SUPPORT MY CLAIM	NOTES THAT OPPOSE MY CLAIM	NOTES THAT MAKE ME RETHINK MY CLAIM

🐚 **TIP**

CONVENTIONS
Be sure to quote sources correctly.

- Run a short quotation from a source into the text and enclose it in quotation marks.

- Set off a long quotation in a block with all lines indented from the left. Such block quotations do not use quotation marks.

Notes That Support My Claim Some information you find may offer direct and fairly obvious support for your claim. Other information may require some interpretation or explanation on your part. For example, in the excerpt from the Launch Text, the writer analyzed the researched information about Roosevelt's speech and demonstrated how it supports the claim.

Notes That Oppose My Claim As you read and review sources, you may find some material that contradicts your claim. Consider working that material into the discussion of a counterclaim. You might start in one of these ways:

- Although [research source] states that _____, I believe that _____.

- [Research source] claims that _____. Nevertheless, it is clear that _____.

- Despite [research source]'s assertion that _____, it seems more likely that _____.

Remember to supply evidence that supports your rejection of any counterclaim that you mention.

Notes That Make Me Rethink My Claim Sometimes, your research will send you in a new direction. It may change your original ideas and make you rethink your claim. Do not be afraid to scrap your original plan if new evidence changes your mind. Just as architects or engineers do, good writers frequently discard a flawed plan and start over.

📑 STANDARDS

Writing
- Develop claim(s) and counterclaims fairly and thoroughly, supplying the most relevant evidence for each while pointing out the strengths and limitations of both in a manner that anticipates the audience's knowledge level, concerns, values, and possible biases.
- Gather relevant information from multiple authoritative print and digital sources, using advanced searches effectively; assess the strengths and limitations of each source in terms of the task, purpose, and audience; integrate information into the text selectively to maintain the flow of ideas, avoiding plagiarism and overreliance on any one source and following a standard format for citation.

Drafting

Organize Your Text Your text should include three parts:

- the **introduction**, in which you state your claim
- the **body**, in which you provide analysis, supporting reasons, and evidence. Each paragraph of your body should focus on one idea and evidence that directly supports it.
- the **conclusion**, in which you summarize or restate your claim

Use a formal style to get your points across. Avoid slang, contractions, and personal ("I") statements. The following chart will help you organize your thoughts.

Topic: _____	
Question: _____	
CLAIM	**COUNTERCLAIM**
EVIDENCE	**EVIDENCE**
1. _____ 2. _____ 3. _____	1. _____ 2. _____ 3. _____
REASONS/SUPPORT FOR EVIDENCE	**REASONS/SUPPORT FOR EVIDENCE**
1. _____ 2. _____ 3. _____	1. _____ 2. _____ 3. _____

Write a First Draft Refer to your chart as you write your first draft. Make sure to include a precise claim and to address counterclaims where possible. Write a conclusion that follows logically from your argument, supports your claim, and adds interest to your writing.

Use Rhetorical Devices **Rhetorical devices** are patterns of language that create emphasis and build emotion. While they do not replace sound reasoning and evidence, they can help to present your ideas in a memorable way. Consider using one or more of the following rhetorical devices in your essay:

- **Repetition:** Repeat key words to focus your argument.
- **Parallelism:** Repeat related ideas in the same grammatical structures.
- **Analogy:** Use comparisons to help readers grasp ideas.

Copyright © SAVVAS Learning Company LLC. All Rights Reserved.

STANDARDS
Writing
• Introduce precise, knowledgeable claim(s), establish the significance of the claim(s), distinguish the claim(s) from alternate or opposing claims, and create an organization that logically sequences claim(s), counterclaims, reasons, and evidence.
• Provide a concluding statement or section that follows from and supports the argument presented.

64 UNIT 1 • WRITING FREEDOM

Create Cohesion: Tense Sequence

A **sequence of tenses** means that there is agreement among the tenses of verbs in related sentences or clauses. In formal writing, it is important to maintain **consistency of tense** from one sentence to the next unless the time frame of the action changes.

Read It

The Launch Text uses verbs correctly to point to both past and current situations.

> President Franklin Roosevelt **identified** four key freedoms... (past)

> These **are** not freedoms that one **finds** in a dictatorship. (present)

Within a sentence, verbs are consistent in tense if the actions are consistent in time.

> Because we **live** in a society, we **need** to consider other people's rights and needs as we **exercise** our own freedoms.
> (all present tense)

When actions vary in time, the writer applies logic to sequence the verbs. In this example, the action of developing laws took place in the past but still applies today, and those laws restrict and protect us in the present.

> Our government **has developed** laws that both **restrict** us and **protect** us. (present perfect; present; present)

Write It

As you draft your essay, use logic to sequence verbs. Use the tense of the independent clause plus any key transitional words to determine the tense of dependent clauses. In most compound sentences, keep the tense consistent. Here are some examples.

present + past	I **am** eager to read the biography that you **recommended.**
present perfect + present	Now that she **has mastered** French, Alice **enjoys** Quebec.
present + future	Until the senator **returns,** I **will wait** patiently in her office.
present + present	Actors **recite** the Bill of Rights, and the audience **listens** raptly.
past perfect + past perfect	The colonists **had complained,** but the king **had ignored** them.
future + future	We **will follow** the law, or we **will face** the consequences.
past + past perfect	We **arrived** in plenty of time, but the tour guide **had left.**

 TIP

USAGE
Change tense only when the timing of an action changes. In general:

- Use the present tense when writing about your own ideas and opinions, factual topics that are widely known, or actions in a written work.
- Use the past tense when writing about past events or completed studies or analyses.

STANDARDS
Writing
Use words, phrases, and clauses as well as varied syntax to link the major sections of the text, create cohesion, and clarify the relationships between claim(s) and reasons, between reasons and evidence, and between claim(s) and counterclaims.

Language
Demonstrate command of the conventions of standard English grammar and usage when writing or speaking.

Revising

Evaluating Your Draft

Use this checklist to evaluate the effectiveness of your first draft. Then, use your evaluation and the instructions on this page to guide your revision.

FOCUS AND ORGANIZATION	EVIDENCE AND ELABORATION	CONVENTIONS
☐ Provides an introduction that establishes a precise claim.	☐ Develops the claim and responds to counterclaims by using facts and details that provide relevant evidence and reasons.	☐ Attends to the norms and conventions of the discipline, especially regarding sequence and consistency of verb tenses.
☐ Distinguishes the claim from opposing claims.	☐ Provides adequate examples for each major idea.	
☐ Provides a conclusion that follows from the argument.	☐ Uses word choices and rhetorical devices effectively.	
☐ Establishes a logical organization and develops a progression throughout the argument.	☐ Establishes and maintains a formal style and an objective tone.	
☐ Uses words, phrases, and clauses to clarify the relationships between and among ideas.		

🔲 WORD NETWORK

Include interesting words from your Word Network in your argument.

Revising for Focus and Organization

Strong, Logical Connections An argument should be built on sound logic that includes strong reasons, definitive evidence, and clear connections. Consider these strong and weak reasons for a pay increase. Connecting words that clarify relationships between ideas are underlined.

- Strong Reasoning: I deserve a raise, <u>as shown by the fact</u> that clients consistently ask to work with me.
- Strong Reasoning: I deserve a raise <u>because</u> my contract calls for an increase after six months.
- Weak Reasoning: <u>Since</u> my brother makes more than I do, I deserve a raise.
- Weak Reasoning: I deserve a raise <u>because</u> I want one.

Revising for Evidence and Elaboration

Word Choice and Style As you work to create an objective, formal tone, consider replacing informal words and phrases with more formal choices. Here are some examples of informal and formal transitional words and phrases.

INSTEAD OF . . .	USE . . .
also	in addition
anyway	nevertheless
basically	in summary
plus	furthermore
so	therefore

▤ STANDARDS

Writing
Establish and maintain a formal style and objective tone while attending to the norms and conventions of the discipline in which they are writing.

PEER REVIEW

Exchange arguments with a classmate. Use the checklist to evaluate your classmate's argument and provide supportive feedback.

1. Is the claim clear?

☐ yes ☐ no   If no, explain what confused you.

2. Do you find the argument convincing?

☐ yes ☐ no   If no, tell what you think might be missing.

3. Does the essay conclude in a logical way?

☐ yes ☐ no   If no, indicate what you might change.

4. What is the strongest part of your classmate's argument? Why?

Editing and Proofreading

Edit for Conventions Reread your draft for accuracy and consistency. Correct errors in grammar and word usage. Check for consistency of verb tense in related sentences and clauses.

Proofread for Accuracy Read your draft carefully, looking for errors in spelling and punctuation. Be sure to capitalize place names and names of documents correctly.

Publishing and Presenting

Post your claim and your strongest reason or piece of evidence on your class's online discussion board. Ask classmates to comment on your post. Review others' posts and point out what you like best about what you read.

Reflecting

Consider what you learned by writing your text. Did you use research effectively to find support for your claim? What did you find to be the most difficult part of this assignment? Why? Think about what you might do differently the next time you write an argument.

▤ STANDARDS

Writing
Develop and strengthen writing as needed by planning, revising, editing, rewriting, or trying a new approach, focusing on addressing what is most significant for a specific purpose and audience.

ESSENTIAL QUESTION:

What is the meaning of freedom?

As you read these selections, work with your group to explore the meaning of freedom.

From Text to Topic The colonies had gained their independence and created a free nation, but freedom had not come to all. The Constitution had not settled the issue of slavery—and by 1790, when the first census in the United States was taken, approximately 700,000 African Americans were enslaved. The issue of slavery laid the foundation for the Civil War, arguably the most tragic time in the history of the United States. As you read, consider what these selections show about the nation's continuing efforts to define freedom.

Small-Group Learning Strategies

Throughout your life, in school, in your community, and in your career, you will continue to learn and work with others. Use these strategies during Small-Group Learning. Add ideas of your own at each step.

STRATEGY	ACTION PLAN
Prepare	• Complete your assignments so you are prepared for group work. • Take notes on your reading so you can contribute to your group's discussions. •
Participate fully	• Make eye contact to signal that you are listening and taking in what is being said. • Use text evidence when making a point. •
Support others	• Build on ideas from others in your group. • State the relationship of your points to those of others—whether you are supporting someone's point, refuting it, or taking the conversation in a new direction. •
Clarify	• Paraphrase the ideas of others to ensure that your understanding is correct. • Ask follow-up questions. •

CONTENTS

COMPARE

EXPOSITORY NONFICTION

from America's Constitution: A Biography

Akhil Reed Amar

The United States needed a Constitution, but the road to its ratification was by no means smooth.

MEDIA: GRAPHIC NOVEL

from The United States Constitution: A Graphic Adaptation

Jonathan Hennessey and Aaron McConnell

We can read about the ratification process—and we can "see" it, too!

AUTOBIOGRAPHY

from The Interesting Narrative of the Life of Olaudah Equiano

Olaudah Equiano

What does it mean to be a slave in a land that takes pride in its freedom?

LETTER | BIOGRAPHY

Letter to John Adams   *Abigail Adams*

from Dear Abigail: The Intimate Lives and Revolutionary Ideas of Abigail Adams and Her Two Remarkable Sisters   *Diane Jacobs*

Letter-writing connects a famous couple when circumstances force them apart.

SPEECH

Gettysburg Address

Abraham Lincoln

What do the founders' ideals mean when the nation is torn apart by war?

PERFORMANCE TASK

SPEAKING AND LISTENING FOCUS

Present an Argument

The Small-Group readings provide further glimpses into the concept of freedom. After reading, your group will present a panel discussion about the usefulness of narratives as evidence in arguments about freedom.

Working as a Team

1. **Take a Position** In your group, discuss the following question:

   Do you think teenagers today should have more freedom—or less—than they do now?

   As you take turns sharing your positions, be sure to provide reasons for your choice. After all group members have shared, discuss the convictions that students expressed and the arguments they proposed to support their views.

2. **List Your Rules** As a group, decide on the rules that you will follow as you work together. Two samples are provided. Add two more of your own. As you work together, you may add or revise rules based on your experience.

   - Everyone should have a chance to speak.
   - Group members should not interrupt each other.

   - _____

     _____

   - _____

     _____

3. **Apply the Rules** Share what you have learned about the meaning of freedom. Make sure each person in the group contributes. Take notes and be prepared to share with the class something you learned from another member of your group.

4. **Name Your Group** Choose a name that reflects the unit topic.

   Our group's name: _____

5. **Create a Communication Plan** Decide how you want to communicate with one another. For example, you might use email, an online bulletin board, or a collaborative annotation tool.

   Our group's decision: _____

   _____

Making a Schedule

First, find out the due dates for the small-group activities. Then, preview the texts and activities with your group, and make a schedule for completing the tasks.

SELECTION	ACTIVITIES	DUE DATE
from America's Constitution: A Biography		
from The United States Constitution: A Graphic Adaptation		
from The Interesting Narrative of the Life of Olaudah Equiano		
Letter to John Adams *from* Dear Abigail: The Intimate Lives and Revolutionary Ideas of Abigail Adams and Her Two Remarkable Sisters		
Gettysburg Address		

Working on Group Projects

As your group works together, you'll find it more effective if each person has a specific role. Different projects require different roles. Before beginning a project, discuss the necessary roles, and choose one for each group member. Some possible roles are listed here. Add your ideas to the list.

Project Manager: monitors the schedule and keeps everyone on task

Researcher: organizes research activities

Recorder: takes notes during group meetings

_____

_____

_____

_____

AMERICA'S CONSTITUTION:
A BIOGRAPHY

Comparing Text to Media

You will read and compare an excerpt from *America's Constitution: A Biography* and an excerpt from the graphic novel *The United States Constitution: A Graphic Adaptation*. First, complete the first-read and close-read activities for *America's Constitution: A Biography*.

THE UNITED STATES
CONSTITUTION:
A GRAPHIC ADAPTATION

About the Author

Akhil Reed Amar (b. 1958), an expert on constitutional law, has been called one of the nation's top legal thinkers. Amar graduated from Yale Law School, where he was an editor for the *Yale Law Journal.* He has written several books and articles about the law—works important enough to have been referenced in a number of Supreme Court cases.

from America's Constitution: A Biography

Concept Vocabulary

As you perform your first read, you will encounter these words.

conclave	eminent	populist

Context Clues An unfamiliar word may become clearer if you use **context clues**—that is, helpful words and phrases in the surrounding text. Here are two types of context clues.

> **Synonyms:** New Hampshire became the ninth state to **ratify** the Constitution, approving the document by a margin of 57 to 47.
>
> **Antonyms:** Opponents of the new Constitution were relatively **rigid**, but proponents such as Madison and Franklin were resourceful and flexible.

Apply your knowledge of context clues and other vocabulary strategies to determine the meanings of unfamiliar words you encounter during your first read.

First Read NONFICTION

Apply these strategies as you conduct your first read. You will have an opportunity to complete a close read after your first read.

NOTICE the general ideas of the text. *What* it is about? *Who* is involved?

ANNOTATE by marking vocabulary and key passages you want to revisit.

CONNECT ideas within the selection to what you already know and what you have already read.

RESPOND by completing the Comprehension Check and by writing a brief summary of the selection.

≣ STANDARDS

Reading Informational Text
By the end of grade 11, read and comprehend literary nonfiction in the grades 11–CCR text complexity band proficiently, with scaffolding as needed at the high end of the range.

Language
Use context as a clue to the meaning of a word or phrase.

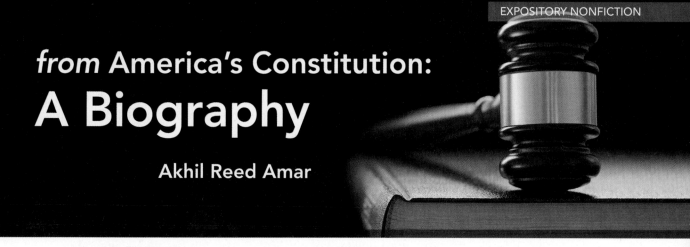

from America's Constitution:
A Biography

Akhil Reed Amar

BACKGROUND

Between 1777 and 1787, the United States used a constitution called the Articles of Confederation rather than the Constitution we use today. The Articles of Confederation created a very weak federal government. It soon became apparent that a document demonstrating more clarity would be helpful. There was great debate about whether to simply change the Articles of Confederation or replace them, as well as what this replacement might look like.

1 It started with a bang. Ordinary citizens would govern themselves across a continent and over the centuries, under rules that the populace would ratify and could revise. By uniting previously independent states into a vast and indivisible nation, New World republicans would keep Old World monarchs at a distance and thus make democracy work on a scale never before dreamed possible.

"We . . . do"

With simple words placed in the document's most prominent location, the Preamble laid the foundation for all that followed. "We the People of the United States, . . . do ordain[1] and establish this Constitution . . ."

2 These words did more than promise popular self-government. They also embodied and enacted it. Like the phrases "I do" in an exchange of wedding vows and "I accept" in a contract, the Preamble's words actually performed the very thing they described. Thus the Founders' "Constitution" was not merely a text but a deed—a *constituting*. We the People *do* ordain. In the late 1780s, this was the most democratic deed the world had ever seen.

3 Behind this act of ordainment and establishment stood countless ordinary American voters who gave their consent to the Constitution via specially elected ratifying conventions held in the thirteen states beginning in late 1787. Until these ratifications took place, the Constitution's words were a mere proposal—the text of a contract yet to be accepted, the script of a wedding still to be performed.

4 The proposal itself had emerged from a special **conclave** held in Philadelphia during the summer of 1787. Twelve state governments— all except Rhode Island's—had tapped several dozen leading public

NOTES

Mark context clues or indicate another strategy you used that helped you determine meaning.

conclave (KON klayv) *n.*

MEANING:

---

1. **ordain** *v.* officially order or decree.

Mark context clues or indicate another strategy you used that helped you determine meaning.

eminent (EHM uh nuhnt) *adj.*

MEANING:

servants and private citizens to meet in Philadelphia and ponder possible revisions of the Articles of Confederation, the interstate compact that Americans had formed during the Revolutionary War. After deliberating behind closed doors for months, the Philadelphia conferees unveiled their joint proposal in mid-September in a document signed by thirty-nine of the continent's most **eminent** men, including George Washington, Benjamin Franklin, James Wilson, Roger Sherman, James Madison, Alexander Hamilton, Gouverneur Morris, John Rutledge, and Nathaniel Gorham. When these notables put their names on the page, they put their reputations on the line.

5   An enormous task of political persuasion lay ahead. Several of the leaders who had come to Philadelphia had quit the conclave in disgust, and others who had stayed to the end had refused to endorse the final script. Such men—John Lansing, Robert Yates, Luther Martin, John Francis Mercer, Edmund Randolph, George Mason, and Elbridge Gerry—could be expected to oppose ratification and to urge their political allies to do the same. No one could be certain how the American people would ultimately respond to the competing appeals. Prior to 1787, only two states, Massachusetts and New Hampshire, had ever brought proposed state constitutions before the people to be voted up or down in some special way. The combined track record from this pair of states was sobering: two successful popular ratifications out of six total attempts.

6   In the end, the federal Constitution proposed by Washington and company would barely squeak through. By its own terms, the document would go into effect only if ratified by specially elected conventions in at least nine states, and even then only states that said yes would be bound. In late 1787 and early 1788, supporters of the Constitution won relatively easy ratifications in Delaware, Pennsylvania, New Jersey, Georgia, and Connecticut. Massachusetts joined their ranks in February 1788, saying "we do" only after weeks of debate and by a close vote, 187 to 168. Then came lopsided yes votes in Maryland and South Carolina, bringing the total to eight ratifications, one shy of the mark. Even so, in mid-June 1788, a full nine months after the publication of the Philadelphia proposal, the Constitution was still struggling to be born, and its fate remained uncertain. Organized opposition ran strong in all the places that had yet to say yes, which included three of America's largest and most influential states. At last, on June 21, tiny New Hampshire became the decisive ninth state by the margin of 57 to 47. A few days later, before news from the North had arrived, Virginia voted her approval, 89 to 79.

7   All eyes then turned to New York, where Anti-Federalists initially held a commanding lead inside the convention. Without the acquiescence of this key state, could the new Constitution really work as planned? On the other hand, was New York truly willing to say no and go it alone now that her neighbors had agreed to form a new, more perfect union among themselves? In late July, the state

ultimately said yes by a vote of 30 to 27. A switch of only a couple of votes would have reversed the outcome. Meanwhile, the last two states, North Carolina and Rhode Island, refused to ratify in 1788. They would ultimately join the new union in late 1789 and mid-1790, respectively—well after George Washington took office as president of the new (eleven!) United States.

8   Although the ratification votes in the several states did not occur by direct statewide referenda,[2] the various ratifying conventions did aim to represent "the People" in a particularly emphatic way— more directly than ordinary legislatures. Taking their cue from the Preamble's bold "We the People" language, several states waived standard voting restrictions and allowed a uniquely broad class of citizens to vote for ratification-convention delegates. For instance, New York temporarily set aside its usual property qualifications and, for the first time in its history, invited all free adult male citizens to vote. Also, states generally allowed an especially broad group of Americans to serve as ratifying-convention delegates. Among the many states that ordinarily required upper-house lawmakers to meet higher property qualifications than lower-house members, none held convention delegates to the higher standard, and most exempted delegates even from the lower. All told, eight states elected convention delegates under special rules that were more **populist** and less property-focused than normal, and two others followed standing rules that let virtually all taxpaying adult male citizens vote. No state employed special election rules that were more property-based or less populist than normal.

9   In the extraordinarily extended and inclusive ratification process envisioned by the Preamble, Americans regularly found themselves discussing the Preamble itself. At Philadelphia, the earliest draft of the Preamble had come from the quill of Pennsylvania's James Wilson, and it was Wilson who took the lead in explaining the Preamble's principles in a series of early and influential ratification speeches. Pennsylvania Anti-Federalists complained that the Philadelphia notables had overreached in proposing an entirely new Constitution rather than a mere modification of the existing Articles of Confederation. In response, Wilson—America's leading lawyer and one of only six men to have signed both the Declaration of Independence and the Constitution—stressed the significance of popular ratification. "This Constitution, proposed by [the Philadelphia draftsmen], claims no more than a production of the same nature would claim, flowing from a private pen. It is laid before the citizens of the United States, unfettered by restraint. . . . By their *fiat*,[3] it will become of value and authority; without it, it will never receive the character of authenticity and power." James Madison agreed, as he made clear in a mid-January 1788 New York newspaper essay today known as *The Federalist* No. 40—one of a long series

NOTES

Mark context clues or indicate another strategy you used that helped you determine meaning.

populist (POP yuh lihst) *adj.*

MEANING:

---

2. **referenda** *n.* public votes on particular issues.
3. **fiat** (FEE uht) *n.* command that creates something.

of columns that he wrote in partnership with Alexander Hamilton and John Jay under the shared pen name "Publius." According to Madison/Publius, the Philadelphia draftsmen had merely "proposed a Constitution which is to be of no more consequence than the paper on which it is written, unless it be stamped with the approbation[4] of those to whom it is addressed. [The proposal] was to be submitted *to the people themselves*, [and] the disapprobation of this supreme authority would destroy it forever; its approbation blot out antecedent errors and irregularities." Leading Federalists across the continent reiterated the point in similar language.

10   With the word *fiat*, Wilson gently called to mind the opening lines of Genesis. In the beginning, God said, *fiat lux*, and—behold!—there was light. So, too, when the American people (Publius's "supreme authority") said, "We do ordain and establish," that very statement would do the deed. "Let there be a Constitution"—and there would be one. As the ultimate sovereign of all had once made man in his own image, so now the temporal sovereign of America, the people themselves, would make a constitution in their own image.

11   All this was breathtakingly novel. In 1787, democratic self-government existed almost nowhere on earth. Kings, emperors, czars, princes, sultans, moguls, feudal lords, and tribal chiefs held sway across the globe. Even England featured a limited monarchy and an entrenched aristocracy alongside a House of Commons that rested on a restricted and uneven electoral base. The vaunted English Constitution that American colonists had grown up admiring prior to the struggle for independence was an imprecise hodgepodge of institutions, enactments, cases, usages, maxims, procedures, and principles that had accreted[5] and evolved over many centuries. This Constitution had never been reduced to a single composite writing and voted on by the British people or even by Parliament.

12   The ancient world had seen small-scale democracies in various Greek city-states and pre-imperial Rome, but none of these had been founded in fully democratic fashion. In the most famous cases, one man—a celebrated lawgiver such as Athens's Solon or Sparta's Lycurgus—had unilaterally ordained his countrymen's constitution. Before the American Revolution, no people had ever explicitly voted on their own written constitution.

13   Nor did the Revolution itself immediately inaugurate popular ordainments and establishments. True, the 1776 Declaration of Independence proclaimed the "self-evident" truth that "Governments are instituted among Men, deriving their just Powers from the Consent of the Governed." The document went on to assert that "whenever any Form of Government becomes destructive of [its legitimate] Ends, it is the Right of the People to alter and abolish it, and to institute new Government." Yet the Declaration only

---

4. **approbation** *n.* praise or approval.
5. **accreted** *v.* grown or accumulated gradually.

imperfectly acted out its bold script. Its fifty-six acclaimed signers never put the document to any sort of popular vote.

14   Between April and July 1776, countless similar declarations issued from assorted towns, counties, parishes, informal assemblies, grand juries, militia units, and legislatures across America. By then, however, the colonies were already under military attack, and conditions often made it impossible to achieve inclusive deliberation or scrupulous tabulation. Many patriots saw Crown loyalists in their midst not as fellow citizens free to vote their honest judgment with impunity, but rather as traitors deserving tar and feathers, or worse. (Virtually no arch-loyalist went on to become a particularly noteworthy political leader in independent America. By contrast, many who would vigorously oppose the Constitution in 1787–88—such as Maryland's Samuel Chase and Luther Martin, Virginia's Patrick Henry and James Monroe, and New York's George Clinton and John Lansing—moved on to illustrious post-ratification careers.)

15   Shortly before and after the Declaration of Independence, new state governments began to take shape, filling the void created by the ouster of George III. None of the state constitutions ordained in the first months of the Revolution was voted on by the electorate or by a specially elected ratifying convention of the people. In many states, sitting legislatures or closely analogous Revolutionary entities declared themselves solons[6] and promulgated or revised constitutions on their own authority, sometimes without even waiting for new elections that might have given their constituents more say in the matter, or at least advance notice of their specific constitutional intentions.

16   In late 1777, patriot leaders in the Continental Congress proposed a set of Articles of Confederation to govern relations among the thirteen states. This document was then sent out to be ratified by the thirteen state legislatures, none of which asked the citizens themselves to vote in any special way on the matter.

17   Things began to change as the Revolution wore on. In 1780, Massachusetts enacted a new state constitution that had come directly before the voters assembled in their respective townships and won their approval. In 1784, New Hampshire did the same. These local dress rehearsals (for so they seem in retrospect) set the stage for the Preamble's great act of continental popular sovereignty in the late 1780s.

18   As Benjamin Franklin and other Americans had achieved famous advances in the natural sciences—in Franklin's case, the invention of bifocals, the lightning rod, and the Franklin stove—so with the Constitution America could boast a breakthrough in political science. Never before had so many ordinary people been invited to

NOTES

America could boast a breakthrough in political science.

---

6. **solons** (SOH luhnz) *n.* lawmakers, especially wise ones. Refers to Solon, the statesman who framed the democratic laws of Athens.

deliberate and vote on the supreme law under which they and their posterity would be governed. James Wilson fairly burst with pride in an oration delivered in Philadelphia to some twenty thousand merrymakers gathered for a grand parade on July 4, 1788. By that date, enough Americans had said "We do" so as to guarantee that the Constitution would go into effect (at least in ten states—the document was still pending in the other three). The "spectacle, which we are assembled to celebrate," Wilson declared, was "the most dignified one that has yet appeared on our globe," namely, a

> people free and enlightened, establishing and ratifying a system of government, which they have previously considered, examined, and approved! . . .
> . . . You have heard of Sparta, of Athens, and of Rome; you have heard of their admired constitutions, and of their high-prized freedom. . . . But did they, in all their pomp and pride of liberty, ever furnish, to the astonished world, an exhibition similar to that which we now contemplate? Were their constitutions framed by those, who were appointed for that purpose, by the people? After they were framed, were they submitted to the consideration of the people? Had the people an opportunity of expressing their sentiments concerning them? Were they to stand or fall by the people's approving or rejecting vote?

19   The great deed was done. The people had taken center stage and enacted their own supreme law. ❧

Comprehension Check

Complete the following items after you finish your first read. Review and clarify details with your group.

1. When and where was the Constitution drafted?

2. Once the Constitution was approved, what more had to happen before it could go into effect?

3. What was *The Federalist*, and who was "Publius"?

4. 📓 **Notebook** Confirm your understanding of the text by writing a summary.

- -

RESEARCH

Research to Explore Choose something that interested you from the text, and formulate a research question.

Close Read the Text

With your group, revisit sections of the text you marked during your first read. **Annotate** details that you notice. What **questions** do you have? What can you **conclude**?

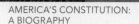

AMERICA'S CONSTITUTION: A BIOGRAPHY

Analyze the Text

> CITE TEXTUAL EVIDENCE
> to support your answers.

 Notebook Complete the activities.

1. **Review and Clarify** With your group, reread paragraphs 4 and 5 of the selection. What kind of document was the Constitution in the summer of 1787? What does this fact indicate about the power of "We the People"?

2. **Present and Discuss** Now, work with your group to share the passages from the selection that you found especially important. Take turns presenting your passages. Discuss what you noticed in the selection, what questions you asked, and what conclusions you reached.

3. **Essential Question:** *What is the meaning of freedom?* What has this text taught you about American freedoms? Discuss with your group.

TIP

GROUP DISCUSSION
Keep in mind that readers often have differing interpretations of a text. Use the varying perspectives to encourage group members to learn from one another and to clarify their own views.

LANGUAGE DEVELOPMENT

Concept Vocabulary

conclave	eminent	populist

Why These Words? The three concept vocabulary words from the text are related. With your group, determine what the words have in common. How do these word choices contribute to the meaning of the text?

Practice

Notebook Confirm your understanding of these words by writing a two- or three-sentence paragraph that includes all three words. Make their meaning clear from the context.

Word Study

Notebook Latin Suffix: -ist The Latin suffix *-ist* identifies a word as an adjective or a noun. It often appears in words that relate to attitudes or philosophies. For example, the word *realist* means "a person who sees thing as they really are."

1. Write two definitions for the concept vocabulary word *populist*—one for the word's meaning as a noun and the other for the word's meaning as an adjective.

2. Use a dictionary to find definitions for *naturist, feminist,* and *idealist.* Then, choose one of the words and write two sentences—one using the word as a noun and the other using it as an adjective.

WORD NETWORK

Add words related to freedom from the text to your Word Network.

STANDARDS

Language
Consult general and specialized reference materials, both print and digital, to find the pronunciation of a word or determine or clarify its precise meaning, its part of speech, its etymology, or its standard usage.

AMERICA'S CONSTITUTION:
A BIOGRAPHY

Analyze Craft and Structure

Author's Choices: Rhetoric An **analogy** is an extended comparison. It is based on the idea that the relationship between one pair of things is like the relationship between another pair. The use of an analogy can clarify complex ideas by explaining an unfamiliar notion in terms of a familiar one. For example, in paragraph 4, Amar introduces the idea that the Preamble to the Constitution is like the words "I accept" in a contract:

> Like the phrases "I do" in an exchange of wedding vows and "I accept" in a contract, the Preamble's words actually performed the very thing they described.

Using this analogy, Amar makes the point that the Constitution represented a binding commitment that affected how people live their lives.

Practice

CITE TEXTUAL EVIDENCE to support your answers.

Reread the passages noted in the chart. For each analogy, identify the two things being compared. Then, explain the idea the analogy helps to clarify. Work independently. Then, share your analysis with your group.

TEXTUAL DETAILS	TWO THINGS BEING COMPARED	MEANING
"I do" / "we do" (paragraphs 1, 2, 3, 6, 18)		
fiat lux (paragraph 10)		
invention of bifocals, the lightning rod, and the Franklin stove (paragraph 18)		

STANDARDS

Reading Informational Text
Determine an author's point of view or purpose in a text in which the rhetoric is particularly effective, analyzing how style and content contribute to the power, persuasiveness, or beauty of the text.

Author's Style

Historical Narrative as Argument A **biography** is a type of narrative nonfiction that tells the story of someone's life. By calling his book a "biography" of the Constitution, Amar indicates that he is telling a story. However, it is not the story of a life, but of a document. Within that story, Amar presents his point of view or position on the Constitution's significance. The story he tells, then, is not just a historical narrative—it is also an argument. Amar states his main idea or principal claim at the end of paragraph 2:

> In the late 1780s, this [the drafting of the U. S. Constitution] was the most democratic deed the world had ever seen.

Amar goes on to present an in-depth description of the conflicts and drama that arose around the ratification of the Constitution, using varied techniques and evidence to tell the story and develop his claim.

- **Historical Details:** Amar is writing for an audience of general readers, not scholars. He includes historical details that provide important background information for such readers. For example, in paragraph 8, he shows how the rules of the ratifying conventions were based on groundbreaking democratic principles.
- **Numerical Data:** Amar presents numerical facts to support his interpretation of events.
- **Quotations:** Amar interweaves quotations from historical figures. These passages add drama to the story he is telling and reinforce the argument he is presenting.

Read It

Work on your own to identify examples of Amar's use of historical details, numerical data, and quotations. Explain how each example helps to tell the story of the Constitution and build Amar's argument. Share and discuss your responses with your group.

TYPE OF EVIDENCE	EFFECT
Historical Details	
Numerical Data	
Quotations	

Write It

🖵 **Notebook** Choose a favorite song, graphic novel or comic book, movie, game, or other text. Write a "biography" of the work in which you both tell the story of its development and defend a claim about its importance. Weave in historical details, facts, and quotations.

✏ EVIDENCE LOG

Before moving on to a new selection, go to your Evidence Log and record what you have learned from the excerpt from *America's Constitution: A Biography*.

☰ STANDARDS

Reading Informational Text
- Analyze a complex set of ideas or sequence of events and explain how specific individuals, ideas, or events interact and develop over the course of the text.
- Analyze and evaluate the effectiveness of the structure an author uses in his or her exposition or argument, including whether the structure makes points clear, convincing, and engaging.

AMERICA'S CONSTITUTION: A BIOGRAPHY

Comparing Text to Media

This graphic adaptation focuses on the ratification process of the Constitution and the creation of the Bill of Rights. After reviewing this selection, you will look for similarities and differences between the selections.

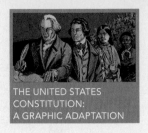

THE UNITED STATES CONSTITUTION: A GRAPHIC ADAPTATION

About the Author

As an adult, **Jonathan Hennessey** gained a new appreciation for his childhood in historic New England, and he notes that "I often find nothing more entertaining than some scrupulously researched historical account." *The United States Constitution: A Graphic Adaptation* is his first published work.

from The United States Constitution: A Graphic Adaptation

Media Vocabulary

These words or concepts will be useful to you as you analyze, discuss, and write about graphic novels.

Layout: overall design and look of a graphic presentation	• Layout deals with the arrangement of graphic panels on a page and with the relationship of text and images within each panel.
Speech Balloon: shape used in graphic novels and comic books to show what a character says	• A "tail" points from the balloon to the person speaking. If the tail is a series of small bubbles, the balloon expresses a thought. • An artist may use a dotted balloon outline to indicate whispered words or jagged "spikes" in the outline to indicate shouting or screaming.
Caption: separate text that presents information that cannot be expressed quickly and easily in dialogue	• A caption may appear anywhere inside or outside a panel. It may be broken into several boxes for a panel.

First Review MEDIA: ART AND PHOTOGRAPHY

Apply these strategies as you conduct your first review.

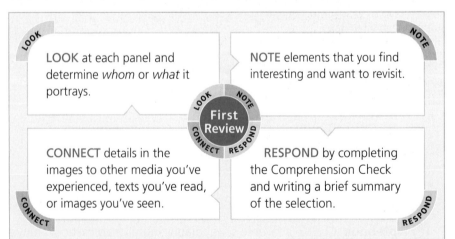

LOOK at each panel and determine *whom* or *what* it portrays.

NOTE elements that you find interesting and want to revisit.

CONNECT details in the images to other media you've experienced, texts you've read, or images you've seen.

RESPOND by completing the Comprehension Check and writing a brief summary of the selection.

First Review

LOOK NOTE CONNECT RESPOND

📓 **Notebook** As you study the graphic novel, record your observations and questions, noting which panel they refer to for later reference.

Copyright © SAVVAS Learning Company LLC. All Rights Reserved.

≣ STANDARDS

Reading Informational Text
By the end of grade 11, read and comprehend literary nonfiction in the grades 11–CCR text complexity band proficiently, with scaffolding as needed at the high end of the range.

Language
Acquire and use accurately general academic and domain-specific words and phrases, sufficient for reading, writing, speaking, and listening at the college and career readiness level; demonstrate independence in gathering vocabulary knowledge when considering a word or phrase important to comprehension or expression.

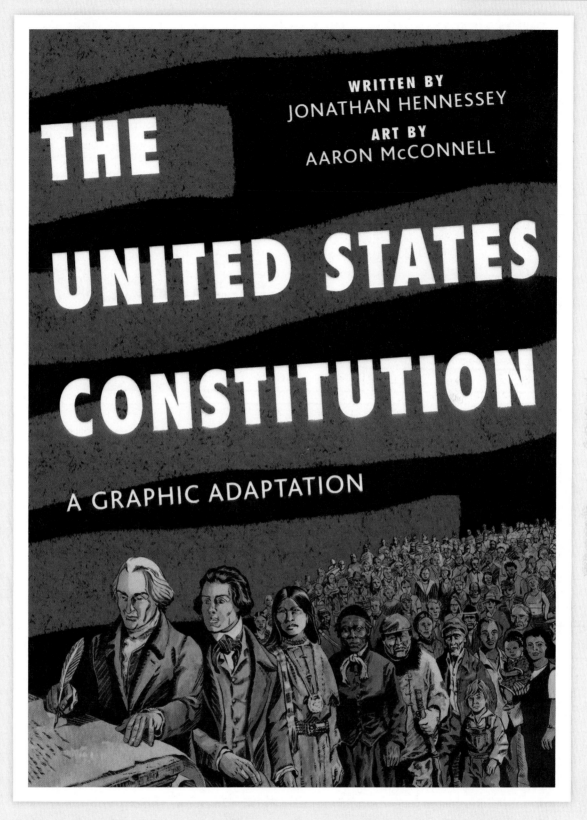

THE

UNITED STATES

CONSTITUTION

A GRAPHIC ADAPTATION

WRITTEN BY
JONATHAN HENNESSEY
ART BY
AARON McCONNELL

BACKGROUND

While the Articles of Confederation created Congress, it did not create a capable national government. Individual states continued to conduct foreign diplomacy, and Georgia was threatening its own war with Spain. Furthermore, Congress failed to deal effectively with Shays's Rebellion in Massachusetts. These and other weaknesses convinced leaders that revisions to the Articles were necessary to form a stronger national government.

from The United States Constitution: A Graphic Adaptation **83**

RATIFICATION: Federalists vs. Anti-Federalists

1 IN THE VOTE TO SEND DELEGATES TO RATIFY THE CONSTITUTION, MORE PEOPLE WOULD HAVE A SAY ON THEIR LAWS—AND THE SHAPE OF THEIR FUTURE—THAN EVER BEFORE.

AND FOR THIS VOTE, MOST STATES REDUCED OR ABOLISHED THEIR RULES ABOUT OWNING PROPERTY.

2 UP TO THAT TIME A *FEDERALIST* WAS SOMEONE WHO BELIEVED FIRST AND FOREMOST IN THE SOVEREIGNTY OF THE STATES, WHILE AN *ANTI-FEDERALIST* WANTED A STRONG, CENTRAL GOVERNMENT TO RULE OVER THEM, JUST AS THE CONSTITUTION WOULD ESTABLISH...

...BUT IN WHAT TODAY WOULD BE CALLED POLITICAL SPIN, THE ONES PUSHING HARDEST TO RATIFY THE CONSTITUTION TOOK THE FEDERALIST NAME FOR THEIR OWN PURPOSE, TO HELP WIN OVER THE COMMON PEOPLE.

3 UNDER THE PEN NAME PUBLIUS, HAMILTON, MADISON, AND JOHN JAY WROTE 85 ESSAYS NOW KNOWN AS *THE FEDERALIST PAPERS* TO EXPLAIN AND CHAMPION THEIR CAUSE.

To the people of the state of New York: you are called upon to deliberate on a new Constitution for the United States of America ...

4 NOW STUCK WITH THE ANTI-FEDERALIST NAME, OPPONENTS OF RATIFICATION—MANY PEOPLE, MANY DIFFERENT IDEAS—ATTACKED!

SOME THOUGHT THE CONSTITUTION, WHICH NEVER MENTIONS GOD, WAS ANTIRELIGIOUS.

MANY RESENTED THAT THE FRAMERS HAD OVERSTEPPED THEIR JOB OF SIMPLY FIXING THE ARTICLES OF CONFEDERATION...

WITH NO RELIGIOUS TEST FOR OFFICE, PAGANS, DEISTS, AND MAHOMETANS MIGHT OBTAIN OFFICE!

...WHAT RIGHT HAD THEY TO SAY, WE, THE PEOPLE...WHO AUTHORIZED THEM TO SPEAK THE LANGUAGE OF WE, THE PEOPLE, INSTEAD OF WE, THE STATES?

THE GREATNESS OF THE POWERS GIVEN... PRODUCE A COALITION OF MONARCHY MEN, MILITARY MEN, ARISTOCRATS AND DRONES, WHOSE NOISE, IMPUDENCE AND ZEAL EXCEEDS ALL BELIEF!

...AND HAD SET UP A POWERFUL NEW GOVERNMENT TO DOMINATE THE STATES.

THEY WERE SUSPICIOUS OF ALL POLITICAL POWER AND WANTED TO KEEP AMERICA A COUNTRY OF LANDOWNING FARMERS FOREVER.

85

"PUBLIUS" VIVIDLY POINTED OUT THE IMMINENT DANGER IF THE STATES FAILED TO JOIN IN A STRONG UNION.

5 ON THEIR OWN OR IN SMALL GROUPS, THE STATES COULD EASILY BE BROUGHT TO THEIR KNEES BY FOREIGN INVADERS...

...America, if not connected at all, or only by the feeble tie of a simple league... would... be gradually entangled in all the pernicious labyrinths of European politics and wars...

FROM THE FEDERALIST, NO. 7.

...OR, GIVEN ALL THE FIERCE COMPETITION BETWEEN THEM, BY EACH OTHER.

6 OVER TIME BLOODSHED BETWEEN THEM COULD BECOME AS COMMON AS AMONG EUROPE'S MANY COUNTRIES IN THEIR CENTURIES OF ARMED CONFLICTS.

...we shall be... an infinity of little jealous, clashing, tumultuous commonwealths, the wretched nurseries of unceasing discord...

FROM THE FEDERALIST, NO 9.

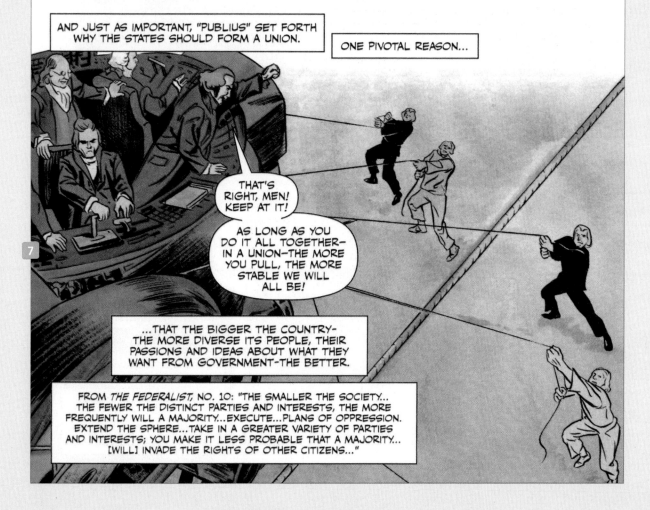

AND JUST AS IMPORTANT, "PUBLIUS" SET FORTH WHY THE STATES SHOULD FORM A UNION.

ONE PIVOTAL REASON...

7 THAT'S RIGHT, MEN! KEEP AT IT!

AS LONG AS YOU DO IT ALL TOGETHER— IN A UNION—THE MORE YOU PULL, THE MORE STABLE WE WILL ALL BE!

...THAT THE BIGGER THE COUNTRY— THE MORE DIVERSE ITS PEOPLE, THEIR PASSIONS AND IDEAS ABOUT WHAT THEY WANT FROM GOVERNMENT—THE BETTER.

FROM THE FEDERALIST, NO. 10: "THE SMALLER THE SOCIETY... THE FEWER THE DISTINCT PARTIES AND INTERESTS, THE MORE FREQUENTLY WILL A MAJORITY...EXECUTE...PLANS OF OPPRESSION. EXTEND THE SPHERE...TAKE IN A GREATER VARIETY OF PARTIES AND INTERESTS; YOU MAKE IT LESS PROBABLE THAT A MAJORITY... [WILL] INVADE THE RIGHTS OF OTHER CITIZENS..."

The Bill of Rights: AMENDMENTS 1-10

14 THE POWER OF A GOVERNMENT CAN BE ENORMOUS. IF LEFT UNCHECKED, DANGEROUS.

ARTICLES I-VII OF THE CONSTITUTION MOSTLY GIVE GOVERNMENT POWER. BUT WITH THE BILL OF RIGHTS...

15 ...PROPOSED BY THE FIRST CONGRESS, DRAFTED BY MADISON, AND SWIFTLY RATIFIED IN 1791...

...GOVERNMENT VOLUNTARILY GIVES UP POWER. IT RESTRAINS ITSELF.

16 AFTER ALL, ONE OF THE CORNERSTONE IDEAS OF THE AMERICAN REVOLUTION ITSELF IS THAT PEOPLE HAVE CERTAIN RIGHTS *BY BIRTH.*

AND SO THE BILL OF RIGHTS CONFIRMS THIS. THUS, THE CONSTITUTION REASSERTS THAT IT IS THE PEOPLE — NOT THEIR GOVERNMENT — WHO RULE.

17 THE RIGHT TO TRIAL BY JURY?

THANKS... I ALREADY HAVE ONE.

THE BILL OF RIGHTS SPELLS OUT WHAT FREEDOMS THE GOVERNMENT MAY NOT TAKE AWAY. IT IS THERE TO PROTECT YOUR RIGHTS, NOT TO GIVE THEM TO YOU.

18 TODAY MOST THINK ABOUT THE BILL OF RIGHTS AS EXCLUSIVELY PROTECTING THE RIGHTS OF THE INDIVIDUAL AGAINST THE MAJORITY.

19 BUT THE ANTI-FEDERALISTS WERE EQUALLY CONCERNED ABOUT PROTECTING THE MAJORITY.

...THAT IS, THE PEOPLE, OR GROUPS OF PEOPLE—FROM GOVERNMENT.

FROM *THE FEDERALIST, NO. 51:* "IT IS OF GREAT IMPORTANCE IN A REPUBLIC...TO GUARD THE SOCIETY AGAINST THE OPPRESSION OF ITS RULERS."

Comprehension Check

Complete the following items after you finish your first review. Review and clarify details with your group.

1. As the fight for ratification began, how did the meaning of the word *federalist* change? Refer to panels 1–4.

2. How does the artist visually depict the three branches of government? Refer to panels 4 and 11.

3. Identify three reasons "Publius" gave in support of a strong federal government. Refer to panels 5–7.

4. According to the author, what assumption about human rights does the Bill of Rights reflect?

5. 🗒 **Notebook** Write a summary to confirm your understanding of the ratification of the Constitution, as presented in the graphic adaptation.

- -

RESEARCH

Research to Clarify Choose at least one unfamiliar detail from the graphic adaptation. Briefly research that detail. In what way does the information you found shed light on your understanding of the Constitution or the Bill of Rights?

Research to Explore Choose something that interested you from the graphic adaptation, and formulate a research question about it.

MAKING MEANING

Close Review

With your group, review your notes and, if necessary, revisit the graphic adaptation. Record any new observations that seem important. What **questions** do you have? What can you **conclude**?

REVIEW · QUESTION · **Close Review** · CONCLUDE

THE UNITED STATES CONSTITUTION: A GRAPHIC ADAPTATION

- -

Analyze the Media

CITE TEXTUAL EVIDENCE to support your answers.

Complete the activities.

1. **Present and Discuss** Choose the part of the graphic adaptation you find most interesting or powerful. Share your choice with the group and discuss why you chose it. Explain what you noticed about that part, what questions it raised for you, and what conclusions you reached about it.

2. **Synthesize** With your group, review the entire graphic adaptation. How do the images, speech balloons, and captions work together to reveal the difficult moments in this part of the Constitution's "story"? Do they inform, entertain, or both? Explain.

3. 🗐 **Notebook** **Essential Question:** *What is the meaning of freedom?* How did the Constitution and the Bill of Rights clarify the meaning of freedom for Americans? Support your response with evidence from the graphic adaptation.

LANGUAGE DEVELOPMENT

Media Vocabulary

layout	speech balloon	caption

Use these vocabulary words in your responses to the following questions.

1. **(a)** Which panel presents a caption with no image? **(b)** What do readers learn from that panel? **(c)** How does the arrangement of the caption text reflect its content?

2. **(a)** Which appears more often in this excerpt—speech balloons or captions? **(b)** Why do you think that Hennessey and McConnell chose to present so much information in one way instead of the other?

3. Choose the series of panels that you think most clearly conveys a large amount of information. Explain the visual choices that make those panels effective.

⊞ STANDARDS

Reading Informational Text
- Analyze a complex set of ideas or sequence of events and explain how specific individuals, ideas, or events interact and develop over the course of the text.

- Analyze and evaluate the effectiveness of the structure an author uses in his or her exposition or argument, including whether the structure makes points clear, convincing, and engaging.

from The United States Constitution: A Graphic Adaptation **89**

AMERICA'S CONSTITUTION:
A BIOGRAPHY

THE UNITED STATES
CONSTITUTION: A GRAPHIC
ADAPTATION

Writing to Compare

You have read two works that provide historical information about the ratification of the U.S. Constitution. Now, deepen your understanding by comparing and writing about the two works.

Assignment

An informative text explains how or why something is true. Write an **informative essay** in which you explain how reading both *America's Constitution: A Biography* and *The United States Constitution: A Graphic Adaptation* helps a person more fully understand the ratification of the U.S. Constitution. Your essay should address these questions:

- What are the strengths of each medium?
- What unique kinds of information does each text present, and how?

To support your central idea, cite evidence from both texts. Support may take the form of quotations, paraphrases, summaries, or descriptions.

Planning and Prewriting

Analyze the Texts With your group, discuss how each text presents different types of information about the Constitution. Use the chart to gather your notes. Generate your own topic for the last row.

TOPIC	AMERICA'S CONSTITUTION: A BIOGRAPHY	THE UNITED STATES CONSTITUTION: A GRAPHIC ADAPTATION
the need for a Constitution		
objections to the Constitution		
the ratification process		

📓 **Notebook Respond to these questions.**

1. What strategies or techniques are used to communicate key ideas in each text?

2. Which gives a more thorough account of the Constitution's origins? How?

3. Which gives a more memorable account? How so?

STANDARDS

Reading Informational Text
Integrate and evaluate multiple sources of information presented in different media or formats as well as in words in order to address a question or solve a problem.

Writing
• Write informative/explanatory texts to examine and convey complex ideas, concepts, and information clearly and accurately through the effective selection, organization, and analysis of content.
• Apply *grades 11–12 Reading standards* to literary nonfiction.

Drafting

Develop a Main Idea Review your Prewriting notes. With your group, draw some conclusions about the main strengths of each text. Then, work independently to draft a main idea for your essay by completing the following frame.

> **Main Idea:** Reading both the historical narrative and the graphic novel can help a person better understand the origins of the Constitution. This is because the historical narrative _____, whereas the graphic novel _____.

Take turns sharing your completed main idea with the group. Discuss which versions are stronger, and why. Use group members' feedback to revise your main idea.

Choose Evidence Your main idea contains a general statement about each text. In your essay, you must support each general statement with evidence—quotations, descriptions, summaries, or paraphrases. One possible general statement and two pieces of supporting evidence are shown here.

EXAMPLE

General Statement: The graphic novel communicates key ideas in memorable ways.

- **Evidence:** Panel 8 showing shaded stamps of states that had ratified the Constitution and unshaded stamps of those that had not
- **Evidence:** vivid image in panel 5 of the U.S. flag being sliced like a cake

---

Work with your group to identify strong pieces of evidence for each of your general statements. Take notes in a chart like this one.

GENERAL STATEMENT	EVIDENCE	PAGE/PANEL NUMBER

Write a Draft Draft your essay independently. Include your main idea in the introduction. Include each general statement and your evidence for it in a separate body section. In your conclusion, make an observation about one or both texts that leaves your reader with some food for thought.

Review, Revise, and Edit

When you are finished drafting, exchange papers with a group member. Ask your peer to comment on both the content and organization of your essay. Use the feedback to guide your revisions. Finally, edit and proofread your work. Replace vague language with more specific words and phrases. Correct any errors in grammar, spelling, or punctuation that you discover.

EVIDENCE LOG

Before moving on to a new selection, go to your Evidence Log and record what you learned from the excerpts from *America's Constitution: A Biography* and *The United States Constitution: A Graphic Adaptation*.

About the Author

The son of a West African tribal elder, **Olaudah Equiano** (1745–1797) might have followed in his father's footsteps had he not been sold into slavery. He was taken first to the West Indies and later brought to Virginia, where he was purchased by a British captain and employed at sea. Renamed Gustavus Vassa, Equiano was enslaved for nearly ten years. After managing his master's finances and making his own money in the process, he amassed enough to buy his own freedom. In later years, he settled in England and devoted himself to the abolition of slavery. In addition to writing his two-volume autobiography to publicize the plight of slaves, he lectured and rallied public sympathy against the cruelties of slavery.

▤ STANDARDS

Reading Informational Text
By the end of grade 11, read and comprehend literary nonfiction in the grades 11–CCR text complexity band proficiently, with scaffolding as needed at the high end of the range.

Language
Determine or clarify the meaning of unknown and multiple-meaning words and phrases based on *grades 11–12 reading and content*, choosing flexibly from a range of strategies.

from The Interesting Narrative of the Life of Olaudah Equiano

Concept Vocabulary

As you perform your first read of this excerpt from *The Interesting Narrative of the Life of Olaudah Equiano*, you will encounter these words.

loathsome	wretched	dejected

Base Words Words that seem unfamiliar may actually contain words you know. Try looking for such familiar base words "inside" unfamiliar words. The word *insupportable*, for example, contains the base word *support*. You know that *support* means "to bear" or "to hold up." In this word, the prefix *in-* means "not," and the suffix *-able* means "capable of being." *Insupportable* means "not capable of being borne or held up."

Note how the addition of prefixes or suffixes affects the meaning of the base word in these words.

un**merci**fully	in a manner without mercy
heightened	made higher or more intense
mariners	sailors

Apply your knowledge of base words and other vocabulary strategies to determine the meanings of unfamiliar words you encounter during your first read.

First Read NONFICTION

Apply these strategies as you conduct your first read. You will have an opportunity to complete a close read after your first read.

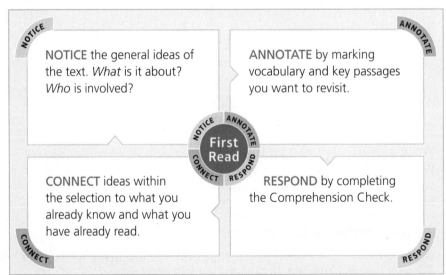

NOTICE the general ideas of the text. *What* is it about? *Who* is involved?

ANNOTATE by marking vocabulary and key passages you want to revisit.

CONNECT ideas within the selection to what you already know and what you have already read.

RESPOND by completing the Comprehension Check.

First Read

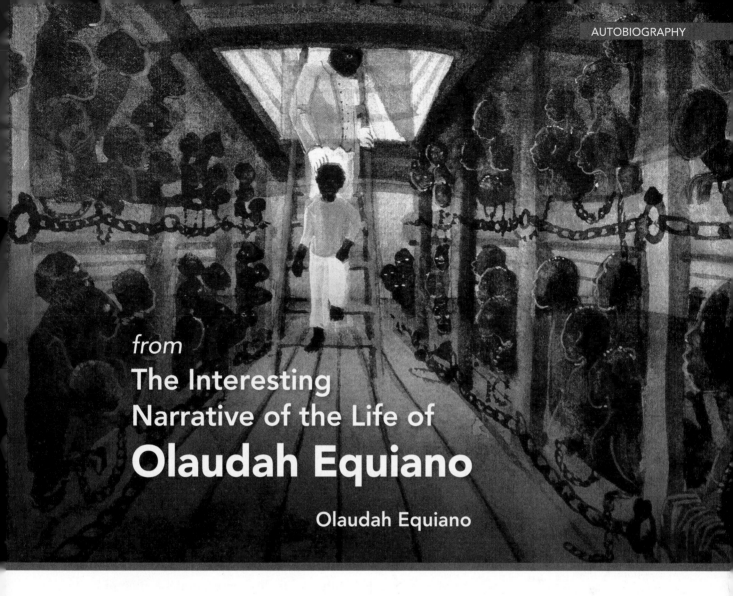

from

The Interesting Narrative of the Life of

Olaudah Equiano

Olaudah Equiano

BACKGROUND

In the first several chapters of his autobiography, Olaudah Equiano describes how slave traders kidnapped him and his sister from their home in West Africa and transported them to the African coast. During this six- or seven-month journey, Equiano was separated from his sister and held at a series of way stations. After reaching the coast, Equiano was shipped with other captives to North America. The following account describes this horrifying journey.

1   At last when the ship we were in, had got in all her cargo, they made ready with many fearful noises, and we were all put under deck, so that we could not see how they managed the vessel. But this disappointment was the least of my sorrow. The stench of the hold while we were on the coast was so intolerably **loathsome**, that it was dangerous to remain there for any time, and some of us had been permitted to stay on the deck for the fresh air; but now that the whole ship's cargo were confined together, it became absolutely pestilential. The closeness of the place, and the heat of the climate, added to the number in the ship, which was so crowded that each had scarcely room to turn himself, almost suffocated us.

NOTES

Mark base words or indicate another strategy you used that helped you determine meaning.

loathsome (LOHTH suhm) *adj.*

MEANING:

NOTES

Mark base words or indicate another strategy you used that helped you determine meaning.

wretched (REHCH ihd) *adj.*

MEANING:

2   This produced copious perspirations, so that the air soon became unfit for respiration, from a variety of loathsome smells, and brought on a sickness among the slaves, of which many died—thus falling victims to the improvident avarice, as I may call it, of their purchasers. This **wretched** situation was again aggravated by the galling of the chains, now become insupportable, and the filth of the necessary tubs, into which the children often fell, and were almost suffocated. The shrieks of the women, and the groans of the dying, rendered the whole a scene of horror almost inconceivable. Happily perhaps, for myself, I was soon reduced so low here that it was thought necessary to keep me almost always on deck; and from my extreme youth I was not put in fetters.[1] In this situation I expected every hour to share the fate of my companions, some of whom were almost daily brought upon deck at the point of death, which I began to hope would soon put an end to my miseries. Often did I think many of the inhabitants of the deep much more happy than myself.

3   I envied them the freedom they enjoyed, and as often wished I could change my condition for theirs. Every circumstance I met with, served only to render my state more painful, and heightened my apprehensions, and my opinion of the cruelty of the whites.

4   One day they had taken a number of fishes; and when they had killed and satisfied themselves with as many as they thought fit, to our astonishment who were on deck, rather than give any of them to us to eat, as we expected, they tossed the remaining fish into the sea again, although we begged and prayed for some as well as we could, but in vain; and some of my countrymen, being pressed by hunger, took an opportunity, when they thought no one saw them, of trying to get a little privately; but they were discovered, and the attempt procured them some very severe floggings. One day, when we had a smooth sea and moderate wind, two of my wearied countrymen who were chained together (I was near them at the time), preferring death to such a life of misery, somehow made through the nettings and jumped into the sea; immediately, another quite **dejected** fellow, who, on account of his illness, was suffered to be out of irons, also followed their example; and I believe many more would very soon have done the same, if they had not been prevented by the ship's crew, who were instantly alarmed. Those of us that were the most active, were in a moment put down under the deck; and there was such a noise and confusion amongst the people of the ship as I never heard before, to stop her, and get the boat out to go after the slaves. However, two of the wretches were drowned, but they got the other, and afterwards flogged him unmercifully, for thus attempting to prefer death to slavery. In this manner we continued to undergo more hardships than I can now relate, hardships which are inseparable from this accursed trade. Many a time we were near suffocation from the want of fresh

Mark base words or indicate another strategy you used that helped you determine meaning.

dejected (dee JEHK tihd) *adj.*

MEANING:

---

1. **fetters** (FEHT uhrz) *n.* chains.

air, which we were often without for whole days together. This, and the stench of the necessary tubs, carried off many.

5   During our passage, I first saw flying fishes, which surprised me very much; they used frequently to fly across the ship, and many of them fell on the deck. I also now first saw the use of the quadrant;[2] I had often with astonishment seen the mariners make observations with it, and I could not think what it meant. They at last took notice of my surprise; and one of them, willing to increase it, as well as to gratify my curiosity, made me one day look through it. The clouds appeared to me to be land, which disappeared as they passed along. This heightened my wonder; and I was now more persuaded than ever, that I was in another world, and that every thing about me was magic. At last, we came in sight of the island of Barbados, at which the whites on board gave a great shout, and made many signs of joy to us. We did not know what to think of this; but as the vessel drew nearer, we plainly saw the harbor, and other ships of different kinds and sizes, and we soon anchored amongst them, off Bridgetown.[3] Many merchants and planters now came on board, though it was in the evening. They put us in separate parcels,[4] and examined us attentively. They also made us jump, and pointed to the land, signifying we were to go there.

2. **quadrant** (KWOD ruhnt) *n.* instrument used by navigators to determine the position of a ship.
3. **Bridgetown** capital of Barbados.
4. **parcels** (PAHR suhlz) *n.* groups.

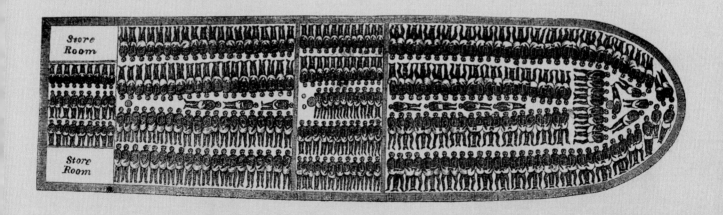

This portion of a 1788 British abolitionist poster depicts the *Brookes*, a slave ship, and the maximum number of slaves that it could transport legally. Slave traders carried as many slaves as the law allowed, knowing that many would die during the journey.

6   We thought by this, we should be eaten by these ugly men, as they appeared to us; and, when soon after we were all put down under the deck again, there was much dread and trembling among us, and nothing but bitter cries to be heard all the night from these apprehensions, insomuch, that at last the white people got some old slaves from the land to pacify us. They told us we were not to be eaten, but to work, and were soon to go on land, where we should see many of our country people. This report eased us much. And sure enough, soon after we were landed, there came to us Africans of all languages.

7   We were conducted immediately to the merchant's yard, where we were all pent up together, like so many sheep in a fold, without regard to sex or age. . . . We were not many days in the merchant's custody, before we were sold after their usual manner, which is this: On a signal given (as the beat of a drum), the buyers rush at once into the yard where the slaves are confined, and make choice of that parcel they like best. . . . ❧

Comprehension Check

Complete the following items after you finish your first read. Review and clarify details with your group.

1. According to Equiano, what physical hardships do the captives suffer during their passage across the Atlantic Ocean?

2. What do some captives do to escape the misery of the Atlantic crossing?

3. Why does Equiano blame the illness aboard ship on the "improvident avarice" of the slave traders?

4. How does Equiano's youth affect his treatment during the voyage?

5. What happens to the captives when the ship reaches Barbados?

6. 📓 **Notebook** Confirm your understanding of the text by creating a timeline of the narrative's events.

- -

RESEARCH

Research to Clarify Choose at least one unfamiliar detail from the text. Briefly research that detail. In what way does the information you learned shed light on an aspect of the narrative?

Research to Explore This autobiographical account may spark your curiosity to learn more about the author, the era, or the topic. You may want to share what you discover with your group.

THE INTERESTING NARRATIVE OF
THE LIFE OF OLAUDAH EQUIANO

GROUP DISCUSSION

In order to have a successful discussion, everyone should participate. Encourage group members to take turns offering their ideas and opinions.

 WORD NETWORK

Add words related to freedom from the text to your Word Network.

STANDARDS

Reading Informational Text
Determine an author's point of view or purpose in a text in which the rhetoric is particularly effective, analyzing how style and content contribute to the power, persuasiveness, or beauty of the text.

Language
Consult general and specialized reference materials, both print and digital, to find the pronunciation of a word or determine or clarify its precise meaning, its part of speech, its etymology, or its standard usage.

Close Read the Text

With your group, revisit sections of the text you marked during your first read. **Annotate** details that you notice. What **questions** do you have? What can you **conclude**?

Analyze the Text

CITE TEXTUAL EVIDENCE
to support your answers.

Complete the activities.

1. **Review and Clarify** With your group, reread paragraph 1 of the selection. Discuss the conditions that the African captives endured aboard the ship. Why were so many people crowded below deck?

2. **Present and Discuss** Now, work with your group to share the passages from the selection that you found especially important. Take turns presenting your passages. Discuss what you noticed in the selection, what questions you asked, and what conclusions you reached.

3. **Essential Question:** *What is the meaning of freedom?* What have you learned about American freedoms from reading this text? Discuss with your group.

LANGUAGE DEVELOPMENT

Concept Vocabulary

loathsome	wretched	dejected

Why These Words? The three concept vocabulary words from the text are related. With your group, discuss the words and determine what they have in common. How do these word choices enhance the impact of the text?

Practice

Notebook Confirm your understanding of these words from the text by using them in sentences. Be sure to include context clues that hint at each word's meaning.

Word Study

Notebook **Latin Root: *-ject-*** The Latin root *-ject-* means "to throw." It contributes to the meaning of the concept vocabulary word *dejected*, as well as many other words in English.

1. Explain how the meaning of the root *-ject-* is evident in the meaning of the word *dejected*.

2. Look up each of these words in a dictionary: *conjecture, trajectory,* and *projection*. Explain how the root *-ject-* contributes to the meaning of each of the words.

Analyze Craft and Structure

Literary Nonfiction: Persuasive Purpose *The Interesting Narrative of the Life of Olaudah Equiano* is an example of a **slave narrative**, or an autobiographical account of a person's life as a slave. Most slave narratives, written when slavery was a legal practice, have an implicit, or unstated, persuasive purpose: to expose the evils of slavery and, in so doing, turn the public against the practice. Equiano's account combines factual details and personal reflections with powerful descriptive language that constitute **emotional appeals** to his readers. Notice, for example, how words such as *shrieks* and *groans* evoke readers' sympathy and outrage in this depiction of the ship that brought Equiano from Africa:

> The shrieks of the women, and the groans of the dying, rendered the whole a scene of horror almost inconceivable.

The abolitionist movement in the United States owed much to the revelations of former slaves. Only the hardest of hearts could fail to be moved by Equiano's narrative.

Practice

CITE TEXTUAL EVIDENCE
to support your answers.

As a group, complete this chart. Identify passages from the autobiography that give factual details, passages that convey personal reflections, and passages that feature strong descriptive language. Then, explain the persuasive impact of each passage.

ELEMENT OF SLAVE NARRATIVE	EXAMPLES FROM TEXT	PERSUASIVE IMPACT
Factual details		
Personal reflections		
Strong descriptive language		

THE INTERESTING NARRATIVE OF
THE LIFE OF OLAUDAH EQUIANO

Conventions and Style

Eighteenth-Century Narrative Style Equiano's account is an example of eighteenth-century narrative style. The formal language of the period has several characteristics that distinguish it from modern style.

CHARACTERISTIC	EIGHTEENTH-CENTURY STYLE	MODERN STYLE
Sentence Length: the number of words, phrases, and clauses in a sentence	Sentences are long and contain multiple clauses and phrases.	Sentences vary in length, and most have fewer than three clauses.
Usage: the ways in which words are commonly used	Word meanings change over time, as do word forms, including formation of singular and plural nouns. Modern readers may contest usage or need to confirm archaic meanings.	Word meanings and forms continue to change over time. In addition, new words continue to enter the English language from other languages or are coined to refer to new situations, ideas, or objects.
Mechanics: punctuation and spelling	Eighteenth-century writers punctuated text however they chose.	Punctuation marks are used according to established conventions.

Read It

📓 **Notebook** Work individually. Read the passage from Equiano's narrative carefully, and then answer the questions that follow.

> One day they had taken a number of fishes; and when they had killed and satisfied themselves with as many as they thought fit, to our astonishment who were on deck, rather than give any of them to us to eat, as we expected, they tossed the remaining fish into the sea again, although we begged and prayed for some as well as we could, but in vain; and some of my countrymen, being pressed by hunger, took an opportunity, when they thought no one saw them, of trying to get a little privately; but they were discovered, and the attempt procured them some very severe floggings.

- How many sentences does the passage contain?
- Identify an example of eighteenth-century usage.
- What punctuation marks does the author use to separate details regarding the plight of the captives?

Write It

📓 **Notebook** Rewrite the passage in modern style. Then, share passages with your group and discuss whether or not the change in style lessened the persuasive impact of the original passage.

🏛 STANDARDS

Writing
• Write arguments to support claims in an analysis of substantive topics or texts, using valid reasoning and relevant and sufficient evidence.

• Establish and maintain a formal style and objective tone while attending to the norms and conventions of the discipline in which they are writing.

Language
• Demonstrate command of the conventions of standard English grammar and usage when writing or speaking.

• Apply the understanding that usage is a matter of convention, can change over time, and is sometimes contested.

Writing to Sources

Assignment

With your group, prepare an **argument** related to the abolitionist cause. Choose from the following options.

☐ a **literary review** of Equiano's autobiography, arguing that the events he describes, and the manner in which he describes them, provide powerful support for the abolitionist movement

☐ a **letter** to the British Parliament, using evidence from the selection to urge its members to abolish the slave trade

☐ an **advertisement** for the British abolitionist movement that uses graphics and text, inspired by specific details from the autobiography, to make a strong point about the need for change

TIP

COLLABORATION

Group members responsible for preparing the reasons that support the claim should work together to decide the order in which to list the reasons.

Project Plan Work with your group to divide the option that you chose into manageable sections or parts. Discuss your ideas and consider the types of supporting evidence you will use, including those that appeal to readers' emotions. Then, assign each member one part of the writing.

Working Title: _____

EVIDENCE LOG

Before moving on to a new selection, go to your Evidence Log and record what you learned from *The Interesting Narrative of the Life of Olaudah Equiano.*

SECTION OR PART	ASSIGNED GROUP MEMBER
Claim	
Reason 1	
Supporting details from the selection	
Reason 2	
Supporting details from the selection	
Reason 3	
Supporting details from the selection	

Tying It Together Work together to draft an introduction that touches on all the sections that you plan to write. Once everyone has written his or her section, work together to draft a logical and memorable conclusion.

LETTER | BIOGRAPHY

Letter to John Adams

from Dear Abigail: The Intimate Lives and Revolutionary Ideas of Abigail Adams and Her Two Remarkable Sisters

Concept Vocabulary

As you perform your first read of these two texts, you will encounter the following words.

vassals	foment	dissented

Context Clues When you come to an unfamiliar word in a text, you can often determine its meaning by using **context clues**—nearby words and phrases that provide hints to a word's meaning. Such hints may come in the form of descriptions.

> **Description as Context Clue:**
> **Passage:** "Others have committed abominable **ravages** . . . both the house and furniture of the Solicitor General have fallen prey to their own merciless party."
>
> **Explanation:** The description of a person's house and furniture as "prey" to a "merciless party" suggests that ravages means something like "destruction."

Apply your knowledge of context clues and other vocabulary strategies to determine the meanings of unfamiliar words you encounter during your first read.

First Read NONFICTION

Apply these strategies as you conduct your first read. You will have an opportunity to complete a close read after your first read.

NOTICE the general ideas of the text. *What* is it about? *Who* is involved?

ANNOTATE by marking vocabulary and key passages you want to revisit.

First Read

CONNECT ideas within the selection to what you already know and what you have already read.

RESPOND by completing the Comprehension Check.

Copyright © SAVVAS Learning Company LLC. All Rights Reserved.

STANDARDS

Reading Informational Text
By the end of grade 11, read and comprehend literary nonfiction in the grades 11–CCR text complexity band proficiently, with scaffolding as needed at the high end of the range.

Language
Use context as a clue to the meaning of a word or phrase.

About the Authors

Abigail Adams (1744–1818) was the wife of John Adams, the second president of the United States, and the mother of John Quincy Adams, the sixth president. She was also one of the most important and influential women of her time. A dedicated supporter of women's rights and the American Revolutionary movement, Adams wrote many letters to her husband and others expressing her opinions. In these letters, she included vivid descriptions that capture the essence of life in early America.

Adams was born Abigail Smith in Weymouth, Massachusetts. At the age of nineteen, she married John Adams. The couple had three sons and two daugthers. Abigail, who had not been educated as a child, made sure all of her children—including a daughter—received a thorough education. This was something few American girls enjoyed at the time.

Abigail died in 1818, after spending the last seventeen years of her life at the Adams family home in Massachusetts. In 1840, a first volume of her letters was published. In the ensuing decades, other collections, biographies, and histories have followed. Today, Abigail Adams is widely recognized as a writer and a pioneer of the American women's movement.

Diane Jacobs, who lives in New York City, is the author of several acclaimed biographies. In addition to *Dear Abigail*, Jacobs has written about the contemporary filmmaker Woody Allen and about Mary Wollstonecraft, the eighteenth-century British author of *A Vindication of the Rights of Woman*.

Backgrounds

Letter to John Adams

Throughout their courtship and marriage, John and Abigail Adams wrote more than one thousand letters to one another. Although their letters are often affectionate and even playful, they also reflect the couple's underlying awareness that they were key players in the unfolding of history. Abigail wrote this and several other letters to her husband while he attended the Second Continental Congress in Philadelphia.

From Dear Abigail: The Intimate Lives and Revolutionary Ideas of Abigail Adams and Her Two Remarkable Sisters

The correspondence between Abigail and John Adams sheds light on Revolutionary-era America. This selection by a modern historian sets their letters within the context of the work of the Continental Congress and the adoption of the Declaration of Independence.

Letter to
John Adams

Abigail Adams

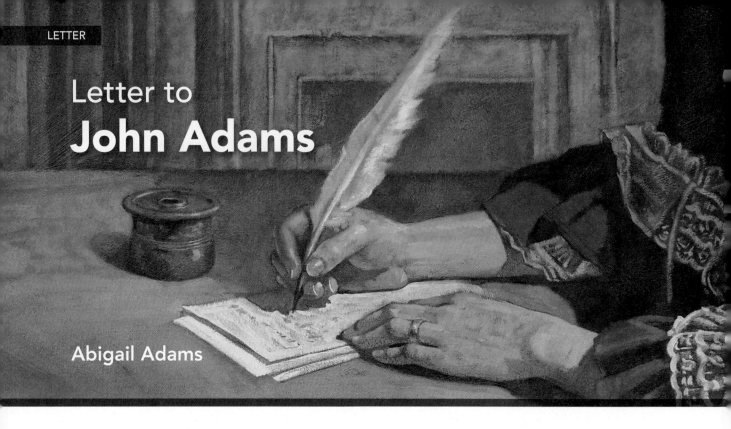

NOTES

Mark context clues or indicate another strategy you used that helped you determine meaning.

vassals (VAS uhlz) *n.*

MEANING:

Braintree[1] March 31, 1776

1   I wish you would ever write me a letter half as long as I write you; and tell me if you may where your fleet are gone? What sort of defense Virginia can make against our common enemy? Whether it is so situated as to make an able defense? Are not the gentry[2] lords and the common people vassals, are they not like the uncivilized natives Britain represents us to be? I hope their rifle men who have shown themselves very savage and even blood thirsty; are not a specimen of the generality of the people.

2   I am willing to allow the Colony great merit for having produced a Washington but they have been shamefully duped by a Dunmore.[3]

3   I have sometimes been ready to think that the passion for liberty cannot be equally strong in the breasts of those who have been accustomed to deprive their fellow creatures of theirs. Of this I am certain that it is not founded upon that generous and Christian principal of doing to others as we would that others should do unto us.

4   Do not you want to see Boston; I am fearful of the small pox, or I should have been in before this time. I got Mr. Crane to go to our

---

1. **Braintree** town in eastern Massachusetts that was the home of John and Abigail Adams.
2. **gentry** (JEHN tree) *n.* people of high social standing.
3. **Dunmore** John Murray, 4th earl of Dunmore, was the British colonial governor of Virginia. He provoked strong feelings among Virginians when he dissolved the legislature and later used troops loyal to the British throne to attack the colony's troops in late 1775 and early 1776.

house and see what state it was in. I find it has been occupied by one of the doctors of a regiment, very dirty, but no other damage has been done to it. The few things which were left in it are all gone. Cranch has the key which he never delivered up. I have wrote to him for it and am determined to get it cleaned as soon as possible and shut it up. I look upon it a new acquisition of property, a property which one month ago I did not value at a single shilling,[4] and could with pleasure have seen it in flames.

5   The town in general is left in a better state than we expected, more owing to a percipitate[5] flight than any regard to the inhabitants, though some individuals discovered a sense of honor and justice and have left the rent of the houses in which they were, for the owners and the furniture unhurt, or if damaged sufficient to make it good.

6   Others have committed abominable ravages. The mansion house of your President [John Hancock] is safe and the furniture unhurt whilst both the house and furniture of the Solicitor General [Samuel Quincy] have fallen a prey to their own merciless party. Surely the very fiends feel a reverential awe for virtue and patriotism, whilst they detest the paricide[6] and traitor.

7   I feel very differently at the approach of spring to what I did a month ago. We knew not then whether we could plant or sow with safety, whether when we had toiled we could reap the fruits of our own industry, whether we could rest in our own cottages, or whether we should not be driven from the sea coasts to seek shelter in the wilderness, but now we feel as if we might sit under our own vine and eat the good of the land.

8   I feel a gaieti de Coar[7] to which before I was a stranger. I think the sun looks brighter, the birds sing more melodiously, and nature puts on a more cheerful countenance. We feel a temporary peace, and the poor fugitives are returning to their deserted habitations.

9   Though we felicitate[8] ourselves, we sympathize with those who are trembling least the lot of Boston should be theirs. But they cannot be in similar circumstances unless pusillanimity and cowardice should take possession of them. They have time and warning given them to see the evil and shun it.—I long to hear that you have declared an independency—and by the way in the new code of laws which I suppose it will be necessary for you to make I desire you would remember the ladies, and be more generous and favorable to them than your ancestors. Do not put such unlimited power into the hands of the husbands. Remember all men would be tyrants if they could. If particuliar care and attention is not paid

I desire you would remember the ladies, and be more generous and favourable to them than your ancestors.

4. **shilling** *n.* former British coin worth one twentieth of a pound.
5. **percipitate** *adj.* precipitate; done very hastily or rashly.
6. **paricide** *n.* parricide; person who kills a parent or other relative.
7. **gaieti de Coar** *gaieté de coeur;* French for "joy of heart."
8. **felicitate** *v.* wish happiness; to congratulate.

to the ladies we are determined to **foment** a rebellion, and will not hold ourselves bound by any laws in which we have no voice, or representation.

10   That your sex are naturally tyrannical is a truth so thoroughly established as to admit of no dispute, but such of you as wish to be happy willingly give up the harsh title of master for the more tender and endearing one of friend. Why then, not put it out of the power of the vicious and the lawless to use us with cruelty and indignity with impunity. Men of sense in all ages abhor those customs which treat us only as the vassals of your sex. Regard us then as beings placed by providence under your protection and in imitation of the supreme being make use of that power only for our happiness.

April 5

11   Not having an opportunity of sending this I shall add a few lines more; though not with a heart so gay. I have been attending the sick chamber of our neighbor Trot whose affliction I most sensibly feel but cannot describe, stripped of two lovely children in one week. George the eldest died on Wednesday and Billy the youngest on Friday, with the canker fever, a terrible disorder so much like the throat distemper, that it differs but little from it. Betsy Cranch has been very bad, but upon the recovery. Becky Peck they do not expect will live out the day. Many grown persons are now sick with it, in this street. It rages much in other towns. The mumps too are very frequent. Isaac is now confined with it. Our own little flock are yet well. My heart trembles with anxiety for them. God preserve them.

12   I want to hear much oftener from you than I do. March 8 was the last date of any that I have yet had.—You inquire of whether I am making salt peter.[9] I have not yet attempted it, but after soap making believe I shall make the experiment. I find as much as I can do to manufacture clothing for my family which would otherwise be naked. I know of but one person in this part of the town who has made any, that is Mr. Tertias Bass as he is called who has got very near a hundred weight which has been found to be very good. I have heard of some others in the other parishes. Mr. Reed of Weymouth has been applied to, to go to Andover to the mills which are now at work, and has gone. I have lately seen a small manuscript describing the proportions for the various sorts of powder, fit for cannon, small arms and pistols. If it would be of any service your way I will get it transcribed and send it to you.—Every one of your friends send their regards, and all the little ones. Your brother's youngest child lies bad with convulsion fits. Adieu. I need not say how much I am your ever faithful friend.

---

9. **salt peter** *n.* saltpeter; a form of potassium nitrate used to make gunpowder.

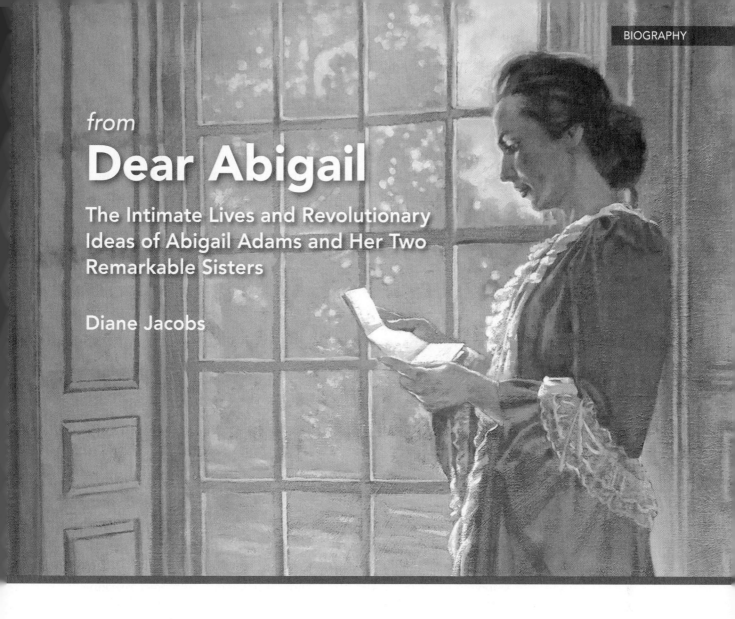

from

Dear Abigail

The Intimate Lives and Revolutionary Ideas of Abigail Adams and Her Two Remarkable Sisters

Diane Jacobs

1   Writing to Abigail about the fierce effort it took him to compose *Thoughts on Government*[1] at the same time that he was working day and night at Congress, John lamented that none of his present endeavors would bring them an easier life. "I shall get nothing [for writing this pamphlet], I believe, because I never get any thing by any thing that I do," he complained, while assuring her he was not above commiserating her lack of help on the farm or writing paper for all his preoccupation with posterity and the greater good. Strawberries and an early spring in the dirty city did little to console him. He longed, he said, to walk in their garden and to the cornfields, the orchards, and the Common.[2] "Instead of domestic felicity, I am destined to public contentions," he brooded. "Instead of rural felicity, I must reconcile myself to the smoke and noise of a city."

2   So he wished to be home. And yet his overriding desire at the moment was for Congress to make a declaration of independence

NOTES

1. **Thoughts on Government** document written by John Adams in 1776, notable for proposing the three branches of American government, including a system of checks and balances.
2. **the Common** large public park in Boston, Massachusetts.

from Great Britain. It had to be sooner rather than later because without it there was no hope for the foreign assistance—from France in particular—which was crucial to winning the war. On June 7, the Virginia delegate Richard Henry Lee of Virginia raised a motion for independence in Congress; it was supported by Massachusetts and six other colonies, while another six—Pennsylvania, Delaware, Maryland, South Carolina, New Jersey, and New York—remained unsure.

3   With everyone hoping for a unanimous verdict, the vote was set three weeks in the future, while a committee to consider the tone and nature of the prospective document immediately convened. It consisted of five members: the most prominent being John, Benjamin Franklin, and the redheaded Virginian who shared Thomas Paine's[3] veneration for the passions: Thomas Jefferson. Considered to be even more eloquent than the far better-known authors of *Poor Richard* and *Thoughts on Government*, 33-year-old Jefferson was chosen to write the text.

4   Like Franklin, Jefferson was a scientist and inventor. He had created a retractable bed and a tilt-top table as well as an indoor weather vane and his own Palladian estate, Monticello. Educated at William and Mary, he was as steeped in history and philosophy as Adams and also adored his wife, a wealthy widow, who was currently pregnant and in poor health. He was a slaveholder who professed to dislike slavery, a statesman ambitious to succeed on the large stage who hated leaving home. As he began drafting the American declaration—in the middle state of Pennsylvania, on a desk of his own design—he longed for southern Monticello as Adams longed for northern Braintree. Though Jefferson was a deist, rejecting Christ and original sin, he shared Adams's obsession with goodness. "Everything is useful which contributes to fix in the mind principles and practices of virtue," he believed.

5   Jefferson was gangly, fidgety, six-foot-two-and-a-half, and as quiet as Franklin in Congress. But he rode his horse elegantly, spoke up regularly in committees, and, despite his aversion to arguing, proved impregnable to opposing views. For better and for worse, no one and nothing swayed him. He had little use for either the vagaries[4] of individuals or venerated ideals.

6   "We are hastening rapidly to great events," John had written Abigail at the end of April, adding that "It requires . . . serenity of temper, a deep . . . understanding and . . . courage . . . to ride in this whirlwind" of Congressional discord. By the end of May, he was telling her that affairs were in a critical state. Then, in the middle of June, exultant after Henry Lee raised a motion for separation from England, he wrote, "These throes will usher in the birth of a fine boy."

---

3. **Thomas Paine's** Thomas Paine was a highly influential writer who argued passionately
   for American independence from England.
4. **vagaries** (VAY guh reez) *n.* unpredictable actions or ideas.

7   On July 1, twenty days after that initial motion, Congress resumed its debate on independence with John Dickinson of Pennsylvania arguing against and John Adams for an immediate break from both Parliament and King George III. John spoke fervidly for two hours to a rapt audience. A clear majority of nine colonies sided with him, but in a preliminary vote the delegates from Pennsylvania (out of respect for Dickinson, though most of its citizens favored independence), South Carolina, and Delaware **dissented**, while New York, with its high percentage of loyalists, abstained. Still hoping for unanimity, Congress agreed to delay the formal vote until the following morning.

8   That night word arrived that a flotilla of British boats had sailed into New York Harbor, panicking George Washington's unprepared Army and adding pressure for some buoying news. The next day John Dickinson, for the sake of unity, announced he would abstain from the voting, throwing Pennsylvania to the majority. South Carolina and Delaware joined Pennsylvania, while New York continued to abstain. The motion was called to the floor and carried.

9   July 3 was spent amending Jefferson's declaration—much to the proprietary writer's chagrin. The most significant change, insisted on by South Carolina and Georgia, was the elimination of a passage implicitly condemning slavery. Jefferson had accused the King of waging "cruel war against human nature" by capturing and transporting innocent Africans "into slavery in another hemisphere, or to incur miserable death in their transportation thither." This was a daring, if bewildering, opinion from a southern slaveholder. Jefferson claimed to be proud of it and to rue its loss. Other of his favorite passages were also cut or tightened during the nearly twelve-hour debate over wording, but Jefferson's voice remained, and on the afternoon of July 4, all of Congress endorsed it.

"We are hastening rapidly to great events"

10   John Adams could hardly contain his exuberance. "Yesterday the greatest question was decided, which ever was debated in America, and a greater, perhaps, never was or will be decided among men," he wrote Abigail. What felt hopelessly slow just a month ago now seemed remarkably expeditious. Looking back to the first arguments with England in the early 1760s, "and recollect[ing] the series of political events, the chain of causes and effects, I am surprised at the suddenness as well as the greatness of this Revolution," he exulted. And, of course, "calamities" and "distresses" might lie in the future; surely the threat of tyranny by the majority, which he had warned against in *Thoughts on Government*, would pose a threat in the coming years. And, yes, it would be far better for the war if independence had been declared seven months before and foreign alliances were set in place. And yet: "July [of] 1776, will be the most memorable

NOTES

Mark context clues or indicate another strategy you used that helped you determine meaning.

dissented (dih SEHNT ihd) *v.*

MEANING:

Drafting the Declaration of Independence in 1776 This 1859 painting by Alonzo Chappel depicts the work of the "Committee of Five": (*right to left*) Roger Sherman, Robert Livingston, John Adams, Thomas Jefferson, and Benjamin Franklin.

epocha,[5] in the history of America.—I am apt to believe that it will be celebrated, by succeeding generations, as the great anniversary." It ought, John declared, to be commemorated and "solemnized with pomp and parade, with shews,[6] sports, guns, bells, bonfires and illuminations from one end of this continent to the other from this time forward forever."

11   On July 18, a week after they were inoculated for smallpox, and with no one yet showing symptoms of the disease, Mary and Richard, Abigail, and Betsy joined masses of patriots lining King Street in front of the Boston State House, the seat of the first elected legislature in the New World. The ragtag troops who had chased the British out of Boston four months earlier stood before them, respectably armed at least for the moment. An officer, Colonel Crafts, appeared on the balcony and began to read:

5. **epocha** (EHP uh kuh) *n.* archaic form of "epoch," a distinct and significant era in history.
6. **shews** *n.* archaic form of "shows."

NOTES

12   When in the course of human events, it becomes necessary for one people to dissolve the political bands which have connected them with another, and to assume among the powers of the earth a separate and equal station to which the Laws of Nature and of Nature's God entitle them, a decent respect to the opinions of mankind requires that they should declare the causes which impel them to the separation.

13   The Smith sisters'[7] lives spoke volumes on the causes for separation, and the spirit of the declaration was familiar, for they had avidly read the great thinkers of the Enlightenment[8] who so informed Jefferson's view. Yet, if his concepts were not original, the occasion was a first in history, and Richard Cranch as well as Mary, Abigail, and Betsy stood spellbound at the beautiful expression of what they felt and knew. "We hold these truths to be self-evident, that all men are created equal, that they are endowed by their Creator with certain unalienable Rights, that among these are Life, Liberty, and the pursuit of Happiness." And on it went.

14   "God Save the King" was already a memory. When Colonel Crafts finished reading the Declaration of Independence, he shouted, "God Save our American States." The people picked up this chant and ran with it, as Richard Cranch reported to John in a letter the following week. There were three cheers that "rended the air," Abigail wrote in her own description, and they were followed by an elated ringing of bells; the cannons roared, and rifles' shots rang in the air. "After dinner the king's arms were taken down from the State House and every vestige of him from every place in which it appeared and burnt in King Street. Thus ends royal authority in this State," she concluded, "and all the people shall say Amen."

15   By July 22, Abigail was ill with the "excruciating pain in my head and every limb" that was said to "portend[9] a speedy eruption," which occurred a few days later, and though she produced only one pox, her symptoms were sufficiently grueling for the doctor to declare her immune. John Quincy's case too was mild but conclusive, while Mary's eldest daughter, Betsy Cranch, the frailest of them all, fainted and lay listless in bed. Her mother and brothers, on the other hand, produced no symptoms. By the end of July, Mary had been inoculated four times and was still healthy as the day she left Braintree, as were Charles and Tommy Adams, who had been inoculated twice. It seemed fitting when Nabby, the calmest of them all, came through with almost no suffering. The doctor, however, insisted that she be inoculated a second time, on the odd chance that her symptoms were "false."

16   Even after her single pox dissipated, Abigail felt light-headed from the disease. "The smallpox is a great confuser of the mind, I am really

7. **Smith sisters** Abigail Adams and her sisters; Smith was their family surname.
8. **the Enlightenment** European intellectual movement in the seventeenth and eighteenth centuries that emphasized the power of reason.
9. **portend** (pawr TEHND) *v.* foreshadow; indicate.

put to it to spell the commonest word," she told John. Yet when John gave her an opening, she had no trouble expounding on her favorite topic of women in the new nation. "If you complain of neglect of education in sons, What shall I say with regard to daughters, who every day experience the want of it," she began. And continued:

17   I most sincerely wish that some more liberal plan might be laid and executed for the benefit of the rising generation, and that our new constitution may be distinguished for learning and virtue. If we mean to have heroes, statesmen, and philosophers, we should have learned women. The world perhaps will laugh at me, and accuse me of vanity, but you know I have a mind too enlarged and liberal [to be vain]. If much depends as is allowed upon the early education of youth and the first principals which are instilled take deepest root, great benefit must arise from literary accomplishments in women.

18   This time John assured Abigail "Your sentiments of the importance of education in women are exactly agreeable to my own," though women who displayed their wits were contemptible, he felt impelled to add. ❧

Comprehension Check

Complete the following items after you finish your first read. Review and clarify details with your group.

LETTER TO JOHN ADAMS

1. In her letter of March 31, 1776, what does Abigail Adams ask that John provide?

2. What does Abigail report to John about the state of homes in Boston?

3. What advice does Abigail Adams give her husband regarding women's rights?

4. 📓 **Notebook** Confirm your understanding of the text by writing a summary.

from DEAR ABIGAIL

1. Cite two reasons for John Adams's unhappiness in the late spring of 1776.

2. Name two contradictions regarding Thomas Jefferson that the text explores.

3. What document does Colonel Crafts, an army officer, read to a crowd assembled in front of the Boston State House?

4. 📓 **Notebook** Confirm your understanding of the text by drawing a storyboard of events.

- -

RESEARCH

Research to Clarify Choose at least one unfamiliar detail from one of the texts. Briefly research that detail. In what way does the information you found shed light on an aspect of that text?

LETTER TO JOHN ADAMS
from DEAR ABIGAIL

TIP

GROUP DISCUSSION
Encourage group members to be positive, encouraging, and open to divergent viewpoints and opinions.

WORD NETWORK

Add words related to freedom from the text to your Word Network.

STANDARDS

Reading Informational Text
Analyze seventeenth-, eighteenth-, and nineteenth-century foundational U.S. documents of historical and literary significance for their themes, purposes, and rhetorical features.

Language
Identify and correctly use patterns of word changes that indicate different meanings or parts of speech.

Close Read the Text

With your group, revisit sections of the text you marked during your first read. **Annotate** details that you notice. What **questions** do you have? What can you **conclude**?

Analyze the Text

CITE TEXTUAL EVIDENCE
to support your answers.

Complete the activities.

1. **Review and Clarify** With your group, reread paragraph 14 from *Dear Abigail*, in which the author discusses the public reading of the Declaration of Independence. Why do you think the Bostonians reacted as they did?

2. **Present and Discuss** Now, work with your group to share the passages from the two selections that you found especially important. Take turns presenting your passages. Discuss what you noticed in the selections, what questions you asked, and what conclusions you reached.

3. **Essential Question:** *What is the meaning of freedom?* What have you learned about American freedoms from reading these texts? Discuss with your group.

LANGUAGE DEVELOPMENT

Concept Vocabulary

vassals	foment	dissented

Why These Words? The three concept words from the texts are related. With your group, discuss the words and determine what they have in common. How do these word choices enhance the impact of the texts?

Practice

📓 **Notebook** Confirm your understanding of these words by using each one in a sentence. Include context clues that help readers figure out what each word means.

Word Study

📓 **Notebook** **Word Families** Groups of words that share a common base but have different prefixes, suffixes, or both, are called **word families**. The concept word *dissented*, for instance, is built upon the base word *dissent*.

Complete the following activities.

1. Use an online dictionary or other source to identify other members of the word family that includes *dissented*. Write three of those related words, and identify their parts of speech.

2. Choose a word from one of these texts that you think is part of a word family. Research the word and verify your choice. Write the original word and two related words. Identify each word's part of speech.

Analyze Craft and Structure

Primary and Secondary Sources Research sources can be classified into one of two categories—primary sources or secondary sources.

- **Primary sources**, created by people who directly participated in or observed an event, give readers first-hand information about a topic. They include diaries, journals, letters, newspaper articles, and speeches. They may also include functional texts, such as government forms, schedules, or blueprints.
- **Secondary sources**, written by people with indirect knowledge, rely on primary sources or other secondary sources for information. Secondary sources include biographies, encyclopedias, and book reviews.

These classifications into primary and secondary categories are not absolutely set, but depend largely on how a text is used by a researcher.

TIP

CLARIFICATION
Original drawings, paintings, news footage, pottery, and photographs are some non-text items that are categorized as primary sources. These can be excellent research sources, and they should be documented with citations.

Practice

CITE TEXTUAL EVIDENCE to support your answers.

Analyze and evaluate how Jacobs uses primary sources to add interest, clarity, and legitimacy to the points she is making. For example, ask: "What does this quotation from a primary source do? Does it make the point clearer?" Work individually to gather your notes in this chart. Then, share your observations with your group.

DEAR ABIGAIL	PRIMARY SOURCE INFORMATION	EFFECT
Paragraph 1		
Paragraph 6		
Paragraph 10		
Paragraph 17		

📓 Notebook Respond to these questions.

1. Which use of a primary source in the excerpt from *Dear Abigail* did you find most effective? Why?

2. Review or scan the two secondary sources related to Abigail Adams in this text—the brief biography and the excerpt from *Dear Abigail*. Identify one trait each secondary source attributes to Abigail Adams. Then, cite a passage from Adams's letter that either supports that interpretation of her character or challenges it. Explain your choices.

LETTER TO JOHN ADAMS
from DEAR ABIGAIL

Author's Style

Voice A writer's **voice** is the way in which his or her personality is revealed on the page. It is the sense the reader gains of the person behind the words. Voice is created through a combination of elements:

- **diction:** the types of words a writer uses
- **syntax:** the types of sentences a writer uses, including structure, length, and variety
- **tone:** the writer's attitude toward the topic or audience

Voice is also influenced by the writer's consideration of his or her **audience**, or readers, and **purpose**, or reason for writing. Since writers adapt their diction, syntax, and tone to suit specific audiences and purposes, a writer's voice can vary from one text to another. For example, John Adams's voice is warm and personal in letters to his wife, but impersonal and formal in public documents.

Read It

Work individually. Use this chart to explore aspects of Abigail Adams's voice as a writer. Cite examples from both texts, and briefly explain how her combination of diction, syntax, and tone creates a sense of her personal qualities. Discuss your findings with your group.

PASSAGES FROM LETTER TO JOHN ADAMS	TYPE(S) OF DICTION, SYNTAX, AND TONE	PERSONALITY TRAIT(S) OF ADAMS
PASSAGES QUOTED IN *DEAR ABIGAIL*		

STANDARDS

Reading Informational Text
Determine an author's point of view or purpose in a text in which the rhetoric is particularly effective, analyzing how style and content contribute to the power, persuasiveness or beauty of the text.

Write It

🗒 **Notebook** Review your notes from the chart. Then, write a paragraph in which you describe Abigail Adams's voice as a writer. Use textual examples to support your view. Share your paragraph with your group, and discuss.

Speaking and Listening

Assignment

Create an **oral presentation** based on the selections and present it to the whole class. Choose from the following options.

☐ **Dialogue** Write and present a dramatization of a conversation between John and Abigail Adams in which the two discuss the colonies' struggle for freedom from Great Britain. Base the conversation on the information provided in the texts. Strive to capture each speaker's unique opinions and point of view.

☐ **Dramatic Reading** Present a reading of the March 31st portion of Abigail Adams's letter to John Adams. Decide how you will divide the text among members of your group so that everyone participates. Then, discuss your interpretation of the text, and consider how you will use your voices and gestures to capture its distinct qualities.

☐ **Public Announcement** Both Abigail Adams's letter and the excerpt from *Dear Abigail* mention the threat that smallpox posed in Revolutionary-era America. Research the symptoms of smallpox; the types of people who are especially vulnerable; its progression, treatment, and potential outcomes. Then, write and deliver the announcement that might have been read to citizens of Boston in 1776 warning them of the presence of the disease in their community. Refer to Adams's letter for ideas about diction and tone.

Project Plan First, identify the information, details, or passages you will use from the texts. Use the chart to determine which details you will include, why they are important, and how you will use them in the presentation. If you feel that you need additional material, decide which group members will do the research.

Detail from Text(s)	Reason to Use Detail	How Group Will Present Detail

Presentation Plan Decide which members of the group will produce the writing required for the assignment, and which members will deliver the presentation. Make sure that all members have an equal role, and allow all members to contribute their ideas before finalizing the presentation.

EVIDENCE LOG

Before moving on to the next selection, go to your Evidence Log and record what you learned from Abigail Adams's letter to John Adams and the excerpt from *Dear Abigail*.

STANDARDS

Speaking and Listening
Present information, findings, and supporting evidence, conveying a clear and distinct perspective and a logical argument, such that listeners can follow the line of reasoning, alternative or opposing perspectives are addressed, and the organization, development, substance, and style are appropriate to purpose, audience, and a range of formal and informal tasks.

Gettysburg Address

Concept Vocabulary

As you perform your first read of the Gettysburg Address, you will encounter these words.

> dedicated consecrate hallow

Familiar Word Parts When determining the meaning of an unfamiliar word, look for word parts, such as roots or affixes, that you know. Doing so may help you unlock word meanings.

> **Unfamiliar Word:** *prologue*
>
> **Familiar Word Parts:** You may recognize the prefix *pro-*, which means "forward" or "forth." Likewise, you may recognize the root *-log-*, which means "word" or "reason" and appears in the words *dialogue*, *logic*, and *eulogy*.
>
> **Possible Meaning:** When you combine your knowledge of the two word parts, you can figure out that *prologue* means something like "words that come first."
>
> **Confirm Meaning:** Use a dictionary or other language resource to check your analysis of a word's meaning. One dictionary definition of *prologue* is "an introductory part of a text; a preface."

Apply your knowledge of familiar word parts and other vocabulary strategies to determine the meanings of unfamiliar words you encounter during your first read.

First Read NONFICTION

Apply these strategies as you conduct your first read. You will have an opportunity to complete a close read after your first read.

NOTICE general ideas of the text. *What* is it about? *Who* is involved?

ANNOTATE by marking vocabulary and key passages you want to revisit.

First Read

CONNECT ideas within the selection to what you already know and what you have already read.

RESPOND by completing the Comprehension Check and by writing a brief summary of the selection.

Copyright © SAVVAS Learning Company LLC. All Rights Reserved.

STANDARDS

Reading Informational Text
By the end of grade 11, read and comprehend literary nonfiction in the grades 11–CCR text complexity band proficiently, with scaffolding as needed at the high end of the range.

Language
• Determine or clarify the meaning of unknown and multiple meaning words and phrases based on *grades 11–12 reading and content*, choosing flexibly from a range of strategies.
• Verify the preliminary determination of the meaning of a word or phrase.

About the Author

Abraham Lincoln

Serving as president during one of the most tragic periods in American history, Abraham Lincoln (1809–1865) fought to reunite a nation torn apart by war. His courage, strength, and dedication in the face of an overwhelming national crisis made him one of the most admired and respected American presidents.

Lincoln was born into a family of humble means. As a child, his duties on his parents' farm limited his opportunities to receive a formal education. Still, he was an avid reader and developed an early interest in politics. He served in the Illinois state legislature and ran for the United States Senate against Stephen Douglas. Lincoln lost the election, but his heated debates with Douglas brought him national recognition and helped him win the presidency in 1860.

Troubled Times Shortly after his election, the Civil War erupted. Throughout the war, Lincoln showed great strength and courage. He also demonstrated his gift for oratory. He was invited to make "a few appropriate remarks" in November 1863 for a dedication of the Gettysburg battlefield as a national cemetery. The world has long remembered what he said there.

Lincoln's great care as a writer shows in the Gettysburg Address, as it does in many of his other speeches. He worked diligently and thoughtfully to prepare messages that would have the effect he desired. Two important aspects of the Gettysburg speech are its brevity—just 272 words—and its reaffirmation of the democratic principles at the heart of American government.

Stories abound regarding Lincoln's drafting of the speech: He wrote it the week before; he wrote it the night before; he wrote it on the train while traveling to the event; he wrote it on a scrap of paper. Certainly, he was still revising as he spoke, adding key words, such as "under God," that he knew would stir his listeners.

A Life Cut Short While the Civil War continued to rage, Lincoln was elected to a second term as President. He was killed by an assassin's bullet in 1865 while attending the theater with his wife.

Gettysburg Address

Abraham Lincoln

BACKGROUND

Abraham Lincoln gave this speech to 15,000 people at the consecration of a new military cemetery in the town of Gettysburg, Pennsylvania—the site of the bloodiest battle ever fought on American soil, and the turning point of the Civil War. At the time of this speech, the war had been raging for more than two years. Lincoln needed to gain continuing support for a bloody conflict that was far from over.

November 19, 1863

1   Four score and seven years ago our fathers brought forth on this continent a new nation, conceived in Liberty, and **dedicated** to the proposition that all men are created equal.

2   Now we are engaged in a great civil war, testing whether that nation, or any nation so conceived and so dedicated, can long endure. We are met on a great battle-field of that war. We have come to dedicate a portion of that field, as a final resting place for those who here gave their lives that that nation might live. It is altogether fitting and proper that we should do this.

3   But, in a larger sense, we cannot dedicate—we cannot **consecrate**—we cannot **hallow**—this ground. The brave men, living and dead, who struggled here, have consecrated it, far above our poor power to add or detract. The world will little note, nor long remember what we say here, but it can never forget what they did here. It is for us the living, rather, to be dedicated here to the unfinished work which they who fought here have thus far so nobly advanced. It is rather for us to be here dedicated to the great task remaining before us—that from these honored dead we take increased devotion to that cause for which they gave the last full measure of devotion—that we here highly resolve that these dead shall not have died in vain—that this nation, under God, shall have a new birth of freedom—and that government of the people, by the people, for the people, shall not perish from the earth.

NOTES

Mark familiar word parts or indicate another strategy you used that helped you determine meaning.

dedicated (DEHD uh kayt ihd) *adj.*

MEANING:

consecrate (KON suh krayt) *v.*

MEANING:

hallow (HAL oh) *v.*

MEANING:

Comprehension Check

Complete the following items after you finish your first read. Review and clarify details with your group.

1. According to Lincoln, what did "our fathers" create eighty-seven years ago?

2. According to Lincoln, the Civil War is a test of what idea?

3. Why have the speaker and the audience met on the battlefield at Gettysburg?

4. According to Lincoln, why are they unable to "dedicate," "consecrate," or "hallow" the battlefield?

5. At the end of the speech, how does Lincoln characterize the American system of government?

6. ⊟ **Notebook** Confirm your understanding of the text by writing a summary.

- -

RESEARCH

Research to Clarify Choose at least one unfamiliar detail from the text. Briefly research that detail. In what way does the information you learned shed light on an aspect of the speech?

Research to Explore Ask one focused question you would like answered about the Battle of Gettysburg. Then, do some research to find the answer.

Close Read the Text

With your group, revisit sections of the text you marked during your first read. **Annotate** details that you notice. What **questions** do you have? What can you **conclude**?

- -

Analyze the Text

CITE TEXTUAL EVIDENCE
to support your answers.

Complete the activities.

1. **Review and Clarify** With your group, reread paragraph 2. How does Lincoln build upon his introduction and prepare the audience for his main points in paragraph 3?

2. **Present and Discuss** Now, work with your group to share the passages from the selection that you found especially important. Take turns presenting your passages. Discuss what you noticed in the selection, what questions you asked, and what conclusions you reached.

3. **Essential Question:** *What is the meaning of freedom?* What has this text revealed about American freedoms? Discuss with your group.

TIP

CLARIFICATION

The Gettysburg Address is short, but it is by no means a group of random comments. As a group, discuss the purpose of each paragraph and the main idea it expresses. How would an outline of the speech look?

 WORD NETWORK

Add words related to freedom from the text to your Word Network.

LANGUAGE DEVELOPMENT

Concept Vocabulary

dedicate	consecrate	hallow

Why These Words? The three concept vocabulary words are related. With your group, discuss the words and determine what they have in common. How do these word choices enhance the impact of the text?

Practice

📓 **Notebook** Confirm your understanding of the vocabulary words by using them in sentences. Use context clues that hint at each word's meaning.

Word Study

📓 **Notebook** **Denotation and Connotation** In his address, Lincoln says that he cannot *dedicate, consecrate,* or *hallow* the battlefield ground. The three concept vocabulary words have similar **denotations**, or definitions, but different **connotations**, or nuances in meaning.

1. Write the denotations of the three words. Then, explain the connotations each one conveys. Note that connotations may involve slightly different meanings, or simply intensity of meaning.

2. Use a thesaurus to find two other words that share denotations with *dedicate*. Then, explain how their connotations differ.

STANDARDS

Reading Informational Text
• Determine an author's point of view or purpose in a text in which the rhetoric is particularly effective, analyzing how style and content contribute to the power, persuasiveness, or beauty of the text.

• Analyze seventeenth-, eighteenth-, and nineteenth-century foundational U.S. documents of historical and literary significance for their themes, purposes, and rhetorical features.

Language
Analyze nuances in the meaning of words with similar denotations.

Analyze Craft and Structure

Author's Choices: Diction A writer's choice and arrangement of words, known as **diction**, helps to express the writer's ideas clearly and precisely and to give the writing a unique quality. Diction may be formal or informal, technical or plain, elevated or simple. A speaker's choice of diction is intimately connected to his or her purpose for writing, as well as to considerations of the audience and the occasion.

Consider the solemn, serious formality of Lincoln's diction at the beginning of his address at Gettysburg—and imagine how he might have expressed the same ideas more informally.

> **FORMAL:** Four score and seven years ago, our fathers brought forth on this continent a new nation. . . .

> **INFORMAL:** Eighty-seven years ago, our early leaders created a new nation, right here. . . .

Practice

CITE TEXTUAL EVIDENCE to support your answers.

Identify passages in the Gettysburg Address that include diction you find powerful or beautiful. Consider how the passage might sound with less formality by rewriting it. Then, explain the impact of Lincoln's diction. One example has been done for you. Complete the chart independently, and then share with your group.

PASSAGE WITH POWERFUL DICTION	REWRITTEN PASSAGE	IMPACT OF LINCOLN'S DICTION
Four score and seven years ago, our fathers brought forth on this continent a new nation.	Eighty-seven years ago, our early leaders created a new nation, right here.	adds power, grandeur to the speech

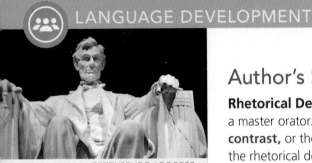

GETTYSBURG ADDRESS

Author's Style

Rhetorical Devices: Antithesis Lincoln was both a master writer and a master orator. In the Gettysburg Address, he makes insightful use of **contrast,** or the juxtaposition of opposing ideas. In some cases, he uses the rhetorical device of **antithesis,** which is a type of parallelism. Antithesis presents contrasting ideas in similar grammatical structures, such as the same types of phrases or clauses. Thus, antithesis allows a speaker to make use of the rhythmic effects of parallelism, while drawing readers' or listeners' attention to powerful oppositions.

EXAMPLES

Parallelism: I stand here today humbled by the task before us, grateful for the trust you have bestowed, mindful of the sacrifices borne by our ancestors. —Barack Obama

Antithesis: My fellow Americans, ask not what your country can do for you, ask what you can do for your country. —John F. Kennedy

---

Read It

Mark the contrasting or opposing elements in each passage from the address. Then, note whether or not each is an example of formal antithesis. Share your work with your group, and discuss and clarify any points of confusion.

1. We have come to dedicate a portion of that field, as a final resting place for those who here gave their lives that the nation might live.

2. The brave men, living and dead, who struggled here…

3. The world will little note, nor long remember what we say here, but it can never forget what they did here.

4. …we here highly resolve that these dead shall not have died in vain—that this nation, under God, shall have a new birth of freedom…

Write It

Write a paragraph in which you describe a speech, performance, artwork, concert, or other cultural work that you saw live, on television, or online. Use at least two examples of antithesis in your paragraph.

STANDARDS

Reading Informational Text
Determine an author's point of view or purpose in a text in which the rhetoric is particularly effective, analyzing how style and content contribute to the power, persuasiveness, or beauty of the text.

Speaking and Listening
Evaluate a speaker's point of view, reasoning, and use of evidence and rhetoric, assessing the stance, premises, links among ideas, word choice, points of emphasis, and tone used.

Research

Assignment

With your group, prepare a **research report** that focuses on an aspect of Lincoln's speech. Choose from the following options.

☐ a **comparison-and-contrast presentation** about the five different known versions of the Gettysburg Address, showing the changes that Lincoln made each time and evaluating their effectiveness

☐ a **review** of three eyewitness accounts of the ceremony at Gettysburg that day, summarizing each account and noting details that shed light upon the address itself

☐ an **analysis of the historical context** of the address, sharing information about the Battle of Gettysburg (July 1863) and considering how that context shaped the content of Lincoln's address

Project Plan Before you begin, identify the tasks you will need to accomplish in order to complete your report. Start with the tasks noted in the chart, and add others that you consider important. Then, assign individual group members to each task. Finally, determine how you will present the report. For example, will you include historical images—and, if so, where will you find them, and how will you show them?

Working Title: _____

TASK	ASSIGNED TO
researching texts for factual information	
researching images (if used)	

Tying It Together Work together to organize the information all group members collect. Write paragraphs incorporating this information. Then, write an introduction and a conclusion for the report. Read the report aloud within the group, and decide together on revisions. Then, share your finished product with the whole class.

✎ EVIDENCE LOG

Before moving on to a new selection, go to your Evidence Log and record what you learned from the Gettysburg Address.

▤ STANDARDS

Writing

• Write informative/explanatory texts to examine and convey complex ideas, concepts, and information clearly and accurately through the effective selection, organization, and analysis of content.

• Conduct short as well as more sustained research projects to answer a question or solve a problem; narrow or broaden the inquiry when appropriate; synthesize multiple sources on the subject, demonstrating understanding of the subject under investigation.

SOURCES

- *from* AMERICA'S CONSTITUTION: A BIOGRAPHY

- *from* THE UNITED STATES CONSTITUTION: A GRAPHIC ADAPTATION

- *from* THE INTERESTING NARRATIVE OF THE LIFE OF OLAUDAH EQUIANO

- LETTER TO JOHN ADAMS

- *from* DEAR ABIGAIL: THE INTIMATE LIVES AND REVOLUTIONARY IDEAS OF ABIGAIL ADAMS AND HER TWO REMARKABLE SISTERS

- GETTYSBURG ADDRESS

Present an Argument

Assignment
You have read a variety of texts, both historic and contemporary, in a range of different genres. Several of these texts are narratives that the writers use to support or imply positions on questions of American freedom. Work with your group to present a **panel discussion** that addresses this question:

> Do narratives provide strong evidence to support arguments about American freedoms?

Use examples from the texts in this section to support your positions.

Plan With Your Group

Analyze the Texts With your group, identify the texts in this section that are either fully narratives or include narrative elements. Consider the arguments about freedom that are either directly stated or that readers can infer from the narrative details. Use the chart to gather your observations.

NARRATIVE DETAILS	RELATED ARGUMENT

Make a Generalization Using your analysis, write a generalization about the use of narrative as evidence to support an argument.

Generalization: Narratives do/do not provide strong evidence to support an argument because _____

_____

Gather Evidence Prepare for the discussion by identifying additional examples from the texts that you might use to illustrate your ideas during the panel discussion.

STANDARDS
Speaking and Listening
Work with peers to promote civil, democratic discussions and decision-making, set clear goals and deadlines, and establish individual roles as needed.

Organize Your Discussion Assign roles, including a role for a moderator who will keep panelists on point and ask questions if there is a lull in the conversation. Have each person in your group use the evidence you gathered to write his or her own talking points for the presentation. Then, meet to decide how you will begin the discussion, the amount of time each speaker will talk, how you will deal with follow-up questions, and how you will end the discussion.

Rehearse With Your Group

Practice With Your Group Once you have established the rules for your discussion, try a run-through. Use this checklist to evaluate how well your process works and whether your ideas and evidence are sound. Then, use your evaluation and these instructions to make changes before you present your discussion to the class.

CONTENT	COLLABORATION	PRESENTATION TECHNIQUES
☐ The discussion responds to the question in the assignment.	☐ The discussion flows smoothly and seems well-planned.	☐ Panelists have equal opportunities to speak, and respond appropriately to one another's insights or questions.
☐ Speakers present a position and supporting evidence.	☐ Speakers interact with each other naturally.	☐ Speakers speak clearly and at an appropriate volume.
☐ Speakers support their observations with evidence from the texts.	☐ The moderator introduces the speakers and keeps the conversation on track.	☐ Speakers use gestures and eye contact effectively.

Fine-Tune the Content Does one panelist dominate the conversation? Make sure that every group member has a chance to present his or her views. If necessary, go back to the texts to gather additional details that will help balance the presentation.

Brush Up on Your Presentation Techniques Remember that you are holding a conversation that is also, to some extent, a performance. Modify your tone and volume so that your audience understands your ideas and evidence. Explain your observations clearly, using language that is appropriate for an academic setting.

Present and Evaluate

As you present your panel discussion, consider your audience's response. Do listeners seem convinced by your argument? Are they interested in the ideas? Watch the presentations by other groups and discuss how yours is similar to or different from theirs.

STANDARDS
Speaking and Listening
Present information, findings, and supporting evidence, conveying a clear and distinct perspective, such that listeners can follow the line of reasoning, alternative or opposing perspectives are addressed, and the organization, development, substance, and style are appropriate to purpose, audience, and a range of formal and informal tasks.

ESSENTIAL QUESTION:

What is the meaning of freedom?

Ideas about what freedom means, and who is or is not free, may depend on time, place, and the person telling the story. In this section, you will complete your study of writings about American freedom by exploring an additional selection related to the topic. You'll then share what you learn with classmates. To choose a text, follow these steps.

Look Back Think about the selections you have already studied. Which aspects of the meaning of freedom do you wish to explore further?

Look Ahead Preview the texts by reading the descriptions. Which one seems most interesting and appealing to you?

Look Inside Take a few minutes to scan the text you chose. Choose a different one if this text doesn't meet your needs.

Independent Learning Strategies

Throughout your life, in school, in your community, and in your career, you will need to rely on yourself to learn and work on your own. Review these strategies and the actions you can take to practice them during Independent Learning. Add ideas of your own for each category.

STRATEGY	ACTION PLAN
Create a schedule	• Understand your goals and deadlines. • Make a plan for what to do each day. •
Practice what you have learned	• Use first-read and close-read strategies to deepen your understanding. • After reading, evaluate the usefulness of the evidence to help you understand the topic. • After reading, consult reference sources for background information that can help you clarify meaning. •
Take notes	• Record important ideas and information. • Review your notes before preparing to share with a group. •

CONTENTS

Choose one selection. Selections are available online only.

ESSAY

from Democracy Is Not a Spectator Sport

Arthur Blaustein with Helen Matatov

How much does freedom depend on civic engagement?

SPEECH

Reflections on the Bicentennial of the United States Constitution

Thurgood Marshall

Supreme Court Justice Marshall observes that the U.S. Constitution is a living document.

POETRY

Speech to the Young
Speech to the Progress-Toward *Gwendolyn Brooks*

The Fish *Elizabeth Bishop*

Is freedom physical, psychological, or perhaps both?

SHORT STORY

The Pedestrian *Ray Bradbury*

In a highly restrictive society, what acts of freedom become acts of crime?

POLITICAL DOCUMENT

from the Iroquois Constitution

Dekanawidah, translated by Arthur C. Parker

Before the arrival of Europeans, the Iroquois Nations developed a constitution of their own.

ARGUMENT

from Common Sense *Thomas Paine*

British-born American patriot Thomas Paine wrote that "the sun never shined on a cause of greater worth" than America's independence.

PERFORMANCE-BASED ASSESSMENT PREP

Review Evidence for an Argument

Complete your Evidence Log for the unit by evaluating what you've learned and synthesizing the information you have recorded.

First-Read Guide

Use this page to record your first-read ideas.

🔧 **Tool Kit**
First-Read Guide and
Model Annotation

Selection Title: _____

NOTICE new information or ideas you learned about the unit topic as you first read this text.

ANNOTATE by marking vocabulary and key passages you want to revisit.

First Read
NOTICE · ANNOTATE · CONNECT · RESPOND

CONNECT ideas within the selection to other knowledge and the selections you have read.

RESPOND by writing a brief summary of the selection.

Copyright © SAVVAS Learning Company LLC. All Rights Reserved.

≔ STANDARD
Reading Read and comprehend complex literary and informational texts independently and proficiently.

Close-Read Guide

Use this page to record your close-read ideas.

Selection Title: _____

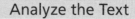

Tool Kit
Close-Read Guide and
Model Annotation

Close Read the Text

Revisit sections of the text you marked during your first read. Read these sections closely and **annotate** what you notice. Ask yourself **questions** about the text. What can you **conclude**? Write down your ideas.

Analyze the Text

Think about the author's choices of patterns, structure, techniques, and ideas included in the text. Select one and record your thoughts about what this choice conveys.

QuickWrite

Pick a paragraph from the text that grabbed your interest. Explain the power of this passage.

_____

_____

_____

_____

_____

_____

_____

_____

:: STANDARD
Reading Read and comprehend complex literary and informational texts independently and proficiently.

Share Your Independent Learning

Prepare to Share

What is the meaning of freedom?

Even when you read something independently, your understanding continues
to grow when you share what you have learned with others. Reflect on the
text you explored independently and write notes about its connection to the
unit. In your notes, consider why this text belongs in this unit.

Learn From Your Classmates

Discuss It Share your ideas about the text you explored on your own.
As you talk with your classmates, jot down ideas that you learn from them.

Reflect

Review your notes, and mark the most important insight you gained from
these writing and discussion activities. Explain how this idea adds to your
understanding of the meaning of freedom.

STANDARDS

Speaking and Listening
Initiate and participate effectively in
a range of collaborative discussions
(one-on-one, in groups, and
teacher-led) with diverse partners
on *grades 11–12 topics, texts, and
issues*, building on others' ideas and
expressing their own clearly and
persuasively.

Review Evidence for an Argument

At the beginning of this unit, you took a position on the following question:

What are the most effective tools for establishing and preserving freedom?

Review your Evidence Log and your QuickWrite from the beginning of the unit. Have your ideas changed?

☐ YES	☐ NO
Identify at least three pieces of evidence that have caused you to reevaluate your ideas.	Identify at least three pieces of evidence that have reinforced your initial position.
1.	1.
2.	2.
3.	3.

State your position now: _____

_____

_____

Identify a possible counterclaim: _____

_____

_____

Evaluate the Strength of Your Evidence Consider your argument. Do you have enough evidence to support your claim? Do you have enough evidence to refute a counterclaim? If not, make a plan.

☐ Do online research.　　☐ Skim a textbook.

☐ Reread a selection.　　☐ Speak with an expert.

☐ Other:_____

⊞ STANDARDS

Writing
Introduce precise, knowledgeable claim(s), establish the significance of the claim(s), distinguish the claim(s) from alternate or opposing claims, and create an organization that logically sequences claim(s), counterclaims, reasons, and evidence.

SOURCES

• WHOLE-CLASS SELECTIONS

• SMALL-GROUP SELECTIONS

• INDEPENDENT-LEARNING SELECTION

PART 1
Writing to Sources: Argument

In this unit, you read a variety of texts that considered the meaning of American freedom. You saw the Founders' concerns about how to establish a nation that offered freedom to at least some of its citizens, and you read other texts that demonstrated how a nation "conceived in liberty" was tested over time.

Assignment

Write an **argumentative essay** in which you respond to this question:

> What are the most effective tools for establishing and preserving freedom?

Use the Anchor Texts to identify some of the most successful tools (processes, government institutions, value systems, documents, and so on) that the Founders established. Use other texts from the unit to demonstrate how well those tools have stood the test of time. Supplement your ideas with examples from your own research that confirm your argument. Consider and address possible counterclaims.

Reread the Assignment Review the assignment to be sure you fully understand it. The task may reference some of the academic words presented at the beginning of the unit. Be sure you understand each of the words given below in order to complete the assignment correctly.

Academic Vocabulary

confirm	supplement	conviction
demonstrate	establish	

Review the Elements of Effective Argument Before you begin writing, read the Argument Rubric. Once you have completed your first draft, check it against the rubric. If one or more of the elements are missing or not as strong as they could be, revise your essay to add or strengthen those components.

WORD NETWORK

As you write and revise your argument, use your Word Network to help vary your word choices.

STANDARDS
Writing
• Write arguments to support claims in an analysis of substantive topics or texts, using valid reasoning and relevant and sufficient evidence.
• Write routinely over extended time frames and shorter time frames for a range of tasks, purposes, and audiences.

Argument Rubric

	Focus and Organization	Evidence and Elaboration	Language Conventions
4	The introduction is engaging and establishes the claim in a compelling way. Valid reasons and evidence address and support the claim. Counterclaims are clearly acknowledged. The ideas progress logically, connected by a variety of sentence transitions. The conclusion offers fresh insight into the claim.	The sources of evidence are comprehensive and specific and contain relevant information. The tone of the argument is formal and objective. Vocabulary is used strategically and appropriately for the audience and purpose.	The argument consistently uses standard English conventions of usage and mechanics.
3	The introduction is engaging and establishes the claim in a way that grabs readers' attention. Reasons and evidence address and support the claim. Counterclaims are acknowledged. The ideas progress logically, and sentence transitions connect readers to the argument. The conclusion restates important information.	The sources of evidence contain relevant information. The tone of the argument is mostly formal and objective. Vocabulary is generally appropriate for the audience and purpose.	The argument demonstrates accuracy in standard English conventions of usage and mechanics.
2	The introduction establishes the claim. Some reasons and evidence address and support the claim. Counterclaims are briefly acknowledged. The ideas progress somewhat logically. A few sentence transitions connect readers to the argument. The conclusion offers some insight into the claim and restates information.	The sources of evidence contain some relevant information. The tone of the argument is occasionally formal and objective. Vocabulary is somewhat appropriate for the audience and purpose.	The argument demonstrates some accuracy in standard English conventions of usage and mechanics.
1	The claim is not clearly stated. No reasons or evidence for the claim are included, and counterclaims are not acknowledged. The ideas do not progress logically. The sentences are often short and choppy and do not connect readers to the argument. The conclusion does not restate any information that is important.	No reliable or relevant evidence is included. The tone of the argument is informal. The vocabulary is limited or ineffective.	The argument contains mistakes in standard English conventions of usage and mechanics.

PART 2

Speaking and Listening: Video Commentary

Assignment

Imagine that representatives of a television station have called on you to be their expert on the concept of freedom. Present a **video commentary,** based on the final draft of your argument, to be used during coverage of a presidential debate.

Follow these steps to make your presentation lively and engaging.

- Read your text aloud, keeping the television audience in mind. Highlight the material you most want to emphasize for that audience.
- Practice your delivery. Remember to look up at the camera regularly instead of staring down at your paper.
- Have a classmate operate the camera as you deliver your commentary.

Review the Rubric The criteria by which your commentary will be evaluated appear in the rubric below. Review the criteria before delivering your commentary to ensure that you are prepared.

	Content	Use of Media	Presentation Techniques
3	The content and delivery are appropriate for a television audience. The commentary is clearly organized and easy to follow.	The voice on the recording is consistent and audible. The camera holds steady, and facial expressions are clearly visible.	Speech is clear and at an appropriate volume. Tone and pace vary to maintain interest. The speaker looks regularly at the camera to engage the audience.
2	The content and delivery are consistent, although some content may not be clearly meant for a television audience. The commentary is organized and fairly easy to follow.	The voice on the recording may vary but is mostly audible. The camera generally holds steady, so most facial expressions are visible.	Speech is clear most of the time and usually has an appropriate volume. Tone and pace are inconsistent. The speaker looks occasionally at the camera.
1	The content and delivery are generic, with no specific audience in mind. The commentary is disorganized and may be difficult to follow.	The voice on the recording sometimes fades in and out. The camera does not hold steady or is not focused on the face, so the expressions are rarely visible.	The speaker mumbles occasionally, speaks too quickly, and/or does not speak loudly enough. The speaker fails to look at the camera.

Reflect on the Unit

Now that you've completed the unit, take a few moments to reflect on your learning.

Reflect on the Unit Goals

Look back at the goals at the beginning of the unit. Use a different colored pen to rate yourself again. Think about readings and activities that contributed the most to the growth of your understanding. Record your thoughts.

Reflect on the Learning Strategies

Discuss It Write a reflection on whether you were able to improve your learning based on your Action Plans. Think about what worked, what didn't, and what you might do to keep working on these strategies. Record your ideas before joining a class discussion.

Reflect on the Text

Choose a selection that you found challenging, and explain what made it difficult.

Explain something that surprised you about a text in the unit.

Which activity taught you the most about the meaning of American freedoms? What did you learn?

The Individual and Society

Fitting In, or Standing Out?

Richard Blanco Reads
"One Today"

Discuss It This poem, read by its author at President Barack Obama's 2013 inaugural, praises America as a society of individuals. How do the details of the poem present individual Americans? What connections among individuals does Blanco see?

Write your response before sharing your ideas.

UNIT 2

ESSENTIAL QUESTION: **What role does individualism play in American society?**

LAUNCH TEXT
NARRATIVE MODEL
from Up from Slavery
Booker T. Washington

WHOLE-CLASS LEARNING

HISTORICAL PERSPECTIVES

Focus Period: 1800–1870
An American Identity

ANCHOR TEXT: ESSAY | POETRY

The Writing of Walt Whitman
Walt Whitman

ANCHOR TEXT: POETRY COLLECTION

The Poetry of Emily Dickinson
Emily Dickinson

COMPARE

MEDIA: RADIO BROADCAST

from Emily Dickinson
from Great Lives
BBC Radio 4

SMALL-GROUP LEARNING

PHILOSOPHICAL WRITING

from **Nature**

from **Self-Reliance**
Ralph Waldo Emerson

PHILOSOPHICAL WRITING

from **Walden**

from **Civil Disobedience**
Henry David Thoreau

MEDIA: PUBLIC DOCUMENTS

Innovators and Their Inventions

POETRY

The Love Song of J. Alfred Prufrock
T. S. Eliot

SHORT STORY

A Wagner Matinée
Willa Cather

INDEPENDENT LEARNING

NEWS ARTICLE

Sweet Land of . . . Conformity?
Claude Fischer

LITERARY CRITICISM

Reckless Genius
Galway Kinnell

SHORT STORY

Hamadi
Naomi Shihab Nye

SHORT STORY

Young Goodman Brown
Nathaniel Hawthorne

PERFORMANCE TASK

WRITING FOCUS:
Write a Personal Narrative

PERFORMANCE TASK

SPEAKING AND LISTENING FOCUS:
Present a Personal Narrative

PERFORMANCE-BASED ASSESSMENT PREP

Review Evidence for a Personal Narrative

PERFORMANCE-BASED ASSESSMENT

Narrative: Personal Narrative and Storytelling Session

PROMPT:
What significant incident helped me realize that I am a unique individual?

Unit Goals

Throughout this unit, you will deepen your perspective on the concept of individualism by reading, writing, speaking, listening, and presenting. These goals will help you succeed on the Unit Performance-Based Assessment.

Rate how well you meet these goals right now. You will revisit your ratings later when you reflect on your growth during this unit.

SCALE	1	2	3	4	5
	NOT AT ALL WELL	NOT VERY WELL	SOMEWHAT WELL	VERY WELL	EXTREMELY WELL

READING GOALS

	1	2	3	4	5
• Read a variety of texts to gain the knowledge and insight needed to write about individualism.	○	○	○	○	○
• Expand your knowledge and use of academic and concept vocabulary.	○	○	○	○	○

WRITING AND RESEARCH GOALS

	1	2	3	4	5
• Write a personal narrative that establishes a clear point of view and uses a variety of narrative techniques to develop a personal experience.	○	○	○	○	○
• Conduct research projects of various lengths to explore a topic and clarify meaning.	○	○	○	○	○

LANGUAGE GOALS

	1	2	3	4	5
• Make effective style choices regarding diction and sentence variety.	○	○	○	○	○
• Correctly use concrete, abstract, and compound nouns.	○	○	○	○	○

SPEAKING AND LISTENING GOALS

	1	2	3	4	5
• Collaborate with your team to build on the ideas of others, develop consensus, and communicate.	○	○	○	○	○
• Integrate audio, visuals, and text to present information.	○	○	○	○	○

▤ STANDARDS

Language
Acquire and use accurately general academic and domain-specific words and phrases, sufficient for reading, writing, speaking, and listening at the college and career readiness level; demonstrate independence in gathering vocabulary knowledge when considering a word or phrase important to comprehension or expression.

Academic Vocabulary: Personal Narrative

Academic terms appear in all subjects and can help you read, write, and discuss with more precision. Here are five academic words that will be useful to you in this unit as you analyze and write personal narratives.

Complete the chart.

1. Review each word, its root, and the mentor sentences.

2. Use the information and your own knowledge to predict the meaning of each word.

3. For each word, list at least two related words.

4. Refer to a dictionary or other resources if needed.

TIP

FOLLOW THROUGH

Study the words in this chart, and mark them or their forms wherever they appear in the unit.

WORD	MENTOR SENTENCES	PREDICT MEANING	RELATED WORDS
significant ROOT: ***-sign-*** "sign"	1. The fire was a *significant* event in our town's history. 2. Ms. Barnes made no *significant* changes to my report.		signify; significance
incident ROOT: ***-cid-*** "fall"	1. Myron described the *incident* in great detail to the reporter. 2. We avoided an embarrassing *incident* by leaving the room.		
unique ROOT: ***-uni-*** "one"	1. Each of these tables is a *unique*, handmade item. 2. My hairstyle is *unique*; no one would dare to copy it.		
sequence ROOT: ***-sequ-*** "follow"	1. A first-grader should be able to recite numbers in *sequence* to 100. 2. Follow the *sequence* of directions, and the recipe will turn out well.		
impact ROOT: ***-pact-*** "press"; "fasten"	1. His books had a strong *impact* on my beliefs and interests. 2. The *impact* of vaccines on public health has been considerable, and has lead to a healthier population.		

LAUNCH TEXT | NARRATIVE MODEL

This selection is an example of a **narrative text.** It is a **personal narrative**—the author tells a story about himself, using a first-person point of view. This is the type of writing you will develop in the Performance-Based Assessment at the end of the unit.

As you read, notice the author's use of specific details. Mark words and phrases that convey his experiences and feelings with vividness and clarity.

About the Author

Booker T. Washington (1856–1915) was born into slavery and overcame enormous obstacles to become a noted author, educator, and advisor to two American presidents. This excerpt is from chapter 3 of his autobiography *Up From Slavery*, in which Washington describes his experiences at Hampton Institute in the early 1870s.

from

Up From Slavery

Booker T. Washington

NOTES

1   When I had saved what I considered enough money with which to reach Hampton, I thanked the captain of the vessel for his kindness, and started again. Without any unusual occurrence I reached Hampton, with a surplus of exactly fifty cents with which to begin my education. To me it had been a long, eventful journey; but the first sight of the large, three-story, brick school building seemed to have rewarded me for all that I had undergone in order to reach the place. . . .

2   As soon as possible after reaching the grounds of the Hampton Institute, I presented myself before the head teacher for assignment to a class. Having been so long without proper food, a bath, and change of clothing, I did not, of course, make a very favorable impression upon her, and I could see at once that there were doubts in her mind about the wisdom of admitting me as a student. I felt that I could hardly blame her if she got the idea that I was a worthless loafer or tramp. For some time she did not refuse to admit me, neither did she decide in my favor, and I continued to linger about her, and

to impress her in all the ways I could with my worthiness. In the meantime I saw her admitting other students, and that added greatly to my discomfort, for I felt, deep down in my heart, that I could do as well as they, if I could only get a chance to show what was in me.

3   After some hours had passed, the head teacher said to me: "The adjoining recitation-room needs sweeping. Take the broom and sweep it."

4   It occurred to me at once that here was my chance. Never did I receive an order with more delight. I knew that I could sweep, for Mrs. Ruffner had thoroughly taught me how to do that when I lived with her.

5   I swept the recitation-room three times. Then I got a dusting-cloth and I dusted it four times. All the woodwork around the walls, every bench, table, and desk, I went over four times with my dusting-cloth. Besides, every piece of furniture had been moved and every closet and corner in the room had been thoroughly cleaned. I had the feeling that in a large measure my future depended upon the impression I made upon the teacher in the cleaning of that room. When I was through, I reported to the head teacher. She was a "Yankee" woman who knew just where to look for dirt. She went into the room and inspected the floor and closets; then she took her handkerchief and rubbed it on the woodwork about the walls, and over the table and benches. When she was unable to find one bit of dirt on the floor, or a particle of dust on any of the furniture, she quietly remarked, "I guess you will do to enter this institution."

6   I was one of the happiest souls on earth. The sweeping of that room was my college examination, and never did any youth pass an examination for entrance into Harvard or Yale that gave him more genuine satisfaction. I have passed several examinations since then, but I have always felt that this was the best one I ever passed.

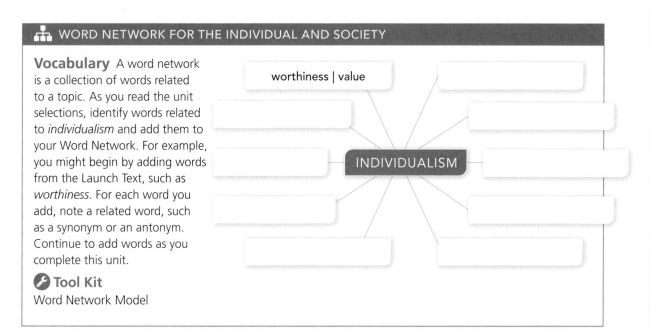

WORD NETWORK FOR THE INDIVIDUAL AND SOCIETY

Vocabulary A word network is a collection of words related to a topic. As you read the unit selections, identify words related to *individualism* and add them to your Word Network. For example, you might begin by adding words from the Launch Text, such as *worthiness*. For each word you add, note a related word, such as a synonym or an antonym. Continue to add words as you complete this unit.

worthiness | value

INDIVIDUALISM

🔧 **Tool Kit**
Word Network Model

Summary

Write a summary of the excerpt from *Up From Slavery*. A **summary** is a concise, complete, and accurate overview of a text. It should not include a statement of your opinion or an analysis.

Launch Activity

Tell a Story Form a talk circle. One by one, take an object from a bag of assorted everyday objects. Then, return to your seat in the circle.

- If you like, trade objects with the person to your left or right.
- Think about a time when you used the object you are holding, or think about what a similar object meant to you at some point in your life. What story could you tell that springs from that incident or moment?
- When your turn comes, tell a one-minute story triggered by the object you chose.
- As you listen to classmates' stories, consider whether your own story about each object would be similar or different. Once everyone has had a turn, discuss what those similarities and differences mean about each person's uniqueness and about the connections among people.

QuickWrite

Consider class discussions, the video, and the Launch Text as you think about the prompt. Record your first thoughts here.

PROMPT: **What significant incident helped me realize that I am a unique individual?**

✐ EVIDENCE LOG FOR THE INDIVIDUAL AND SOCIETY

Review your QuickWrite and summarize your initial idea in one sentence to record in your Evidence Log. Then, record evidence from the excerpt from *Up From Slavery* that connects to your idea.

After each selection, you will continue to use your Evidence Log to record the evidence you gather and the connections you make. The graphic shows what your Evidence Log looks like.

🔧 **Tool Kit**
Evidence Log Model

Title of Text: _____   Date: _____

CONNECTION TO PROMPT	TEXT EVIDENCE/DETAILS	ADDITIONAL NOTES/IDEAS

How does this text change or add to my thinking?   Date: _____

ESSENTIAL QUESTION:

What role does individualism play in American society?

As you read these selections, work with your whole class to explore the meaning of individualism.

From Text to Topic For Walt Whitman, individualism formed the cornerstone of life in America. His writing celebrates the promise of America, in which all people can make an impact by developing their unique abilities. For Emily Dickinson, individualism meant looking inward to express the deepest musings of the soul. As you read, consider what the selections show about perceptions of individualism in American society in the nineteenth century. Also, consider how these works influence American attitudes toward individualism today.

Whole-Class Learning Strategies

Throughout your life, in school, in your community, and in your career, you will continue to learn and work in large-group environments.

Review these strategies and the actions you can take to practice them. Add ideas of your own for each step. Get ready to use these strategies during Whole-Class Learning.

STRATEGY	ACTION PLAN
Listen actively	• Eliminate distractions. For example, put your cellphone away. • Record brief notes on main ideas and points of confusion. •
Clarify by asking questions	• If you're confused, other people probably are, too. Ask a question to help your whole class. • Ask follow-up questions as needed—for example, if you do not understand the clarification or if you want to make an additional connection. •
Monitor understanding	• Notice what information you already know and be ready to build on it. • Ask for help if you are struggling. •
Interact and share ideas	• Share your ideas and answer questions, even if you are unsure. • Build on the ideas of others by adding details or making a connection. •

CONTENTS

HISTORICAL PERSPECTIVES

Focus Period: 1800–1870

An American Identity

During the early to mid-nineteenth century, Americans looked both inward and outward, determining their identity and shaping a distinctly "American" character.

ANCHOR TEXT: ESSAY | POETRY

The Writing of Walt Whitman

Walt Whitman

With its bold, energetic language and embracing vision, Whitman's work is for many readers America's epic poem.

COMPARE

ANCHOR TEXT: POETRY COLLECTION

The Poetry of Emily Dickinson

Emily Dickinson

In brief, precise poems, this great American writer describes sweeping vistas of thought and feeling.

MEDIA: RADIO BROADCAST

from Emily Dickinson

from Great Lives

BBC Radio 4

A poem written in the mid-1860s remains fresh and meaningful for contemporary readers.

PERFORMANCE TASK

WRITING FOCUS

Write a Personal Narrative

The Whole-Class readings were written during a time when American literature celebrated the individual. After reading, you will write a personal narrative that shows how a life experience has shaped your understanding of individuality.

An American Identity

Voices of the Period

"I have always supported measures and principles and not men. I have acted fearless and independent and I never will regret my course."

—Davy Crockett,
frontiersman, folk hero, and statesman

"I have an almost complete disregard of precedent, and a faith in the possibility of something better. It irritates me to be told how things have always been done. I defy the tyranny of precedent. I go for anything new that might improve the past."

—Clara Barton,
founder of the American Red Cross

"There will never be a really free and enlightened State until the State comes to recognize the individual as a higher and independent power, from which all its own power and authority are derived, and treats him accordingly."

—Henry David Thoreau,
author of "Civil Disobedience" and *Walden*

History of the Period

What Is an American? French writer Alexis de Tocqueville came to America in the early 1830s with a colleague to study and write about American prisons. Instead, they ended up traveling extensively and studying American democracy. In his book *Democracy in America*, de Tocqueville coined the word *individualism* as a way of describing the attitudes he found in America, where people are "always considering themselves as standing alone, [imagining] that their whole destiny is in their own hands."

Jefferson's Bargain In 1803, President Thomas Jefferson purchased from France 828,000 square miles of North America for $15 million—about three cents per acre—and in the process, more than doubled the size of the United States. Jefferson sent explorers Meriwether Lewis and William Clark, with their Corps of Discovery, to investigate the land, people, and plants and animals of the new territory. They crossed the continent, reached the Pacific Ocean, and led the way for decades of westward-bound settlers.

The War of 1812 In the War of 1812, the United States once again defeated Great Britain, asserting its independence from European control. However, the most important effect of the war may have been the sense of solidarity it fostered within the young nation.

The People's President The 1828 election of Andrew Jackson, "the People's President," ushered in the era of the "common man." The center of power began to shift west, even as a two-party system was emerging.

TIMELINE

1803: The Louisiana Purchase nearly doubles the size of the United States.

1804: France Napoleon Bonaparte declares himself emperor.

1808–1833: Latin America Independence movements result in wars and the creation of new governments.

1800

1804–1806: Lewis and Clark lead an exploration of the Louisiana Purchase, reaching the Pacific Ocean.

1807: Robert Fulton's steamboat makes its first trip, from New York City to Albany.

Integration of Knowledge and Ideas

Notebook From which countries did the United States acquire land during this era? How do you think these acquisitions influenced the way that Americans viewed themselves and their nation's future by the 1850s?

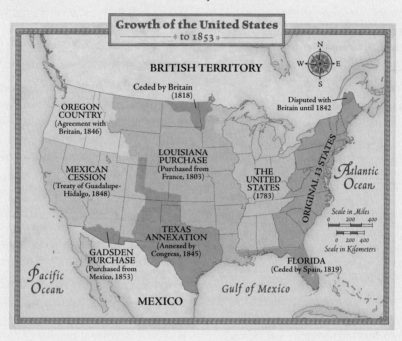

Growth of the United States
to 1853

BRITISH TERRITORY

Ceded by Britain (1818)

OREGON COUNTRY (Agreement with Britain, 1846)

Disputed with Britain until 1842

LOUISIANA PURCHASE (Purchased from France, 1803)

MEXICAN CESSION (Treaty of Guadalupe-Hidalgo, 1848)

THE UNITED STATES (1783)

ORIGINAL 13 STATES

Atlantic Ocean

TEXAS ANNEXATION (Annexed by Congress, 1845)

GADSDEN PURCHASE (Purchased from Mexico, 1853)

FLORIDA (Ceded by Spain, 1819)

Pacific Ocean

MEXICO

Gulf of Mexico

Scale in Miles
0 200 400
Scale in Kilometers
0 200 400

Manifest Destiny Many Americans believed in Manifest Destiny, the idea that it was their right to settle America's lands across the continent. By 1840, about 40 percent of the U.S. population lived west of the Appalachian Mountains. By 1860, following the great pioneer migrations to Oregon, California, and Texas, only about half of the population lived in the eastern part of the United States. Westward expansion inspired an upsurge of national pride and self-awareness.

Trail of Tears The tragic policy of "Indian removal," a result of westward expansion, resulted in the confiscation of tribal lands and the relocation of more than 100,000 Native Americans. On the 1838 Trail of Tears, for example, thousands of Cherokee perished on the trek from Georgia to Oklahoma, where the promise of freedom from white settlement would last for only about 15 years.

1812: The United States declares war on Great Britain; a treaty ends the war in 1814.

1831: Cyrus McCormick invents the mechanical reaper.

1840

1813: England Jane Austen's *Pride and Prejudice* is published.

1825: The Erie Canal is completed, spurring canal building across the nation.

1838: Cherokees are forced from Georgia to Oklahoma Territory on the "Trail of Tears."

On the Move Travel was transformed in the nineteenth century by new methods and routes of transportation. The National Road, begun in 1811, reached St. Louis and the Mississippi River by mid-century. In 1860, nearly 1,000 steamboats were plying the Mississippi, and some 30,000 miles of railroad track had been spread across the nation. The lure of the West motivated this revolution in transportation, which created a bond between existing and new states.

Coming to America In the first half of the nineteenth century, hundreds of thousands of immigrants—mostly European—were arriving on American shores. By the 1850s, the number was in the millions. Pushed from home by hardships and revolutions, these people were lured by a land of opportunity.

The Industrial Revolution A machine called the cotton gin, which separated cotton fibers from seeds, invented in 1793, revolutionized American industry. By 1860, more than 1,000 factories, mainly in New England, were turning more than 400 million pounds of Southern cotton into cloth, which was then sold around the world. However, while factories boomed in the North, enlarging the job market for women and immigrants, slavery grew stronger in the South.

A Flood of New Ideas Buoyed by a sense of their power to improve society, Americans set out to reform what they saw as problems or failures. Voters demanded better schools and public education slowly began to expand. Reform movements sprang up in religion, in temperance, and in women's rights. All brought important changes, but the most revolutionary movement was the drive to end slavery.

Slavery and the Civil War States in the North had declared slavery illegal by 1804 and had begun the gradual emancipation of enslaved African Americans within their borders. By 1860, however, slavery was more entrenched than ever in the South. Out of a population of 31.5 million, there were four million enslaved African Americans and about 500,000 free blacks. In six states in the Deep South, the slave population accounted for approximately half of the total population.

Abolitionists—people who worked to end slavery—were black and white, Northern and sometimes Southern. They organized, preached, spoke, published newspapers, and wrote books. They also helped fugitives flee slavery via a network of secret escape routes into the North and into Canada, known as the Underground Railroad. As their actions intensified, they helped push the nation to the breaking point—the eruption of the Civil War. The war lasted for four years and remains to date the deadliest conflict in American history.

Individualism in the Reconstruction Era
America emerged from the Civil War with many questions unresolved. Chief among these was how to guarantee the rights of millions whom law and tradition had previously treated as property rather than people. The Reconstruction Era that followed the war was a tumultuous period in which former slaves capitalized on their newfound freedoms, including sending a record number of African Americans into government. The period did not last long, however, as a backlash ensued that included widespread violence. Freedoms for African Americans were rolled back and the rights of individuals were quashed, as the gains of Reconstruction evaporated and the Jim Crow system became firmly established throughout the South.

TIMELINE

1837: Samuel F. B. Morse patents the telegraph.

1845: Ireland Potato famine begins, leading to massive immigration to North America.

1849: The Gold Rush begins in California.

1850: Nathaniel Hawthorne's *The Scarlet Letter* is published.

1851: Herman Melville's *Moby-Dick* is published.

1836

Literature Selections

Literature of the Focus Period A number of the selections in this unit were written during the Focus Period and pertain to the expansion of the United States, the reforms of American society, and the actions of individuals who influenced its history and culture:

The Writing of Walt Whitman

The Poetry of Emily Dickinson

from "Nature" • from "Self-Reliance," Ralph Waldo Emerson

from *Walden* • from "Civil Disobedience," Henry David Thoreau

"Young Goodman Brown," Nathaniel Hawthorne

Connections Across Time A consideration of the importance of American individualism both preceded and continued past the Focus Period. Indeed, it has influenced writers and commentators in many times and places.

"The Love Song of J. Alfred Prufrock," T. S. Eliot

"A Wagner Matinée," Willa Cather

"Sweet Land of . . . Conformity?" Claude Fischer

"Reckless Genius," Galway Kinnell

"Hamadi," Naomi Shihab Nye

ADDITIONAL FOCUS PERIOD LITERATURE

UNIT 1
The Gettysburg Address, Abraham Lincoln

UNIT 3
"What to the Slave Is the Fourth of July?," Frederick Douglass

Second Inaugural Address, Abraham Lincoln

"Ain't I a Woman?," Sojourner Truth

Declaration of Sentiments, Elizabeth Cady Stanton

UNIT 4
"The Notorious Jumping Frog of Calaveras County," Mark Twain

UNIT 6
"The Tell-Tale Heart," Edgar Allan Poe

1854: Japan The Treaty of Kanagawa opens Japan to trade with the United States.

1861–1865: The Union and the Confederacy fight the Civil War.

1865: The Reconstruction Era begins in the South.

1870

1860: Abraham Lincoln is elected the sixteenth U.S. President.

ESSAY | POETRY COLLECTION

The Writing of Walt Whitman

- *from* the Preface to the 1855 Edition of *Leaves of Grass*
- *from* Song of Myself
- I Hear America Singing
- On the Beach at Night Alone
- America

Concept Vocabulary

You will encounter the following words as you read part of an essay and a number of poems by Walt Whitman. Before reading, note how familiar you are with each word. Then, rank the words in order from most familiar (1) to least familiar (6).

WORD	YOUR RANKING
ampler	
teeming	
vast	
breadth	
prolific	
multitudes	

After completing the first read, come back to the concept vocabulary and review your rankings. Mark changes to your original rankings as needed.

First Read NONFICTION and POETRY

Apply these strategies as you conduct your first read. You will have an opportunity to complete the close-read notes after your first read.

🔧 Tool Kit
First-Read Guide and Model Annotation

NOTICE new information or ideas you learn about the unit topic as you first read this text.

ANNOTATE by marking vocabulary and key passages you want to revisit.

First Read

CONNECT ideas within the selection to other knowledge and the selections you have read.

RESPOND by completing the Comprehension Check.

:= STANDARDS

Reading Literature
By the end of grade 11, read and comprehend literature, including stories, dramas, and poems, in the grades 11–CCR text complexity band proficiently, with scaffolding as needed at the high end of the range.

Reading Informational Text
By the end of grade 11, read and comprehend literary nonfiction in the grades 11–CCR text complexity band proficiently, with scaffolding as needed at the high end of the range.

About the Author
Walt Whitman

Walt Whitman (1819–1892) was born on Long Island and raised in Brooklyn, New York. His education was not formal, but he read widely, including the works of Sir Walter Scott, Shakespeare, Homer, and Dante. Trained to be a printer, Whitman spent his early years working at times as a printer and at other times as a journalist. When he was twenty-seven, he became the editor of the *Brooklyn Eagle*, a respected newspaper, but the paper fired him in 1848 because of his opposition to slavery. After accepting a job at a newspaper in New Orleans, Whitman traveled across the country for the first time, observing the diversity of America's landscapes and people.

A New Vocation Whitman soon returned to New York City, however, and in 1850, he quit journalism to devote his energy to writing poetry. Impressed by Ralph Waldo Emerson's prophetic description of a new kind of American poet, Whitman had been jotting down ideas and fragments of verse in a notebook for years. His work broke every poetic tradition of rhyme and meter as it celebrated America and the common person. When the first edition of *Leaves of Grass* was published in 1855, critics attacked Whitman's subject matter and abandonment of traditional poetic devices and forms. Noted poet John Greenleaf Whittier hated Whitman's poems so much that he hurled his copy of *Leaves of Grass* into the fireplace. Emerson, on the other hand, responded with great enthusiasm, remarking that the collection was "the most extraordinary piece of wit and wisdom that America has yet contributed."

His Life's Work Though Whitman did publish other works in the course of his career, his life's work proved to be *Leaves of Grass*, which he continually revised, reshaped, and expanded until his death in 1892. The poems in later editions became less confusing, repetitious, and raucous, and more symbolic, expressive, and universal. He viewed the volume as a single long poem that expressed his evolving vision of the world, and in its poems he captured the diversity of the American people and conveyed the energy and intensity of all forms of life. Today, *Leaves of Grass* is regarded as one of the most important and influential collections of poetry ever written.

Background

The Writing of Walt Whitman

During the nineteenth century, American writers found their own voices and began to produce literature that no longer looked to Europe. Emerson, Thoreau, Poe, Dickinson— each contributed to a recognizably American style, but no one sounded as utterly American as Whitman. His style incorporates the plain and the elegant, the high and the low, the foreign and the native. It mixes grand opera, political oratory, journalistic punch, everyday conversation, and biblical cadences. Whitman's sound is the American sound. From its first appearance as twelve unsigned and untitled poems, *Leaves of Grass* grew to include 383 poems in its final, "death-bed" edition (1892). In the preface to the 1855 edition, Whitman wrote: "The proof of a poet is that his country absorbs him as affectionately as he absorbed it." There is little doubt that, according to his own definition, Whitman proved himself a poet.

from the
Preface to the 1855 Edition of

Leaves
of **Grass**

Walt Whitman

1   America does not repel the past or what it has produced under its forms or amid other politics or the idea of castes or the old religions . . . accepts the lesson with calmness . . . is not so impatient as has been supposed that the slough still sticks to opinions and manners and literature while the life which served its requirements has passed into the new life of the new forms . . . perceives that the corpse is slowly borne from the eating and sleeping rooms of the house . . . perceives that it waits a little while in the door . . . that it was fittest for its days . . . that its action has descended to the stalwart and well-shaped heir who approaches . . . and that he shall be fittest for his days.

2   The Americans of all nations at any time upon the earth have probably the fullest poetical nature. The United States themselves are essentially the greatest poem. In the history of the earth hitherto the largest and most stirring appear tame and orderly to their **ampler** largeness and stir. Here at last is something in the doings of man that corresponds with the broadcast doings of the day and night. Here is not merely a nation but a **teeming** nation of nations. Here is action untied from strings necessarily blind to particulars and details magnificently moving in **vast** masses. Here is the hospitality that forever indicates heroes. . . . Here are the roughs and beards and space and ruggedness and nonchalance that the soul loves. Here the performance disdaining the trivial unapproached in the tremendous audacity of its crowds and groupings and the push of its perspective spreads with crampless and flowing **breadth** and showers its **prolific** and splendid extravagance. One sees it must indeed own the riches of the summer and winter, and need never be bankrupt while corn grows from the ground or the orchards drop apples or the bays contain fish or men beget children upon women. . . . 🍃

NOTES

CLOSE READ
ANNOTATE: Mark details in paragraph 1 that relate to death and other details that relate to new life or rebirth.

QUESTION: Why does Whitman include these details? What is dying and what is being born?

CONCLUDE: What impression of America do these references create?

ampler (AM pluhr) *adj.* more abundant

teeming (TEE mihng) *adj.* full

vast (vast) *adj.* very great in size

breadth (brehdth) *n.* wide range; expansive extent

prolific (pruh LIHF ihk) *adj.* fruitful; abundant

from
Song of
Myself

Walt Whitman

1

I celebrate myself, and sing myself,
And what I assume you shall assume,
For every atom belonging to me as good belongs to you.

I loaf and invite my soul,
5 I lean and loaf at my ease observing a spear of summer grass.

My tongue, every atom of my blood, formed from this soil, this air.
Born here of parents born here from parents the same, and
        their parents the same,
I, now thirty-seven years old in perfect health begin,
Hoping to cease not till death.

10 Creeds and schools in abeyance,[1]
Retiring back a while sufficed at what they are, but never forgotten,
I harbor for good or bad, I permit to speak at every hazard,
Nature without check with original energy.

6

A child said *What is the grass?* fetching it to me with full hands,
How could I answer the child? I do not know what it is any
        more than he.

I guess it must be the flag of my disposition, out of hopeful
        green stuff woven.

Or I guess it is the handkerchief of the Lord,
5 A scented gift and remembrancer[2] designedly dropped,
Bearing the owner's name someway in the corners, that we may see
        and remark, and say *Whose?*

. . .

What do you think has become of the young and old men?
And what do you think has become of the women and children?

They are alive and well somewhere,
10 The smallest sprout shows there is really no death,
And if ever there was it led forward life, and does not wait at the
        end to arrest it,
And ceas'd the moment life appear'd.

All goes onward and outward, nothing collapses,
And to die is different from what anyone supposed, and luckier.

CLOSE READ

ANNOTATE: In Section 6, mark the questions.

QUESTION: Why does Whitman choose to present these ideas as questions?

CONCLUDE: What is the effect of these questions?

---

1. **abeyance** (uh BAY uhns) *n.* temporary suspension.
2. **remembrancer** *n.* reminder.

9

The big doors of the country barn stand open and ready,
The dried grass of the harvest-time loads the slow-drawn wagon.
The clear light plays on the brown gray and green intertinged,
The armfuls are pack'd to the sagging mow.

5 I am there, I help, I came stretch'd atop of the load,
I felt its soft jolts, one leg reclined on the other,
I jump from the crossbeams and seize the clover and timothy,
And roll head over heels and tangle my hair full of wisps.

14

The wild gander leads his flock through the cool night,
Ya-honk he says, and sounds it down to me like an invitation,
The pert may suppose it meaningless, but I listening close,
Find its purpose and place up there toward the wintry sky.

5 The sharp-hoof'd moose of the north, the cat on the house-sill,
    the chickadee, the prairie dog,
The litter of the grunting sow as they tug at her teats,
The brood of the turkey hen and she with her half-spread wings,
I see in them and myself the same old law.

The press of my foot to the earth springs a hundred affections,
10 They scorn the best I can do to relate them.

I am enamor'd of growing outdoors,
Of men that live among cattle or taste of the ocean or woods,
Of the builders and steerers of ships and the wielders of axes and
    mauls, and the drivers of horses,
I can eat and sleep with them week in and week out.

15 What is commonest, cheapest, nearest, easiest, is Me,
Me going in for my chances, spending for vast returns,
Adorning myself to bestow myself on the first that will take me,
Not asking the sky to come down to my good will,
Scattering it freely forever.

17

These are really the thoughts of all men in all ages and lands,
    they are not original with me,
If they are not yours as much as mine they are nothing, or next
    to nothing,
If they are not the riddle and the untying of the riddle they are nothing,
If they are not just as close as they are distant they are nothing.

5 This is the grass that grows wherever the land is and the water is,
This is the common air that bathes the globe.

51

The past and present wilt—I have fill'd them, emptied them,
And proceed to fill my next fold of the future.

Listener up there! what have you to confide to me?
Look in my face while I snuff the sidle of evening,[3]
5 (Talk honestly, no one else hears you, and I stay only a minute longer.)

Do I contradict myself?
Very well then I contradict myself,
(I am large, I contain **multitudes**.)

I concentrate toward them that are nigh,[4] I wait on the door-slab.

10 Who has done his day's work? who will soonest be through with
    his supper?
Who wishes to walk with me?

Will you speak before I am gone? will you prove already too late?

52

The spotted hawk swoops by and accuses me, he complains of
    my gab and my loitering.

I too am not a bit tamed, I too am untranslatable,
I sound my barbaric yawp[5] over the roofs of the world.

The last scud[6] of day holds back for me,
5 It flings my likeness after the rest and true as any on the shadow'd wilds,
It coaxes me to the vapor and the dusk.

I depart as air, I shake my white locks at the runaway sun,
I effuse[7] my flesh in eddies, and drift it in lacy jags.

I bequeath[8] myself to the dirt to grow from the grass I love,
10 If you want me again look for me under your boot soles.

You will hardly know who I am or what I mean,
But I shall be good health to you nevertheless,
And filter and fiber your blood.

Failing to fetch me at first keep encouraged,
15 Missing me one place search another,
I stop somewhere waiting for you. ❧

---

3. **snuff . . . evening** put out the last light of day, which moves sideways across the sky.
4. **nigh** *adj.* near.
5. **yawp** *n.* hoarse cry or shout.
6. **scud** *n.* low, dark, wind-driven clouds.
7. **effuse** (ih FYOOZ) *v.* pour out.
8. **bequeath** (bih KWEETH) *v.* hand down or pass on.

from Song of Myself **159**

NOTES

CLOSE READ
ANNOTATE: In Section 51, mark details that suggest the speaker is talking to a specific person or group of people.

QUESTION: Why does the speaker include these references? Whom is the speaker addressing?

CONCLUDE: What is the effect of this approach?

multitudes (MUHL tuh toodz) *n.* large number of people or things; masses

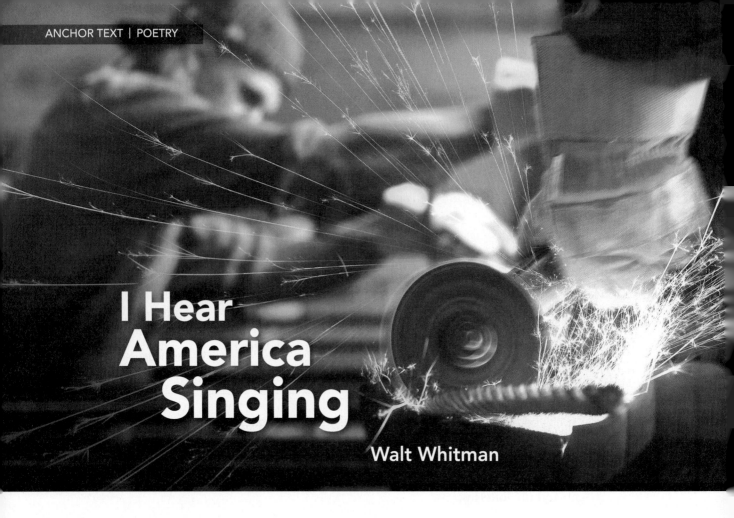

I Hear America Singing

Walt Whitman

NOTES

CLOSE READ

ANNOTATE: Mark the various kinds of workers mentioned in lines 2–8.

QUESTION: Why does the speaker name so many kinds of workers?

CONCLUDE: What is the effect of these references?

I hear America singing, the varied carols I hear,
Those of mechanics, each one singing his as it should be blithe
    and strong,
The carpenter singing his as he measures his plank or beam,
The mason singing his as he makes ready for work, or leaves
    off work.
5 The boatman singing what belongs to him in his boat, the
    deckhand singing on the steamboat deck,
The shoemaker singing as he sits on his bench, the hatter[1]
    singing as he stands,
The woodcutter's song, the plowboy's on his way in the
    morning, or at noon intermission or at sundown,
The delicious singing of the mother, or of the young wife at work,
    or of the girl sewing or washing,
Each singing what belongs to him or her and to none else,
10 The day what belongs to the day—at night the party of young
    fellows, robust, friendly,
Singing with open mouths their strong melodious songs.

---

1. **hatter** *n.* person who makes, sells, or cleans hats.

On the Beach at Night Alone

Walt Whitman

On the beach at night alone,
As the old mother sways her to and fro singing her husky song,
As I watch the bright stars shining, I think a thought of the clef[1]
    of the universes and of the future.

A vast similitude[2] interlocks all,
5 All spheres, grown, ungrown, small, large, suns, moons, planets,
All distances of place however wide,
All distances of time, all inanimate forms,
All souls, all living bodies though they be ever so different, or in
    different worlds,
All gaseous, watery, vegetable, mineral processes, the fishes, the
    brutes,
10 All nations, colors, barbarisms, civilizations, languages,
All identities that have existed or may exist on this globe, or any
    globe,
All lives and deaths, all of the past, present, future,
This vast similitude spans them, and always has spann'd,
And shall forever span them and compactly hold and enclose them.

NOTES

---

1. **clef** *n.* symbol that is placed at the beginning of a line of written music to indicate the pitch of the notes.
2. **similitude** (suh MIHL uh tood) *n.* similarity or likeness.

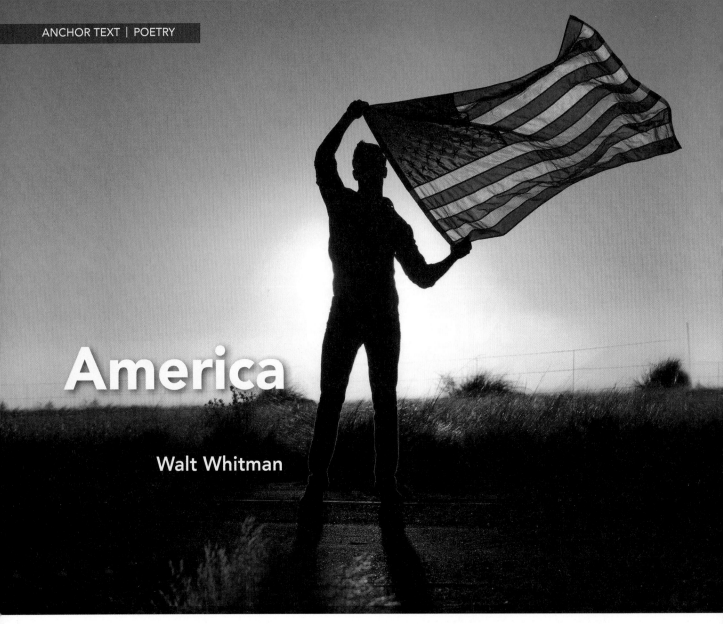

America

Walt Whitman

NOTES

Center of equal daughters, equal sons,
All, all alike endear'd, grown, ungrown, young or old,
Strong, ample, fair, enduring, capable, rich,
Perennial[1] with the Earth, with Freedom, Law and Love,
5 A grand, sane, towering, seated Mother,
Chair'd in the adamant[2] of Time.

---

1. **perennial** *adj.* enduring; consistently recurring or returning.
2. **adamant** *n.* legendary rock of impenetrable hardness.

Comprehension Check

Complete the following items after you finish your first read.

1. In his Preface to *Leaves of Grass*, how does Whitman define America's attitude toward the past?

2. In Section 1 of "Song of Myself," what does the speaker celebrate and sing?

3. In Section 52 of "Song of Myself," what does the speaker "bequeath" to the dirt?

4. Cite three types of songs the speaker hears in "I Hear America Singing."

5. According to the speaker in "On the Beach at Night Alone," what connects all things?

6. In the opening line of "America," how does the speaker describe the nation?

- -

RESEARCH

Research to Clarify Choose at least one unfamiliar detail from the text. Briefly research that detail. In what way does the information you learned shed light on an aspect of Walt Whitman's work?

Research to Explore Conduct research to find out why Whitman was regarded as a revolutionary writer in his time.

THE WRITING OF WALT WHITMAN

🔧 **Tool Kit**
Close-Read Guide and
Model Annotation

Close Read the Text

1. This model, from paragraph 2 of the Preface to *Leaves of Grass*, shows two sample annotations, along with questions and conclusions. Close read the passage and find another detail to annotate. Then, write a question and your conclusion.

> **ANNOTATE:** The passage contains some repeated words.
>
> **QUESTION:** What idea does the repetition emphasize?
>
> **CONCLUDE:** Whitman emphasizes a "right now" picture of America.

Here at last is something in the doings of man that corresponds with the broadcast doings of the day and night. Here is not merely a nation but a teeming nation of nations. . . . Here are the roughs and beards and space and ruggedness and nonchalance that the soul loves.

> **ANNOTATE:** This list juxtaposes concrete and abstract nouns.
>
> **QUESTION:** Why does Whitman include these particular nouns?
>
> **CONCLUDE:** He is painting a diverse and exuberant picture of America.

2. For more practice, go back into the text and complete the close-read notes.

3. Revisit a section of the text you found important during your first read. Read this section closely and **annotate** what you notice. Ask yourself **questions** such as "Why did the author make this choice?" What can you **conclude**?

Analyze the Text

CITE TEXTUAL EVIDENCE to support your answers.

📓 **Notebook** Respond to these questions.

1. (a) **Interpret** In the Preface to *Leaves of Grass*, what does Whitman mean when he calls America a "nation of nations"? (b) **Connect** How does he develop that idea in "I Hear America Singing"?

2. (a) In Section 51 of "Song of Myself," what attitude toward time does the speaker express? Cite time-related details to support your answer. (b) **Analyze** What does the speaker seem to want of the listener? Explain.

3. **Summarize** What main idea does the speaker express in lines 2–3 of Section 52 of "Song of Myself"?

4. **Interpret** In "On the Beach at Night Alone," how does the second stanza state and develop the "thought" the speaker has in the third line of the poem? Explain.

5. **Historical Perspectives** The French political thinker Alexis de Tocqueville wrote that Americans are "always considering themselves as standing alone, [imagining] that their whole destiny is in their own hands." To what extent do you think Walt Whitman's writing illustrates that idea?

6. **Essential Question: *What role does individualism play in American society?*** What have you learned about American individualism from reading Whitman's writings?

📋 STANDARDS
Reading Literature
• Cite strong and thorough textual evidence to support analysis of what the text says explicitly as well as inferences drawn from the text, including determining where the text leaves matters uncertain.
• Analyze how an author's choices concerning how to structure specific parts of a text contribute to its overall structure and meaning as well as its aesthetic impact.
• Demonstrate knowledge of eighteenth-, nineteenth-, and early-twentieth-century foundational works of American literature, including how two or more texts from the same period treat similar themes or topics.

Analyze Craft and Structure

Poetic Structures Traditional epic poetry tells a long story about a hero whose adventures embody the values of a nation. Today, many readers consider *Leaves of Grass* an American epic because it expresses national ideals. Underlying the poem's diverse subjects is the constant echo of an **epic theme**—that all people are inherently equal and connected by the shared experience of being alive. Whitman uses specific poetic structures to establish a sense of epic sweep suitable for this theme.

- **Free Verse:** Unlike formal verse, which has strict rules, free verse has irregular meter, no rhyme scheme, and varying line lengths. It simulates natural speech. Free verse allows Whitman to shape every line and stanza to suit his meaning, rather than fitting his message to a form:

  Do I contradict myself?

  Very well then I contradict myself, . . .

- **Anaphora:** A type of rhetorical device, anaphora is the repetition of a word or group of words at the beginnings of successive sentences or sections of text. It creates a majestic tone and rhythm.

  If they are not yours as much as mine . . .

  If they are not the riddle and the untying of the riddle . . .

  If they are not just as close as they are distant . . .

- **Catalogue:** Whitman's use of catalogues, or lists, of people, objects, or situations evokes the infinite range of elements that make up human experience. "I am enamor'd," he writes,

  Of the builders and steerers of ships and the wielders of axes and mauls, and the drivers of horses . . .

Practice

CITE TEXTUAL EVIDENCE to support your answers.

📓 **Notebook** Answer the questions, and complete the activity.

1. (a) How does line 1 of Section 17 of "Song of Myself" express Whitman's epic theme? (b) How does "On the Beach at Night Alone" relate to this theme?

2. (a) Cite specific lines from Section 51 of "Song of Myself" that sound like natural speech. Explain your choices. (b) What does this speech-like quality suggest about the speaker's attitudes toward the listener and the topic?

3. (a) Identify at least one example of each poetic structure as it appears in the Preface or poems. (b) For each example, explain how it contributes to the expansive, epic-like quality of the work.

POETIC STRUCTURE	EFFECT
free verse:	
anaphora:	
catalogues:	

Concept Vocabulary

ampler	vast	prolific
teeming	breadth	multitudes

Why These Words? These concept words are used to describe abundance, even overabundance. Whitman believes that all people of all times are connected. As he writes in "On the Beach at Night Alone," a "*vast* similitude interlocks all." America is a "*teeming* nation of nations," Whitman declares, that "showers its *prolific* and splendid extravagance."

1. How does the concept vocabulary clarify the reader's understanding of Whitman's worldview?

2. What other words in these selections connect to this concept?

Practice

 Notebook **Answer these questions.**

1. Which is the *ampler* unit of measure: a pint or a cup? Explain.
2. Why might life in a *teeming* urban area be challenging?
3. How would you feel if you were set adrift on a raft in a *vast* ocean? Why?
4. Why might a job candidate emphasize his or her *breadth* of experience?
5. What would a songwriter need to do to be considered *prolific*?
6. Why do *multitudes* of people sometimes gather in sports stadiums?

Word Study

Latin Combining Form: *multi-* A **combining form** is a word part that can be added to a word or to another word part—such as a root or an affix—to create a new word. The Latin combining form *multi-* means "many" or "much." In the word *multitudes*, it combines with *-tude*, another word-forming element that means "state or quality of." *Multitudes*, thus, means "the state or quality of being multiple or many."

1. *Multi-* is part of some words that relate to math or science. Write a definition of *multiply* that demonstrates your understanding of the combining form *multi-*. Check your answer in a college-level dictionary.

2. Identify and define two other words that include *multi-* and relate to math or science. Consult etymological references in a dictionary to verify your choices.

WORD NETWORK

Add words related to individualism from the text to your Word Network.

STANDARDS

Reading Literature
Determine the meaning of words and phrases as they are used in the text, including figurative and connotative meanings; analyze the impact of specific word choices on meaning and tone, including words with multiple meanings or language that is particularly fresh, engaging, or beautiful.

Language
• Identify and correctly use patterns of word changes that indicate different meanings or parts of speech.
• Verify the preliminary determination of the meaning of a word or phrase.

from NATURE
from SELF-RELIANCE

Copyright © SAVVAS Learning Company LLC. All Rights Reserved.

Reading aloud from the text can help all group members focus on the writer's ideas and style. Take turns reading interesting, confusing, or thought-provoking passages. After each reading, discuss the meaning and then dig deeper with thorough analysis.

Add words related to individualism from the texts to your Word Network.

Reading Informational Text
• Determine two or more central ideas of a text and analyze their development over the course of the text, including how they interact and build on one another to produce a complex analysis; provide an objective summary of the text.
• Analyze and evaluate the effectiveness of the structure an author uses in his or her exposition or argument, including whether the structure makes points clear, convincing, and engaging.
• Analyze seventeenth-, eighteenth-, and nineteenth-century foundational U.S. documents of historical and literary significance for their themes, purposes, and rhetorical features.

Language
Consult general and specialized reference materials, both print and digital, to find the pronunciation of a word or determine or clarify its precise meaning, its part of speech, its etymology, or its standard usage.

CITE TEXTUAL EVIDENCE to support your answers.

from WALDEN
from CIVIL DISOBEDIENCE

▤ STANDARDS

Reading Informational Text
By the end of grade 11, read and comprehend literary nonfiction in the grades 11–CCR text complexity band proficiently, with scaffolding as needed at the high end of the range.

Language
Acquire and use accurately general academic and domain-specific words and phrases, sufficient for reading, writing, speaking, and listening at the college and career readiness level; demonstrate independence in gathering vocabulary knowledge when considering a word or phrase important to comprehension or expression.

PEER REVIEW

Exchange narratives with a classmate. Use the checklist to evaluate your classmate's personal narrative and provide supportive feedback.

1. Did the narrative explain how the experience shaped the writer's views about individualism?

☐ yes ☐ no If no, explain what might be added.

2. Did the sequence of events lead naturally to the writer's views on individualism?

☐ yes ☐ no If no, tell what needs clarifying.

3. Are the writer's views on individualism clear to you now?

☐ yes ☐ no If no, suggest what you might change.

4. What is the strongest part of your classmate's narrative? Why?

Editing and Proofreading

Edit for Conventions Reread your draft for accuracy and consistency. Correct errors in grammar and word usage. Be sure that any shifts in time between past and present are clear.

Proofread for Accuracy Reread your draft carefully, looking for errors in spelling and punctuation. Be sure to punctuate dialogue correctly.

Publishing and Presenting

Use an app of your choice to save your personal narrative as an ebook. Depending on the app, you may include illustrations, and you may have a choice of preserving it in print or as a vocal recording. Share your ebook with others in your class. Ask your classmates to leave comments on a comment sheet that you provide. As you read classmates' ebooks, remember to keep your comments positive and helpful.

Reflecting

Consider what you learned by writing your personal narrative. Would a different incident from your life have provided a stronger response to the prompt? Does your narrative accurately reflect what happened to you and explain its importance in shaping your view about individualism? Think about what you might do differently the next time you write a personal narrative.

▤ STANDARDS

Writing
• Develop and strengthen writing as needed by planning, revising, editing, rewriting, or trying a new approach, focusing on addressing what is most significant for a specific purpose and audience.
• Use technology, including the Internet, to produce, publish, and update individual or shared writing products in response to ongoing feedback, including new arguments or information.

ESSENTIAL QUESTION:

What role does individualism play in American society?

As you read these selections, work with your group to explore the meaning of individualism.

From Text to Topic In the nineteenth century, America's spirit of individualism was evident in every sphere of activity, from the arts to exploration to the development of new technologies. For instance, the completion of the Erie Canal in 1825—the first transportation system between New York City and the Great Lakes that did not require carrying cargo over land—helped open the West to settlers. In 1844, Samuel Morse sent the first telegraph message, pioneering the first near-instant means of communication between cities. As you read, consider how these selections show individualism in all realms of American life.

Small-Group Learning Strategies

Throughout your life, in school, in your community, and in your career, you will continue to develop strategies when you work in teams. Use these strategies during Small-Group Learning. Add ideas of your own for each step.

STRATEGY	ACTION PLAN
Prepare	• Complete your assignment so that you are prepared for group work. • Organize your thinking so you can contribute to your group's discussions.
Participate fully	• Make eye contact to signal that you are listening and taking in what is being said. • Use text evidence when making a point.
Support others	• Build on ideas from others in your group. • Invite others who have not yet spoken to join the discussion.
Clarify	• Paraphrase the ideas of others to ensure that your understanding is correct. • Ask follow-up questions.

CONTENTS

PHILOSOPHICAL WRITING

from Nature

from Self-Reliance

Ralph Waldo Emerson

An important American philosopher praises the power of nature—and nonconformity.

PHILOSOPHICAL WRITING

from Walden

from Civil Disobedience

Henry David Thoreau

Can we maintain both a sense of individuality and a commitment to community at the same time?

MEDIA: PUBLIC DOCUMENTS

Innovators and Their Inventions

Inventors stand out from and often defy "the crowd." How does "the crowd" then benefit from their creativity and perseverance?

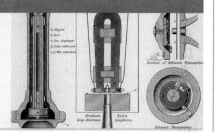

POETRY

The Love Song of J. Alfred Prufrock

T. S. Eliot

What does it mean to be an individual in the modern world?

SHORT STORY

A Wagner Matinée

Willa Cather

What happens to a woman's sense of self when she must give up all she loves most?

PERFORMANCE TASK

SPEAKING AND LISTENING FOCUS

Present a Personal Narrative

The Small-Group readings explore the complex relationship between individuality and community in American life. After reading, your group will deliver a speech in which you describe what is difficult and rewarding about nonconformity.

Working as a Team

1. **Take a Position** In your group, discuss the following question:

   Do you think American teenagers today would rather fit in than stand out? Explain.

   As you take turns sharing your positions, provide reasons for your choice. After all group members have shared, discuss connections among the ideas that were presented.

2. **List Your Rules** As a group, decide on the rules that you will follow as you work together. Two samples are provided. Add two more of your own. As you work together, you may add or revise rules based on your experience together.

   • Be open to multiple perspectives and creative responses.

   • Give reasons for your opinions and encourage others to do so as well.

   • _____

   _____

   • _____

   _____

3. **Apply the Rules** Share what you have learned about individualism in America. Make sure each person in the group contributes. Take notes as you listen to others and be prepared to share with the class one thing that you heard from another member of your group.

4. **Name Your Group** Choose a name that reflects the unit topic.

   Our group's name: _____

5. **Create a Communication Plan** Decide how you want to communicate with one another. For example, you might text, set up an online chat, or use the private messaging feature on a social media website.

   Our group's decision: _____

   _____

Making a Schedule

First, find out the due dates for the Small-Group activities. Then, preview the texts and activities with your group and make a schedule for completing the tasks.

SELECTION	ACTIVITIES	DUE DATE
from Nature *from* Self-Reliance		
from Walden *from* Civil Disobedience		
Innovators and Their Inventions		
The Love Song of J. Alfred Prufrock		
A Wagner Matinée		

Working on Group Projects

As your group works together, you'll find it more effective if each person has a specific role. Different projects require different roles. Before beginning a project, discuss the necessary roles and choose one for each group member. Some possible roles are listed here. Add your ideas to the list.

Project Manager: monitors the schedule and keeps everyone on task

Researcher: organizes research activities

Recorder: takes notes during group meetings

_____

_____

_____

_____

About the Author

Ralph Waldo Emerson
(1803–1882) was born
in Boston, the son of a
Unitarian minister. He
entered Harvard at the age of
fourteen. After postgraduate
studies at Harvard Divinity
School, he became pastor
of the Second Church of
Boston. Emerson's career as a
minister, however, was short-
lived. Grief-stricken at his
wife's death, and dissatisfied
with his faith, Emerson
resigned after three years
and went to Europe. There,
he met many of the leading
thinkers of the day. Upon
his return to the United
States, Emerson settled in
Concord, Massachusetts,
and began to write seriously.
His ideas helped forge the
Transcendentalist movement,
which celebrated the
individual and the power
of the human mind. Using
material from his lectures
and journals, Emerson
published *Essays* in 1841.
The collection brought him
international fame. Even
today, Emerson is one of
the most quoted writers in
American literature.

▤ STANDARDS

Reading Informational Text
By the end of grade 11, read and
comprehend literary nonfiction in
the grades 11–CCR text complexity
band proficiently, with scaffolding as
needed at the high end of the range.
Language
Use context as a clue to the meaning
of a word or phrase.

from Nature
from Self-Reliance

Concept Vocabulary

As you perform your first read of these excerpts from "Nature" and
"Self-Reliance," you will encounter these words:

sanctity	transcendent	redeemers

Context Clues To find the meaning of an unfamiliar word, look for **context
clues.** Words and phrases that appear in the same sentence or in nearby
sentences may help you determine the meaning of the unfamiliar word.

> **Example:** At all times she acts with respectful *decorum*, even when
> others try to anger her.
>
> **Context clues:** According to the sentence, *decorum* is a respectful
> way to behave—something that would be difficult for most people to
> maintain when angered.
>
> **Possible meaning:** *Decorum* means "dignity or control appropriate to
> an occasion."

Apply your knowledge of context clues and other vocabulary strategies to
determine the meanings of unfamiliar words you encounter during your
first read.

First Read NONFICTION

Apply these strategies as you conduct your first read. You will have an
opportunity to complete a close read after your first read.

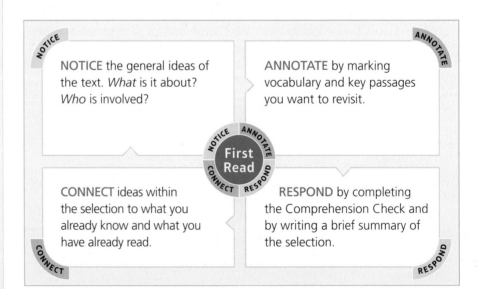

NOTICE the general ideas of the text. *What* is it about? *Who* is involved?

ANNOTATE by marking vocabulary and key passages you want to revisit.

CONNECT ideas within the selection to what you already know and what you have already read.

RESPOND by completing the Comprehension Check and by writing a brief summary of the selection.

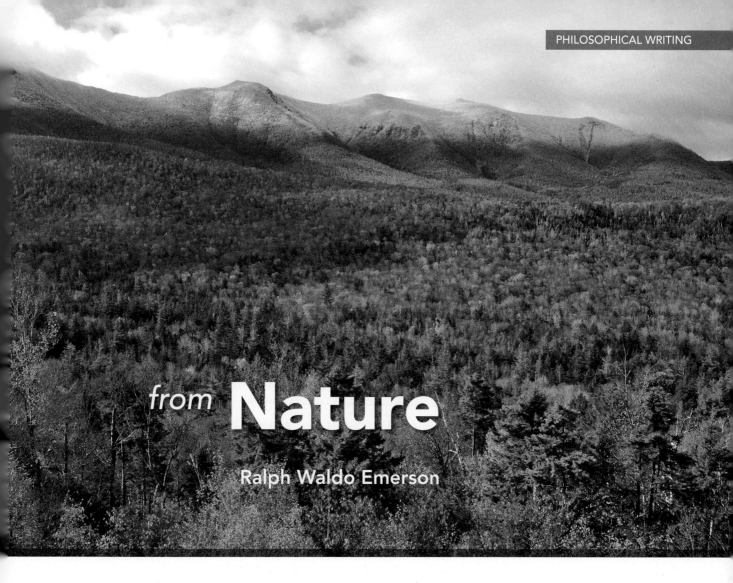

from Nature

Ralph Waldo Emerson

BACKGROUND

During the 1830s and 1840s, Emerson and a small group of like-minded friends gathered regularly in his study to discuss philosophy, religion, and literature. The Transcendental Club developed a philosophical system that stressed intuition, individuality, and self-reliance. In 1836, Emerson published "Nature," the Transcendental Club's unofficial statement of belief.

1   Nature is a setting that fits equally well a comic or a mourning piece. In good health, the air is a cordial[1] of incredible virtue. Crossing a bare common,[2] in snow puddles, at twilight, under a clouded sky, without having in my thoughts any occurrence of special good fortune, I have enjoyed a perfect exhilaration. I am glad to the brink of fear. In the woods, too, a man casts off his years, as the snake his slough, and at what period soever of life is always a child. In the woods is perpetual youth. Within these plantations of God, a decorum and **sanctity** reign, a perennial festival is dressed, and the guest sees not how he should tire of them in a thousand years. In

NOTES

Mark context clues or indicate another strategy you used that helped you determine meaning.

sanctity (SANGK tuh tee) *n.*

MEANING:

---

1. **cordial** (KAWR juhl) *n.* a strong, sweet liquor.
2. **common** *n.* piece of open public land.

the woods, we return to reason and faith. There I feel that nothing can befall me in life—no disgrace, no calamity (leaving me my eyes), which nature cannot repair. Standing on the bare ground—my head bathed by the blithe air and uplifted into infinite space—all mean egotism vanishes. I become a transparent eyeball; I am nothing; I see all; the currents of the Universal Being circulate through me; I am part or parcel of God. The name of the nearest friend sounds then foreign and accidental: to be brothers, to be acquaintances, master or servant, is then a trifle and a disturbance. I am the lover of uncontained and immortal beauty. In the wilderness, I find something more dear and connate[3] than in the streets or villages. In the tranquil landscape, and especially in the distant line of the horizon, man beholds somewhat as beautiful as his own nature.

2   The greatest delight which the fields and woods minister is the suggestion of an occult relation between man and the vegetable. I am not alone and unacknowledged. They nod to me, and I to them. The waving of the boughs in the storm is new to me and old. It takes me by surprise, and yet is not unknown. Its effect is like that of a higher thought or a better emotion coming over me, when I deemed I was thinking justly or doing right.

3   Yet it is certain that the power to produce this delight does not reside in nature, but in man, or in a harmony of both. It is necessary to use these pleasures with great temperance. For nature is not always tricked[4] in holiday attire, but the same scene which yesterday breathed perfume and glittered as for the frolic of the nymphs is overspread with melancholy today. Nature always wears the colors of the spirit. To a man laboring under calamity, the heat of his own fire hath sadness in it. Then there is a kind of contempt of the landscape felt by him who has just lost by death a dear friend. The sky is less grand as it shuts down over less worth in the population. ❧

---

3. **connate** (KON ayt) *adj.* existing within someone since birth; inborn.
4. **tricked** *v.* dressed.

from Self-Reliance

Ralph Waldo Emerson

BACKGROUND

Individuality, independence, and an appreciation for the wonders of nature are just a few of the principles that Ralph Waldo Emerson helped to instill in our nation's identity. His essay "Self-Reliance" grew out of a series of lectures that he conducted in the 1830s.

1   There is a time in every man's education when he arrives at the conviction that envy is ignorance; that imitation is suicide; that he must take himself for better, for worse, as his portion; that though the wide universe is full of good, no kernel of nourishing corn can come to him but through his toil bestowed on that plot of ground which is given to him to till. The power which resides in him is new in nature, and none but he knows what that is which he can do, nor does he know until he has tried. Not for nothing one face, one character, one fact makes much impression on him, and another none. This sculpture in the memory is not without preestablished harmony. The eye was placed where one ray should fall, that it might testify of that particular ray. We but half express ourselves, and are ashamed of that divine idea which each of us represents. It may be safely trusted as proportionate and of good issues, so it be faithfully imparted, but God will not have his work made manifest by cowards. A man is relieved and gay when he has put his heart into his work and done his best; but what he has said or done otherwise, shall give him no peace. It is a deliverance which does not deliver. In the attempt his genius deserts him; no muse befriends; no invention, no hope.

NOTES

transcendent (tran SEHN duhnt) *adj.*

MEANING:

redeemers (rih DEE muhrz) *n.*

MEANING:

2   Trust thyself: every heart vibrates to that iron string. Accept the place the divine providence has found for you; the society of your contemporaries, the connection of events. Great men have always done so and confided themselves childlike to the genius of their age, betraying their perception that the absolutely trustworthy was stirring at their heart, working through their hands, predominating in all their being. And we are now men, and must accept in the highest mind the same **transcendent** destiny; and not minors and invalids in a protected corner, but guides, **redeemers**, and benefactors. Obeying the Almighty effort and advancing on chaos and the Dark. . . .

3   Society everywhere is in conspiracy against the manhood of every one of its members. Society is a joint-stock company[1] in which the members agree for the better securing of his bread to each shareholder, to surrender the liberty and culture of the eater. The virtue in most request is conformity. Self-reliance is its aversion. It loves not realities and creators, but names and customs.

4   Whoso[2] would be a man must be a nonconformist. He who would gather immortal palms must not be hindered by the name of goodness, but must explore if it be goodness. Nothing is at last sacred but the integrity of your own mind. Absolve you to yourself, and you shall have the suffrage of the world. . . .

5   A foolish consistency is the hobgoblin of little minds, adored by little statesmen and philosophers and divines. With consistency a great soul has simply nothing to do. He may as well concern himself with his shadow on the wall. Speak what you think now in hard words and tomorrow speak what tomorrow thinks in hard words again, though it contradict everything you said today. "Ah, so you shall be sure to be misunderstood?"—is it so bad, then, to be misunderstood? Pythagoras was misunderstood, and Socrates, and Jesus, and Luther, and Copernicus, and Galileo, and Newton,[3] and every pure and wise spirit that ever took flesh. To be great is to be misunderstood. . . . ❧

---

1. **joint-stock company** similar to a publicly owned corporation, in which risk is spread among numerous investors.
2. **Whoso** *pr.* archaic term for "whoever."
3. **Pythagoras ... Newton** individuals who made major contributions to scientific, philosophical, or religious thinking.

Comprehension Check

Complete the following items after you finish your first read. Review and clarify details with your group.

from NATURE

1. Under what circumstances, according to Emerson, does "mean egotism" vanish?

2. What does Emerson say is "the greatest delight" of being in contact with nature?

3. Under what circumstances, according to Emerson, does nature appear to be melancholy and sad?

4. 🗐 **Notebook** Confirm your understanding of the text by writing a summary.

from SELF-RELIANCE

1. According to Emerson, what idea makes "every heart" vibrate?

2. What virtue does society demand, and what does Emerson recommend in its place?

3. According to Emerson, what is the "hobgoblin of little minds"?

4. 🗐 **Notebook** Confirm your understanding of the excerpt by writing two sentences that summarize its key content.

- -

RESEARCH

Research to Clarify Choose at least one unfamiliar detail from one of these texts. Briefly research that detail. In what way does the information you learned shed light on an aspect of the text?

Research to Explore Conduct research on an aspect of the text you find interesting. For example, you may want to learn more about Emerson's abolitionist politics. Share what you discover with your group.

Close Read the Text

With your group, revisit sections of the texts you marked during your first read. **Annotate** details that you notice. What **questions** do you have? What can you **conclude?**

Analyze the Text

CITE TEXTUAL EVIDENCE
to support your answers.

📝 **Notebook** Complete the activities.

1. **Review and Clarify** With your group, reread paragraph 1 of the excerpt from "Nature." Describe how Emerson is affected by nature. Is his experience in nature universal to all people, or is it unique to him?

2. **Present and Discuss** Now, work with your group to share the passages from the selections that you found especially important. Take turns presenting your passages. Discuss what you noticed in the selection, what questions you asked, and what conclusions you reached.

3. **Essential Question:** *What role does individualism play in American society?* What have these texts taught you about the individual and society? Discuss with your group.

TIP

⚏ WORD NETWORK

Add words related to individualism from the texts to your Word Network.

☰ STANDARDS

LANGUAGE DEVELOPMENT

Concept Vocabulary

| sanctity | transcendent | redeemers |

Why These Words? The three concept vocabulary words are related. With your group, determine what the words have in common. How do these word choices enhance the impact of the essays?

Practice

📝 **Notebook** Confirm your understanding of these words by answering the questions. Use the vocabulary word in your answer.

1. What might people do to preserve the *sanctity* of a special place?

2. When might a person experience a *transcendent* moment?

3. How might *redeemers* help other people?

Word Study

📝 **Notebook Latin Root: -sanct-** The word *sanctity* contains the Latin root -*sanct*-, which means "holy," and the suffix -*ity*, which turns adjectives into abstract nouns. Write several other words that you suspect contain the Latin root -*sanct*-. Use etymological information in a college-level dictionary to verify your choices. Record the words and their meanings.

Analyze Craft and Structure

Development of Ideas An **essay** is a short work of nonfiction in which an author presents ideas on a specific topic. Often, an essay involves an open-ended exploration of ideas. Reading Emerson's essays, you may feel as if you are walking beside him as he converses, continually discovering new connections. Through his explorations, Emerson elaborates a **philosophical vision,** or interpretation of humanity's situation in the world. To help readers see life from his perspective, he employs strategies such as these:

- **Setting the Scene:** Emerson grounds his discussion in a shared experience—a walk in the woods, or a moment when one takes charge of one's life.

- **Re-envisioning the Ordinary:** Starting from shared experience, Emerson transforms it, showing its larger implications. In "Nature," for example, he finds that a walk in the woods restores youth and connects him more deeply to the world. He re-envisions this walk as a journey into the infinite.

- **Re-defining Words:** Emerson develops specific associations for key terms. In "Nature," for example, the term *nature* grows from a reference to fields and woods to include associations with the spirit.

- **Finding Limits:** Emerson may reflect on how far his vision should extend. In "Nature," for example, he concludes that the power of nature to delight is not unlimited.

Practice

Notebook Work on your own to analyze Emerson's presentation of his vision in these two essays. Complete a chart like this one. Then, share and discuss your findings with your group.

from NATURE	from SELF-RELIANCE
Summary of Vision humanity's relationship to nature:	Summary of Vision significance of being an individual:
References to Shared Experience	References to Shared Experience
How the Shared Experience Reflects the Vision	How the Shared Experience Reflects the Vision
Meanings and Associations of Key Terms nature: harmony:	Meanings and Associations of Key Terms self-reliance: great men: manhood: society: conformity: consistency:
Limits/Lack of Limits	Limits/Lack of Limits

from NATURE
from SELF-RELIANCE

Conventions and Style

Sentence Variety One way in which writers hold the attention of their readers is by varying the types of sentences they use. There are four kinds of sentences, categorized by the number and types of clauses they contain. **Independent clauses** have a subject and verb and can stand alone as complete thoughts. **Subordinate** (or **dependent**) **clauses** also have a subject and verb but cannot stand alone as complete thoughts. This chart shows the components of the four kinds of sentences. (Independent clauses are underlined once; dependent clauses are underlined twice.)

KIND OF SENTENCE	COMPONENTS	EXAMPLES
simple	a single independent clause	I have enjoyed a perfect exhilaration. In the woods is perpetual youth.
compound	two or more independent clauses	They nod to me, and I [nod] to them. It takes me by surprise, and yet [it] is not unknown.
complex	one independent clause + at least one subordinate clause	The sky is less grand as it shuts down over less worth in the population.
compound-complex	two or more independent clauses + at least one subordinate clause	Within these plantations of God, a decorum and sanctity reign, a perennial festival is dressed, and the guest sees not how he should tire of them in a thousand years.

Emerson often uses the complex, compound, and compound-complex sentences typical of formal nineteenth-century prose. However, he also includes shorter, simple sentences to vary the flow of the text. The result is a text that is more conversational—and, therefore, more engaging.

Read It

🔲 **Notebook** Identify each sentence in this paragraph as simple, compound, complex, or compound-complex. Explain each choice.

(1) Although society thrives on conformity, progress depends on individuality. (2) Emerson may celebrate individuality, but he does not address progress, and we should not ignore it. (3) While we need strong leaders, those leaders would be ineffective without loyal followers. (4) Every person must assume both roles. (5) No one can lead all the time, so we should become leaders in our areas of strength and follow others when they have greater experience and knowledge.

Write It

🔲 **Notebook** Write a paragraph consisting of at least four sentences. Include at least one example of each kind of sentence: simple, compound, complex, and compound-complex.

≔ STANDARDS

Writing
Write narratives to develop real or imagined experiences or events using effective technique, well-chosen details, and well-structured event sequences.

Language
• Apply knowledge of language to understand how language functions in different contexts, to make effective choices for meaning or style, and to comprehend more fully when reading or listening.
• Vary syntax for effect, consulting references for guidance as needed; apply an understanding of syntax to the study of complex texts when reading.

Writing to Sources

Assignment

Respond to one of Emerson's essays by writing a **story element** for a first-person narrative related to Emerson's ideas. Work initially with other group members to use them as a sounding board for your ideas, but then write individually. The narrative can be either fiction or nonfiction. Choose from the following options. Check the box of the one you chose.

☐ **Setting:** Write a vivid description of a place in which a character feels the "perpetual youth" that Emerson describes in "Nature." For your narrative, choose a setting that is different from the forest that Emerson describes.

☐ **Character:** Create a personality profile of someone who fits Emerson's idea of a nonconformist in today's society. Describe in detail the types of things he or she eats, loves, writes, listens to, says, and so on. Make explicit connections to ideas in Emerson's essays where you can.

☐ **Dialogue:** Write a dialogue for a scene including two or more characters in which you capture what it means to "speak what you think now in hard words." Include a brief introduction explaining who the characters are and what the situation is.

Narrative Plan Work with your group to plan the narrative element that you chose. Discuss how your story element connects to Emerson's ideas, and consider integrating some quotations from his essays into your writing.

Working Title: _____

NARRATIVE ELEMENT
Details to include:
Ideas to express:
Quotation(s) from Emerson's writing to use:

Tying It Together Work individually to draft your writing. Then, read your work aloud to a partner or your group and discuss revisions. Look for ways to make your writing stronger. Also, consider additional ideas or quotations from Emerson's essays that support the idea you are developing.

✎ EVIDENCE LOG

Before moving on to a new selection, go to your Evidence Log and record what you learned from the excerpts from "Nature" and "Self-Reliance."

About the Author

Henry David Thoreau
(1817–1862) was born in
Concord, Massachusetts,
where he spent most of his
life. After graduating from
Harvard, he became a teacher.
In 1841, Thoreau moved into
the home of another famous
Concord resident, Ralph Waldo
Emerson, where he lived for two
years. Fascinated by Emerson's
Transcendentalist ideas, Thoreau
became Emerson's friend and
disciple. Rather than return to
teaching, he decided to devote
his energies to living by his
beliefs. The literary results of that
decision include his masterwork,
Walden (1854). When Thoreau
died at the age of forty-four, he
had published little and received
no public recognition. Emerson,
however, knew that future
generations would cherish his
friend. Speaking at Thoreau's
funeral, Emerson said: "The
country knows not yet, or in
the least part, how great a son
it has lost. . . . [W]herever there
is knowledge, wherever there is
virtue, wherever there is beauty,
he will find a home."

STANDARDS

Reading Informational Text
By the end of grade 11, read and
comprehend literary nonfiction in
the grades 11–CCR text complexity
band proficiently, with scaffolding as
needed at the high end of the range.

Language
Identify and correctly use patterns of
word changes that indicate different
meanings or parts of speech.

from Walden
from Civil Disobedience

Concept Vocabulary

As you perform your first read of the excerpts from *Walden* and "Civil
Disobedience," you will encounter these words.

sufficed	superfluous	vital

Familiar Word Parts Words that seem unfamiliar may contain **familiar
word parts,** such as roots, prefixes, or suffixes, that you already know.
When you encounter an unfamiliar word, identify any familiar word parts,
and consider how they might contribute to the meaning of the unfamiliar
word. Then, draw a conclusion about the word's likely meaning.

Unfamiliar Word: *insensibly*

Word in Context: It is remarkable how easily and *insensibly* we fall
into a particular route, . . .

Familiar Word Parts: the prefix *in-*, which often means "not"; the
root *-sens-*, which means "sense"; and the suffix *-ly*, which often
appears in adverbs that tell how something is done

Conclusion: *Insensibly* has a meaning related to *sense*. The word
probably means "in a way that is not connected to the senses" or
possibly "in a way that does not make sense."

Apply your knowledge of familiar word parts and other vocabulary strategies
to determine the meanings of unfamiliar words you encounter during your
first read.

First Read NONFICTION

Apply these strategies as you conduct your first read. You will have an
opportunity to complete a close read after your first read.

NOTICE the general ideas of
the text. *What* is it about?
Who is involved?

ANNOTATE by marking
vocabulary and key passages
you want to revisit.

First Read

CONNECT ideas within
the selection to what you
already know and what
you've already read.

RESPOND by completing the
Comprehension Check and by
writing a brief summary of the
selection.

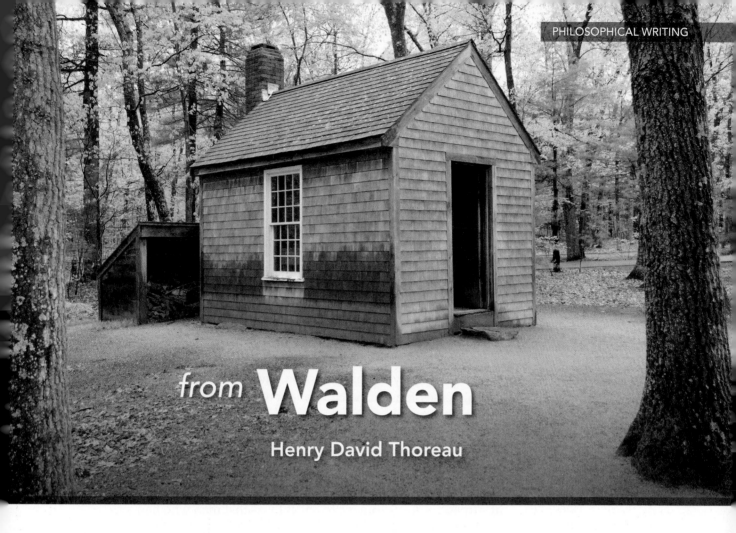

from Walden

Henry David Thoreau

BACKGROUND

From 1845 to 1847, Henry David Thoreau lived alone in a one-room cabin he built at Walden Pond near Concord, Massachusetts. This experience led him to write *Walden*, a blend of natural observation, social criticism, and philosophical insight. It remains one of the greatest examples of nature writing in American literature.

from Where I Lived, and What I Lived For

1   At a certain season of our life we are accustomed to consider every spot as the possible site of a house. I have thus surveyed the country on every side within a dozen miles of where I live. In imagination I have bought all the farms in succession, for all were to be bought, and I knew their price. I walked over each farmer's premises, tasted his wild apples, discoursed on husbandry[1] with him, took his farm at his price, at any price, mortgaging it to him in my mind; even put a higher price on it—took everything but a deed of it—took his word for his deed, for I dearly love to talk—cultivated it, and him too to some extent, I trust, and withdrew when I had enjoyed it long enough, leaving him to carry it on. This experience entitled me to be regarded as a sort of real-estate broker by my friends. Wherever I sat, there I might live, and the landscape radiated

NOTES

1. **husbandry** (HUHZ buhn dree) *n.* farming.

Mark familiar word parts or indicate
another strategy you used that
helped you determine meaning.

sufficed (suh FYST) *v.*

MEANING:

from me accordingly. What is a house but a sedes, a seat?—better if a country seat. I discovered many a site for a house not likely to be soon improved, which some might have thought too far from the village, but to my eyes the village was too far from it. Well, there might I live, I said; and there I did live, for an hour, a summer and a winter life; saw how I could let the years run off, buffet the winter through, and see the spring come in. The future inhabitants of this region, wherever they may place their houses, may be sure that they have been anticipated. An afternoon **sufficed** to lay out the land into orchard woodlot and pasture, and to decide what fine oaks or pines should be left to stand before the door, and whence each blasted tree could be seen to the best advantage; and then I let it lie, fallow[2] perchance, for a man is rich in proportion to the number of things which he can afford to let alone.

2   My imagination carried me so far that I even had the refusal of several farms—the refusal was all I wanted—but I never got my fingers burned by actual possession. The nearest that I came to actual possession was when I bought the Hollowell Place, and had begun to sort my seeds, and collected materials with which to make a wheelbarrow to carry it on or off with; but before the owner gave me a deed of it, his wife—every man has such a wife—changed her mind and wished to keep it, and he offered me ten dollars to release him. Now, to speak the truth, I had but ten cents in the world, and it surpassed my arithmetic to tell, if I was that man who had ten cents, or who had a farm, or ten dollars, or all together. However, I let him keep the ten dollars and the farm too, for I had carried it far enough; or rather, to be generous, I sold him the farm for just what I gave for it, and, as he was not a rich man, made him a present of ten dollars, and still had my ten cents, and seeds, and materials for a wheelbarrow left. I found thus that I had been a rich man without any damage to my poverty. But I retained the landscape, and I have since annually carried off what it yielded without a wheelbarrow. With respect to landscapes:

3   "I am monarch of all I *survey*,
           My right there is none to dispute."[3]

4   I have frequently seen a poet withdraw, having enjoyed the most valuable part of a farm, while the crusty farmer supposed that he had got a few wild apples only. Why, the owner does not know it for many years when a poet has put his farm in rhyme, the most admirable kind of invisible fence, has fairly impounded it, milked it, skimmed it, and got all the cream, and left the farmer only the skimmed milk.

5   The real attractions of the Hollowell farm, to me, were: its complete retirement, being about two miles from the village, half a mile from the nearest neighbor, and separated from the highway by a broad field; its bounding on the river, which the owner said protected

2. **fallow** (FAL oh) *adj.* left uncultivated or unplanted.
3. **"I ... dispute"** from William Cowper's *Verses Supposed to Be Written by Alexander Selkirk*.

it by its fogs from frosts in the spring, though that was nothing to me; the gray color and ruinous state of the house and barn, and the dilapidated fences, which put such an interval between me and the last occupant; the hollow and lichen-covered apple trees, gnawed by rabbits, showing what kind of neighbors I should have; but above all, the recollection I had of it from my earliest voyages up the river, when the house was concealed behind a dense grove of red maples, through which I heard the house-dog bark. I was in haste to buy it, before the proprietor finished getting out some rocks, cutting down the hollow apple trees, and grubbing up some young birches which had sprung up in the pasture, or, in short, had made any more of his improvements. To enjoy these advantages I was ready to carry it on; like Atlas,[4] to take the world on my shoulders—I never heard what compensation he received for that—and do all those things which had no other motive or excuse but that I might pay for it and be unmolested in my possession of it; for I knew all the while that it would yield the most abundant crop of the kind I wanted if I could only afford to let it alone. But it turned out as I have said.

6   All that I could say, then, with respect to farming on a large scale (I have always cultivated a garden) was that I had had my seeds ready. Many think that seeds improve with age. I have no doubt that time discriminates between the good and the bad; and when at last I shall plant, I shall be less likely to be disappointed. But I would say to my fellows, once for all, As long as possible live free and uncommitted. It makes but little difference whether you are committed to a farm or the county jail.

7   Old Cato,[5] whose "De Re Rustica" is my "Cultivator," says, and the only translation I have seen makes sheer nonsense of the passage, "When you think of getting a farm, turn it thus in your mind, not to buy greedily; nor spare your pains to look at it, and do not think it enough to go round it once. The oftener you go there the more it will please you, if it is good." I think I shall not buy greedily, but go round and round it as long as I live, and be buried in it first, that it may please me the more at last. . . .

8   I do not propose to write an ode to dejection, but to brag as lustily as chanticleer[6] in the morning, standing on his roost, if only to wake my neighbors up.

9   When first I took up my abode in the woods, that is, began to spend my nights as well as days there, which, by accident, was on Independence Day, or the fourth of July, 1845, my house was not finished for winter, but was merely a defense against the rain, without plastering or chimney, the walls being of rough weatherstained boards, with wide chinks, which made it cool at night. The upright white hewn studs and freshly planed door

---

4. **Atlas** (AT luhs) from Greek mythology, a Titan who supported the heavens on his shoulders.
5. **Old Cato** (KAY toh) Roman statesman (234–149 B.C.). "De Re Rustica" is Latin for "Of Things Rustic."
6. **chanticleer** (CHAN tuh klihr) *n.* rooster.

and window casings gave it a clean and airy look, especially in the morning, when its timbers were saturated with dew, so that I fancied that by noon some sweet gum would exude from them. To my imagination it retained throughout the day more or less of this auroral[7] character, reminding me of a certain house on a mountain which I had visited the year before. This was an airy and unplastered cabin, fit to entertain a traveling god, and where a goddess might trail her garments. The winds which passed over my dwelling were such as sweep over the ridges of mountains, bearing the broken strains, or celestial parts only, of terrestrial music. The morning wind forever blows, the poem of creation is uninterrupted; but few are the ears that hear it. Olympus is but the outside of the earth everywhere. . . .

10   I went to the woods because I wished to live deliberately, to front only the essential facts of life, and see if I could not learn what it had to teach, and not, when I came to die, discover that I had not lived. I did not wish to live what was not life, living is so dear; nor did I wish to practice resignation, unless it was quite necessary. I wanted to live deep and suck out all the marrow of life, to live so sturdily and Spartanlike[8] as to put to rout all that was not life, to cut a broad swath and shave close, to drive life into a corner, and reduce it to its lowest terms, and, if it proved to be mean, why then to get the whole and genuine meanness of it, and publish its meanness to the world; or if it were sublime, to know it by experience, and be able to give a true account of it in my next excursion. For most men, it appears to me, are in a strange uncertainty about it, whether it is of the devil or of God, and have *somewhat hastily* concluded that it is the chief end of man here to "glorify God and enjoy him forever."[9]

11   Still we live meanly, like ants; though the fable tells us that we were long ago changed into men; like pygmies we fight with cranes:[10] it is error upon error, and clout upon clout, and our best virtue has for its occasion a **superfluous** and evitable wretchedness. Our life is frittered away by detail. An honest man has hardly need to count more than his ten fingers, or in extreme cases he may add his ten toes, and lump the rest. Simplicity, simplicity, simplicity! I say, let your affairs be as two or three, and not a hundred or a thousand; instead of a million count half a dozen, and keep your accounts on your thumbnail. In the midst of this chopping sea of civilized life, such are the clouds and storms and quicksands and thousand-and-one items to be allowed for, that a man has to live, if he would not founder and go to the bottom and not make his port at all, by dead reckoning,[11] and he must be a great calculator indeed who succeeds. Simplify, simplify. Instead of three meals

Mark familiar word parts or indicate another strategy you used that helped you determine meaning.

superfluous (suh PUR floo uhs) *adj.*

MEANING:

---

7. **auroral** (aw RAWR uhl) *adj.* resembling the dawn.
8. **Spartanlike** *adj.* like the people of Sparta, an ancient Greek state whose citizens were known to be hardy, stoical, simple, and highly disciplined.
9. **"glorify ... forever"** the answer to the question "What is the chief end of man?" in the Westminster catechism.
10. **like ... cranes** In the *Iliad*, the Trojans are compared to cranes fighting against pygmies.
11. **dead reckoning** navigating without the assistance of stars.

a day, if it be necessary eat but one; instead of a hundred dishes, five; and reduce other things in proportion. Our life is like a German Confederacy,[12] made up of petty states, with its boundary forever fluctuating, so that even a German cannot tell you how it is bounded at any moment. The nation itself, with all its so-called internal improvements, which, by the way, are all external and superficial, is just such an unwieldy and overgrown establishment, cluttered with furniture and tripped up by its own traps, ruined by luxury and heedless expense, by want of calculation and a worthy aim, as the million households in the land; and the only cure for it as for them is in a rigid economy, a stern and more than Spartan simplicity of life and elevation of purpose. It lives too fast. Men think that it is essential that the *Nation* have commerce, and export ice, and talk through a telegraph, and ride thirty miles an hour, without a doubt, whether *they* do or not; but whether we should live like baboons or like men, is a little uncertain. If we do not get out sleepers,[13] and forge rails, and devote days and nights to the work, but go to tinkering upon our *lives* to improve *them*, who will build railroads? And if railroads are not built, how shall we get to heaven in season? But if we stay at home and mind our business, who will want railroads? We do not ride on the railroad; it rides upon us. . . .

> I have always been regretting that I was not as wise as the day I was born.

12   Time is but the stream I go a-fishing in. I drink at it; but while I drink I see the sandy bottom and detect how shallow it is. Its thin current slides away, but eternity remains. I would drink deeper; fish in the sky, whose bottom is pebbly with stars. I cannot count one. I know not the first letter of the alphabet. I have always been regretting that I was not as wise as the day I was born. The intellect is a cleaver; it discerns and rifts its way into the secret of things. I do not wish to be any more busy with my hands than is necessary. My head is hands and feet. I feel all my best faculties concentrated in it. My instinct tells me that my head is an organ for burrowing, as some creatures use their snout and forepaws, and with it I would mine and burrow my way through these hills. I think that the richest vein is somewhere here-abouts; so by the divining rod[14] and thin rising vapors I judge; and here I will begin to mine. . . .

from The Conclusion

13 I left the woods for as good a reason as I went there. Perhaps it seemed to me that I had several more lives to live, and could not spare any more time for that one. It is remarkable how easily and

---

12. **German Confederacy** At the time, Germany was a loose union of thirty-nine independent states with no common government.
13. **sleepers** *n.* ties supporting railroad tracks.
14. **divining rod** a forked branch or stick alleged to reveal underground water or minerals.

insensibly we fall into a particular route, and make a beaten track for ourselves. I had not lived there a week before my feet wore a path from my door to the pondside; and though it is five or six years since I trod it, it is still quite distinct. It is true, I fear that others may have fallen into it, and so helped to keep it open. The surface of the earth is soft and impressible by the feet of men; and so with the paths which the mind travels. How worn and dusty, then, must be the highways of the world, how deep the ruts of tradition and conformity! I did not wish to take a cabin passage, but rather to go before the mast and on the deck of the world, for there I could best see the moonlight amid the mountains. I do not wish to go below now.

14   I learned this, at least, by my experiment; that if one advances confidently in the direction of his dreams, and endeavors to live the life which he has imagined, he will meet with a success unexpected in common hours. He will put some things behind, will pass an invisible boundary; new, universal, and more liberal laws will begin to establish themselves around and within him; or the old laws be expanded, and interpreted in his favor in a more liberal sense, and he will live with the license of a higher order of beings. In proportion as he simplifies his life, the laws of the universe will appear less complex, and solitude will not be solitude, nor poverty poverty, nor weakness weakness. If you have built castles in the air, your

work need not be lost; that is where they should be. Now put the foundations under them. . . .

15   Why should we be in such desperate haste to succeed, and in such desperate enterprises? If a man does not keep pace with his companions, perhaps it is because he hears a different drummer. Let him step to the music which he hears, however measured or far away. It is not important that he should mature as soon as an apple tree or an oak. Shall he turn his spring into summer? If the condition of things which we were made for is not yet, what were any reality which we can substitute? We will not be shipwrecked on a vain reality. Shall we with pains erect a heaven of blue glass over ourselves, though when it is done we shall be sure to gaze still at the true ethereal heaven far above, as if the former were not? . . .

16   However mean your life is, meet it and live it; do not shun it and call it hard names. It is not so bad as you are. It looks poorest when you are richest. The faultfinder will find faults even in paradise. Love your life, poor as it is. You may perhaps have some pleasant, thrilling, glorious hours, even in a poorhouse. The setting sun is reflected from the windows of the almshouse[15] as brightly as from the rich man's abode; the snow melts before its door as early in the spring. I do not see but a quiet mind may live as contentedly there, and have as cheering thoughts, as in a palace. The town's poor seem to me often to live the most independent lives of any. Maybe they are simply great enough to receive without misgiving. Most think that they are above being supported by the town; but it oftener happens that they are not above supporting themselves by dishonest means, which should be more disreputable. Cultivate poverty like a garden herb, like sage. Do not trouble yourself much to get new things, whether clothes or friends. Turn the old; return to them. Things do not change; we change. Sell your clothes and keep your thoughts. God will see that you do not want society. If I were confined to a corner of a garret[16] all my days, like a spider, the world would be just as large to me while I had my thoughts about me. The philosopher said: "From an army of three divisions one can take away its general, and put it in disorder; from the man the most abject and vulgar one cannot take away his thought." Do not seek so anxiously to be developed, to subject yourself to many influences to be played on; it is all dissipation. Humility like darkness reveals the heavenly lights. The shadows of poverty and meanness gather around us, "and lo! creation widens to our view."[17] We are often reminded that if there were bestowed on us the wealth of Croesus,[18] our aims must still be the same, and our means essentially the same. Moreover, if you are restricted in your range by poverty, if you cannot buy books and

---

15. **almshouse** (OMZ hows) *n.* government-run home for people too poor to support themselves.
16. **garret** (GAR iht) *n.* attic.
17. **"and ... view"** from the sonnet "To Night" by the British poet Joseph Blanco White (1775–1841).
18. **Croesus** (KREE suhs) King of Lydia (d. 546 B.C.), believed to be the wealthiest person of his time.

NOTES

Mark familiar word parts or indicate another strategy you used that helped you determine meaning.

vital (VY tuhl) *adj.*

newspapers, for instance, you are but confined to the most significant and **vital** experiences; you are compelled to deal with the material which yields the most sugar and the most starch. It is life near the bone where it is sweetest. You are defended from being a trifler. No man loses ever on a lower level by magnanimity[19] on a higher. Superfluous wealth can buy superfluities only. Money is not required to buy one necessary of the soul. . . .

17   The life in us is like the water in the river. It may rise this year higher than man has ever known it, and flood the parched uplands; even this may be the eventful year, which will drown out all our muskrats. It was not always dry land where we dwell. I see far inland the banks which the stream anciently washed, before science began to record its freshets.[20] Everyone has heard the story which has gone the rounds of New England, of a strong and beautiful bug which came out of the dry leaf of an old table of apple-tree wood, which had stood in a farmer's kitchen for sixty years, first in Connecticut, and afterward in Massachusetts—from an egg deposited in the living tree many years earlier still, as appeared by counting the annual layers beyond it; which was heard gnawing out for several weeks, hatched perchance by the heat of an urn. Who does not feel his faith in a resurrection and immortality strengthened by hearing of this? Who knows what beautiful and winged life, whose egg has been buried for ages under many concentric layers of woodenness in the dead dry life of society, deposited at first in the alburnum[21] of the green and living tree, which has been gradually converted into the semblance of its well-seasoned tomb—heard perchance gnawing out now for years by the astonished family of man, as they sat round the festive board— may unexpectedly come forth from amidst society's most trivial and handselled furniture, to enjoy its perfect summer life at last!

18   I do not say that John or Jonathan[22] will realize all this; but such is the character of that morrow[23] which mere lapse of time can never make to dawn. The light which puts out our eyes is darkness to us. Only that day dawns to which we are awake. There is more day to dawn. The sun is but a morning star. ❧

---

19. **magnanimity** (mag nuh NIHM uh tee) *n.* generosity.
20. **freshets** (FREHSH its) *n.* river floods resulting from heavy rain or melted snow.
21. **alburnum** (al BUR nuhm) *n.* soft wood between the bark and the heartwood, where water is conducted.
22. **John or Jonathan** average person.
23. **morrow** *n.* literary term for "tomorrow;" archaic term for "morning."

from Civil Disobedience

Henry David Thoreau

BACKGROUND

The Mexican War was a conflict between Mexico and the United States that took place from 1846 to 1848. The war was caused by a dispute over the boundary between Texas and Mexico, as well as by Mexico's refusal to discuss selling California and New Mexico to the United States. Believing that President Polk had intentionally provoked the conflict before gaining congressional approval, Thoreau and many other Americans strongly objected to the war. In protest, Thoreau refused to pay his taxes and was forced to spend a night in jail. Afterward, he wrote "Civil Disobedience," urging people to resist governmental policies with which they disagree.

1   I heartily accept the motto, "That government is best which governs least";[1] and I should like to see it acted up to more rapidly and systematically. Carried out, it finally amounts to this, which also I believe: "That government is best which governs not at all"; and when men are prepared for it, that will be the kind of government which they will have. Government is at best but an expedient; but most governments are usually, and all governments are sometimes, inexpedient. The objections which have been brought against a standing army, and they are many and weighty, and deserve to prevail, may also at last be brought against a standing government.

NOTES

---

1. **"That ... least"** the motto of the *United States Magazine and Democratic Review*, a literary-political journal.

The standing army is only an arm of the standing government. The government itself, which is only the mode which the people have chosen to execute their will, is equally liable to be abused and perverted before the people can act through it. Witness the present Mexican war, the work of comparatively a few individuals using the standing government as their tool; for in the outset, the people would not have consented to this measure.

2   This American government—what is it but a tradition, though a recent one, endeavoring to transmit itself unimpaired to posterity, but each instant losing some of its integrity? It has not the vitality and force of a single living man; for a single man can bend it to his will. It is a sort of wooden gun to the people themselves; and, if ever they should use it in earnest as a real one against each other, it will surely split. But it is not the less necessary for this; for the people must have some complicated machinery or other, and hear its din, to satisfy that idea of government which they have. Governments show thus how successfully men can be imposed on, even impose on themselves, for their own advantage. It is excellent, we must all allow; yet this government never of itself furthered any enterprise, but by the alacrity with which it got out of its way. *It* does not keep the country free. *It* does not settle the West. *It* does not educate. The character inherent in the American people has done all that has been accomplished; and it would have done somewhat more, if the government had not sometimes got in its way. For government is an expedient by which men would fain[2] succeed in letting one another alone; and, as has been said, when it is most expedient, the governed are most let alone by it. Trade and commerce, if they were not made of India rubber,[3] would never manage to bounce over the obstacles which legislators are continually putting in their way; and, if one were to judge these men wholly by the effects of their actions, and not partly by their intentions, they would deserve to be classed and punished with those mischievous persons who put obstructions on the railroads.

3   But, to speak practically and as a citizen, unlike those who call themselves no government men, I ask for, not at once no government, but *at once* a better government. Let every man make known what kind of government would command his respect, and that will be one step toward obtaining it. . . . 🐚

---

2. **fain** *adv.* gladly.
3. **India rubber** form of crude rubber.

Comprehension Check

Complete the following items after you finish your first read. Review and clarify details with your group.

from WALDEN

1. What advice does Thoreau offer to his "fellows" about ownership of land or property?

2. What did Thoreau hope to discover by living in the woods?

3. What advice does Thoreau give to those living in poverty?

4. 🗒 **Notebook** Confirm your understanding of the text by writing a summary.

from CIVIL DISOBEDIENCE

1. What motto does Thoreau endorse at the beginning of this selection?

2. How does Thoreau define the best possible kind of government?

3. At the end of the text, what does Thoreau ask his readers to do?

4. 🗒 **Notebook** Confirm your understanding of the text by writing two sentences that summarize its key content.

- -

RESEARCH

Research to Clarify Choose at least one unfamiliar detail from one of the texts. Briefly research that detail. In what way does the information you learned shed light on an aspect of the text?

Research to Explore The excerpt from *Walden* may have sparked your curiosity to learn more. For example, you may want to know what Walden Pond is like today. Share what you discover with your group.

from WALDEN
from CIVIL DISOBEDIENCE

TIP

GROUP DISCUSSION

Be sure to follow rules for participating in group discussions, speaking in turn, and addressing each participant with respect. In a discussion, it is often unlikely that all group members will agree, but everyone deserves to be heard and to receive thoughtful consideration.

🔀 **WORD NETWORK**

Add words related to individualism from the texts to your Word Network.

:≡ **STANDARDS**

Reading Informational Text
• Cite strong and thorough textual evidence to support analysis of what the text says explicitly as well as inferences drawn from the text, including determining where the text leaves matters uncertain.
• Determine an author's point of view or purpose in a text in which the rhetoric is particularly effective, analyzing how style and content contribute to the power, persuasiveness, or beauty of the text.

Language
Identify and correctly use patterns of word changes that indicate different meanings or parts of speech.

Close Read the Text

With your group, revisit sections of the texts you marked during your first read. **Annotate** what you notice. What **questions** do you have? What can you **conclude?**

Analyze the Text

> **CITE TEXTUAL EVIDENCE**
> to support your answers.

📓 **Notebook** Complete the activities.

1. **Review and Clarify** With your group, reread paragraph 1 of the excerpt from *Walden*. Describe Thoreau's attitude toward home ownership. How does this outlook relate to his experience in the woods and to his overall view of how life should be lived?

2. **Present and Discuss** Now, work with your group to share the passages from the selections that you found especially important. Take turns presenting your passages. Discuss what you noticed in the selections, what questions you asked, and what conclusions you reached.

3. **Essential Question:** *What role does individualism play in American society?* What have these texts taught you about the relationship between the individual and society? Discuss with your group.

LANGUAGE DEVELOPMENT

Concept Vocabulary

sufficed	superfluous	vital

Why These Words? The concept vocabulary words from these texts are related. With your group, determine what the words have in common. How do these word choices enhance the impact of the texts?

Practice

📓 **Notebook** Confirm your understanding of these words by answering these questions. Use the vocabulary word from each question in your answer.

1. If everything in someone's life *sufficed,* would he or she most likely be content? Explain.

2. How would refusing to purchase *superfluous* items help your budget?

3. In the modern world, is technology *vital* to survival?

Word Study

📓 **Notebook Latin Prefix: *super-*** The Latin prefix *super-* means "above" or "over." Explain how the meaning of the prefix contributes to the meaning of *superfluous*. Then, find four other words that have this same prefix. Record the words and their meanings.

Analyze Craft and Structure

Author's Point of View An author's **point of view** is the perspective the writer adopts toward a situation or set of issues. In both *Walden* and "Civil Disobedience," Thoreau presents arguments that build on **philosophical assumptions,** or principles and beliefs that he takes for granted and that form a foundation for his ideas. Some assumptions are **explicit,** or directly stated. Other assumptions, however, are **implicit,** or not stated outright.

For example, a writer might hold certain beliefs about human nature, divine or spiritual matters, the nature of society, or another aspect of life. A writer may not explain these fundamental beliefs; nevertheless, they may be the basis for his or her ideas. In order to identify and consider these implicit assumptions, the reader must tease them out from details the writer does supply. Then, the reader must consider how these assumptions contribute to the author's overall position or ideas.

Practice

CITE TEXTUAL EVIDENCE to support your answers.

📓 **Notebook** Respond to these questions.

1. (a) What implicit assumption does Thoreau rely on when he discusses the relationship of money and the soul in *Walden*? (b) Do you believe Thoreau's assumption is valid? Why or why not?

2. (a) Identify the explicit assumption with which Thoreau begins his discussion in "Civil Disobedience." (b) What counterarguments, or opposing views, to this assumption might someone present?

3. (a) In *Walden,* how does Thoreau support his point that "It makes but little difference whether you are committed to a farm or the county jail"? (b) What implicit assumption does this statement suggest? (c) Do you agree? Explain.

4. Record Thoreau's implicit assumptions on a variety of issues as they are revealed in *Walden*. List specific details that allow you to identify each assumption.

ISSUE	IMPLICIT ASSUMPTION	DETAILS
Desire for freedom		
Simplicity of life		
Nonconformity		

Conventions and Style

Author's Style A writer's **style** is the unique manner in which he or she puts thoughts into words. In his philosophical writing, Thoreau uses a broad range of devices to establish a **conversational style,** as if he were talking informally to a friend.

- Typically, Thoreau's **diction,** or **word choice,** is simple and direct: *I went to the woods because I wished to live deliberately . . .*

- Thoreau often combines plain statements with **figures of speech**— imaginative comparisons that engage the thinking of his readers: *In the midst of this chopping sea of civilized life, such are the clouds and storms and quicksands . . .*

- By using **analogy,** or extended comparison, Thoreau highlights related ideas or explains the unfamiliar in terms of the familiar: *Our life is like a German Confederacy, made up of petty states, with its boundary forever fluctuating . . .*

Other devices that contribute to Thoreau's conversational style include **direct address of the reader** (*Let your affairs be as two or three*), **brief anecdotes** (short, illustrative stories, like that of the Hollowell Place), and **pithy statements** (wise and concise statements—*we do not ride upon the railroad; it rides upon us*).

Read It

1. Work individually. In a sentence or two, explain how each underlined part of this passage from *Walden* contributes to Thoreau's conversational style and to his overall point. Then, meet with your group to compare your responses.

> Moreover, <u>if you are restricted in your range by poverty,</u> if you cannot buy books and newspapers, for instance, you are but confined to the most significant and vital experiences; you are compelled to deal with the material <u>which yields the most sugar and the most starch.</u> <u>It is life near the bone where it is sweetest.</u>

2. **Connect to Style** Reread paragraph 13 of the excerpt from *Walden*. Mark and then label two words or phrases that contribute to Thoreau's conversational style.

3. 📓 **Notebook** In a sentence or two, explain why a conversational style might be especially useful for a philosophical writer such as Thoreau.

Write It

📓 **Notebook** Write a paragraph-long review of the excerpt from "Civil Disobedience." Create a conversational style in your review by using some of the techniques discussed above.

STANDARDS

Reading Informational Text
Determine an author's point of view or purpose in a text in which the rhetoric is particularly effective, analyzing how style and content contribute to the power, persuasiveness, or beauty of the text.

Speaking and Listening

Assignment

With your group, hold a **discussion** in which you respond to these excerpts from Thoreau's philosophical writings. Choose from the following options:

☐ Brainstorm for a **list** of current or past events in which citizens have followed Thoreau's advice in "Civil Disobedience" to stand up and *make known what kind of government would command [their] respect.* Explain your reasons for including each example.

☐ Prepare a **response** to this statement adapted from Thoreau: *It is always better to march to the beat of one's own drummer.* Take turns offering and supporting your opinions.

☐ Formulate a **prosecution** or a **defense** of Thoreau's decision to withhold payment of his taxes. Marshal evidence and reasons to support your perspective, making sure that you deal directly with Thoreau's rationale for civil disobedience.

Finding Evidence Most of the evidence you will use during this discussion should come from Thoreau's writings. However, you may need additional information to have a lively conversation. This decision will depend on the topic you have chosen to discuss. For example, you may need to conduct some research about American or world history, or U.S. tax laws.

Holding the Discussion Make sure that everyone has a chance to speak and to express opinions that are supported with evidence from the text or from related research. If questions emerge from your discussion, decide together how you will locate the answers.

Considering All Responses Philosophical ideas can generate a wide variety of responses—and that can make a discussion exciting. Be open to the idea that many interpretations can be valid.

Asking Questions Get in the habit of asking questions to clarify your understanding of another reader's ideas. You can also use questions to call attention to areas of confusion, debatable points, or errors. In addition, offer elaboration on the points that others make by providing examples. To move a discussion forward, summarize and evaluate tentative conclusions reached by the group members.

Notes:

✎ EVIDENCE LOG

Before moving on to a new selection, go to your Evidence Log and record what you learned from the excerpts from *Walden* and "Civil Disobedience."

▤ STANDARDS

Speaking and Listening
• Work with peers to promote civil and democratic discussions and decision-making, set clear goals and deadlines, and establish individual roles as needed.
• Propel conversations by posing and responding to questions that probe reasoning and evidence; ensure a hearing for a full range of positions on a topic or issue; clarify, verify, or challenge ideas and conclusions; and promote divergent and creative perspectives.
• Respond thoughtfully to diverse perspectives; synthesize comments, claims, and evidence made on all sides of an issue; resolve contradictions when possible; and determine what additional information or research is required to deepen the investigation or complete the task.

About Technical Drawings

Some public documents include **technical drawings,** which are scale diagrams that show how something is constructed or how it functions. Individual inventors often create technical drawings to explain their innovations to a wider audience. Multiple views, including close-up details of key parts, are usually required to fully illustrate a new invention. When applying for a **patent**—the exclusive right to sell a product—inventors include technical drawings that show each important part in detail.

Innovators and Their Inventions

Media Vocabulary

These words will be useful to you as you analyze, discuss, and write about visual public documents and the text features that they contain.

Specifications: section of a patent application in which the inventor fully describes the invention	• Specifications include both verbal descriptions and detailed diagrams that illustrate the invention's parts and functions. • Patent specifications come before the claims, in which the applicant defines the scope of protection being requested (such as the right to prevent others from selling the invention).
Cross-section: view of a three-dimensional object that shows the interior as if a cut has been made across the object	• A cross-section shows the parts inside a solid shape, revealing details that are not visible from the outside. • Labels or callouts may identify parts revealed within. • Details are shown using an exact scale, or ratio that compares the size of the illustration with the actual size of the invention.
Figure: one of a set of drawings or illustrations	• Figures are usually given consecutive numbers or letters so they can be referred to in accompanying text. • The term is often abbreviated as *fig.*

First Review MEDIA: PUBLIC DOCUMENT

Apply these strategies as you conduct your first review. You will have an opportunity to complete a close review after your first review.

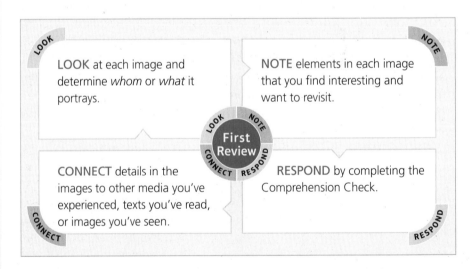

LOOK at each image and determine *whom* or *what* it portrays.

NOTE elements in each image that you find interesting and want to revisit.

CONNECT details in the images to other media you've experienced, texts you've read, or images you've seen.

RESPOND by completing the Comprehension Check.

Innovators and Their Inventions

BACKGROUND

A patent documents the government's recognition that a person has invented something. Nobody else is allowed to make, use, or sell that invention without the inventor's permission until the patent expires. The federal government has been issuing patents, including those for the inventions discussed here, since George Washington signed the Patent Act of 1790.

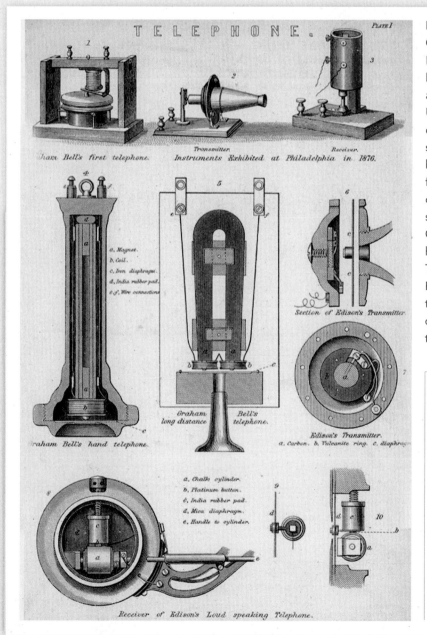

IMAGE 1: Diagram of Telephone Components Alexander Graham Bell was born in Scotland, but he did his most famous work as a scientist and inventor in the United States. After many years of experimenting with sound—specifically, how sound could be transmitted electrically—Bell filed a patent for the telephone on February 14, 1876. On the same day, another inventor, Elisha Gray, also submitted a claim that he had invented the telephone. The controversy was settled when Bell received the patent for the telephone, now considered one of the most valuable patents in the world.

NOTES

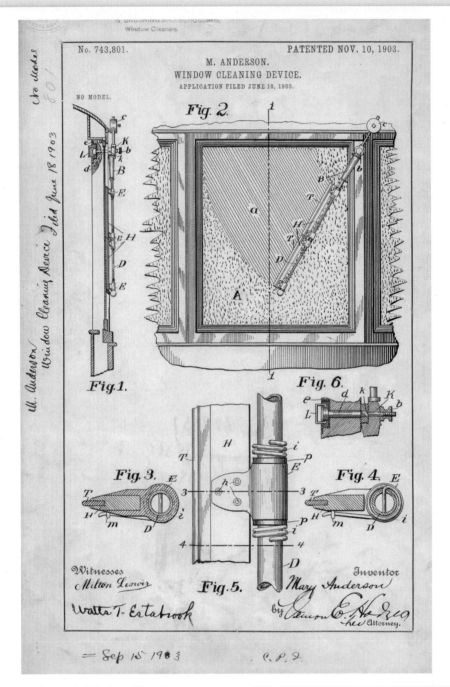

No. 743,801.

PATENTED NOV. 10, 1903.

M. ANDERSON.
WINDOW CLEANING DEVICE.
APPLICATION FILED JUNE 18, 1903.

NO MODEL.

Fig. 2.

Fig.1.

Fig. 6.

Fig. 3.

Fig. 4.

Fig.5.

Witnesses
Milton Lenoir

Walter T. Estabrook

Inventor
Mary Anderson

by
her Attorney.

IMAGE 2: Mary Anderson's Window-Cleaning Device Patent applications often include detailed images to clarify the design and use of the device in the application. This image is a diagram of the first windshield wiper, patented by Mary Anderson. It is operated by pulling a lever inside of the vehicle. Before her invention, drivers would reach out and wipe down windshields by hand— sometimes stopping the vehicle to do so, and sometimes doing so while driving.

NOTES

Comprehension Check

Complete the following items after you finish your first review. Review and clarify details with your group.

1. In the technical drawings of Bell's telephone, which components are labeled 2 and 3?

2. In Figure 4 of the telephone components, what do the labels lettered *a* to *e* name?

3. According to information included on the diagrams of the window-cleaning device, when did Anderson apply for this patent, and when was it awarded?

4. In Figure 2 of the diagrams for the window-cleaning device, what is part A?

- -

RESEARCH

Research to Clarify Choose at least one unfamiliar element in the technical drawings. Briefly research that element. In what way does the information you learned shed light on an aspect of the drawings or on the work of inventing a new technology?

Research to Explore These technical drawings might make you curious about the patent application process. Find out what a patent application includes, where it is filed, who determines whether the patent is granted, and how that decision is made. You may want to share what you discover with your group.

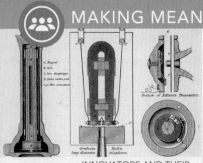

INNOVATORS AND THEIR
INVENTIONS

Close Review

With your group, revisit the technical drawings and your first-review notes. Write down any new observations that seem important. What **questions** do you have? What can you **conclude?**

- -

Analyze the Media

CITE TEXTUAL EVIDENCE
to support your answers.

📓 **Notebook** Complete the activities.

1. **Present and Discuss** Choose the drawing you find more interesting or informative. Share your choice with the group and discuss why you chose it. Explain what you noticed in the drawing, what questions it raised for you, and what conclusions you reached about it.

2. **Review and Synthesize** With your group, review both technical drawings. How do they provide information about the inventions they illustrate? What do the drawings alone tell you about how these inventions work? What information might accompanying text provide that would help you understand each device's function?

3. **Essential Question:** *What role does individualism play in American society?* What have these public documents taught you about the role that innovative individuals play in society? Discuss with your group.

TIP

GROUP DISCUSSION
Begin your discussion of the technical drawings by reviewing all titles, captions, and labels as a group. Refer to the labels to make sure each group member is looking at the same image or part during the discussion.

LANGUAGE DEVELOPMENT

Media Vocabulary

specifications	cross-section	figure

Use these words as you discuss and write about the technical drawings.

1. Why is it useful to have more than one technical drawing of an early telephone to understand the parts of this invention, as well as its origins?

2. In addition to the drawings shown here, what information did Anderson probably include in her patent application for a window-cleaning device? Explain.

3. Both drawings include multiple views of the invention. Why are multiple views needed to show how something works?

▤ STANDARDS

Speaking and Listening
Present information, findings, and supporting evidence, conveying a clear and distinct perspective, such that listeners can follow the line of reasoning, alternative or opposing perspectives are addressed, and the organization, development, substance, and style are appropriate to purpose, audience, and a range of formal and informal tasks.

Speaking and Listening

Assignment

Consider this question with your group: How have each of the two inventions pictured in these public documents affected people's lives in different ways? Then, discuss other inventions that have changed people's lives. Consider surprising inventions, such as sticky notes, as well as more obvious ones. Decide which invention of all the ones you discussed has had the greatest impact on society. Then, write a one-minute **speech** in which you state and support your position. Deliver your speech to the class.

Choose a Position Begin to answer the question by considering as many impacts as possible. Ask yourselves how life would be different without each invention. Collect your thoughts in a chart.

	INVENTION	INVENTION	INVENTION
Use and function			
Importance			

Plan Your Argument After you have determined your position, plan your speech. Begin with a strong statement of your claim about the impact of the invention you chose, and then provide support. Aim to include at least three ideas that support your position. Finally, end your speech with a conclusion that restates your claim.

PLAN YOUR ARGUMENT
Claim:
Support: 1.   2.   3.
Conclusion:

Present Your Speech and Debate Deliver your speeches, and have your classmates score them. After the initial speeches, allow time for discussion, in which students compare their positions and make some generalizations about the impact of technical innovation on society.

 EVIDENCE LOG

Before moving on to a new selection, go to your Evidence Log and record what you learned from "Innovators and Their Inventions."

The Love Song of J. Alfred Prufrock

Concept Vocabulary

As you perform your first read of "The Love Song of J. Alfred Prufrock," you will encounter these words.

tedious	indecisions	digress

Context Clues Use **context clues** to find the meanings of unfamiliar words in a text. Context clues include the words, punctuation, and images that surround an unknown word.

> **Example:** "the evening, sleeps so peacefully! / Smoothed by long, fingers. / Asleep . . . tired . . . or it *malingers,* / Stretched on the floor, here beside you and me."
>
> **Context clues:** The word *malingers* appears to be related to "asleep," "tired," and "stretched on the floor," but the word *or* suggests that it's not quite sleep.
>
> **Possible meaning:** *Malinger*s may mean "lazes about, sleepily."

Apply your knowledge of context clues and other vocabulary strategies to determine the meanings of unfamiliar words you encounter during your first read.

First Read POETRY

Apply these strategies as you conduct your first read. You will have an opportunity to complete a close read after your first read.

NOTICE *who* or *what* is "speaking" the poem and whether the poem tells a story or describes a single moment.

ANNOTATE by marking vocabulary and key passages you want to revisit.

CONNECT ideas within the selection to what you already know and what you have already read.

RESPOND by completing the Comprehension Check.

First Read

NOTICE ANNOTATE CONNECT RESPOND

STANDARDS

Reading Literature
By the end of grade 11, read and comprehend literature, including stories, dramas, and poems, in the grades 11–CCR text complexity band proficiently, with scaffolding as needed at the high end of the range.

Language
Use context as a clue to the meaning of a word or phrase.

About the Poet
T. S. Eliot

T. S. Eliot (1888–1965) was born into a wealthy family in St. Louis and grew up in an environment that promoted intellectual development. He attended Harvard University, where he published a number of poems in the school's literary magazine. In 1910, the year Eliot received his master's degree in philosophy, he completed "The Love Song of J. Alfred Prufrock."

A Literary Sensation Just before the outbreak of World War I, Eliot moved to England, where he became acquainted with Ezra Pound, another young American poet. Pound convinced Harriet Monroe, the editor of *Poetry* magazine, to publish "Prufrock." Shortly thereafter, Eliot published a collection entitled *Prufrock and Other Observations* (1917). Eliot's use of innovative poetic techniques and his focus on the despair of modern urban life caused a sensation in the literary world.

Facing a New World Eliot made his literary mark against the backdrop of a rapidly changing society. Disillusioned with the ideologies that produced the devastation of World War I, many people were searching for new ideas and values. Eliot was among a group of such writers and visual artists who called themselves Modernists. Modernist poets believed that poetry had to reflect the genuine, fractured experience of life in the twentieth century, not a romanticized idea of what life was once like.

In 1922, Eliot published *The Waste Land*, a profound critique of the spiritual barrenness of the modern world. Filled with allusions to classics of world literature and to Eastern culture and religion, it was widely read and greatly affected writers and critics.

A Return to Tradition In his search for something beyond the "waste land" of modern society, Eliot became a member of the Church of England in 1927. He began to explore religious themes in poems such as "Ash Wednesday" (1930) and *Four Quartets* (1943)— works that suggest a belief that religion can heal the wounds inflicted by society. In later years, Eliot wrote several plays and a sizable body of literary criticism. In 1948, he received the Nobel Prize in Literature.

Background

The Love Song of J. Alfred Prufrock

In this poem, J. Alfred Prufrock, a stuffy and inhibited man who is pained by his own passivity, invites the reader, or some unnamed visitor, to join him on a journey. Where Prufrock is and where he is going are open to debate. The most important part of this journey takes place within the inner landscape of Prufrock's emotions, memory, and intellect as he meditates on his life.

The **Love Song**
of **J. Alfred Prufrock**

T. S. Eliot

S'io credessi che mia risposta fosse
a persona che mai tornasse al mondo,
questa fiamma staria senza più scosse.
Ma per ciò che giammai di questo fondo
non tornò vivo alcun, s'i'odo il vero,
senza tema d'infamia ti rispondo.[1]

Let us go then, you and I,
When the evening is spread out against the sky
Like a patient etherized[2] upon a table;
Let us go, through certain half-deserted streets,
5 The muttering retreats
Of restless nights in one-night cheap hotels
And sawdust restaurants with oyster-shells:
Streets that follow like a **tedious** argument
Of insidious intent
10 To lead you to an overwhelming question . . .
Oh, do not ask, "What is it?"
Let us go and make our visit.

In the room the women come and go
Talking of Michelangelo.[3]

15 The yellow fog that rubs its back upon the window-panes,
The yellow smoke that rubs its muzzle on the window-panes,
Licked its tongue into the corners of the evening,
Lingered upon the pools that stand in drains,
Let fall upon its back the soot that falls from chimneys,
20 Slipped by the terrace, made a sudden leap,
And seeing that it was a soft October night,
Curled once about the house, and fell asleep.

And indeed there will be time[4]
For the yellow smoke that slides along the street
25 Rubbing its back upon the window-panes;
There will be time, there will be time
To prepare a face to meet the faces that you meet;
There will be time to murder and create,
And time for all the works and days[5] of hands

Mark context clues or indicate another strategy you used that helped you determine meaning.

tedious (TEE dee uhs) *adj.*

MEANING:

---

1. ***S'io credessi . . . ti rispondo*** This epigraph is a passage from Dante's *Inferno,* in which one of the damned, upon being asked to tell his story, says, "If I believed my answer were being given to someone who could ever return to the world, this flame [his voice] would shake no more. But since no one has ever returned alive from this depth, if what I hear is true, I will answer you without fear of disgrace."
2. **etherized** (EE thuh ryzd) *adj.* anesthetized with ether.
3. **Michelangelo** (my kuhl AN juh loh) famous Italian artist and sculptor (1475–1564).
4. **there will be time** These words echo the speaker's plea in the English poet Andrew Marvell's "To His Coy Mistress": "Had we but world enough and time . . . "
5. **works and days** The ancient Greek poet Hesiod wrote a poem about farming called "Works and Days."

30 That lift and drop a question on your plate;
Time for you and time for me,
And time yet for a hundred **indecisions**,
And for a hundred visions and revisions.
Before the taking of a toast and tea.

35 In the room the women come and go
Talking of Michelangelo.

And indeed there will be time
To wonder, "Do I dare?" and, "Do I dare?"
Time to turn back and descend the stair,
40 With a bald spot in the middle of my hair—
(They will say: "How his hair is growing thin!")
My morning coat, my collar mounting firmly to the chin,
My necktie rich and modest, but asserted by a simple pin—
(They will say: "But how his arms and legs are thin!")
45 Do I dare
Disturb the universe?
In a minute there is time
For decisions and revisions which a minute will reverse.

For I have known them all already, known them all—
50 Have known the evenings, mornings, afternoons,
I have measured out my life with coffee spoons;
I know the voices dying with a dying fall
Beneath the music from a farther room.
        So how should I presume?

55 And I have known the eyes already, known them all—
The eyes that fix you in a formulated phrase,
And when I am formulated, sprawling on a pin,
When I am pinned and wriggling on the wall,
Then how should I begin
60 To spit out all the butt-ends of my days and ways?
        And how should I presume?

And I have known the arms already, known them all—
Arms that are braceleted and white and bare
(But in the lamplight, downed with light brown hair!)
65 Is it perfume from a dress
That makes me so **digress**?
Arms that lie along a table, or wrap about a shawl.
        And should I then presume?
        And how should I begin?

⌘ ⌘ ⌘

70 Shall I say, I have gone at dusk through narrow streets
    And watched the smoke that rises from the pipes
    Of lonely men in shirt-sleeves, leaning out of windows? . . .

    I should have been a pair of ragged claws
    Scuttling across the floors of silent seas.[6]

⌘ ⌘ ⌘

75 And the afternoon, the evening, sleeps so peacefully!
    Smoothed by long fingers,
    Asleep . . . tired . . . or it malingers,
    Stretched on the floor, here beside you and me.
    Should I, after tea and cakes and ices,
80 Have the strength to force the moment to its crisis?
    But though I have wept and fasted, wept and prayed,
    Though I have seen my head (grown slightly bald) brought in
        upon a platter,[7]
    I am no prophet—and here's no great matter;
    I have seen the moment of my greatness flicker,
85 And I have seen the eternal Footman[8] hold my coat, and snicker.
    And in short, I was afraid.

    And would it have been worth it, after all,
    After the cups, the marmalade, the tea,
    Among the porcelain, among some talk of you and me,
90 Would it have been worth while,
    To have bitten off the matter with a smile,
    To have squeezed the universe into a ball
    To roll it towards some overwhelming question.
    To say: "I am Lazarus,[9] come from the dead,
95 Come back to tell you all. I shall tell you all"—
    If one, settling a pillow by her head,
        Should say: "That is not what I meant at all.
        That is not it, at all."

    And would it have been worth it, after all,
100 Would it have been worth while,
    After the sunsets and the dooryards and the sprinkled streets,
    After the novels, after the teacups, after the skirts that trail
        along the floor—
    And this, and so much more?—

---

6. **I should . . . seas** In Shakespeare's *Hamlet,* the hero, Hamlet, mocks the aging Lord
   Chamberlain, Polonius, saying, "You yourself, sir, should be old as I am, if like a crab you
   could go backward" (II. ii. 205–206).
7. **head . . . platter** a reference to the prophet John the Baptist, whose head was delivered
   on a platter to Salome as a reward for her dancing (Matthew 14:1–11).
8. **eternal Footman** death.
9. **Lazarus** (LAZ uh ruhs) Lazarus is resurrected from the dead by Jesus in John 11:1–44.

It is impossible to say just what I mean!
105 But as if a magic lantern[10] threw the nerves in patterns
    on a screen:
Would it have been worth while
If one, settling a pillow or throwing off a shawl,
And turning toward the window, should say:
    "That is not it at all,
110 That is not what I meant, at all."

❁ ❁ ❁

No! I am not Prince Hamlet, nor was meant to be;
Am an attendant lord, one that will do
To swell a progress,[11] start a scene or two,
Advise the prince; no doubt, an easy tool,
115 Deferential, glad to be of use,
Politic, cautious, and meticulous;
Full of high sentence,[12] but a bit obtuse;
At times, indeed, almost ridiculous—
Almost, at times, the Fool.

120 I grow old . . . I grow old . . .
I shall wear the bottoms of my trousers rolled.

Shall I part my hair behind? Do I dare to eat a peach?
I shall wear white flannel trousers, and walk upon the beach.
I have heard the mermaids singing, each to each.

125 I do not think that they will sing to me.

I have seen them riding seaward on the waves
Combing the white hair of the waves blown back
When the wind blows the water white and black.

We have lingered in the chambers of the sea
130 By sea-girls wreathed with seaweed red and brown
Till human voices wake us, and we drown.

---

10. **magic lantern** early device used to project images on a screen.
11. **To swell a progress** to add to the number of people in a parade or scene from a play.
12. **Full of high sentence** speaking in a very ornate manner, often offering advice.

Comprehension Check

Complete the following items after you finish your first read. Review and clarify details with your group.

1. At what time of day are the opening lines of the poem set?

2. In the opening stanza, Prufrock invites someone to go with him. Describe the place he plans to visit.

3. What atmospheric condition does Prufrock describe in lines 15–25?

4. Name three questions that Prufrock asks himself.

5. Whom does Prufrock say he has heard singing "each to each"?

6. 🗐 **Notebook** Confirm your understanding by drawing an illustration of one or more key moments from the poem.

- -

RESEARCH

Research to Clarify Choose at least one unfamiliar detail from the text. Briefly research that detail. In what way does the information you learned shed light on an aspect of the poem?

Research to Explore Find out more about Modernism, the artistic movement embraced by Eliot and other early-twentieth-century writers and artists. Find out how this movement broke with the past—and how the work of its pioneers was received at the time.

THE LOVE SONG OF
J. ALFRED PRUFROCK

TIP

GROUP DISCUSSION

When discussing poetry, begin by reading a passage for sense. Follow the sentence structure and identify the subject and verb, if necessary. After your group understands the basic meaning, continue your analysis by looking at the poetic techniques, such as rhythm and rhyme, imagery, and figurative language.

⬡ WORD NETWORK

Add words related to individualism from the text to your Word Network.

☰ STANDARDS

Reading Literature
• Analyze how an author's choices concerning how to structure specific parts of a text contribute to its overall structure and meaning as well as its aesthetic impact.
• Analyze a case in which grasping point of view requires distinguishing what is directly stated in a text from what is really meant.

Language
Identify and correctly use patterns of word changes that indicate different meanings or parts of speech.

Close Read the Text

With your group, revisit sections of the text you marked during your first read. **Annotate** details that you notice. What **questions** do you have? What can you **conclude**?

Analyze the Text

CITE TEXTUAL EVIDENCE
to support your answers.

Complete the activities.

1. **Review and Clarify** With your group, reread lines 1–12 of the poem. The speaker of the poem, J. Alfred Prufrock, invites someone to join him on a journey. What is unusual about his invitation? Is it likely to be accepted? Why or why not?

2. **Present and Discuss** Now, work with your group to share the passages from the poem that you found especially important. Take turns presenting your passages. Discuss what you noticed in the selection, what questions you asked, and what conclusions you reached.

3. **Essential Question:** *What role does individualism play in American society?* What has this poem taught you about the individual and society? Discuss with your group.

LANGUAGE DEVELOPMENT

Concept Vocabulary

tedious	indecisions	digress

Why These Words? The three concept vocabulary words from the text are related. With your group, discuss the words and determine what they have in common. How do these word choices enhance the impact of the poem?

Practice

📓 **Notebook** Confirm your understanding of the concept vocabulary words by answering these questions. Use the vocabulary word in your answer.

1. Would you like to have a *tedious* conversation? Explain.

2. How can *indecisions* affect someone's efficiency?

3. What are some signs that a speaker is beginning to *digress*?

Word Study

Latin Prefix: *di- / dis-* The Latin prefix *di-* or *dis-* means "not" or "away." This prefix (not to be confused with the Greek prefix *di-*, meaning "two") occurs in many common English words, as well as in some mathematical and scientific terms.

1. Write the meaning of the mathematical term *diverge*.

2. Write the meaning of the scientific term *dilate*.

Use a dictionary to confirm your definitions for both words.

Analyze Craft and Structure

Poetic Structure A troubled J. Alfred Prufrock invites an unidentified companion, perhaps a part of his own personality, to walk with him as he considers how life and love are passing him by. His so-called love song is a **dramatic monologue,** a poem or speech in which a character addresses a silent listener. Images, dialogue, and other details reveal Prufrock's inner conflicts as he continues through his evening.

Prufrock is the **speaker,** or voice of the poem. Details reflect his **point of view,** the perspective or vantage point from which the monologue is told. To understand the speaker's point of view, consider details that describe the following elements:

- *Physical Traits:* What words does Prufrock use to describe his own appearance? How do others perceive him—or how does Prufrock feel he is perceived?

- *Emotional Traits:* What is Prufrock's overall mood? Which details reveal that mood?

- *Verbal Traits:* What is the speaker's unique way of talking? When Prufrock repeats himself, what kinds of things does he say? How does this reflect his values or preoccupations?

Practice

CITE TEXTUAL EVIDENCE
to support your answers.

1. (a) Work together to complete the chart. Identify details that reveal Prufrock's personal qualities. (b) What do these details suggest about Prufrock's view of himself and life as a whole?

PHYSICAL TRAITS	EMOTIONAL TRAITS	VERBAL TRAITS

2. (a) How can the first line of the poem be interpreted to suggest that Prufrock sees himself as divided, both seeking and fearing action? (b) At what other points does he express a deeply conflicted sense of self?

3. (a) In lines 49–54, what image does Prufrock use to describe how he has "measured out" his life? (b) In your own words, explain how Prufrock has lived.

THE LOVE SONG OF
J. ALFRED PRUFROCK

Conventions and Style

Compound Nouns Eliot uses many compound nouns in "The Love Song of J. Alfred Prufrock," including some that he invented just for use in this poem. A **compound noun** is a noun that is made with two or more words. In a **closed compound,** there is no space between the words. In a **hyphenated compound,** a hyphen separates the words.

CLOSED COMPOUNDS	HYPHENATED COMPOUNDS
From "Prufrock":	**From "Prufrock":**
necktie	oyster-shells
afternoons	window-panes
lamplight	shirt-sleeves
Other examples:	**Other examples:**
basketball	brother-in-law
sunrise	house-builder
keyboard	six-year-old

Closed compounds are words that have been long accepted as single nouns. Hyphenated compounds often are newer forms, or words that are used less frequently.

Hyphens may be used to join words and avoid ambiguity. In some cases, hyphens are not required but are a matter of style. For example, Prufrock describes mermaids as "sea-girls." Eliot could have presented the phrase without a hyphen: "sea girls." By creating an original, hyphenated noun, Eliot may be suggesting Prufrock's skill with words, his need to categorize and classify, or his precise nature.

Read It

Mark the compound nouns in these sentences. Identify each one as closed or hyphenated.

1. Prufrock hears a conversation among women who seem to be partygoers.

2. He worries that he has spent his lifetime focused on trivial, unimportant matters.

3. The speaker's walk-through at nighttime seems to take place in isolation, without passers-by or companions other than the unnamed listener.

4. Prufrock's digressions might suggest daydreaming or woolgathering, but the precise way he presents his word-pictures makes that unlikely.

Write It

🖘 **Notebook** Write four sentences that include compound nouns. Include at least one compound noun that is not commonly used. Decide whether your new compound noun will be closed or hyphenated, and explain your reasoning.

:≡ STANDARDS

Speaking and Listening
Make strategic use of digital media in presentations to enhance understanding of findings, reasoning, and evidence and to add interest.

Language
• Demonstrate command of the conventions of standard English grammar and usage when writing or speaking.
• Observe hyphenation conventions.

Writing to Sources

Assignment

With your group, create a **digital presentation** that explains, amplifies, or extends key ideas about J. Alfred Prufrock's worldview. Choose from these options:

☐ a **slide show** that presents images reflecting phrases from the poem or your mental picture of Prufrock, accompanied by appropriate music

☐ an **oral recitation and discussion** in which readers recite important lines from the poem and then discuss how those lines reflect Prufrock's character and concerns

☐ a **filmed oral response** in which group members share their reactions to the poem by citing specific lines and explaining their meaning and effect

Project Plan Work with your group to plan your digital presentation. Use this chart to determine how you will integrate content and media elements, including audio and visual materials. Also, consider how you will organize your presentation to include a strong introduction, a complete body, and an effective conclusion. Choose transitions that will make the organization of your presentation clear.

EVIDENCE LOG

Before moving on to a new selection, go to your Evidence Log and record what you learned from "The Love Song of J. Alfred Prufrock."

PART	CONTENT		MEDIA	
	Ideas	Related lines from Eliot's poem	Visual	Audio
Introduction				
Transition				
Body				
Transition				
Conclusion				

About the Author

As a child, **Willa Cather** (1873–1947) moved from her birthplace in Virginia to the Nebraska frontier, where many of her neighbors were immigrant farmers. Cather went on to receive a college degree, work as an editor at a Pittsburgh newspaper, and become a full-time writer in New York City. Still, it was prairie life that inspired many of her best-known works, including *O! Pioneers, My Ántonia,* and *One of Ours,* which won the Pulitzer Prize in 1923.

A Wagner Matinée

Concept Vocabulary

As you perform your first read of "A Wagner Matinée," you will encounter these words.

overture	motifs	prelude

Familiar Word Parts When you come to an unfamiliar word in a text, see whether the word contains any familiar word parts you can use to determine the word's meaning. A familiar word part may be a prefix, a suffix, a base word, or a root. Consider this example of the strategy:

Unfamiliar Word: *physiognomy*

Word in Context: The most striking thing about her *physiognomy,* however, was an incessant twitching of the mouth and eyebrows, . . .

Familiar Word Part: the root *-phys-,* which appears in words such as *physical* and *physician*

Conclusion: *Physiognomy* has a meaning related to a person's body. Context clues, such as "incessant twitching," support that assumption. You can then verify the meaning in a reliable dictionary.

Apply your knowledge of familiar word parts and other vocabulary strategies to determine the meanings of unfamiliar words you encounter during your first read.

First Read FICTION

Apply these strategies as you conduct your first read. You will have an opportunity to complete a close read after your first read.

NOTICE *whom* the story is about, *what* happens, *where* and *when* it happens, and *why* those involved react as they do.

ANNOTATE by marking vocabulary and key passages you want to revisit.

First Read

CONNECT ideas within the selection to what you already know and what you have already read.

RESPOND by completing the Comprehension Check and by writing a brief summary of the selection.

STANDARDS

Reading Literature
By the end of grade 11, read and comprehend literature, including stories, dramas, and poems, in the grades 11–CCR text complexity band proficiently, with scaffolding as needed at the high end of the range.

Language
Identify and correctly use patterns of word changes that indicate different meanings or parts of speech.

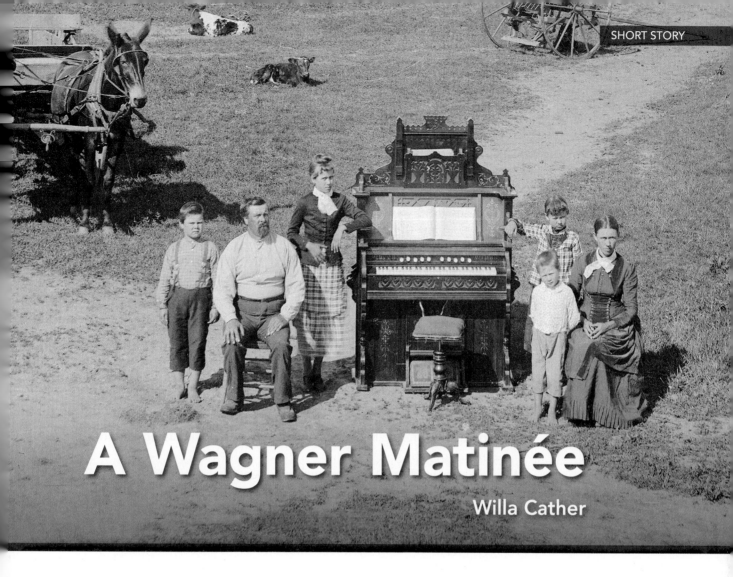

A Wagner Matinée

Willa Cather

SHORT STORY

BACKGROUND

Richard Wagner was one of the nineteenth century's great composers. His operas are characterized by adventurous harmonies and an innovative blend of music and drama. To many, Wagner's music represents the idea of high culture. In this story, Cather contrasts the stark realities of frontier life with life in a more cultured world.

NOTES

1　I received one morning a letter written in pale ink, on glassy, blue-lined notepaper, and bearing the postmark of a little Nebraska village. This communication, worn and rubbed, looking as though it had been carried for some days in a coat pocket that was none too clean, was from my Uncle Howard. It informed me that his wife had been left a small legacy by a bachelor relative who had recently died, and that it had become necessary for her to come to Boston to attend to the settling of the estate. He requested me to meet her at the station, and render her whatever services might prove necessary. On examining the date indicated as that of her arrival, I found it no later than tomorrow. He had characteristically delayed writing until, had I been away from home for a day, I must have missed the good woman altogether.

A Wagner Matinée **249**

Copyright © SAVVAS Learning Company LLC. All Rights Reserved.

2   The name of my Aunt Georgiana called up not alone her own figure, at once pathetic and grotesque, but opened before my feet a gulf of recollections so wide and deep that, as the letter dropped from my hand, I felt suddenly a stranger to all the present conditions of my existence, wholly ill at ease and out of place amid the surroundings of my study. I became, in short, the gangling farmer boy my aunt had known, scourged with chilblains and bashfulness, my hands cracked and raw from the corn husking. I felt the knuckles of my thumb tentatively, as though they were raw again. I sat again before her parlor organ, thumbing the scales with my stiff, red hands, while she beside me made canvas mittens for the huskers.

3   The next morning, after preparing my landlady somewhat, I set out for the station. When the train arrived I had some difficulty in finding my aunt. She was the last of the passengers to alight, and when I got her into the carriage she looked not unlike one of those charred, smoked bodies that firemen lift from the *débris* of a burned building. She had come all the way in a day coach; her linen duster[1] had become black with soot and her black bonnet gray with dust during the journey. When we arrived at my boardinghouse the landlady put her to bed at once, and I did not see her again until the next morning.

4   Whatever shock Mrs. Springer experienced at my aunt's appearance she considerately concealed. Myself, I saw my aunt's misshapen figure with that feeling of awe and respect with which we behold explorers who have left their ears and fingers north of Franz Josef Land,[2] or their health somewhere along the upper Congo.[3] My Aunt Georgiana had been a music teacher at the Boston Conservatory, somewhere back in the latter sixties. One summer, which she had spent in the little village in the Green Mountains[4] where her ancestors had dwelt for generations, she had kindled the callow[5] fancy of the most idle and shiftless of all the village lads, and had conceived for this Howard Carpenter one of those absurd and extravagant passions which a handsome country boy of twenty-one sometimes inspires in a plain, angular, spectacled woman of thirty. When she returned to her duties in Boston, Howard followed her; and the upshot of this inexplicable infatuation was that she eloped with him, eluding the reproaches of her family and the criticism of her friends by going with him to the Nebraska frontier. Carpenter, who of course had no money, took a homestead in Red Willow County,[6] fifty miles from the railroad. There they measured off their eighty acres by driving across the prairie in a wagon, to the wheel of which they had tied a red cotton handkerchief, and counting its revolutions. They built a dugout in the red hillside, one of those

---

1. **duster** *n.* short, loose smock worn while traveling to protect clothing from dust.
2. **Franz Josef Land** group of islands in the Arctic Ocean.
3. **Congo** river in central Africa.
4. **Green Mountains** mountains in Vermont.
5. **callow** (KAL oh) *adj.* immature; inexperienced.
6. **Red Willow County** county in southwestern Nebraska that borders on Kansas.

cave dwellings whose inmates usually reverted to the conditions of primitive savagery. Their water they got from the lagoons where the buffalo drank, and their slender stock of provisions was always at the mercy of bands of roving Indians. For thirty years my aunt had not been farther than fifty miles from the homestead.

5   But Mrs. Springer knew nothing of all this, and must have been considerably shocked at what was left of my kinswoman. Beneath the soiled linen duster, which on her arrival was the most conspicuous feature of her costume, she wore a black stuff dress whose ornamentation showed that she had surrendered herself unquestioningly into the hands of a country dressmaker. My poor aunt's figure, however, would have presented astonishing difficulties to any dressmaker. Her skin was yellow from constant exposure to a pitiless wind, and to the alkaline water which transforms the most transparent cuticle into a sort of flexible leather. She wore ill-fitting false teeth. The most striking thing about her physiognomy, however, was an incessant twitching of the mouth and eyebrows, a form of nervous disorder resulting from isolation and monotony, and from frequent physical suffering.

6   In my boyhood this affliction had possessed a sort of horrible fascination for me, of which I was secretly very much ashamed, for in those days I owed to this woman most of the good that ever came my way, and had a reverential affection for her. During the three winters when I was riding herd for my uncle, my aunt, after cooking three meals for half a dozen farmhands, and putting the six children to bed, would often stand until midnight at her ironing board, hearing me at the kitchen table beside her recite Latin declensions and conjugations, and gently shaking me when my drowsy head sank down over a page of irregular verbs. It was to her, at her ironing or mending, that I read my first Shakespeare; and her old textbook of mythology was the first that ever came into my empty hands. She taught me my scales and exercises, too, on the little parlor organ which her husband had bought her after fifteen years, during which she had not so much as seen any instrument except an accordion, that belonged to one of the Norwegian farmhands. She would sit beside me by the hour, darning and counting, while I struggled with the "Harmonious Blacksmith"; but she seldom talked to me about music, and I understood why. She was a pious woman; she had the consolation of religion; and to her at least her martyrdom was not wholly sordid. Once when I had been doggedly beating out some passages from an old score of "Euryanthe" I had found among her music books, she came up to me and, putting her hands over my eyes, gently drew my head back upon her shoulder, saying tremulously, "Don't love it so well, Clark, or it may be taken from you. Oh! dear boy, pray that whatever your sacrifice be it is not that."

7   When my aunt appeared on the morning after her arrival, she was still in a semi-somnambulant[7] state. She seemed not to realize that

---

7. **semi-somnambulant** (SEHM ee som NAM byuh luhnt) *adj.* resembling a sleepwalker.

she was in the city where she had spent her youth, the place longed for hungrily for half a lifetime. She had been so wretchedly trainsick throughout the journey that she had no recollection of anything but her discomfort, and, to all intents and purposes, there were but a few hours of nightmare between the farm in Red Willow County and my study on Newbury Street. I had planned a little pleasure for her that afternoon, to repay her for some of the glorious moments she had given me when we used to milk together in the straw-thatched cowshed, and she, because I was more than usually tired, or because her husband had spoken sharply to me, would tell me of the splendid performance of Meyerbeer's *Les Huguenots*[8] she had seen in Paris in her youth. At two o'clock the Boston Symphony Orchestra was to give a Wagner program, and I intended to take my aunt, though as I conversed with her I grew doubtful about her enjoyment of it. Indeed, for her own sake, I could only wish her taste for such things quite dead, and the long struggle mercifully ended at last. I suggested our visiting the Conservatory and the Common[9] before lunch, but she seemed altogether too timid to wish to venture out. She questioned me absently about various changes in the city, but she was chiefly concerned that she had forgotten to leave instructions about feeding half-skimmed milk to a certain weakling calf, "Old Maggie's calf, you know, Clark," she explained, evidently having forgotten how long I had been away. She was further troubled because she had neglected to tell her daughter about the freshly opened kit of mackerel in the cellar, that would spoil if it were not used directly.

8   I asked her whether she had ever heard any of the Wagnerian operas, and found that she had not, though she was perfectly familiar with their respective situations and had once possessed the piano score of *The Flying Dutchman*. I began to think it would have been best to get her back to Red Willow County without waking her, and regretted having suggested the concert.

9   From the time we entered the concert hall, however, she was a trifle less passive and inert, and seemed to begin to perceive her surroundings. I had felt some trepidation[10] lest one might become aware of the absurdities of her attire, or might experience some painful embarrassment at stepping suddenly into the world to which she had been dead for a quarter of a century. But again I found how superficially I had judged her. She sat looking about her with eyes as impersonal, almost as stony, as those with which the granite Ramses[11] in a museum watches the froth and fret that ebbs and flows about his pedestal, separated from it by the lonely stretch of centuries. I have seen this same aloofness in old miners who drift into the Brown Hotel at Denver, their pockets full of bullion, their linen soiled, their

---

8. **Les Huguenots** (lay oo guh NOH) opera written in 1836 by Giacomo Meyerbeer (1791–1864).
9. **Common** Boston Common, a small park in Boston.
10. **trepidation** (trehp uh DAY shuhn) *n.* fearful anxiety; apprehension.
11. **Ramses** (RAM seez) one of the eleven Egyptian kings by that name who ruled from c. 1292 B.C. to 1075 B.C.

haggard faces unshorn, and who stand in the thronged corridors as solitary as though they were still in a frozen camp on the Yukon, or in the yellow blaze of the Arizona desert, conscious that certain experiences have isolated them from their fellows by a gulf no haberdasher could conceal.

10   The audience was made up chiefly of women. One lost the contour of faces and figures, indeed any effect of line whatever, and there was only the color contrast of bodices past counting, the shimmer and shading of fabrics soft and firm, silky and sheer, resisting and yielding: red, mauve, pink, blue, lilac, purple, ecru, rose, yellow, cream, and white, all the colors that an impressionist finds in a sunlit landscape, with here and there the dead black shadow of a frock coat. My Aunt Georgiana regarded them as though they had been so many daubs of tube paint on a palette.

11   When the musicians came out and took their places, she gave a little stir of anticipation, and looked with quickening interest down over the rail at that invariable grouping; perhaps the first wholly familiar thing that had greeted her eye since she had left old Maggie and her weakling calf. I could feel how all those details sank into her soul, for I had not forgotten how they had sunk into mine when I came fresh from plowing forever and forever between green aisles of corn, where, as in a treadmill, one might walk from daybreak to dusk without perceiving a shadow of change in one's environment. I reminded myself of the impression made on me by the clean profiles of the musicians, the gloss of their linen; the dull black of their coats, the beloved shapes of the instruments, the patches of yellow light thrown by the green-shaded stand-lamps on the smooth, varnished bellies of the cellos and the bass viols in the rear, the restless, wind-tossed forest of fiddle necks and bows; I recalled how, in the first orchestra I had ever heard, those long bow strokes seemed to draw the soul out of me, as a conjuror's stick reels out paper ribbon from a hat.

> I could feel how
> all those details sank
> into her soul, . . .

12   The first number was the Tannhäuser **overture**. When the violins drew out the first strain of the Pilgrims' chorus, my Aunt Georgiana clutched my coat sleeve. Then it was that I first realized that for her this singing of basses and stinging frenzy of lighter strings broke a silence of thirty years, the inconceivable silence of the plains. With the battle between the two **motifs**, with the bitter frenzy of the Venusberg[12] theme and its ripping of strings, came to me an overwhelming sense of the waste and wear we are so powerless to combat. I saw again the tall, naked house on the prairie, black and grim as a wooden fortress; the black pond where I had learned to swim, the rain-gullied clay about the naked house; the four dwarf ash seedlings on which the dishcloths were always hung to dry before

Mark familiar word parts or indicate another strategy you used that helped you determine meaning.

overture (OH vuhr chuhr) *n.*

MEANING:

motifs (moh TEEFS) *n.*

MEANING:

12. **Venusberg** (VEE nuhs buhrg) legendary mountain in Germany where Venus, the Roman goddess of love, held court.

the kitchen door. The world there is the flat world of the ancients; to the east, a cornfield that stretched to daybreak; to the west, a corral that stretched to sunset; between, the sordid conquests of peace, more merciless than those of war.

13   The overture closed. My aunt released my coat sleeve, but she said nothing. She sat staring at the orchestra through a dullness of thirty years, through the films made, little by little, by each of the three hundred and sixty-five days in every one of them. What, I wondered, did she get from it? She had been a good pianist in her day, I knew, and her musical education had been broader than that of most music teachers of a quarter of a century ago. She had often told me of Mozart's operas and Meyerbeer's, and I could remember hearing her sing, years ago, certain melodies of Verdi. When I had fallen ill with a fever she used to sit by my cot in the evening, while the cool night wind blew in through the faded mosquito netting tacked over the window, and I lay watching a bright star that burned red above the cornfield, and sing "Home to our mountains, oh, let us return!" In a way fit to break the heart of a Vermont boy near dead of homesickness already.

14   I watched her closely through the **prelude** to *Tristan and Isolde*, trying vainly to conjecture what that warfare of motifs, that seething turmoil of strings and winds, might mean to her. Had this music any message for her? Did or did not a new planet swim into her ken? Wagner had been a sealed book to Americans before the sixties. Had she anything left with which to comprehend this glory that had flashed around the world since she had gone from it? I was in a fever of curiosity, but Aunt Georgiana sat silent upon her peak in Darien.[13] She preserved this utter immobility throughout the numbers from the *Flying Dutchman*, though her fingers worked mechanically upon her black dress, as though of themselves they were recalling the piano score they had once played. Poor old hands! They were stretched and pulled and twisted into mere tentacles to hold, and lift, and knead with; the palms unduly swollen, the fingers bent and knotted, on one of them a thin worn band that had once been a wedding ring. As I pressed and gently quieted one of those groping hands, I remembered, with quivering eyelids, their services for me in other days.

15   Soon after the tenor began the "Prize Song," I heard a quick-drawn breath, and turned to my aunt. Her eyes were closed, but the tears were glistening on her cheeks, and I think in a moment more they were in my eyes as well. It never really dies, then, the soul? It withers to the outward eye only, like that strange moss which can lie on a dusty shelf half a century and yet, if placed in water, grows green again. My aunt wept gently throughout the development and elaboration of the melody.

16   During the intermission before the second half of the concert, I questioned my aunt and found that the "Prize Song" was not new to her. Some years before there had drifted to the farm in Red Willow County a young German, a tramp cow puncher who had sung in the chorus at Bayreuth,[14] when he was a boy, along with the other peasant boys and girls. On a Sunday morning he used to sit on his blue gingham-sheeted bed in the hands' bedroom, which opened off the kitchen, cleaning the leather of his boots and saddle, and singing the "Prize Song," while my aunt went about her work in the kitchen. She had hovered about him until she had prevailed upon him to join the country church, though his sole fitness for this step, so far as I could gather, lay in his boyish face and his possession of this divine melody. Shortly afterward he had gone to town on the Fourth of July, lost his money at a faro[15] table, ridden a saddled Texas steer on a bet, and disappeared with a fractured collarbone.

17   "Well, we have come to better things than the old *Trovatore* at any rate. Aunt Georgie?" I queried, with well-meant jocularity.

---

13. **peak in Darien** mountain on the Isthmus of Panama; from "On First Looking Into Chapman's Homer," by English poet John Keats (1795–1821).
14. **Bayreuth** (by ROYT) city in Germany known for its annual festivals of Wagner's music.
15. **faro** (FAR oh) *n.* gambling game in which players bet on the cards to be turned up from the top of the dealer's deck.

Mark familiar word parts or indicate another strategy you used that helped you determine meaning.

prelude (PRAY lood) *n.*

MEANING:

18   Her lip quivered and she hastily put her handkerchief up to her mouth. From behind it she murmured, "And you've been hearing this ever since you left me, Clark?" Her question was the gentlest and saddest of reproaches.

19   "But do you get it, Aunt Georgiana, the astonishing structure of it all?" I persisted.

20   "Who could?" she said, absently; "why should one?"

21   The second half of the program consisted of four numbers from the *Ring*. This was followed by the forest music from *Siegfried*[16] and the program closed with Siegfried's funeral march. My aunt wept quietly, but almost continuously. I was perplexed as to what measure of musical comprehension was left to her, to her who had heard nothing for so many years but the singing of gospel hymns in Methodist services at the square frame schoolhouse on Section Thirteen. I was unable to gauge how much of it had been dissolved in soapsuds, or worked into bread, or milked into the bottom of a pail.

22   The deluge of sound poured on and on; I never knew what she found in the shining current of it; I never knew how far it bore her, or past what happy islands, or under what skies. From the trembling of her face I could well believe that the *Siegfried* march, at least, carried her out where the myriad graves are, out into the gray, burying grounds of the sea; or into some world of death vaster yet, where, from the beginning of the world, hope has lain down with hope, and dream with dream and, renouncing, slept.

23   The concert was over; the people filed out of the hall chattering and laughing, glad to relax and find the living level again, but my kinswoman made no effort to rise. I spoke gently to her. She burst into tears and sobbed pleadingly, "I don't want to go, Clark, I don't want to go!"

24   I understood. For her, just outside the door of the concert hall, lay the black pond with the cattle-tracked bluffs, the tall, unpainted house, naked as a tower, with weather-curled boards; the crookbacked ash seedlings where the dishcloths hung to dry, the gaunt, moulting turkeys picking up refuse about the kitchen door. ❧

---

16. ***Siegfried*** (SEEG freed) opera based on the adventures of Siegfried, a legendary hero in medieval German literature.

Comprehension Check

Complete the following items after you finish your first read. Review and clarify
details with your group.

1. Why does Aunt Georgiana travel to Boston?

2. When Clark was a boy, what subjects did he learn from Aunt Georgiana?

3. What is Clark's initial feeling about being in public with his aunt?

4. What does Aunt Georgiana do when the violins start playing the Pilgrims' chorus?

5. What does Aunt Georgiana do and say at the end of the concert?

6. 📝 **Notebook** Confirm your understanding of the story by writing a summary.

- -

RESEARCH

Research to Clarify Choose at least one unfamiliar detail from the text. Briefly research
that detail. In what way does the information you learned shed light on an aspect of
the story?

Research to Explore Conduct research on an aspect of the text you find interesting. For
example, you may want to learn more about the operas by Richard Wagner that Cather
mentions in the story. You may want to share what you discover with your group.

A WAGNER MATINÉE

Close Read the Text

With your group, revisit sections of the text you marked during your first read. **Annotate** details that you notice. What **questions** do you have? What can you **conclude?**

ANNOTATE · QUESTION · **Close Read** · CONCLUDE

Analyze the Text

CITE TEXTUAL EVIDENCE
to support your answers.

Complete the activities.

1. **Review and Clarify** With your group, reread paragraph 22. In what sense might Siegfried's funeral march be thought of as Georgiana's funeral march, too? Discuss with your group.

2. **Present and Discuss** Now, work with your group to share the passages from the selection that you found especially significant. Take turns presenting your passages. Discuss what you noticed in the selection, what questions you asked, and what conclusions you reached.

3. **Essential Question:** *What role does individualism play in American society?* What has this text taught you about individualism? Discuss with your group.

LANGUAGE DEVELOPMENT

Concept Vocabulary

overture	motifs	prelude

Why These Words? The three concept vocabulary words are related. With your group, discuss the words and determine which concept they share. How do these words contribute to your understanding of the text?

Practice

⬛ **Notebook** Confirm your understanding of the concept vocabulary words by using them in sentences. Consult reference materials, such as print or online dictionaries, to check the accuracy of your work.

Word Study

⬛ **Notebook Word Derivations** In "A Wagner Matinée," Clark refers to the *motifs* in an opera. The word *motif* descended from the Latin word *motivus*, meaning "moving; impelling."

1. Explain how the meaning of the Latin root word *motivus* contributes to the meaning of *motifs*.

2. Identify two other words that descend from *motivus*. Write their definitions.

🔗 WORD NETWORK

Add words related to individualism from the text to your Word Network.

☰ STANDARDS

Reading Literature
Analyze the impact of the author's choices regarding how to develop and relate elements of a story or drama.

Language
Consult general and specialized reference materials, both print and digital, to find the pronunciation of a word or determine or clarify its precise meaning, its part of speech, its etymology, or its standard usage.

Analyze Craft and Structure

Author's Choices: Character Development The term **characterization** refers to the art of revealing characters' personalities. In **direct characterization,** a writer simply states what a character is like, as in "She was a pious woman." In **indirect characterization,** a writer uses one or more of the following methods to provide clues about a character:

- describing a character's appearance and mannerisms
- presenting a character's words, thoughts, and actions
- showing ways in which other characters react to a character
- including comments that other characters make about a character

The point of view in which a story is told also affects how readers learn about characters. For example, this story uses **first-person point of view**— Clark, the narrator, is part of the action and uses the pronouns *I, me,* and *we.* As a result, readers' impressions filter through Clark's eyes.

Practice

1. Complete this chart independently to analyze Cather's use of Clark to characterize Aunt Georgiana indirectly. Record one example for each method. Then, share with your group.

METHOD OF CHARACTERIZATION	EXAMPLES FROM TEXT
physical description given by Clark	
other comments made by Clark	
Aunt Georgiana's words and actions	

📓 **Notebook** Answer the questions.

2. What do Clark's thoughts and feelings about his aunt indirectly reveal about his personality? Explain.

3. **(a)** How do Clark's feelings toward his aunt change during the story? **(b)** How do his feelings affect your response to Georgiana? **(c)** How do Clark's feelings about his aunt affect your attitude toward him as a character?

A WAGNER MATINÉE

Conventions and Style

Figurative Language Language that is used imaginatively rather than literally is called **figurative language.** Most fiction writers and poets—and many nonfiction writers, as well—use figurative language to convey ideas and emotions in a more nuanced and expressive way than plain statements would allow. Simile, metaphor, and hyperbole are three common types of figurative language.

- A **simile** is a comparison between two dissimilar things using an explicit word of comparison, such as *like, as,* or *resemble.* (Note that some writers may use the expression "not unlike," which actually means "like.") For example, Cather compares the soul to moss in this simile: "It withers to the outward eye only, <u>like</u> that strange moss which can lie on a dusty shelf half a century and yet, if placed in water, grows green again."
- A **metaphor** is a comparison that does not use an explicit word of comparison. Instead, the comparison is either implied or directly stated, often using a form of the verb *to be,* as in this example: "Wagner <u>had been</u> a sealed book to Americans before the sixties." Wagner is a composer, not a book. Cather's metaphor shows that no orchestra played Wagner's music before the 1860s.
- **Hyperbole** is exaggeration for effect. For example, Cather uses hyperbole when Clark comments, "there were but a few hours of nightmare between the farm in Red Willow County and my study on Newbury Street." Georgiana had traveled from Nebraska to Boston, so clearly more than "a few hours" had passed.

Read It

Work individually. Identify each example as a simile, a metaphor, or hyperbole, and explain your response. Then, share and discuss your responses with your group.

EXAMPLE	TYPE OF FIGURATIVE LANGUAGE	EXPLANATION
The deluge of sound poured on and on; I never knew what she found in the shining current of it . . .		
. . . when I came fresh from ploughing forever and forever between green aisles of corn . . .		
. . . she looked not unlike one of those charred, smoked bodies that firemen lift from the *débris* of a burned building		

Write It

🔵 **Notebook** Write a simile, a metaphor, and an example of hyperbole to describe Aunt Georgiana. Label each type of figurative language you use.

■ STANDARDS

Reading Literature
Determine the meaning of words and phrases as they are used in the text, including figurative and connotative meanings; analyze the impact of specific word choices on meaning and tone, including words with multiple meanings or language that is particularly fresh, engaging, or beautiful.

Language
Interpret figures of speech in context and analyze their role in the text.

Writing to Sources

Assignment

Prepare an informative **research report** that will help readers understand the historical context of Cather's story. Choose from the following project options:

☐ a **comparison and contrast** of rural Nebraska and Boston in the early 1900s, in which you include information about population density, living situations, transportation, jobs, clothing, and culture

☐ a **how-to essay** with a diagram that explains in detail how cornhuskers in the early twentieth century husked corn, including what parts of the process were difficult or laborious

☐ a **problem-solution letter** that gives helpful information to someone considering moving far away to a very different locale in the late 1800s, and that includes topics such as ways to maintain communication with friends and relatives, ways to make a living, and possible lifestyle changes

Project Plan As a group, discuss the types of information you will need to find. Then, develop a research plan that assigns responsibilities to individual group members and establishes deadlines for everyone to meet. Consult a variety of sources, including primary, secondary, print, and digital. Use the chart to organize your efforts.

TYPE OF INFORMATION	PRIMARY SOURCES	SECONDARY SOURCES	ASSIGNED TO	DEADLINE

Tying It Together Your research goal is to gather information that will allow you to create a complete picture of the topic. Once you have gathered information, review it as a group. Make sure that the sources are reliable and that all of the information is sufficient, credible, and relevant. Then, organize the writing tasks and complete your report.

EVIDENCE LOG

Before moving on to the next selection, go to your Evidence Log and record what you learned from "A Wagner Matinée."

STANDARDS

Writing
• Write informative/explanatory texts to examine and convey complex ideas, concepts, and information clearly and accurately through the effective selection, organization, and analysis of content.
• Conduct short as well as more sustained research projects to answer a question or solve a problem; narrow or broaden the inquiry when appropriate; synthesize multiple sources on the subject, demonstrating understanding of the subject under investigation.

SOURCES

• *from* NATURE

• *from* SELF-RELIANCE

• *from* WALDEN

• *from* CIVIL DISOBEDIENCE

• INNOVATORS AND THEIR INVENTIONS

• THE LOVE SONG OF J. ALFRED PRUFROCK

• A WAGNER MATINÉE

Present a Personal Narrative

Assignment

Plan and deliver a **group speech** that uses evidence from the texts in Small-Group Learning, as well as your own experiences and observations, to explore the challenges of nonconformity. Use the following prompt to guide your work:

> When is it difficult to march to the beat of a "different drummer" and stand on your own as an individual? What are the risks and rewards of nonconformity?

Draw on both Emerson's and Thoreau's ideas about nonconformity as starting points. Use precise language and quotations from the texts, as well as individual experiences and observations to support your ideas.

Plan With Your Group

Analyze the Texts Discuss the ways in which the texts you have read approach the topic of nonconformity. For example, consider Emerson's experiences in nature, the creativity of inventors who find new solutions to old problems, or Aunt Georgiana's bravery and independence in setting a different course for her life, regardless of the results. Use the chart to record your group's ideas about nonconformity as expressed in these selections.

TEXT	WHAT IT SHOWS ABOUT NONCONFORMITY
from Nature / *from* Self-Reliance	
from Walden / *from* Civil Disobedience	
Innovators and Their Inventions	
The Love Song of J. Alfred Prufrock	
A Wagner Matinée	

Connect Evidence to Experiences Combine textual evidence with your own real-life examples and experiences that support your group's views. Then, complete this statement:

Nonconformity is difficult when _____. Nonconformity

is risky because _____. It can be rewarding when

_____.

STANDARDS

Speaking and Listening
Work with peers to promote civil, democratic discussions and decision-making, set clear goals and deadlines, and establish individual roles as needed.

Organize Your Presentation Work individually to write a three-minute informal speech. Remember to include references to the texts, quotations from the texts, and your own experiences to support your ideas. Then, review each group member's speech. Decide how you will introduce the speeches, provide transitions between them, and conclude your presentation.

Rehearse With Your Group

Practice With Your Group Use this checklist to evaluate the effectiveness of your group's first run-through. Then, use your evaluation and these instructions to guide your revision.

CONTENT	PRESENTATION TECHNIQUES
☐ The speeches respond to the prompt thoroughly and coherently.	☐ Speakers enunciate clearly and use gestures and eye contact effectively.
☐ The speeches are presented in a logical sequence.	☐ Speakers vary pitch and volume to add interest to their words.
☐ Speakers draw on evidence from both the texts and individual experiences and observations.	☐ Speakers speak fluently, without hesitations or repetitions.

Fine-Tune the Content If a speech is too long, too short, off-topic, or incomplete, work together to revise it.

Brush Up on Your Presentation Techniques Although an informal speech may be relaxed and friendly in tone, it should not be sloppy. Make sure that your speech is expressive and articulate, both in its content and in your presentation. Your words should help your audience to understand your ideas and to appreciate the textual evidence and personal experiences you use to support them.

Present and Evaluate

As you present your series of speeches, consider your audience's response. Use questions such as these to evaluate the presentation:

- Does the speech offer clear reasoning and provide enough evidence to support the group's overall position on nonconformity?
- Does the speech bring together real-life experiences with examples from the texts in this section?

Once all the speeches have been delivered, you may wish to select two or three favorite parts. Be ready to explain what you like about each one.

STANDARDS

Speaking and Listening
- Evaluate a speaker's point of view, reasoning, and use of evidence and rhetoric, assessing the stance, premises, links among ideas, word choice, points of emphasis, and tone used.
- Present information, findings, and supporting evidence, conveying a clear and distinct perspective, such that listeners can follow the line of reasoning, alternative or opposing perspectives are addressed, and the organization, development, substance, and style are appropriate to purpose, audience, and a range of formal and informal tasks.

OVERVIEW: INDEPENDENT LEARNING

ESSENTIAL QUESTION:

What role does individualism play in American society?

In this section, you will complete your study of the role of individualism in American life by exploring an additional selection related to the topic. You'll then share what you learn with classmates. To choose a text, follow these steps.

Look Back Think about the selections you have already studied. Which aspects of individualism do you wish to explore further? Which time period interests you the most?

Look Ahead Preview the texts by reading the descriptions. Which one seems most interesting and appealing to you?

Look Inside Take a few minutes to scan the text you chose. Choose a different one if this text doesn't meet your needs.

Independent Learning Strategies

Throughout your life, in school, in your community, and in your career, you will need to rely on yourself to learn and work on your own. Review these strategies and the actions you can take to practice them during Independent Learning. Add ideas of your own for each category.

STRATEGY	ACTION PLAN
Create a schedule	• Understand your goals and deadlines. • Make a plan for what to do each day. •
Practice what you have learned	• Use first-read and close-read strategies to deepen your understanding. • After you read, evaluate the usefulness of the evidence to help you understand the topic. • Consider the quality and reliability of the source. •
Take notes	• Record important ideas and information. • Review your notes before preparing to share with a group. •

Copyright © SAVVAS Learning Company LLC. All Rights Reserved.

CONTENTS

Choose one selection. Selections are available online only.

NEWS ARTICLE

Sweet Land of . . . Conformity?

Claude Fischer

Are we Americans really as individualistic as we like to think?

LITERARY CRITICISM

Reckless Genius

Galway Kinnell

A great contemporary poet explains why the reclusive, private Emily Dickinson is one of America's most intelligent and fearless poets.

SHORT STORY

Hamadi

Naomi Shihab Nye

What makes Hamadi such a remarkable individual?

SHORT STORY

Young Goodman Brown

Nathaniel Hawthorne

A Puritan discovers the dark side of individualism.

PERFORMANCE-BASED ASSESSMENT PREP

Review Evidence for a Personal Narrative

Complete your Evidence Log for the unit by evaluating what you have learned and synthesizing the information you have recorded.

First-Read Guide

Use this page to record your first-read ideas.

🔧 **Tool Kit**
First-Read Guide and
Model Annotation

Selection Title: _____

NOTICE

NOTICE new information or ideas you learn about the unit topic as you first read this text.

ANNOTATE

ANNOTATE by marking vocabulary and key passages you want to revisit.

First Read

CONNECT ideas within the selection to other knowledge and the selections you have read.

CONNECT

RESPOND by writing a brief summary of the selection.

RESPOND

▤ STANDARD

Reading Read and comprehend complex literary and informational texts independently and proficiently.

Close-Read Guide

Use this page to record your close-read ideas.

Selection Title: _____

Close Read the Text

Revisit sections of the text you marked during your first read. Read these sections closely and **annotate** what you notice. Ask yourself **questions** about the text. What can you **conclude?** Write down your ideas.

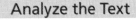

Analyze the Text

Think about the author's choices of patterns, structure, techniques, and ideas included in the text. Select one, and record your thoughts about what this choice conveys.

QuickWrite

Pick a paragraph from the text that grabbed your interest. Explain the power of this passage.

STANDARD

Reading Read and comprehend complex literary and informational texts independently and proficiently.

Share Your Independent Learning

Prepare to Share

What role does individualism play in American society?

Even when you read something independently, your understanding continues to grow when you share what you have learned with others. Reflect on the text you explored independently and write notes about its connection to the unit. In your notes, consider why this text belongs in this unit.

EVIDENCE LOG

Go to your Evidence Log and record what you learned from the text you read.

Learn From Your Classmates

Discuss It Share your ideas about the text you explored on your own. As you talk with your classmates, jot down a few ideas that you learn from them.

Reflect

Review your notes, and mark the most important insight you gained from these writing and discussion activities. Explain how this idea adds to your understanding of the concept of individualism.

STANDARDS

Speaking and Listening
Initiate and participate effectively in a range of collaborative discussions with diverse partners on grades 11–12 topics, texts, and issues, building on others' ideas and expressing their own clearly and persuasively.

Review Evidence for a Personal Narrative

At the beginning of this unit, you responded to the following question:

> **What significant incident helped me realize that I am a unique individual?**

✎ EVIDENCE LOG

Review your Evidence Log and your QuickWrite from the beginning of the unit. Have the texts you read altered your original thoughts about the incident?

☐ YES	☐ NO
Identify at least three ideas from the texts that have caused you to reevaluate your original idea. 1. 2. 3.	Identify at least three ideas from the texts that reinforced your original idea. 1. 2. 3.

Develop your thoughts into a topic sentence: *I first became aware of myself as a unique human being when:*

_____

_____

_____

The incident took place:

WHEN	WHERE	WITH WHOM

STANDARDS

Writing
Engage and orient the reader by setting out a problem, situation, or observation and its significance, establishing one or multiple point(s) of view, and introducing a narrator and/or characters; create a smooth progression of experiences or events.

PERFORMANCE-BASED ASSESSMENT

SOURCES

- WHOLE-CLASS SELECTIONS
- SMALL-GROUP SELECTIONS
- INDEPENDENT-LEARNING SELECTION

🔗 WORD NETWORK

As you write and revise your personal narrative, use your Word Network to help vary your word choices.

PART 1
Writing to Sources: Personal Narrative

In this unit, you read a variety of texts that explore ideas about individuality. Each text, in its own way, sings the praises of nonconformity, independence, and a life of awareness and contemplation.

> **Assignment**
>
> Write a **personal narrative** in which you describe an event from your life that answers this question:
>
> > **What significant incident helped me realize that I am a unique individual?**
>
> Choose an incident that you are comfortable describing and sharing with others. Connect your personal experience to ideas expressed in the texts from this unit. Show how your experience illustrates or departs from the ideas these texts express. End with a conclusion about the ways in which the understanding you gained from the incident affects your life today.

Reread the Assignment Review the writing prompt to be sure you fully understand it. The assignment may reference some of the academic words presented at the beginning of the unit. Be sure you understand each of the words in order to complete the assignment correctly.

Academic Vocabulary

significant	unique	impact
incident	sequence	

Review the Elements of a Personal Narrative Before you begin writing, read the Narrative Rubric. Once you have completed your first draft, check it against the rubric. If one or more of the elements is missing or is not as strong as it could be, revise your narrative to add to or strengthen that component.

⬛ STANDARDS

Writing
Write narratives to develop real or imagined experiences or events using effective technique, well-chosen details, and well-structured event sequences.
- Write routinely over extended time frames and shorter time frames for a range of tasks, purposes, and audiences.

270 UNIT 2 • THE INDIVIDUAL AND SOCIETY

Narrative Rubric

	Focus and Organization	Evidence and Elaboration	Language Conventions
4	The introduction engages the reader and sets the scene for a specific situation. A unique point of view is clearly established and maintained. The events appear in a clear sequence and build toward a particular outcome. The conclusion follows from and reflects on the rest of the narrative.	Dialogue, pacing, reflection, and description adeptly move the narrative forward. Precise details and vivid sensory language give readers a clear picture of events.	The text employs standard English conventions of usage and mechanics consistently and accurately.
3	The introduction is somewhat engaging and sets the scene for a specific situation. A clear point of view is established and maintained. The events appear in a clear sequence and mostly combine to build toward a particular outcome. The conclusion follows from the rest of the narrative.	Dialogue, reflection, and description move the narrative forward. Precise details and some sensory language give readers a clear picture of events.	The text generally employs standard English conventions of usage and mechanics.
2	The introduction sets the scene for a specific situation. A point of view is established and maintained, with occasional lapses. The events appear mostly in sequence, although some events may not belong, and some events that would clarify the narrative do not appear. The conclusion follows from the narrative.	Some dialogue, reflection, or description is used in the narrative. Some details and one or two examples of sensory language are included.	The text inconsistently employs standard English conventions of usage and mechanics.
1	The introduction fails to set a scene or is omitted altogether. The point of view is not always clear. The events do not appear in a clear sequence, and events that would clarify the narrative may not appear. The conclusion does not follow from the narrative or is omitted altogether.	Appropriate narrative techniques such as dialogue, pacing, or reflection, are not used. Details are vague or missing. No sensory language is included.	The text does not employ standard English conventions of usage and mechanics.

PART 2
Speaking and Listening: Storytelling Session

Assignment

Even if you have never seen a professional storyteller, you have probably witnessed great storytelling. Stand-up comedians, lecturers, teachers, and other public speakers tell stories that engage, amuse, and instruct listeners. Use the personal narrative you wrote as the basis for an oral **storytelling session.**

Follow these steps to make your storytelling presentation active and interesting.

- Read your personal narrative aloud, and consider ways to make it stronger as an oral piece. You may want to shorten some sections, or add dramatic detail to others. Make those revisions, and then memorize the story.
- Practice your delivery in front of a mirror. Modulate your voice, adding highs and lows, and use gestures that add meaningful emphasis. If you find yourself stumbling over some words, change them. You do not need to stick to the story exactly as it appears on the page.
- As you deliver your story, relax, avoid rushing, and speak with expression.

Review the Rubric The criteria by which your storytelling will be evaluated appear in the rubric below. Review the criteria before telling your story to ensure that you are prepared.

STANDARDS
Speaking and Listening
- Present information, findings, and supporting evidence, conveying a clear and distinct perspective, such that listeners can follow the line of reasoning, alternative or opposing perspectives are addressed, and the organization, development, substance, and style are appropriate to purpose, audience, and a range of formal and informal tasks.
- Adapt speech to a variety of contexts and tasks, demonstrating a command of formal English when indicated or appropriate.

	Content	Presentation Techniques
3	The story has a clear beginning, middle, and end, and the sequence is easy to follow.	The speaker enunciates clearly and uses an appropriate volume throughout the story.
	The story expresses a significant insight in an engaging, entertaining way.	The speaker varies the tone and pace to maintain interest.
		The speaker uses movement and expression to enliven the performance.
2	The story has a beginning, middle, and end, and the sequence is mostly easy to follow.	The speaker enunciates clearly most of the time and usually uses appropriate volume.
	The story expresses an insight and is somewhat entertaining or engaging.	The speaker varies the tone and pace to some extent.
		The speaker uses some movement and expression.
1	The story does not have a clear beginning, middle, and end, and the sequence is hard to follow.	The speaker does not enunciate clearly and does not use an appropriate volume.
	The story does not express an insight and is not engaging.	The speaker does not vary tone and pace at all.
		The speaker does not use movement or expression.

Reflect on the Unit

Now that you've completed the unit, take a few moments to reflect on your learning.

Reflect on the Unit Goals

Look back at the goals at the beginning of the unit. Use a different colored pen to rate yourself again. Think about readings and activities that contributed the most to the growth of your understanding. Record your thoughts.

Reflect on the Learning Strategies

💬 **Discuss It** Write a reflection on whether you were able to improve your learning based on your Action Plans. Think about what worked, what didn't, and what you might do to keep working on these strategies. Record your ideas before a class discussion.

Reflect on the Text

Choose a selection that you found challenging and explain what made it difficult.

Explain something that surprised you about a text in the unit.

Which activity taught you the most about the concept of individualism? What did you learn?

⊞ STANDARDS

Speaking and Listening
• Initiate and participate effectively in a range of collaborative discussions with diverse partners on *grades 11–12 topics, texts, and issues,* building on others' ideas and expressing their own clearly and persuasively.
• Come to discussions prepared, having read and researched material under study; explicitly draw on that preparation by referring to evidence from texts and other research on the topic or issue to stimulate a thoughtful, well-reasoned exchange of ideas.

UNIT (3)

Power, Protest, and Change

A Spirit of Reform

Civil Rights Marches

💬 **Discuss It** Perhaps more than any other country, the United States was founded on dreams people had of shaping the society in which they lived. What were some of those dreams?

Write your response before sharing your ideas.

UNIT 3

ESSENTIAL QUESTION: In what ways does the struggle for freedom change with history?

LAUNCH TEXT
INFORMATIVE MODEL
The Zigzag Road to Rights

 ## WHOLE-CLASS LEARNING

 ## SMALL-GROUP LEARNING

 ## INDEPENDENT LEARNING

HISTORICAL PERSPECTIVES

Focus Period: 1850–1890
Civil War and Social Change

ANCHOR TEXT: SPEECH

from What to the Slave Is the Fourth of July?
Frederick Douglass

ANCHOR TEXT: SPEECH

Second Inaugural Address
Abraham Lincoln

MEDIA: IMAGE GALLERY

Perspectives on Lincoln

SPEECH

Ain't I a Woman?
*Sojourner Truth,
adapted by Frances Gage*

COMPARE

PUBLIC DOCUMENT

Declaration of Sentiments
Elizabeth Cady Stanton

MEDIA: PODCAST

Giving Women the Vote
Sandra Sleight-Brennan

SHORT STORY

The Story of an Hour
Kate Chopin

LEGAL OPINION

Brown v. Board of Education: Opinion of the Court
Earl Warren

POETRY COLLECTION 1

The Poetry of Langston Hughes
Langston Hughes

POETRY COLLECTION 2

Douglass
Paul Laurence Dunbar

The Fifth Fact
Sarah Browning

Who Burns for the Perfection of Paper   *Martín Espada*

HISTORY

from The Warmth of Other Suns
Isabel Wilkerson

ESSAY

What a Factory Can Teach a Housewife
Ida Tarbell

PERSUASIVE ESSAY

from Books as Bombs
Louis Menand

MEDIA: PODCAST

A Balance Between Nature and Nurture
Gloria Steinem

PERFORMANCE TASK

WRITING FOCUS:
Write an Informative Essay

PERFORMANCE TASKS

SPEAKING AND LISTENING/RESEARCH FOCUS:
Panel Discussion/Research Presentation

PERFORMANCE-BASED ASSESSMENT PREP

Review Evidence for an Informative Essay

PERFORMANCE-BASED ASSESSMENT

Informative Text: Essay and Podcast

PROMPT:
What motivates people to struggle for change?

Unit Goals

Throughout this unit, you will deepen your perspective on power, protest, and change by reading, writing, speaking, listening, and presenting. These goals will help you succeed on the Unit Performance-Based Assessment.

Rate how well you meet these goals right now. You will revisit your ratings later when you reflect on your growth during this unit.

SCALE	1	2	3	4	5
	NOT AT ALL WELL	NOT VERY WELL	SOMEWHAT WELL	VERY WELL	EXTREMELY WELL

READING GOALS

	1	2	3	4	5
• Read and analyze a variety of texts to gain the knowledge and insight needed to write about the struggle for freedom.	○	○	○	○	○
• Expand your knowledge and use of academic and concept vocabulary.	○	○	○	○	○

WRITING AND RESEARCH GOALS

	1	2	3	4	5
• Write an informative essay that has a clear structure and that draws evidence from texts and original research.	○	○	○	○	○
• Conduct research projects of various lengths to explore a topic and clarify meaning.	○	○	○	○	○

LANGUAGE GOAL

	1	2	3	4	5
• Use appropriate and varied sentence structures to create cohesion and clarify relationships.	○	○	○	○	○

SPEAKING AND LISTENING GOALS

	1	2	3	4	5
• Collaborate with your team to build on the ideas of others, develop consensus, and communicate.	○	○	○	○	○
• Integrate audio, visuals, and text to present information.	○	○	○	○	○

:≡ STANDARDS

Language
Acquire and use accurately general academic and domain-specific words and phrases, sufficient for reading, writing, speaking, and listening at the college and career readiness level; demonstrate independence in gathering vocabulary knowledge when considering a word or phrase important to comprehension or expression.

Academic Vocabulary: Informative Text

Academic terms appear in all subjects and can help you read, write, and discuss with precision and clarity. Here are five academic words that will be useful to you in this unit as you analyze and write informative texts.

Complete the chart.

1. Review each word, its root, and the mentor sentences.

2. Use the information and your own knowledge to predict the meaning of each word.

3. For each word, list at least two related words.

4. Refer to a dictionary or other resources if needed.

TIP

FOLLOW THROUGH
Study the words in this chart, and mark them or their forms wherever they appear in the unit.

WORD	MENTOR SENTENCES	PREDICT MEANING	RELATED WORDS
informational ROOT: **-form-** "shape"; "image"	1. This *informational* pamphlet tells about the history of the village. 2. The students found the remarks both *informational* and inspirational.		inform; informative; uninformed; misinformed
inquire ROOT: **-quir-/-quer-** "ask"	1. If you want to find out why your application was denied, you must *inquire*. 2. In my research, I *inquire* about the reasons for certain social customs.		
verbatim ROOT: **-verb-** "word"	1. The actor knew the script so well that he could quote it *verbatim*. 2. The witness's ability to give a *verbatim* account persuaded the jury that her memory was reliable.		
deduction ROOT: **-duc-** "lead"	1. The astronomer's *deduction* was based on years of observation. 2. The writer presented the objective facts and then shared his *deduction* from them.		
specific ROOT: **-spec-** "sort"; "kind"	1. Your report topic is too broad; find one that is more *specific*. 2. Was there one *specific* event that caused the war, or were there many?		

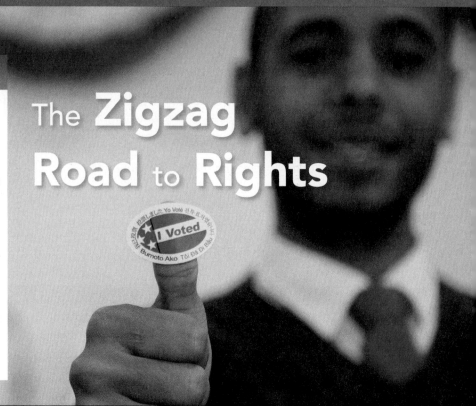

LAUNCH TEXT | INFORMATIVE MODEL

The **Zigzag** Road to **Rights**

This selection is an example of an **informative text,** a type of writing in which an author examines concepts through the careful selection, organization, and analysis of information. This is the type of writing you will develop in the Performance-Based Assessment at the end of the unit.

As you read, think about how the information is shared. Mark the text to help you answer this question: How does the writer help readers understand the main point of the essay?

NOTES

1   When we look back at history, we often like to identify trends. Viewing the big picture, we may see a steady push toward progress. However, every fight for rights involves a series of advances and setbacks. The struggle for equal recognition of African Americans demonstrates a zigzag road to rights.

2   The push-and-pull of this struggle was evident at the birth of the nation. In his original draft of the Declaration of Independence, Thomas Jefferson included a strong condemnation of slavery, protesting this "cruel war against human nature." Jefferson wanted the Declaration of Independence to grant freedom to all men. However, at the Continental Congress in 1776, both northern and southern slaveholders objected to any mention of African American rights. Powerful indeed was their pressure. Any mention of slavery was deleted from the Declaration.

3   Although the removal of Jefferson's antislavery paragraph was a severe setback, reformers did not give up hope. With the ratification of the Constitution, they gained an important tool for change. Article V describes the conditions required for amending the Constitution. Laws can be changed, and rights can be gained.

4   The struggle took another crucial step forward in 1863, when President Abraham Lincoln issued the Emancipation Proclamation. It asserted that "all persons held as slaves" within states that had seceded from the Union "are, and henceforward shall be, free." Still, freedom for slaves depended upon a Union victory. Slavery remained legal in border states loyal to the Union, as well as in Confederate areas under Northern control.

5   The hope of change promised by Article V paid off in 1865. Congress passed the Thirteenth Amendment, abolishing slavery in the United States. "Neither slavery nor involuntary servitude . . . shall exist within the United States, or any place subject to their jurisdiction." The next two amendments, adopted in 1868 and 1870, made African Americans citizens and gave them the right to vote. The expanded Constitution reflects a nation willing to change.

6   Yet these significant advances did not guarantee full rights for black Americans, as evidenced by a landmark decision by the Supreme Court in 1896. In the case of *Plessy v. Ferguson*, seven of eight Supreme Court justices voted in support of Louisiana's Separate Car Act, which made it illegal for blacks to travel in trains reserved for white passengers. This decision set an important legal precedent: "Separate, but equal" facilities were constitutional.

7   That decision was eventually reversed in 1954, when the Supreme Court issued a unanimous decision in the case of *Brown v. Board of Education*. Finding that "separate educational facilities are inherently unequal," the decision promised an end to segregation. Once again, progress toward equal rights surged forward.

8   Nonetheless, no single case, law, or amendment could instantly erase the long tradition of prejudice and inequality. For example, even though the Fifteenth Amendment guaranteed African Americans the right to vote, state and local laws and policies often kept black Americans from voting through tactics such as poll taxes, voter registration exams, and intimidation. These strategies were outlawed by the Voting Rights Act of 1965.

9   The history of African American rights features many crucial victories, from the Emancipation Proclamation through the Voting Rights Act. However, the record of the struggle also includes the difficult stumbling blocks that have had to be overcome. While the path to progress is not smooth, one thing is certain: The zigzag will continue into the future. History teaches us that rights gained can be lost, curtailed, or ignored—and perhaps gained once more. ❧

NOTES

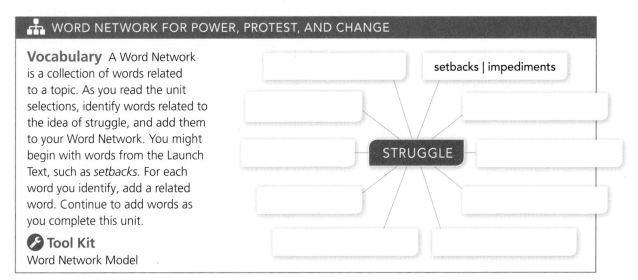

WORD NETWORK FOR POWER, PROTEST, AND CHANGE

Vocabulary A Word Network is a collection of words related to a topic. As you read the unit selections, identify words related to the idea of struggle, and add them to your Word Network. You might begin with words from the Launch Text, such as *setbacks*. For each word you identify, add a related word. Continue to add words as you complete this unit.

🔑 **Tool Kit**
Word Network Model

setbacks | impediments

STRUGGLE

Summary

Write a summary of "The Zigzag Road to Rights." Remember that a **summary** is a concise, complete, and accurate overview of a text. It should contain neither opinion nor analysis.

Launch Activity

Draft a Focus Statement Complete this focus statement: The struggle for freedom is _____, _____, and _____.

- Working individually, choose three words or phrases to complete the statement. Write each one on a separate sticky note.

- Place everyone's sticky notes on a board where they can be seen. Then, work together to group words or phrases that are synonyms or that are otherwise closely related.

- Again working individually, decide which three words or phrases you think best complete the focus statement. Place a tally mark on each sticky note that lists one of your choices.

- As a class, use the tally results to create a single focus statement. Identify the words or phrases that received the most votes. Then, discuss whether those three words or phrases create the strongest statement.

- Once the class has selected three words or phrases, discuss how the order in which they are placed affects the meaning of the focus statement. Choose the best order, and finish the statement.

QuickWrite

Consider class discussions, the video, and the Launch Text as you think about the prompt. Record your first thoughts here.

PROMPT: **What motivates people to struggle for change?**

✎ EVIDENCE LOG FOR POWER, PROTEST, AND CHANGE

Review your QuickWrite. Summarize your initial position in one sentence in your Evidence Log. Then, record evidence from "The Zigzag Road to Rights" that supports your position.

After each selection, you will continue to use your Evidence Log to record the evidence you gather and the connections you make. The graphic shows what your Evidence Log looks like.

🔧 **Tool Kit**
Evidence Log Model

Title of Text: _____ Date: _____

CONNECTION TO PROMPT	TEXT EVIDENCE/DETAILS	ADDITIONAL NOTES/IDEAS

How does this text change or add to my thinking? Date: _____

ESSENTIAL QUESTION:

In what ways does the struggle for freedom change with history?

As you read these selections, work with your whole class to explore the struggle for freedom.

From Text to Topic For Frederick Douglass, the struggle for freedom meant a perilous escape from slavery. For Abraham Lincoln, it meant waging war against his fellow citizens. The issue of slavery polarized the country before the Civil War. As you read, consider what the selections show about the struggle for freedom during the Focus Period—and its relationship to our ideas of freedom today.

Whole-Class Learning Strategies

Throughout your life, in school, in your community, and in your career, you will continue to learn and work in large-group environments.

Review these strategies and the actions you can take to practice them as you work with your whole class. Add ideas of your own for each step. Get ready to use these strategies during Whole-Class Learning.

STRATEGY	ACTION PLAN
Listen actively	• Eliminate distractions. For example, put your cellphone away. • Record brief notes on main ideas and points of confusion. •
Clarify by asking questions	• If you're confused, other people probably are, too. Ask a question to help your whole class. • Ask follow-up questions as needed; for example, if you do not understand the clarification or if you want to make an additional connection. •
Monitor understanding	• Notice what information you already know and be ready to build on it. • Ask for help if you are struggling. •
Interact and share ideas	• Share your ideas and offer answers, even if you are unsure of them. • Build on the ideas of others by adding details or making a connection. •

CONTENTS

HISTORICAL PERSPECTIVES

Focus Period: 1850–1890
Civil War and Social Change

The second half of the nineteenth century was a period of deep political and social conflict, influencing writers, commentators, and activists to fight for freedom and reform.

ANCHOR TEXT: SPEECH

from What to the Slave Is the Fourth of July?

Frederick Douglass

How might America's celebration of liberty affect those Americans who are not yet free?

ANCHOR TEXT: SPEECH

Second Inaugural Address

Abraham Lincoln

Is warfare in the name of freedom and unity worth the sacrifice?

MEDIA: IMAGE GALLERY

Perspectives on Lincoln

How do political cartoons show us what people thought of President Lincoln in his own time?

PERFORMANCE TASK

WRITING FOCUS
Write an Informative Essay

Both Whole-Class readings present powerful arguments concerning the struggle to end slavery in America. After reading, you will write an informative essay in which you provide facts about the goals of these speeches.

Civil War and Social Change

Voices of the Period

" . . . I would write something that would make this whole nation feel what an accursed thing slavery is."

—Harriet Beecher Stowe,
author of *Uncle Tom's Cabin*

"In your hands, my dissatisfied fellow countrymen, and not in mine, is the momentous issue of civil war. The government will not assail you. . . . You have no oath registered in heaven to destroy the government, while I shall have the most solemn one to 'preserve, protect, and defend' it."

—Abraham Lincoln,
President of the United States
from 1861 to 1865

"Those who profess to favor freedom, and yet deprecate agitation, are men who want crops without plowing up the ground. They want rain without thunder and lightning. They want the ocean without the awful roar of its many waters. This struggle may be a moral one, or it may be a physical one, or it may be both moral and physical, but it must be a struggle. Power concedes nothing without a demand. It never did and it never will."

—Frederick Douglass,
abolitionist

History of the Period

Dreams of Shaping Society More than any other nation, the United States was founded on dreams people had of shaping the society in which they lived. The Puritans who colonized New England came to build a new society, a society in which they could freely practice their religion. Some 150 years later, the American revolutionaries wrote a constitution that gave citizens powerful tools to continue reshaping society—tools such as freedom of speech and an elected, representative government. With these tools, citizens could change the course of the country.

The Crisis of Slavery By 1850, though, the question of whether those tools were enough became grave. About 88 percent of the African Americans in the country—approximately 14 percent of the nation's total population—were enslaved: treated as property, forced to work for others, torn in many cases from their own families, and subject to various other abuses and cruelties. Many in the nation cried out for change, but the economy of the South depended on the use of enslaved African Americans for labor. When challenged, many in the South rallied to the defense of the institution.

In the North, industry was replacing agriculture as the motor of the economy. Northern states had begun passing antislavery laws in the eighteenth century, and by 1850 slavery had all but vanished in the North. Critics of slavery were becoming

TIMELINE

1850: China Taiping Rebellion begins.

1857: In the *Dred Scott* decision, the U.S. Supreme Court rules that people of African descent cannot become U.S. citizens.

1860: Abraham Lincoln is elected president.

1850

1852: Harriet Beecher Stowe's *Uncle Tom's Cabin* is published.

1859: John Brown, an abolitionist, leads a raid on the federal arsenal at Harpers Ferry, Virginia.

1861: The Civil War begins with Confederate forces firing on Fort Sumter, South Carolina.

Integration of Knowledge and Ideas

Notebook What does the information shown in these charts help you understand about differences between the North and South in their economies, population densities, and overall lifestyles? How do you think these differences affected the outcome of the Civil War?

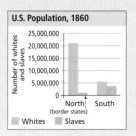

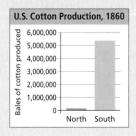

vocal in their opposition, with abolitionists campaigning against slavery and assisting runaway slaves.

Civil War When Abraham Lincoln was elected president in 1860, the divisions between North and South only sharpened. Beginning with South Carolina in 1860, 11 Southern states seceded (separated) from the United States. In 1861, the Civil War began, pitting North against South. After years of suffering and devastation, the North won the war in 1865. This victory set the nation's future course, for it decided the issue of slavery: No longer would anyone be enslaved in the United States. In addition, it made clear the fact that the centers of economic influence in the country had shifted from the agricultural South to the industrial North. Finally, it confirmed the

strength of the country's central government in relation to the states.

Expansion and Progress Before the Civil War, the country had been busily expanding, adding new territories and states as settlers pushed west, seeking land. After the war, the country continued to grow at a furious pace. Settlers continued to move west, forcing Native Americans from their lands. Immigrants flooded the nation's cities, providing labor. For the first time, electricity was being used on a large scale for everything from city lights to factory machines. The nation began linking frontiers to cities with railway tracks and telegraph wires.

Reform Movements While forces such as westward expansion and immigration were reshaping the nation, reformers were attempting to transform society. Pioneers such as Horace

1862: France Louis Pasteur proposes the modern germ theory of disease.

1865: The Thirteenth Amendment, outlawing slavery, is added to the U.S. Constitution.

1867: The United States buys Alaska from Russia.

1870

1863: President Lincoln issues the Emancipation Proclamation.

1865: President Lincoln is assassinated by John Wilkes Booth.

1869: Russia Leo Tolstoy's *War and Peace* is published.

Mann championed public education. Other activists pushed forward reforms of the justice system, leading to the development of the modern prison. During this period, women also began pursuing political and economic rights equal to men's.

A Historic Convention In the years around 1850, women were discouraged from playing most major roles in public life. Their rights to property were limited. In addition, women did not yet have the right to vote. In 1848, Elizabeth Cady Stanton and Lucretia Mott helped organize the Seneca Falls Convention, which met to discuss women's rights. There, Stanton introduced a resolution to pursue the right to vote for women. With the support of Frederick Douglass, a former slave and an active abolitionist, the resolution passed.

The Movement for Women's Rights Reformers such as Stanton, Mott, and Susan B. Anthony campaigned vigorously for women's rights. Their tactics included lobbying politicians, holding public lectures, publishing newspapers, picketing, and marching.

Social Progress Some reforms were seen at the time. Even before the Seneca Falls Convention, some states had passed laws giving women the right to their own property, although their husbands still had the right to manage shared property.

Some states, including ones newly added to the Union, passed laws allowing women to vote. The right to vote was not granted to women nationwide, however, until the ratification of the Nineteenth Amendment to the Constitution in 1920.

A Nation Comes of Age In the decades from 1850 to 1914, the United States grew from a largely agricultural society into a modern industrial giant. During this time, important issues such as the freedom of African Americans, the rights of women, and the rights of workers were discussed and argued. In the end, the society of the United States was reshaped, not just by reformers, but by forces such as war, technological progress, and economic development. These forces laid the foundations of the nation we know today.

A Legacy of Protest The issues of power and change raised during the period were not resolved once and for all, however. Even though slavery had been abolished, injustices against African Americans continued. New eras of protest were born in the effort to end racial discrimination. Women's lives had generally improved but voting equality was still an unachieved goal, and other forms of inequality continued to reign. Protests continued. The literature in this unit tells of the ongoing struggle for social justice.

TIMELINE

1872: Susan B. Anthony is arrested for trying to vote in a presidential election.

1876: Baseball's National League is founded.

1877: The Reconstruction Era ends in the South.

1870

1874: France Claude Monet gathers Impressionist painters for their first exhibit. •

1876: Alexander Graham Bell patents the telephone.

1879: Thomas Edison invents a practical electric light.

Literature Selections

Literature of the Focus Period Several of the selections in this unit were written during the Focus Period and pertain to the deep conflicts of the era over power and change:

from *"What to the Slave Is the Fourth of July?"* Frederick Douglass

Second Inaugural Address, Abraham Lincoln

"Ain't I a Woman?" Sojourner Truth

Declaration of Sentiments, Elizabeth Cady Stanton

"The Story of an Hour," Kate Chopin

"Douglass," Paul Laurence Dunbar

Connections Across Time The struggle against social injustice and for the expansion of rights continued past the Focus Period. In addition, the struggles of the Focus Period have influenced contemporary writers and commentators.

Brown v. Board of Education: Opinion of the Court, Earl Warren

"Was *Brown v. Board* a Failure?" Sarah Garland

"The Fifth Fact," Sarah Browning

"Who Burns for the Perfection of Paper," Martín Espada

from *The Warmth of Other Suns,* Isabel Wilkerson

"What a Factory Can Teach a Housewife," Ida Tarbell

from *Books as Bombs*, Louis Menand

"A Balance Between Nature and Nurture," Gloria Steinem

ADDITIONAL FOCUS PERIOD LITERATURE

Student Edition

UNIT 2
The Writing of Walt Whitman

- *from* The Preface to the 1885 edition of *Leaves of Grass*
- *from* Song of Myself
- "I Hear America Singing"
- "On the Beach at Night Alone"
- "America"

The Poetry of Emily Dickinson

- "The Soul selects her own Society —"
- "The Soul unto itself"
- "Fame is a fickle food"
- "They shut me up in Prose —"
- "There is a solitude of space"
- "I heard a fly buzz — when I died —"
- "I'm Nobody! Who are you?"

1882: Europe The Triple Alliance (Germany, Austria-Hungary, and Italy) is formed.

1884: Mark Twain's *The Adventures of Huckleberry Finn* is published.

1890

1882: The Standard Oil trust becomes the first industrial monopoly.

1883: The Brooklyn Bridge is opened.

1886: The Statue of Liberty is dedicated in New York Harbor.

1890: The U.S. Census Bureau declares the frontier closed.

About the Speaker

Frederick Douglass

(1818–1895) was born into slavery in Maryland. He nevertheless learned to read and write, and at the age of 21 he escaped to Massachusetts. There, he joined the abolitionist cause and quickly became one of its most powerful public speakers, lecturing against slavery and campaigning for civil rights for all people. He published his autobiography, established a newspaper for African Americans, and went on to hold several governmental positions.

 **Tool Kit**
First-Read Guide and Model Annotation

from What to the Slave Is the Fourth of July?

Concept Vocabulary

You will encounter the following words as you read this excerpt from "What to the Slave Is the Fourth of July?" Before reading, note how familiar you are with each word. Then, rank the words in order from most familiar (1) to least familiar (6).

WORD	YOUR RANKING
obdurate	
stolid	
disparity	
denounce	
equivocate	
conceded	

After completing the first read, come back to the concept vocabulary and review your rankings. Mark changes to your original rankings as needed.

First Read NONFICTION

Apply these these strategies as you conduct your first read. You will have an opportunity to complete the close-read notes after your first read.

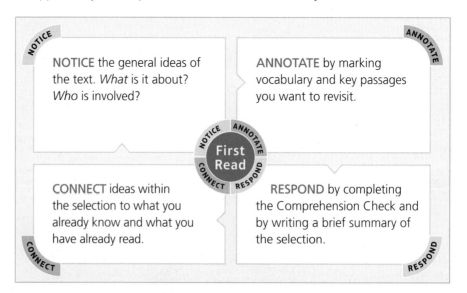

NOTICE the general ideas of the text. *What* is it about? *Who* is involved?

ANNOTATE by marking vocabulary and key passages you want to revisit.

CONNECT ideas within the selection to what you already know and what you have already read.

RESPOND by completing the Comprehension Check and by writing a brief summary of the selection.

from

What to the Slave Is the Fourth of July?

Frederick Douglass

BACKGROUND

On July 5, 1852, Frederick Douglass addressed an audience at the Rochester (New York) Ladies' Anti-Slavery Society. At a time when many people—some who were against slavery in principle—viewed the total abolition of slavery as a radical cause, Douglass pulled no punches in pleading his case.

1   Fellow citizens, pardon me, allow me to ask, why am I called upon to speak here today? What have I, or those I represent, to do with your national independence? Are the great principles of political freedom and of natural justice, embodied in that Declaration of Independence, extended to us? And am I, therefore, called upon to bring our humble offering to the national altar, and to confess the benefits and express devout gratitude for the blessings resulting from your independence to us?

2   Would to God, both for your sakes and ours, that an affirmative answer could be truthfully returned to these questions! Then would my task be light, and my burden easy and delightful. For who is there so cold that a nation's sympathy could not warm him? Who so **obdurate** and dead to the claims of gratitude that would not thankfully acknowledge such priceless benefits? Who so **stolid** and selfish that would not give his voice to swell the hallelujahs of a nation's jubilee,[1] when the chains of servitude had been torn from

NOTES

obdurate (OB dur iht) *adj.*
resistant to persuasion

stolid (STOL ihd) *adj.*
feeling little or no emotion

---

1. **hallelujahs of a nation's jubilee** praises to God at the time of celebrating a national anniversary.

disparity (dih SPAR uh tee) *n.*
great difference or inequality

CLOSE READ
ANNOTATE: Parallelism is the repetition of words or phrases that have similar grammatical structures. In the last two sentences of paragraph 4, mark two examples of parallelism.

QUESTION: What ideas do these examples of parallelism connect?

CONCLUDE: How does the use of parallelism add to the power and meaning of this section of the speech?

denounce (dih NOWNS) *v.*
criticize harshly

equivocate (ih KWIHV uh kayt) *v.* use unclear language to avoid committing oneself to something

his limbs? I am not that man. In a case like that, the dumb might eloquently speak, and the "lame man leap as an hart."[2]

3   But such is not the state of the case. I say it with a sad sense of the **disparity** between us. I am not included within the pale of glorious anniversary! Your high independence only reveals the immeasurable distance between us. The blessings in which you, this day, rejoice are not enjoyed in common. The rich inheritance of justice, liberty, prosperity, and independence, bequeathed[3] by your fathers, is shared by you, not by me. The sunlight that brought light and healing to you has brought stripes and death to me. This Fourth of July is yours, not mine. You may rejoice; I must mourn. To drag a man in fetters[4] into the grand illuminated temple of liberty, and call upon him to join you in joyous anthems, were inhuman mockery and sacrilegious irony. Do you mean, citizens, to mock me, by asking me to speak today? . . .

4   Fellow citizens, above your national, tumultuous joy, I hear the mournful wail of millions! whose chains, heavy and grievous yesterday, are, today, rendered more intolerable by the jubilee shouts that reach them. If I do forget, if I do not faithfully remember those bleeding children of sorrow this day, "may my right hand forget her cunning, and may my tongue cleave to the roof of my mouth!"[5] To forget them, to pass lightly over their wrongs, and to chime in with the popular theme would be treason most scandalous and shocking, and would make me a reproach before God and the world. My subject, then, fellow citizens, is American slavery. I shall see this day and its popular characteristics from the slave's point of view. Standing there identified with the American bondman, making his wrongs mine, I do not hesitate to declare, with all my soul, that the character and conduct of this nation never looked blacker to me than on this Fourth of July! Whether we turn to the declarations of the past or to the professions of the present, the conduct of the nation seems equally hideous and revolting. America is false to the past, false to the present, and solemnly binds herself to be false to the future. Standing with God and the crushed and bleeding slave on this occasion, I will, in the name of humanity which is outraged, in the name of liberty which is fettered, in the name of the Constitution and the Bible, which are disregarded and trampled upon, dare to call into question and to **denounce**, with all the emphasis I can command, everything that serves to perpetuate slavery—the great sin and shame of America! "I will not **equivocate**; I will not excuse;" I will use the severest language I can command; and yet not one word shall escape me that any man, whose judgment is not blinded by prejudice, or who is not at heart a slaveholder, shall not confess to be right and just.

---

2. **"lame man leap as an hart"** reference to the biblical passage Isaiah 35:6, promising God's rescue of the weak and fearful. (A *hart* is a male deer.)
3. **bequeathed** (bih KWEETHT) *adj.* handed down.
4. **fetters** *n.* chains.
5. **"may . . . mouth"** reference to the biblical passage Psalm 137, referencing the grief of Jews who had been taken as captives to Babylon (c. 600 B.C.).

5   But I fancy I hear some one of my audience say, "It is just in this circumstance that you and your brother abolitionists fail to make a favorable impression on the public mind. Would you argue more, and denounce less; would you persuade more, and rebuke[6] less; your cause would be much more likely to succeed." But, I submit, where all is plain, there is nothing to be argued. What point in the antislavery creed would you have me argue? On what branch of the subject do the people of this country need light? Must I undertake to prove that the slave is a man? That point is conceded already. Nobody doubts it. The slaveholders themselves acknowledge it in the enactment of laws for their government. They acknowledge it when they punish disobedience on the part of the slave. There are seventy-two crimes in the State of Virginia which, if committed by a black man (no matter how ignorant he be), subject him to the punishment of death; while only two of the same crimes will subject a white man to the like punishment. What is this but the acknowledgment that the slave is a moral, intellectual, and responsible being? The manhood of the slave is conceded. It is admitted in the fact that Southern statute books are covered with enactments forbidding, under severe fines and penalties, the teaching of the slave to read or to write. When you can point to any such laws in reference to the beasts of the field, then I may consent to argue the manhood of the slave. When the dogs in your streets, when the fowls of the air, when the cattle on your hills, when the fish of the sea, and the reptiles that crawl, shall be unable to distinguish the slave from a brute, then will I argue with you that the slave is a man!

> Must I undertake to prove that the slave is a man?

6   For the present, it is enough to affirm the equal manhood of the Negro race. Is it not astonishing that, while we are plowing, planting, and reaping, using all kinds of mechanical tools, erecting houses, constructing bridges, building ships, working in metals of brass, iron, copper, silver and gold; that, while we are reading, writing and ciphering,[7] acting as clerks, merchants, and secretaries, having among us lawyers, doctors, ministers, poets, authors, editors, orators, and teachers; that, while we are engaged in all manner of enterprises common to other men, digging gold in California, capturing the whale in the Pacific, feeding sheep and cattle on the hillside, living, moving, acting, thinking, planning, living in families as husbands, wives, and children, and, above all, confessing and worshipping the Christian's God, and looking hopefully for life and immortality beyond the grave, we are called upon to prove that we are men!

7   Would you have me argue that man is entitled to liberty? That he is the rightful owner of his own body? You have already declared it. Must I argue the wrongfulness of slavery? Is that a question for Republicans? Is it to be settled by the rules of logic and

---

6. **rebuke** (rih BYOOK) v. criticize.
7. **ciphering** (SY fuhr ihng) v. computing using arithmetic.

argumentation, as a matter beset with great difficulty, involving a doubtful application of the principle of justice, hard to be understood? How should I look today, in the presence of Americans, dividing and subdividing a discourse, to show that men have a natural right to freedom—speaking of it relatively and positively, negatively and affirmatively? To do so would be to make myself ridiculous, and to offer an insult to your understanding. There is not a man beneath the canopy of heaven that does not know that slavery is wrong for him.

8   What, am I to argue that it is wrong to make men brutes, to rob them of their liberty, to work them without wages, to keep them ignorant of their relations to their fellow men, to beat them with sticks, to flay their flesh with the lash, to load their limbs with irons, to hunt them with dogs, to sell them at auction, to sunder their families, to knock out their teeth, to burn their flesh, to starve them into obedience and submission to their masters? Must I argue that a system thus marked with blood, and stained with pollution, is wrong? No! I will not. I have better employment for my time and strength than such arguments would imply.

9   What, then, remains to be argued? Is it that slavery is not divine; that God did not establish it; that our doctors of divinity are mistaken? There is blasphemy in the thought. That which is inhuman cannot be divine! Who can reason on such a proposition? They that can, may; I cannot. The time for such argument is passed.

CLOSE READ

ANNOTATE: In paragraph 10, mark words that suggest how strongly Douglass feels. Mark adjectives, nouns that name forms of expression, and nouns that name natural phenomena.

QUESTION: Why does Douglass compare certain forms of expression to natural phenomena?

CONCLUDE: What is the effect of this language?

10   At a time like this, scorching irony, not convincing argument, is needed. O! had I the ability, and could I reach the nation's ear, I would, today, pour out a fiery stream of biting ridicule, blasting reproach, withering sarcasm, and stern rebuke. For it is not light that is needed, but fire; it is not the gentle shower, but thunder. We need the storm, the whirlwind, and the earthquake. The feeling of the nation must be quickened; the conscience of the nation must be roused; the propriety[8] of the nation must be startled; the hypocrisy of the nation must be exposed; and its crimes against God and man must be proclaimed and denounced.

11   What, to the American slave, is your Fourth of July? I answer: a day that reveals to him, more than all other days of the year, the gross injustice and cruelty to which he is the constant victim. To him, your celebration is a sham; your boasted liberty, an unholy license; your national greatness, swelling vanity; your sounds of rejoicing are empty and heartless; your denunciation of tyrants, brass-fronted impudence; your shouts of liberty and equality, hollow mockery; your prayers and hymns, your sermons and thanksgivings, with all your religious parade and solemnity, are, to Him, mere bombast, fraud, deception, impiety,[9] and hypocrisy—a thin veil to cover up crimes which would disgrace a nation of savages. There is not a nation on the earth guilty of practices more shocking and bloody than are the people of these United States, at this very hour. . . .

---

8. **propriety** (pruh PRY uh tee) *n.* behavior that is accepted as socially correct or proper.
9. **impiety** (ihm PY uh tee) *n.* lack of respect for God.

12   Allow me to say, in conclusion, notwithstanding the dark picture I have this day presented, of the state of the nation, I do not despair of this country. There are forces in operation which must inevitably work the downfall of slavery. "The arm of the Lord is not shortened,"[10] and the doom of slavery is certain. I, therefore, leave off where I began, with hope. While drawing encouragement from the Declaration of Independence, the great principles it contains, and the genius of American institutions, my spirit is also cheered by the obvious tendencies of the age. 🐝

10. **"The arm of the Lord is not shortened"** reference to the biblical passage Isaiah 59:1, assuring that God is able to hear and rescue those who call on him.

Comprehension Check

Complete the following items after you finish your first read.

1. What kind of "easy and delightful" speech does Douglass wish he could present?

2. What is the "mournful wail" that gives Douglass the topic for his speech?

3. According to Douglass, how do laws in the South prove that slaves are human beings?

4. At the end of this excerpt, what encouraging signs does Douglass find?

5. 📝 **Notebook** Write a summary of this excerpt from "What to the Slave Is the Fourth of July?" to confirm your understanding of the speech.

RESEARCH

Research to Clarify Choose at least one unfamiliar detail from the text. Briefly research that detail. In what way does the information you learned shed light on an aspect of the speech?

Research to Explore Choose something that interests you from the text, and formulate a research question about it.

from WHAT TO THE SLAVE IS THE FOURTH OF JULY?

Close Read the Text

1. This model, from paragraph 3 of the text, shows two sample annotations, along with questions and conclusions. Close read the passage, and find another detail to annotate. Then, write a question and your conclusion.

Close Read
ANNOTATE QUESTION CONCLUDE

ANNOTATE: These terms are similar.

QUESTION: What do these words show about Douglass's feelings toward American ideals?

CONCLUDE: They show his reverence. The legacy of freedom is both sacred ("blessings") and a part of every American's identity ("rich inheritance").

ANNOTATE: Here, Douglass is providing contrasts.

QUESTION: What point is Douglass making by this series of contrasts?

CONCLUDE: He is emphasizing the idea that enslaved Americans are denied freedom.

The blessings in which you, this day, rejoice are not enjoyed in common. The rich inheritance of justice, liberty, prosperity, and independence, bequeathed by your fathers, is shared by you, not by me. The sunlight that brought light and healing to you, has brought stripes and death to me. This Fourth of July is yours, not mine.

Tool Kit

Close-Read Guide and Model Annotation

2. For more practice, go back into the text, and complete the close-read notes.

3. Revisit a section of the text you found important during your first read. Read this section closely, and **annotate** what you notice. Ask yourself **questions** such as "Why did the author make this choice?" What can you **conclude**?

Analyze the Text

CITE TEXTUAL EVIDENCE to support your answers.

Notebook Respond to these questions.

1. **Analyze** How does Douglass's opening reference to the Declaration of Independence reinforce his message?

2. **Interpret** Identify two biblical allusions Douglass makes, and then explain how each contributes to Douglass's overall argument.

3. (a) **Analyze** In what ways is Douglass's word choice suited to his audience? (b) **Evaluate** How effective would it be for a modern audience? Explain.

4. **Historical Perspectives** Douglass presented this speech to an antislavery society—an audience that was already on his side. Why, then, did Douglass speak as harshly as he did? Whom was he trying to reach?

5. **Essential Question:** *How does the struggle for freedom change with history?* What have you learned about the struggle for freedom from reading this speech?

Analyze Craft and Structure

Argumentative Structure Frederick Douglass's famous speech "What to the Slave Is the Fourth of July?" is an **argument**, a discussion of a controversial or debatable issue. In an argument, a writer or speaker uses valid reasoning and evidence to support a **claim**—a particular belief, conclusion, or point of view. The person who presents the argument also may anticipate objections and challenges, or **counterclaims**, and then refute them.

In general, an argument addresses at least one of these purposes:

- to change the audience's mind about an issue
- to persuade the audience to accept an idea
- to motivate the audience to take a specific action

Douglass structures his speech to address all three purposes, either directly or by implication.

Practice

CITE TEXTUAL EVIDENCE to support your answers.

📝 **Notebook** Respond to these questions.

1. (a) What main claim shapes Douglass's speech? (b) How early in the speech does he introduce this claim?

2. In paragraph 10, Douglass states that "scorching irony, not convincing argument, is needed." Nevertheless, his speech does make an argument. (a) In one sentence, state Douglass's argument. (b) Up to that point, what evidence has he presented to support his claim?

3. (a) In paragraph 5, what does Douglass acknowledge as a counterclaim to his position? (b) How does he refute that counterclaim?

4. Reread the three purposes that most arguments address. (a) In the left-hand column of the chart, record those purposes in the order in which you think Douglass was effective in addressing them, from most successful to least successful. (b) Use the right-hand column to explain your choices.

PURPOSE	EXPLANATION
addressed **most** effectively:	
addressed **fairly** effectively:	
addressed **least** effectively:	

from WHAT TO THE SLAVE IS THE
FOURTH OF JULY?

⛓ WORD NETWORK

Add words related to
struggle from the text to
your Word Network.

Concept Vocabulary

obdurate	disparity	equivocate
stolid	denounce	conceded

Why These Words? These concept vocabulary words help reveal the nature of the debate over slavery. For example, although many people *conceded* that slavery was profoundly wrong, few were willing to campaign against it. On the other hand, some Americans whose economic success depended on slave labor were *obdurate,* insisting that the institution continue. One word suggests an acknowledgement of another point of view, whereas the other suggests a rejection of it.

1. How does the concept vocabulary sharpen the reader's understanding of the debate over slavery?

2. What other words in the speech connect to this concept?

Practice

📓 **Notebook** **Respond to these questions.**

1. How would you expect *obdurate* people to respond to advertisements?

2. Would you want to have *stolid* friends? Why, or why not?

3. Give an example of a *disparity* that you have noticed between two groups of people.

4. How might a group of people *denounce* a government policy?

5. Suppose that you are trying to get information from people who *equivocate*. What would you ask them to do?

6. If someone *conceded* a point, did he or she continue to argue against it? Explain.

Word Study

📓 **Notebook** **Latin Prefix: *ob-*** The Latin prefix *ob-* often means "against." It combines with the root *-dur-*, which means "hard," to form *obdurate*, which means "hardened against." The word suggests a lack of sympathy toward someone else's difficulty or need and is a good synonym for *hard-hearted*.

1. Write a definition of *obstruction* based on your understanding of the prefix *ob-*. Check your answer in a print or an online college-level dictionary.

2. Identify and define two other words in which the prefix *ob-* means "against." Use etymological information in a dictionary to verify your choices.

📋 STANDARDS

Language
• Demonstrate command of the conventions of standard English grammar and usage when writing or speaking.
• Apply knowledge of language to understand how language functions in different contexts, to make effective choices for meaning or style, and to comprehend more fully when reading or listening.
• Consult general and specialized reference materials, both print and digital, to find the pronunciation of a word or determine or clarify its precise meaning, its part of speech, its etymology, or its standard usage.

Conventions and Style

Types of Phrases A **noun phrase** consists of a noun and all of its modifiers. It functions just as a one-word noun does—as a subject, a direct or indirect object, a predicate nominative, an appositive, or the object of a preposition. A **verb phrase** consists of a main verb and all of its helping, or auxiliary, verbs.

Writers use noun phrases and verb phrases to add precision to their writing. A noun phrase can be quite specific and richly detailed. A verb phrase can indicate the exact tense, mood, and voice of the main verb.

This chart shows examples of noun phrases and verb phrases in the excerpt from "What to the Slave Is the Fourth of July?"

TIP

CLARIFICATION
Refer to the Grammar Handbook to learn more about verb tense, verb mood, and active and passive voice.

TYPE OF PHRASE	COMPOSITION	EXAMPLES
noun phrase	a noun and its modifiers, including articles, adjectives, and adjective phrases	*I am not <u>that man</u>.* (predicate nominative) *<u>Your high independence</u> only reveals <u>the immeasurable distance between us</u>.* (subject; direct object) *To drag . . . into <u>the grand illuminated temple of liberty</u> . . .* (object of a preposition)
verb phrase	a main verb and its helping verbs, but not any interrupting adverbs, such as *not*	*. . . when the chains of servitude <u>had been torn</u> from his limbs?* *In a case like that, the dumb <u>might</u> eloquently <u>speak</u>. . . .* *. . . I <u>do</u> not <u>despair</u> of this country.*

Read It

1. Each of these sentences contains at least one noun phrase or verb phrase—or both. Mark and label those phrases.

   a. Douglass spoke to the Rochester Ladies Anti-Slavery Society.

   b. He felt that listeners had not supported abolitionism strongly enough, and that he could stir them into action.

   c. His powerful words and his urgent tone shocked many and are still resonating with readers today.

2. **Connect to Style** Reread paragraph 4 of the excerpt from "What to the Slave Is the Fourth of July?" Mark and label two noun phrases and two verb phrases. Explain how the use of the phrases you identified shapes Douglass's style—how the reader "hears" the speaker's voice.

Write It

📝 **Notebook** Replace each of these nouns with a noun phrase: *crowd, message, shame.* Replace each of these verbs with a verb phrase: *feel, participate, work.* Then, use each phrase in an original sentence that relates to Douglass's speech.

Writing to Sources

As Douglass's speech demonstrates, you can strengthen an argument by addressing counterclaims. A similar technique can strengthen informative writing as well: By addressing misconceptions or disproven ideas, you can guide readers to a clearer understanding of the information that you present. For example, if you were writing to explain why explorer Christopher Columbus had difficulty gaining support for his first Atlantic voyage, you might correct the following misconception by stating the fact:

Misconception: People thought that the world was flat and that Columbus would sail off the edge.

Fact: People thought that Columbus had underestimated the distance and that the crew would die when supplies ran out.

Assignment
In this speech, Douglass mentions Southern laws that made it a criminal offense to teach a slave to read and write. Briefly research how some slaves, including Douglass himself, learned to read. Then, write an **informative paragraph** in which you draw connections between your research and Douglass's speech. Include these elements in your paragraph:

- a clear introduction to the topic
- a misconception that you correct with a fact
- a formal, objective tone

Vocabulary and Conventions Connection Consider using several of the concept vocabulary words. Also, remember to use noun phrases and verb phrases to make your sentences precise and informative.

obdurate	disparity	equivocate
stolid	denounce	conceded

Copyright © SAVVAS Learning Company LLC. All Rights Reserved.

- -

Reflect on Your Writing

After you have drafted your informative paragraph, answer the following questions.

1. How do you think that refuting a misconception strengthened your presentation?

2. Why These Words? The words you choose make a difference in your writing. Which words helped you convey information precisely?

STANDARDS
Writing
- Write informative/explanatory texts to examine and convey complex ideas, concepts, and information clearly and accurately through the effective selection, organization, and analysis of content.
- Establish and maintain a formal style and objective tone while attending to the norms and conventions of the discipline in which they are writing.

Speaking and Listening
Evaluate a speaker's point of view, reasoning, and use of evidence and rhetoric, assessing the stance, premises, links among ideas, word choice, points of emphasis, and tone used.

Speaking and Listening

Assignment

Tone is the attitude a speaker expresses toward the subject or audience. A speaker's tone may convey any emotion; for instance, it may be loving, angry, scornful, or amused. In this speech, Douglass changes his tone for a variety of reasons. With a partner, identify two passages from the excerpt that convey different tones. Then, take turns giving a **dramatic reading** of each example.

1. **Choose Examples** Together, look for examples of passages in which Douglass emphasizes each of these ideas.

   - He expresses confusion about his purpose for speaking at this occasion.

   - He seeks common ground with his audience.

   - He reaches a turning point.

   - He introduces a counterclaim.

   - He expresses outrage.

2. **Listen to Dramatic Readings** Before you present your dramatic readings, review your examples. Decide which example you will present and which one your partner will present. Then, follow these steps.

   - Practice reciting the passages. Try to convey the tone you feel Douglass wanted to express. Use your voice and body language to emphasize that tone.

   - Introduce each passage by stating the idea that Douglass wanted to present; then, deliver your dramatic reading.

   - After you have both recited, briefly summarize your thoughts about Douglass's use of tone in each passage.

3. **Evaluate the Examples** Use a presentation evaluation guide like the one shown to assess your classmates' readings. Then, as a class, discuss how Douglass's use of tone contributes to his argument.

PRESENTATION EVALUATION GUIDE
Rate each statement on a scale of 1 (not demonstrated) to 5 (demonstrated).
☐ The speaker clearly introduced the passage.
☐ The speaker communicated expressively.
☐ The speaker used body language, including gestures, to emphasize the tone of the passage.
☐ The speaker accurately interpreted the tone of the passage.
☐ The speaker showed a good understanding of the text.

📝 EVIDENCE LOG

Before moving on to a new selection, go to your Evidence Log and record what you learned from "What to the Slave Is the Fourth of July?"

About the Speaker

Abraham Lincoln
(1809–1865) took office
as president on March 4,
1861—just six weeks before
the Civil War began. The war
shaped his presidency, as he
sought to reunify the nation.
Lincoln took a keen interest
in the operations of the war,
appointing senior officers,
following the war's progress
through telegraph updates,
and even visiting Union
encampments. His belief
that slavery was morally
wrong drove him to issue
a preliminary Emancipation
Proclamation in 1862 and a
final version on January 1,
1863. From that point on,
the Civil War was viewed as
a fight to end slavery, as well
as to restore the Union.

🔧 **Tool Kit**
First-Read Guide and
Model Annotation

📋 STANDARDS
Reading Informational Text
• By the end of grade 11, read and
comprehend literary nonfiction in
the grades 11–CCR text complexity
band proficiently, with scaffolding as
needed at the high end of the range.

Second Inaugural Address

Concept Vocabulary

You will encounter the following words as you read Lincoln's second
inaugural address. Before reading, note how familiar you are with each word.
Then, rank the words in order from most familiar (1) to least familiar (6).

WORD	YOUR RANKING
insurgent	
perish	
rend	
scourge	
unrequited	
malice	

After completing the first read, come back to the concept vocabulary and
review your rankings. Mark changes to your original rankings as needed.

First Read NONFICTION

Apply these strategies as you conduct your first read. You will have an
opportunity to complete the close-read notes after your first read.

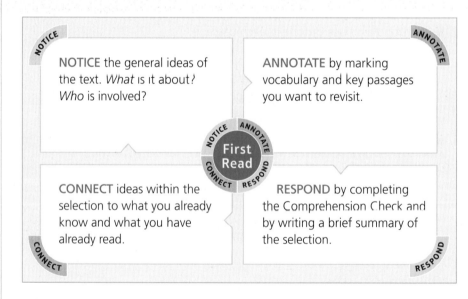

NOTICE the general ideas of the text. *What* is it about? *Who* is involved?

ANNOTATE by marking vocabulary and key passages you want to revisit.

CONNECT ideas within the selection to what you already know and what you have already read.

RESPOND by completing the Comprehension Check and by writing a brief summary of the selection.

First Read

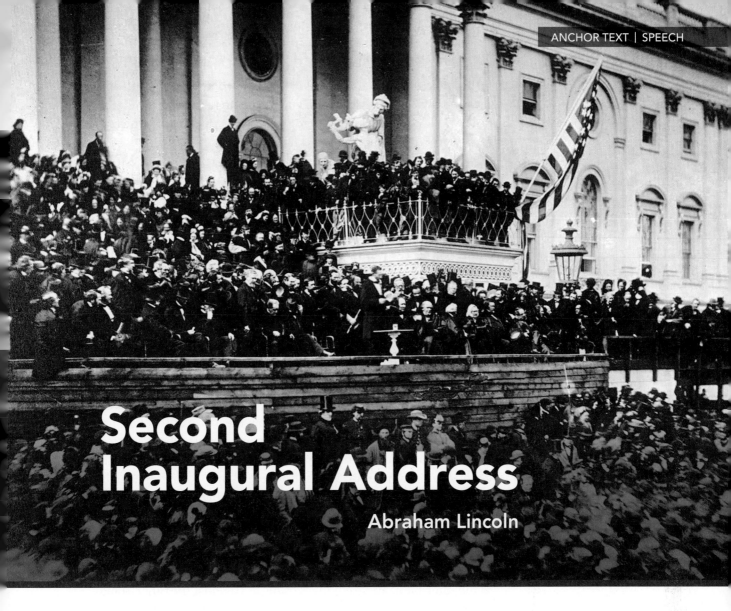

Second Inaugural Address

Abraham Lincoln

BACKGROUND

On March 4, 1865, a crowd of perhaps as many as 40,000 people gathered on the muddy grounds of the United States Capitol to see Abraham Lincoln sworn in for his second term. Despite rain earlier in the morning, the sun broke through the clouds as Lincoln came forward. He gave the following speech to hopeful listeners, who (as one of his bodyguards later said) "seemed to hang on his words as though they were meat and drink." Indeed, Frederick Douglass told Lincoln that the speech had been "a sacred effort." Following the speech, Chief Justice Salmon P. Chase administered the oath of office. Ironically, Lincoln would die a little more than a month later at the hands of John Wilkes Booth, who stood in the crowd on the Capitol steps that day and listened to Lincoln give the speech.

NOTES

Fellow-Countrymen:

1 At this second appearing to take the oath of the presidential office, there is less occasion for an extended address than there was at the first. Then a statement somewhat in detail of a course to be pursued seemed fitting and proper. Now, at the expiration of four years, during which public declarations have been constantly called

insurgent (ihn SUR juhnt) *adj.* rebellious or in revolt against a government in power

perish (PEH rish) *v.* die

rend (rehnd) *v.* tear apart with violent force

CLOSE READ

ANNOTATE: Mark the sentence in paragraph 3 that states the government's policy regarding the expansion of slavery.

QUESTION: Why does the president include this information?

CONCLUDE: What effect does this information have, particularly in shaping the audience's view of the Confederacy?

scourge (SKURJ) *n.* cause of serious trouble or suffering

unrequited (uhn rih KWY tihd) *adj.* not repaid or avenged

forth on every point and phase of the great contest which still absorbs the attention and engrosses the energies of the nation, little that is new could be presented. The progress of our arms, upon which all else chiefly depends, is as well known to the public as to myself, and it is, I trust, reasonably satisfactory and encouraging to all. With high hope for the future, no prediction in regard to it is ventured.

2   On the occasion corresponding to this four years ago, all thoughts were anxiously directed to an impending civil war. All dreaded it; all sought to avert it. While the inaugural address was being delivered from this place, devoted altogether to saving the Union without war, **insurgent** agents were in the city seeking to destroy it without war— seeking to dissolve the Union and divide effects by negotiation. Both parties deprecated war, but one of them would make war rather than let the nation survive, and the other would accept war rather than let it **perish**, and the war came.

3   One-eighth of the whole population were colored slaves, not distributed generally over the Union, but localized in the southern part of it. These slaves constituted a peculiar and powerful interest. All knew that this interest was somehow the cause of the war. To strengthen, perpetuate, and extend this interest was the object for which the insurgents would **rend** the Union even by war, while the government claimed no right to do more than to restrict the territorial enlargement of it. Neither party expected for the war the magnitude or the duration which it has already attained. Neither anticipated that the cause of the conflict might cease with or even before the conflict itself should cease. Each looked for an easier triumph, and a result less fundamental and astounding. Both read the same Bible and pray to the same God, and each invokes his aid against the other. It may seem strange that any men should dare to ask a just God's assistance in wringing their bread from the sweat of other men's faces, but "let us judge not, that we be not judged."[1] The prayers of both could not be answered. That of neither has been answered fully. The Almighty has his own purposes. "Woe unto the world because of offenses; for it must needs be that offenses come, but woe to that man by whom the offense cometh."[2] If we shall suppose that American slavery is one of those offenses which, in the providence of God, must needs come, but which, having continued through his appointed time, he now wills to remove, and that he gives to both North and South this terrible war as the woe due to those by whom the offense came, shall we discern therein any departure from those divine attributes which the believers in a living God always ascribe to him? Fondly do we hope, fervently do we pray, that this mighty **scourge** of war may speedily pass away. Yet, if God wills that it continue until all the wealth piled by the bondsman's two hundred and fifty years of **unrequited** toil

---

1. **"let us judge not, that we be not judged"** reference to the words of Jesus in the biblical passage Matthew 7:1.
2. **"Woe unto the world . . . the offense cometh."** reference to the biblical passage Matthew 18:7, in which Jesus warns about allowing sin into one's life.

shall be sunk, and until every drop of blood drawn with the lash shall be paid by another drawn with the sword, as was said three thousand years ago, so still it must be said "the judgments of the Lord are true and righteous altogether."[3]

4   With **malice** toward none, with charity for all, with firmness in the right as God gives us to see the right, let us strive on to finish the work we are in, to bind up the nation's wounds, to care for him who shall have borne the battle and for his widow and his orphan, to do all which may achieve and cherish a just and lasting peace among ourselves and with all nations. 🖝

malice (MAL ihs) *n.* desire to harm or inflict injury

---

3. **"the judgments of the Lord are true and righteous altogether"** reference to the biblical Psalm 19:9, praising the rightness of God's ways.

Comprehension Check

Complete the following items after you finish your first read.

1. To what event is Lincoln referring when he says, "On the occasion corresponding to this four years ago. . ."?

2. What was on people's minds at the time of the occasion you identified in item 1?

3. What is the "peculiar and powerful interest" that Lincoln says was "somehow the cause of the war?"

4. What does Lincoln intend to do to heal the nation, after the war?

5. 📓 **Notebook** Write a summary of Lincoln's second inaugural address to confirm your understanding of the speech.

- -

RESEARCH

Research to Clarify Choose at least one unfamiliar detail from the text. Briefly research that detail. In what way does the information you learned shed light on an aspect of the speech?

Research to Explore Choose something that interests you from the text, and formulate a research question about it.

SECOND INAUGURAL ADDRESS

Close Read the Text

1. This model, from paragraph 2 of the text, shows two sample annotations, along with questions and conclusions. Close read the passage, and find another detail to annotate. Then, write a question and your conclusion.

ANNOTATE: Lincoln is comparing and contrasting reasons the North and South went to war.

QUESTION: For what purpose might Lincoln do this?

CONCLUDE: By showing insight about the war's causes, Lincoln might be indicating his ability to reunite the nation.

ANNOTATE: The final words are very dramatic.

QUESTION: What is the effect of these words?

CONCLUDE: Appearing at the end of a long, complex sentence, the simple words emphasize the horror of war.

> Both parties deprecated war, but one of them would make war rather than let the nation survive, and the other would accept war rather than let it perish, and the war came.

🔧 **Tool Kit**
Close-Read Guide and Model Annotation

2. For more practice, go back into the text, and complete the close-read notes.

3. Revisit a section of the text you found important during your first read. Read this section closely, and **annotate** what you notice. Ask yourself **questions** such as "Why did the author make this choice?" What can you **conclude**?

- -

Analyze the Text

CITE TEXTUAL EVIDENCE
to support your answers.

📓 **Notebook** Respond to these questions.

1. (a) **Paraphrase**, or state in your own words, Lincoln's comment that "all else chiefly depends" upon "the progress of our arms." (b) **Interpret** To what is Lincoln referring with the words "all else"?

2. **Connect** How do Lincoln's statements in paragraph 2 connect to the rest of the speech?

3. (a) **Make Inferences** The term **irony** refers to a discrepancy between appearances and reality. Think about the irony in paragraph 3. In what way does Lincoln see irony in the abolition of slavery in the United States? (b) **Interpret** What does Lincoln find ironic about the prayers of both sides?

4. **Historical Perspectives** In what ways is this speech a commentary on the issue of slavery?

5. **Essential Question** *How does the struggle for freedom change with history?* What have you learned about the struggle for freedom from reading this speech?

🔑 STANDARDS

Reading Informational Text
• Determine two or more central ideas of a text and analyze their development over the course of the text, including how they interact and build on one another to provide a complex analysis; provide an objective summary of the text.
• Analyze and evaluate the effectiveness of the structure an author uses in his or her exposition or argument, including whether the structure makes points clear, convincing, and engaging.
• Determine an author's point of view or purpose in a text in which the rhetoric is particularly effective, analyzing how style and content contribute to the power, persuasiveness, or beauty of the text.
• Analyze seventeenth-, eighteenth-, and nineteenth-century foundational U.S. documents of historical and literary significance for their themes, purposes, and rhetorical features.

Analyze Craft and Structure

Structure Writers often use a **chronological structure,** or time order, as a framework for their ideas. You may be used to seeing chronological order in the plot of a novel or play, but this kind of structure is also effective in nonfiction. For example, listeners can more easily follow the logic of a speech when ideas are presented within a chronological structure.

- The speaker establishes the chronological structure by discussing the events or actions that led to the present situation—which is often the occasion for the speech.
- The present situation is examined. At this point, the audience understands the central idea of the speech and contemplates the author's reasoning.
- The chronological framework is completed by a discussion of the future. This part can be a persuasive call to action or an explanation of a final step. It is always a clear statement of the speaker's central idea.

In his second inaugural address, Lincoln recalls the past, discusses the present, and looks to the future.

Practice

CITE TEXTUAL EVIDENCE
to support your answers.

Notebook Respond to these questions.

1. (a) What does Lincoln say about the nature of the speech he made when he first took office, four years earlier? (b) How does he contrast that information with the speech that he is making in the present, at his second inauguration?
2. In this chart, briefly record the content of each part of the chronological framework of Lincoln's speech.

LINCOLN'S SECOND INAUGURAL ADDRESS: CHRONOLOGICAL CONTENT	
Past	
Present	
Future	

3. What does the content of the speech tell you about Lincoln's intended policy for his second term?
4. (a) What national issue does Lincoln discuss in paragraph 3? (b) What might have been the effect of the speech if Lincoln had developed it to discuss only this issue? Explain.
5. How does Lincoln's use of chronological structure contribute to the effectiveness of the speech? Explain.

SECOND INAUGURAL ADDRESS

Concept Vocabulary

insurgent	rend	unrequited
perish	scourge	malice

Why These Words? These concept vocabulary words remind the audience of the terrible nature of the conflict that the nation was enduring at the moment. Lincoln says that the *insurgents* would *rend* the nation. He speaks of the *scourge* of war—and, indeed, the war took many American lives and destroyed much of the nation's property.

1. How does the concept vocabulary convey the nature of the conflict?

2. What other words in the speech connect to this concept?

WORD NETWORK

Add words related to struggle from the text to your Word Network.

Practice

Notebook **Complete these activities.**

1. Use each concept vocabulary word in a sentence that demonstrates your understanding of the word's meaning.

2. In two of your sentences, replace the concept word with a synonym. What is the effect of your word change? For example, which sentence seems more powerful? Which one seems more positive or more negative?

Word Study

Synonyms and Nuances In this speech, Lincoln refers to the "scourge" of war. *Scourge* is a very strong word, an example of charged language. Lincoln might have chosen another word with a similar denotation, such as *blight* or *curse*. These words are synonyms because they have similar general meanings. They are also all examples of charged, or emotionally laden language. However, each word has its own **nuance,** or shade of meaning. For example, *blight* suggests disease or withering, whereas *curse* suggests a supernatural source of suffering.

1. Write two sentences, using a synonym for *scourge* in each sentence. Make sure that each sentence demonstrates the shade of meaning of the synonym you choose.

2. Reread the second inaugural address. Which synonym for *scourge* most closely reflects Lincoln's use of the word? Explain.

STANDARDS

Language
• Demonstrate command of the conventions of standard English grammar and usage when writing or speaking.
• Apply knowledge of language to understand how language functions in different contexts, to make effective choices for meaning or style, and to comprehend more fully when reading or listening.
• Analyze nuances in the meaning of words with similar denotations.
• Acquire and use accurately general academic and domain-specific words and phrases, sufficient for reading, writing, speaking, and listening at the college and career readiness level; demonstrate independence in gathering vocabulary knowledge when considering a word or phrase important to comprehension or expression.

Conventions and Style

Types of Phrases A **prepositional phrase** is a group of words that begins with a preposition. Some prepositions are listed here.

about	across	at	beneath	by
concerning	despite	except	for	from
in	into	near	of	on
regarding	than	to	toward	with

A prepositional phrase also includes an object and any modifiers of that object. The object of the preposition may be a noun, a pronoun, a gerund (a verb form that acts as a noun), or, occasionally, a clause. Prepositional phrases function in sentences as either adverbs or adjectives. They help writers and speakers express their ideas with greater clarity and precision.

TYPE OF PHRASE	DEFINITION	EXAMPLES
adverb phrase	a prepositional phrase that modifies a verb, an adjective, or another adverb, by telling *how, where, when,* or *to what degree*	Lincoln was assassinated <u>at Ford's Theatre</u>. (tells *where*) John Wilkes Booth shot him <u>during a play</u>. (tells *when*)
adjective phrase	a prepositional phrase that modifies a noun or pronoun, by telling *what kind, how many,* or *which one*	The president <u>from Illinois</u> died soon after. (tells *which one*) Crowds <u>beyond number</u> mourned his loss. (tells *how many*)

Read It

1. Mark the prepositional phrase in each sentence. Then, label each one as an adverb phrase or an adjective phrase.

   a. Lincoln delivered his address at the White House.

   b. The East Portico of the White House was a historic place.

   c. Lincoln spoke in a clear, strong voice.

2. **Connect to Style** Reread paragraph 3 of Lincoln's speech. Mark and then label two adjective phrases and two adverb phrases. Explain how the use of prepositional phrases contributes to Lincoln's style and helps clarify his ideas.

Write It

🔲 **Notebook** Expand the numbered sentences by adding one or more adverb phrases or adjective phrases. Label each phrase in parentheses.

> **EXAMPLE**
> The sun began shining.
> The sun began shining ***through the clouds*** (adverb phrase) ***at the moment*** (adverb phrase) ***of Lincoln's speech*** (adjective phrase).

1. Lincoln spoke, and everyone paid rapt attention.

2. Most listeners applauded when the words touched their minds and hearts.

SECOND INAUGURAL ADDRESS

Writing to Sources

Eyewitness accounts are important sources of historical information. Historians look for as many such accounts as are available in order to compare what each eyewitness has recorded. In addition to each person's unique insights, historians look for corroboration of descriptions and sequences of events.

Assignment

Imagine that you had been present when Abraham Lincoln delivered this inaugural address. Write an **informative eyewitness account** in the form of a letter or journal entry. Include details such as these:

- personal details, such as where you were standing
- an estimate of how many people were present
- Lincoln's appearance and delivery
- the effect of the speech on the crowd
- your opinion of the speech

Report narrative details in an orderly sequence. You might want to remark, for example, on your difficulties as you looked for a place to stand and observe the occasion. Then, describe the scene from the vantage point you eventually found.

Vocabulary and Conventions Connection Consider including several of the concept vocabulary words. Also, remember to use prepositional phrases to add precision to your account.

insurgent	rend	unrequited
perish	scourge	malice

Reflect on Your Writing

After you have drafted your informative eyewitness account, answer these questions.

1. Did you write as if you had been actually present?

2. What kinds of details did you add to make your account realistic?

3. Why These Words? The words you choose can greatly increase the effect of your writing. Which words do you think are most helpful in conveying the sense that "you had been there"?

STANDARDS

Writing
• Write informative/explanatory texts to examine and convey complex ideas, concepts, and information clearly and accurately through the effective selection, organization, and analysis of content.
• Write narratives to develop real or imagined experiences or events using effective technique, well-chosen details, and well-structured event sequences.

Speaking and Listening
Evaluate a speaker's point of view, reasoning, and use of evidence and rhetoric, assessing the stance, premises, links among ideas, word choice, points of emphasis, and tone used.

Speaking and Listening

Assignment
With a partner, prepare a brief **reading and discussion** of key passages from Lincoln's speech.

1. **Choose the Passages** Work together to choose two passages that you feel express key ideas with particular force or clarity.

   - Read the sentences or passages aloud, pausing to restate, or paraphrase, Lincoln's words.

   - Work together to develop a clear statement about the reasons you chose the two passages: What qualities in the language or ideas make these two passages especially powerful?

2. **Prepare Your Delivery** Read through the passages, and note natural breaks. These may be indicated by punctuation marks, but you also can choose places where you will want to pause for emphasis.

3. **Deliver Your Reading and Analysis** Follow these tips as you read your passages aloud and discuss your choices.

   - Speak slowly so that listeners can follow any challenging language or ideas.

   - Use gestures and body language carefully to emphasize meaning without causing distraction. In addition, vary the volume of your voice and the speed with which you speak to accurately reflect the ideas you are expressing.

   - Remember that the language of Lincoln's speech is formal. In addition, some word choices are different from those in modern speech. Make sure your interpretation reflects the meanings of such words accurately.

   - Pause after you complete your readings of the passages. Then, present your interpretations of the passages in your own words.

4. **Evaluate Presentations** As your classmates deliver their presentations, listen attentively. Use the evaluation guide to analyze their presentations.

PRESENTATION EVALUATION GUIDE

Rate each statement on a scale of 1 (not demonstrated) to 5 (demonstrated).

☐ The speaker read the text with proper emphasis on meaning.

☐ The speaker used appropriate gestures and body language.

☐ The speaker's pace and volume were varied and appropriate for the thoughts and feelings expressed in the text.

☐ The speaker's interpretations and evaluations were accurate and well expressed.

⬛ EVIDENCE LOG

Before moving on to a new selection, go to your Evidence Log and record what you learned from Lincoln's second inaugural address.

About Political Cartoons and Photojournalism

Many **political cartoons**, especially in the nineteenth century, were published anonymously; in fact, of the three cartoons in this gallery, only the pro-Lincoln caricature of the President's height is attributable (to Frank Billew). The others, expressing the dissatisfaction with Lincoln's leadership that seethed in the North among the Democrats and those Republicans unsatisfied with Lincoln's leadership in the war, were published anonymously in various newspapers.

Photojournalism—capturing news in photographs—emerged in the 1840s. The new technology of photography found a use in revealing events and preserving images for history, including battlefield photographs of the Civil War.

Perspectives on Lincoln

Media Vocabulary

The following words will be useful to you as you analyze, discuss, and write about political cartoons and photojournalism.

Composition: arrangement of the parts of an image, whether drawn or recorded in some other visual format	• The composition may emphasize one part of an image more than another. • The composition may offer clues to the political purpose of the image.
Caricature: exaggeration of details relating to people and events, often for humorous effect, in a cartoon or other created image	• In political cartoons, caricature often shows how the cartoonist (or the publication that hired the cartoonist) feels about a particular person, group, or situation. • Sometimes, elements of a public figure's appearance become commonly caricatured, making that person easy to identify.
Labeling and Captions: written labels and other text that often accompany politically charged images to clarify their meanings	• In political cartoons, key details are often labeled to help readers recognize their meaning. • Photographs are more likely to use captions or annotations that present the context in which the photograph was taken.

First Review MEDIA: ART AND PHOTOGRAPHY

Apply these strategies as you conduct your first review. You will have an opportunity to conduct a close review after your first review.

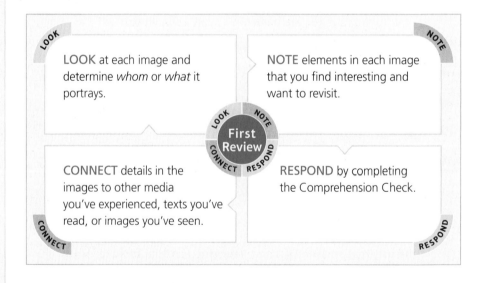

LOOK at each image and determine *whom* or *what* it portrays.

NOTE elements in each image that you find interesting and want to revisit.

First Review

CONNECT details in the images to other media you've experienced, texts you've read, or images you've seen.

RESPOND by completing the Comprehension Check.

STANDARDS

Reading Informational Text
By the end of grade 11, read and comprehend literary nonfiction in the grades 11–CCR text complexity band proficiently, with scaffolding as needed at the high end of the range.

Perspectives on Lincoln

BACKGROUND

As Lincoln's second election campaign approached, he was faced with a Republican party threatening to splinter, a bloody Civil War in its final stages, and a Democratic party ready to capitalize on his apparent vulnerability. However, Lincoln overcame these obstacles by combining the political heft of an impending Union victory, the support of the soldier vote, and political deals brokered within the Republican party. His campaign's slogan was "Don't change horses in the middle of a stream." As you study these images, ask yourself these questions: What opinions did people have of Lincoln in his own time? How is he thought of today?

IMAGE 1: The Union Must Be Preserved at All Hazards This 1864 cartoon depicts Democratic presidential candidate George Brinton McClellan trying to keep a map of the United States from being pulled apart by President Abraham Lincoln and the Confederate president Jefferson Davis. The cartoon depicts both Lincoln and Davis as short-sightedly putting their own political goals (abolition for Lincoln, secession for Davis) ahead of the country's well-being.

NOTES

IMAGE 2: Columbia Demands Her Children! "Columbia," a personification of America, is condemning Abraham Lincoln for the Union casualties of the Civil War. Lincoln's reply refers to a false report that Lincoln had told a joke on the battlefield of Antietam.

NOTES

IMAGE 3: Long Abe a Little Longer In this celebration of Lincoln's reelection, Lincoln is caricatured as being president "even longer"—a play on words regarding his height and his length of time in office, as well as a reference to his "stature," or importance, as president.

NOTES

IMAGE 4: The Body of the Martyr President, Abraham Lincoln, Lying in State Further increasing his stature in the eyes of the nation, Lincoln's assassination made him a martyr, as the North was united in grief. Many historians have called Lincoln's funeral the greatest in the history of the United States.

NOTES

NOTES

IMAGE 5: Funeral Procession in New York City Millions turned out to see Lincoln's funeral train pass on its way to his burial in Springfield, Illinois—and, in some cities, to attend a ceremony in his honor. In this photograph of a funeral procession held during a stop in New York City, a young Theodore Roosevelt (later President Roosevelt) and his brother watch the scene from a window (in the upper left-hand corner of the image).

IMAGE 6: Civil Rights Activists at the Lincoln Memorial Almost a century after Lincoln's death, leaders of the Civil Rights movement, including Dr. Martin Luther King, Jr., (seated, farthest right) gather in front of the Lincoln Memorial during the 1963 March on Washington. The Civil Rights movement often looked to Abraham Lincoln, "the Great Emancipator," for inspiration.

NOTES

Comprehension Check

Use the chart to note details about the subject of each image. Identify people and/or symbols, objects, the setting (if there is one), and activities or events depicted.

IMAGE	PEOPLE AND/OR SYMBOLS	OBJECTS	SETTING	ACTIVITIES AND/OR EVENTS
IMAGE 1				
IMAGE 2				
IMAGE 3				
IMAGE 4				
IMAGE 5				
IMAGE 6				

NOTES

PERSPECTIVES ON LINCOLN

Close Review

Revisit the images and your first-review notes. Write down any new observations that seem important. What **questions** do you have? What can you **conclude?**

Analyze the Media

📋 **Notebook** Complete the activities.

1. **Present and Discuss** Choose the image you find most interesting or persuasive. Share your choice with the class, and discuss why you chose it. Explain what you noticed in the image, the questions it raised for you, and the conclusions you reached about it.

2. **Review and Synthesize** Review all the images. What perspectives do they present? What argument are they making? Are they examples of journalism, art, both, or neither? Explain.

3. **Essential Question:** *In what ways does the struggle for freedom change with history?* What have you learned about the struggle for freedom from these cartoons and photographs?

LANGUAGE DEVELOPMENT

Media Vocabulary

composition	caricature	labeling and captions

Use these vocabulary words in your responses to the following questions.

1. (a) In Image 1, what are the positions of the three people in relation to one another? To the map of the United States? (b) What might the artist have intended to convey through this depiction?

2. (a) In Image 2, what visual details clarify the identity of the woman on the left? (b) On what visual details does Image 3 rely to convey its message?

3. (a) In what sense does Image 6 express a political idea? (b) How does that idea reflect the ideas expressed in Images 4 and 5?

📑 **STANDARDS**

Reading Informational Text
Integrate and evaluate multiple sources of information presented in different media or formats as well as in words in order to address a question or solve a problem.

Speaking and Listening
• Integrate multiple sources of information presented in diverse formats and media in order to make informed decisions and solve problems, evaluating the credibility and accuracy of each source and noting any discrepancies among the data.
• Make strategic use of digital media in presentations to enhance understanding of findings, reasoning, and evidence and to add interest.

Speaking and Listening

Assignment
Create and present an **image gallery.** Choose a person about whom or an event about which Americans had or have varying perspectives. Conduct research, using print and online sources, to find relevant political cartoons and photographs. Create a slide show of your image gallery, and write an informative script to accompany your presentation.

EVIDENCE LOG

Before moving on to a new selection, go to your Evidence Log and record what you learned from "Perspectives on Lincoln."

Plan the Project To help you prepare your image gallery, consider these questions.

- Why is or was the person or event important? What are you trying to show your audience about the perspectives that people had or have of the person or event?

- What sources will you use to conduct your research?

- What technology will you need to present your image slide show?

When choosing photographs, consider how the images reflect attitudes, not just how they preserve a moment in time. When you have chosen your images, make a storyboard.

STORYBOARD TEMPLATE

Prepare the Informative Script Think about the relationships among the images. Consider how you might use the script to point out those relationships.

- Choose a logical sequence of images. Decide how to use transitions in your script to show that sequence.

- Decide how much time to spend on presenting each image. Tailor the length of each section of your script accordingly.

- Once you have written your script, practice reading it aloud.

Present and Discuss Present a slide show of your image gallery to the class, using your script to narrate each image as you show it. Afterward, discuss how well the various perspectives were captured in the images.

WRITING TO SOURCES

• *from* WHAT TO THE SLAVE IS THE FOURTH OF JULY?

• SECOND INAUGURAL ADDRESS

• PERSPECTIVES ON LINCOLN

 **Tool Kit**
Student Model of an
Informative Essay

ACADEMIC
VOCABULARY

As you write your essay, consider using some of the academic vocabulary you learned in the beginning of the unit.

informational
deduction
verbatim
inquire
specific

STANDARDS
Writing
• Write informative/explanatory texts to examine and convey complex ideas, concepts, and information clearly and accurately through the effective selection, organization, and analysis of content.
• Conduct short as well as more sustained research projects to answer a question or solve a problem; narrow or broaden the inquiry when appropriate; synthesize multiple sources on the subject, demonstrating understanding of the subject under investigation.
• Write routinely over extended time frames and shorter time frames for a range of tasks, purposes, and audiences.

Write an Informative Essay

You've just read two important nineteenth-century speeches. In the first, Frederick Douglass looks forward to the liberation of people from slavery. In the second, Abraham Lincoln looks forward to the end of a war and to a just and lasting peace. You've also examined political cartoons and other images from the period that portray differing attitudes about Abraham Lincoln.

Assignment
Write an **informative essay** that looks at American history after the Civil War and that answers this question:

> Did the nation achieve the goals that Douglass and Lincoln desired?

Begin by doing some library or online research. Investigate the period following the Civil War by looking up "Reconstruction" and taking notes on your findings. Include facts, details, and definitions that clarify your response. Connect your findings to specific details from the selections in Whole-Class Learning.

Elements of an Informative Essay

An **informative essay** uses facts, details, data, and other kinds of evidence to present information about a topic. Readers turn to informative texts when they wish to learn about a specific idea, concept, or subject area.

An effective informative essay contains these elements:

• a thesis statement that introduces the concept or subject
• relevant facts and concrete details that expand upon the topic
• extended definitions, quotations, and other examples that support the information presented
• use of varied sentence structures to clarify the relationships among ideas
• precise language and technical vocabulary where appropriate
• a formal style and an objective tone
• a conclusion that follows from and supports the information presented

Model Informative Essay For a model of a well-crafted informative essay, see the Launch Text, "The Zigzag Road to Rights." Review the Launch Text for examples of the elements described above. You will look more closely at these elements as you prepare to write your own informative essay.

Prewriting / Planning

Write a Working Thesis Reread the assignment. Based on the work you have done so far in this unit, think about what you want to say in response to the question that the assignment asks. Write a draft of your **thesis statement** (or **thesis**)—the sentence that presents the controlling idea of your text.

_____

_____ .

Compare and Contrast Douglass and Lincoln had different goals, but some of their concerns were similar. Record some areas of comparison and contrast that you might use to support your thesis statement.

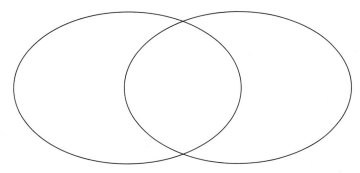

Douglass's Goals   Common Goals   Lincoln's Goals

Gather Evidence Several kinds of information support the thesis developed in the Launch Text. Think about ways in which you can effectively support your thesis. Consider these types of evidence:

- **facts:** relevant statements that can be proved true

- **statistics:** facts presented in the form of numerical data

- **definitions:** explanations of key terms that may be unfamiliar to readers

- **quotations:** statements from authoritative sources (such as historical documents)

- **examples:** specific circumstances that illustrate a general idea

Always confirm your evidence by using more than one source.

Connect Across Texts The prompt asks you to connect your findings to specific details from the speeches by Douglass and Lincoln. Also include details from the political cartoons and other images of Lincoln in your response. Return to those texts, and on note cards record **direct quotations** from the speeches that you might use to support your ideas. Look back at the Launch Text to see how the writer weaves direct quotations from court cases, proclamations, and amendments into the informative essay.

EVIDENCE LOG

Review your Evidence Log and identify key details you may want to cite in your informative essay.

STANDARDS

Writing
- Introduce a topic; organize complex ideas, concepts, and information so that each new element builds on that which precedes it to create a unified whole; include formatting, graphics, and multimedia when useful to aiding comprehension.
- Develop the topic thoroughly by selecting the most significant and relevant facts, extended definitions, concrete details, quotations, or other information and examples appropriate to the audience's knowledge of the topic.

ENRICHING WRITING WITH RESEARCH

Conducting Research Most informative writing requires some research. Find relevant information from reputable sources, and then weave it into your essay.

Assessing Strengths and Limitations of Information Some information is reliable and useful, whereas other information may be suspect or simply not helpful. Evaluate the quality of the information you find by answering these questions:

- Will this information help me develop my topic or thesis?
- Will my audience understand this information, or will I need to provide more background or detail?
- Is this information current, or is it outdated?

Read It

This excerpt from the Launch Text shows how the writer integrates details found through research. The researched information is underlined.

> The writer quotes directly from the researched text to illustrate one of the "zigzag" steps to rights for African Americans.

LAUNCH TEXT EXCERPT

The struggle took another crucial step forward in 1863, when President Abraham Lincoln issued the Emancipation Proclamation. It asserted that "all persons held as slaves" within states that had seceded from the Union "are, and henceforward, shall be free." Still, freedom for slaves depended upon a Union victory. Slavery remained legal in border states loyal to the Union, as well as in Confederate areas under Northern control.

Avoiding Plagiarism *Plagiarism* means taking someone's ideas and words and passing them off as your own. Nobody expects you to be an expert in every subject. However, when you rely on other experts, you must credit them. Follow these steps to avoid plagiarism.

1. **Quote.** If the source uses wording that you find especially strong or apt, quote it directly. Make sure the reader can tell whom you are quoting.

   Example: *In his original draft of the Declaration of Independence, Thomas Jefferson included a strong condemnation of slavery, protesting this "cruel war against human nature."*

2. **Paraphrase.** When an author's ideas are important but the wording is less critical, restate the information in your own words.

   Example:
   Original: *The struggle took another crucial step forward in 1863, when President Abraham Lincoln issued the Emancipation Proclamation.*

   Paraphrase: Lincoln's Emancipation Proclamation of 1863 would prove to be a benchmark in the fight for civil rights.

3. **Cite.** Follow the format your teacher prefers to cite sources for any information you use that is not common public knowledge.

STANDARDS
Writing
Gather relevant information from multiple authoritative print and digital sources, using advanced searches effectively; assess the strengths and limitations of each source in terms of the task, purpose, and audience; integrate information into the text selectively to maintain the flow of ideas, avoiding plagiarism and overreliance on any one source and following a standard format for citation.

Write It

Organize your notes in a way that will best help you support your thesis statement.

Taking and Organizing Notes Develop a system for organizing your notes so that you know which are paraphrased and which are directly quoted. Try using this format for one of your notes to see whether it works well for you. Then, copy it or revise it to use for each of your sources.

TITLE: _____ PAGE _____

AUTHOR: _____

SUMMARY, QUOTATION, OR PARAPHASE? (Circle one)

NOTES:

Evaluating Sources Review your notes, and look for conflicting information. If you find substantial differences, consider the reliability and credibility of the sources: web sites ending with .edu or .gov generally provide more accurate information than sites ending with .com. When two sources conflict, look for a third source to confirm facts.

Weaving Research Into Text As you draft your essay, work to integrate quotations and other information from your sources. Clearly introduce each reference and note its relevance, as in this model.

INTEGRATING QUOTATIONS

Lincoln's proclamation was not guaranteed to have the effects he wanted. In his Lincoln Prize–winning book, *Lincoln's Emancipation Proclamation,* Gettysburg College professor Allen Guelzo called it "one of the biggest political gambles in American history" (7). It might easily have backfired.

TIP

CITATIONS

When citing sources, use a consistent style, such as the one established by the Modern Language Association (MLA):

- Sources are cited following the quotation or reference. The citation appears in parentheses with a page reference, as applicable.

- If the parenthetical citation appears at the end of a sentence, the period follows the final parenthesis.

The writer clearly introduces the quotation, identifying its author and integrating it with surrounding text, and then links it to a main point: *The proclamation might have made a situation worse instead of better.*

Drafting

Organize Your Essay Your essay should include an introduction, a body, and a conclusion. Each section of the essay should build on what has come before.

This outline shows the key sections of the Launch Text. In an informative essay, you have the option of adding headings to separate sections that belong together. Whether or not you use headings, each section of the text should have a specific purpose.

Consider the Launch Text outline as you organize information for your draft.

Model: "The Zigzag Road to Rights" Outline

INTRODUCTION
Paragraph 1 states the thesis: *The struggle for equal recognition of African Americans demonstrates a zigzag road to rights.*

BODY
Paragraph 2 (failure): revisions to the Declaration of Independence

Paragraph 3 (improvement): Article V of the Constitution

Paragraph 4 (improvement): the Emancipation Proclamation

Paragraph 5 (improvement): the Thirteenth *Amendment*

Paragraph 6 (failure): *Plessy v. Ferguson*

Paragraph 7 (improvement): *Brown v. Board of Education*

Paragraph 8 (improvement): the Voting Rights Act of 1965

CONCLUSION
Paragraph 9 recalls the thesis: *History teaches us that rights gained can be lost, curtailed, or ignored— and perhaps gained once more.*

Informative Essay Outline

INTRODUCTION

BODY

CONCLUSION

Copyright © SAVVAS Learning Company LLC. All Rights Reserved.

STANDARDS

Writing
• Develop the topic thoroughly by selecting the most significant and relevant facts, extended definitions, concrete details, quotations, or other information and examples appropriate to the audience's knowledge of the topic.
• Provide a concluding statement or section that follows from and supports the information or explanation presented.

Write a First Draft Use your outline to write your first draft. Include a variety of evidence, and make clear connections among ideas. Be sure that each paragraph has a purpose and follows logically from the paragraphs that come before it. Keep your readers in mind as you craft your text. Consider what they might already know and what might be unfamiliar. Work at making your writing engaging and logical. Include headings if they might clarify things for your readers. Write a conclusion that follows from your thesis and supports the information you presented.

Syntax: Sentence Patterns

Sentences come in a variety of patterns. Some sentence patterns are best suited for simple ideas; some patterns better convey complex, related ideas.

Read It

These sentences from the Launch Text demonstrate a variety of sentence patterns. Subjects are underlined once, and verbs are underlined twice.

- Simple Sentence (one independent clause): *In his original draft of the Declaration of Independence, Thomas Jefferson included a strong condemnation of slavery.*

- Inverted Sentence (verb precedes subject): *Powerful indeed was their pressure.*

- Compound Sentence (two or more independent clauses): *Laws can be changed, and rights can be gained.*

- Complex Sentence (one independent clause and one or more dependent clauses): *The struggle took another crucial step forward in 1863, when President Abraham Lincoln issued the Emancipation Proclamation.*

- Compound-Complex Sentence (two or more independent clauses and one or more dependent clauses): *While the path to progress is not smooth, one thing is certain: The zigzag will continue into the future.*

Write It

As you draft, choose sentence patterns that best match the ideas you want to convey. Here are some strategies and examples.

STRATEGY	EXAMPLES
To convey two closely related ideas, combine simple sentences to make compound sentences.	Today, all adult citizens can vote. Many hold higher office. *Today, all adult citizens can vote, and many hold higher office.*
Invert simple sentences to add interest.	Voting rights are among an American's most important privileges. *Among an American's most important privileges are voting rights.*
Add subordinate clauses to provide detail.	Eighteen-year-olds rarely vote. *Eighteen-year-olds who are not informed rarely vote.* *Even when the polls are nearby, eighteen-year-olds rarely vote.*

PUNCTUATION
Punctuate compound and complex sentences correctly.

- Use a comma before the coordinating conjunction in a compound sentence.
- Use a semicolon between independent clauses in a compound sentence with no coordinating conjunction.
- Use a comma after a subordinate clause that begins a complex sentence.

STANDARDS

Writing
Use appropriate and varied transitions and syntax to link the major sections of the text, create cohesion, and clarify the relationships among complex ideas and concepts.

Language
Vary syntax for effect, consulting references for guidance as needed; apply an understanding of syntax to the study of complex texts when reading.

Revising

Evaluating Your Draft

Use this checklist to evaluate the effectiveness of your first draft. Then, use your evaluation and the revising instructions on this page to guide your revision.

FOCUS AND ORGANIZATION	EVIDENCE AND ELABORATION	CONVENTIONS
☐ Provides an introduction that establishes the topic and thesis statement.	☐ Develops the topic using relevant facts, definitions, details, quotations, examples, and/or other evidence.	☐ Attends to the norms and conventions of the discipline, especially the correct use and punctuation of compound and complex sentences.
☐ Presents main points in a logical order.	☐ Uses vocabulary and word choices that are appropriate for the purpose and audience, including precise words and technical vocabulary where appropriate.	☐ Uses appropriate and varied sentence structures to create cohesion and clarify relationships.
☐ Uses words, phrases, and clauses to clarify relationships among ideas.		
☐ Provides a conclusion that follows logically from the preceding information.		

🔠 WORD NETWORK

Include interesting words from your Word Network in your informative essay.

Revising for Focus and Organization

Strong Conclusion Your conclusion should reflect the information that precedes it, but it also should suggest the topic's importance or somehow connect the topic to a broader view. Notice how the Launch Text writer draws a conclusion about the topic's connection to the past and the future in the conclusion of "The Zigzag Road to Rights."

> **LAUNCH TEXT EXCERPT**
>
> The history of African American rights features many crucial victories, from the Emancipation Proclamation through the Voting Rights Act. However, the record of the struggle also includes the difficult stumbling blocks that have had to be overcome. While the path to progress is not smooth, one thing is certain: The zigzag will continue into the future. History teaches us that rights gained can be lost, curtailed, or ignored— and perhaps gained once more.

Revising for Evidence and Elaboration

Technical Vocabulary If you use topic-specific words, consider how you might define them for your audience. Be sure to spell and use those words correctly.

▤ STANDARDS

Writing
• Use precise language, domain-specific vocabulary and techniques such as metaphor, simile, and analogy to manage the complexity of the topic.
• Provide a concluding statement or section that follows from and supports the information or explanation presented.

PEER REVIEW

Exchange essays with a classmate. Use the checklist to evaluate your classmate's essay and provide supportive feedback.

1. Is the thesis clear?

☐ yes   ☐ no   If no, explain what confused you.

2. Are there sufficient examples and details to support the thesis?

☐ yes   ☐ no   If no, tell what you think might be missing.

3. Does the text conclude in a logical, satisfying way?

☐ yes   ☐ no   If no, indicate what you might change.

4. What is the strongest part of your classmate's essay? Why?

_____

_____

_____

_____

Editing and Proofreading

Edit for Conventions Reread your draft for accuracy and consistency. Correct errors in grammar and word usage. Make sure that you have quoted your sources accurately and indicated your sources.

Proofread for Accuracy Read your draft carefully, looking for errors in spelling and punctuation. If you are including technical vocabulary, use a dictionary to check your spelling.

Publishing and Presenting

Create a final version of your text. Pair up with a classmate (not your peer reviewer), and read each other's work. Discuss ways in which your two essays are alike and different. Are your thesis statements similar? Did you incorporate some of the same details? Even if the content is similar, do your styles differ? Share your findings with the class, and talk about what comparing the texts has taught you about developing a topic and supporting a thesis.

Reflecting

Consider what you learned by writing your text. Was your research sufficient to respond to the prompt, or would you have preferred to spend more time researching the topic? Think about what you will do differently the next time you write an informative essay.

≣ STANDARDS

Writing
Develop and strengthen writing as needed by planning, revising, editing, rewriting, or trying a new approach, focusing on addressing what is most significant for a specific purpose and audience.

OVERVIEW: SMALL-GROUP LEARNING

ESSENTIAL QUESTION:

In what ways does the struggle for freedom change with history?

As you read these selections, work with your group to explore the various ways in which the struggle for freedom has changed over time.

From Text to Topic During the Civil War era, opponents of slavery argued that the nation had not fully lived up to its founding promise of liberty. In the selections in this section, others add their voices to the chorus, clamoring for liberty, justice, and equal rights. As you read, consider what the selections show about how the struggle for freedom has changed and grown over time.

Small-Group Learning Strategies

Throughout your life, in school, in your community, and in your career, you will continue to develop strategies when you work in teams. Use these strategies during Small-Group Learning. Add ideas of your own for each step.

STRATEGY	ACTION PLAN
Prepare	• Complete your assignments so that you are prepared for group work. • Organize your thinking so you can contribute to your group's discussions. •
Participate fully	• Make eye contact to signal that you are listening and taking in what is being said. • Use text evidence when making a point. •
Support others	• Build off ideas from others in your group. • Invite others who have not yet spoken to join the discussion. •
Clarify	• Paraphrase the ideas of others to ensure that your understanding is correct. • Ask follow-up questions. •

CONTENTS

SPEECH

Ain't I a Woman?
Sojourner Truth, adapted by Frances Gage

Haven't women proved over time that they are deserving of power?

PUBLIC DOCUMENT

Declaration of Sentiments
Elizabeth Cady Stanton

The Declaration of Independence did not free us all—a form of tyranny still exists!

COMPARE

MEDIA: PODCAST

Giving Women the Vote
Sandra Sleight-Brennan

The ratification of the Nineteenth Amendment came down to a single vote—and a surprising turn of events.

SHORT STORY

The Story of an Hour
Kate Chopin

What might it mean to a woman to be truly free?

LEGAL OPINION

Brown v. Board of Education: Opinion of the Court   *Earl Warren*

Can educational facilities be equal if they are racially segregated?

PERFORMANCE TASKS

SPEAKING AND LISTENING FOCUS
Panel Discussion

RESEARCH FOCUS:
Research Presentation

Working as a Team

1. **Take a Position** In your group, discuss the following question:

   What issue today might persuade you to join a movement for social change?

   As you take turns sharing your positions, be sure to provide reasons for your response. After all group members have shared, discuss some of the connections among the issues that were presented.

2. **List Your Rules** As a group, decide on the rules that you will follow as you work together. Two samples are provided. Add two more of your own. As you work together, you may add or revise rules based on your experience together.

   • People should respect each other's opinions.

   • No one should dominate the discussion.

   • _____

     _____

     _____

   • _____

     _____

     _____

3. **Apply the Rules** Share what you have learned about power, protest, and change. Make sure each person in the group contributes. Take notes on and be prepared to share with the class one thing that you heard from another member of your group.

4. **Name Your Group** Choose a name that reflects the unit topic.

   Our group's name: _____

5. **Create a Communication Plan** Decide how you want to communicate with one another. For example, you might use online platforms, collaboration apps, video conferencing, email, or group texts.

   Our group's decision: _____

   _____

Making a Schedule

First, find out the due dates for the Small-Group activities. Then, preview the texts and activities with your group, and make a schedule for completing the tasks.

SELECTION	ACTIVITIES	DUE DATE
Ain't I a Woman?		
Declaration of Sentiments		
Giving Women the Vote		
The Story of an Hour		
Brown v. Board of Education: Opinion of the Court		
Was Brown v. Board a Failure?		

Working on Group Projects

As your group works together, you'll find it more effective if each person has a specific role. Different projects require different roles. Before beginning a project, discuss the necessary roles, and choose one for each group member. Here are some possible roles; add your own ideas.

Project Manager: monitors the schedule and keeps everyone on task

Researcher: organizes research activities

Recorder: takes notes during group meetings

_____

_____

_____

_____

_____

About the Author

Sojourner Truth (c. 1797–1883) was born into slavery in Swartekill, New York, as Isabella Baumfree. In 1826, when one of her owners refused to honor his promise to free her, Baumfree fled with Sophia, her infant daughter. In 1843, she changed her name to Sojourner Truth and began her career as an abolitionist. Her memoirs were published in 1850, and she toured the country to promote not only abolitionism but also equal civil rights for women.

Ain't I a Woman?

Concept Vocabulary

As you perform your first read of "Ain't I a Woman?" you will encounter these words.

racket	fix	obliged

Context Clues When you come across unfamiliar words in a text, you can often determine their meanings by using **context clues**—words and phrases Punishment was harsh; many were subjected to the lash, which tore the skin and caused lasting physical and emotional scars that appear in nearby text. There are various kinds of context clues. Some provide information from which you can draw inferences, or reasonable guesses, about a word's meaning.

> **Example Sentence:** Punishment was harsh: Many were subjected to the **lash**, which tore the skin and caused deep physical and emotional scars.
>
> **Inference:** Because it causes the skin to tear and leaves scars, a *lash* must be a whip or cane.
>
> You can verify your preliminary definition by consulting a reliable print or online dictionary.

Apply your knowledge of context clues and other vocabulary strategies to determine the meanings of unfamiliar words you encounter during your first read.

First Read NONFICTION

Apply these these strategies as you conduct your first read. You will have an opportunity to complete a close read after your first read.

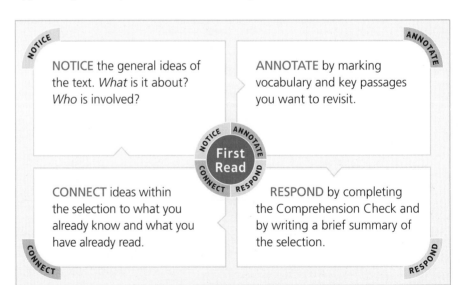

NOTICE the general ideas of the text. *What* is it about? *Who* is involved?

ANNOTATE by marking vocabulary and key passages you want to revisit.

CONNECT ideas within the selection to what you already know and what you have already read.

RESPOND by completing the Comprehension Check and by writing a brief summary of the selection.

First Read

NOTICE ANNOTATE CONNECT RESPOND

STANDARDS
Reading Informational Text
By the end of grade 11, read and comprehend literary nonfiction in the grades 11–CCR Text complexity band proficiently, with scaffolding as needed at the high end of the range.
Language
• Use context as a clue to the meaning of a word or phrase.
• Verify the preliminary determination of the meaning of a word or phrase.

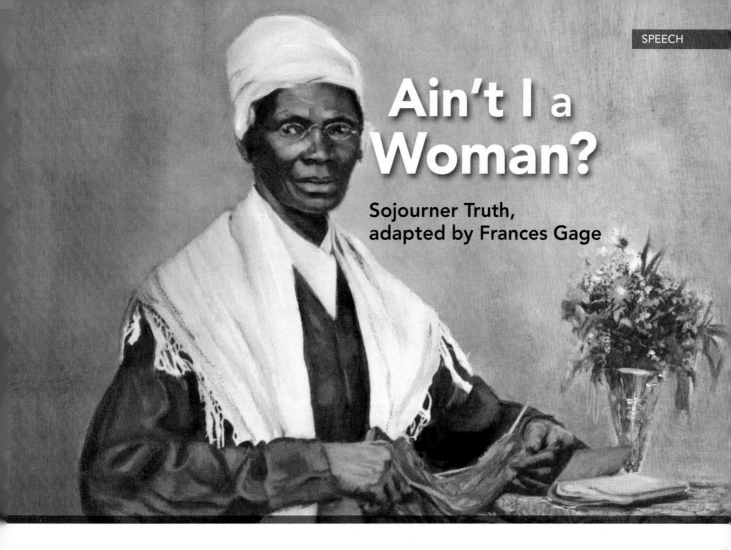

Ain't I a Woman?

Sojourner Truth,
adapted by Frances Gage

BACKGROUND

Sojourner Truth delivered her speech, titled "On Woman's Rights," at the Women's Rights Convention in Akron, Ohio, in 1851. Frances Gage, an abolitionist, published this adapted version in 1863. Though Gage admitted she had "given but a faint sketch" of Truth's speech, her version served the cause of the suffrage movement of the time and has endured. It is by far the best-known version of the speech.

1   Well, children, where there is so much **racket** there must be something out of kilter.[1] I think that 'twixt[2] the Negroes of the South and the women at the North, all talking about rights, the white men will be in a **fix** pretty soon. But what's all this here talking about?

2   That man over there says that women need to be helped into carriages, and lifted over ditches, and to have the best place everywhere. Nobody ever helps me into carriages, or over mudpuddles, or gives me any best place! And ain't I a woman? Look at me! Look at my arm! I have ploughed and planted, and gathered into barns, and no man could head me! And ain't I a woman? I could work as much and eat as much as a man—when I could get it—and bear the lash as well! And ain't I a woman? I have borne thirteen children, and seen them most all sold off to slavery, and when I cried

---

1. **kilter** *n.* proper state or condition.
2. **'twixt** *prep.* between.

out with my mother's grief, none but Jesus heard me! And ain't I a woman? Then they talk about this thing in the head; what's this they call it? [A member of the audience whispers, "Intellect."] That's it, honey. What's that got to do with women's rights or Negroes' rights? If my cup won't hold but a pint, and yours holds a quart, wouldn't you be mean not to let me have my little half measure full? Then that little man in black there, he says women can't have as much rights as men, 'cause Christ wasn't a woman! Where did your Christ come from? Where did your Christ come from? From God and a woman! Man had nothing to do with him.[3] If the first woman God ever made[4] was strong enough to turn the world upside down all alone, these women together ought to be able to turn it back, and get it right side up again! And now they is asking to do it, the men better let them.

3   **Obliged** to you for hearing me, and now old Sojourner ain't got nothing more to say. ❧

---

3. **Man had nothing to do with him** reference to the biblical teaching of the virgin birth of Jesus.

4. **the first woman God ever made** the biblical Eve.

MEDIA CONNECTION

▶ **VIDEO**

"On Woman's Rights," the 1851 Speech by Sojourner Truth

BACKGROUND

Sojourner Truth's original speech was transcribed at the time by her friend Marius Robinson. Truth's dialect was most likely Dutch-accented English because of her regional upstate New York roots.

💬 **Discuss It** Watch this performance of the original speech and compare it to the one you have read. Listen closely and note how the original speech differs from the version adapted by Gage. What do you think might have been Gage's reasoning for making the changes she did?

Write your response before sharing your ideas.

Comprehension Check

Complete the following items after you finish your first read. Review and clarify details with your group.

1. What two reform movements does the speech connect?

2. According to the speech, what privileges do many people think women should enjoy?

3. Identify two hardships that the writer says Truth suffered.

4. What effect does the writer think women can have on the world if they work together?

5. 📝 **Notebook** Confirm your understanding of the text by writing a summary.

- -

RESEARCH

Research to Clarify Choose at least one unfamiliar detail from the text. Briefly research that detail. In what way does the information you learned shed light on an aspect of the speech?

Research to Explore This speech may spark your curiosity to learn more about Sojourner Truth, the era, or the topic. Briefly research a topic that interests you. You may want to share what you discover with your group.

AIN'T I A WOMAN?

Close Read the Text

With your group, revisit sections of the text you marked during your first read. **Annotate** details that you notice. What **questions** do you have? What can you **conclude**?

Analyze the Text

CITE TEXTUAL EVIDENCE
to support your answers.

Complete the activities.

1. **Review and Clarify** With your group, reread paragraph 2 of the selection. Discuss the figurative meanings of "pints" and "cups." What do they have to do with the overall argument in this speech?

2. **Present and Discuss** Now, work with your group to share the passages from the selection that you found especially important. Take turns presenting your passages. Discuss what you noticed in the selection, the questions you asked, and the conclusions you reached.

3. **Essential Question: *In what ways does the struggle for freedom change with history?*** What has this text taught you about power, protest, and change? Discuss with your group.

Concept Vocabulary

racket	fix	obliged

Why These Words? The three concept vocabulary words are related. With your group, determine what the words have in common. How do these word choices enhance the impact of the text?

Practice

 Notebook Confirm your understanding of the concept vocabulary words by using them in sentences. Be sure to use context clues that hint at each word's meaning.

Word Study

Latin Root: *-lig-* At the end of this speech, Gage chooses to use the phrase "Obliged to you for hearing me. . . ." The English word *obliged* is built from the Latin root *-lig-*, which means "to bind." Find several other words that have this same root. Then, write the words and their meanings.

TIP

GROUP DISCUSSION
If you disagree with someone's opinion, allow the speaker to finish his or her point. Then, raise your objection tactfully—for example, you might say, "I see it a little differently." Make sure that you have textual evidence to support your idea.

⛓ WORD NETWORK

Add words related to struggle from the text to your Word Network.

☰ STANDARDS

Reading Informational Text
• Determine two or more central ideas of a text and analyze their development over the course of the text, including how they interact and build on one another to provide a complex analysis; provide an objective summary of the text.
• Determine an author's point of view or purpose in a text in which the rhetoric is particularly effective, analyzing how style and content contribute to the power, persuasiveness, or beauty of the text.

Analyze Craft and Structure

Effective Rhetoric "Ain't I a Woman?" is a speech that makes an **argument**; its message is meant to persuade an audience. The writer of the speech connects ideas and builds the argument to its climax by using a **refrain**, or repeated chorus. This refrain, "And ain't I a woman?" urgently restates the main idea and challenges listeners to rethink their ideas about equality.

Practice

Work on your own to fill in the chart. Track the ways in which the writer uses refrain to build an argument. Find each use of the repeated question, "Ain't I a woman?" Then, list the textual details that lead up to each repetition. Finally, consider how each set of details adds meaning to the question. After you have completed the chart, share and discuss your responses with your group.

TEXTUAL DETAILS THAT LEAD TO . . .	ADDED MEANING
first statement of the refrain:	
first repetition of the refrain:	
second repetition of the refrain:	
third repetition of the refrain:	
fourth repetition of the refrain:	

AIN'T I A WOMAN?

Author's Style

Use of Words and Phrases A writer or speaker's **diction** is his or her choice of words and phrases. Diction is a key element of a speaker's style—his or her distinct way of using language.

- Diction may be formal, informal, elevated, simple, technical, poetic, or have many other qualities.
- Diction may change to reflect the **audience**—the listeners a speaker is attempting to reach.
- A speaker's diction reflects both the occasion and purpose of a speech.

Compare the opening lines of the original Sojourner Truth speech as performed in the Media Connection with the Frances Gage adaptation:

Truth's 1851 speech: May I say a few words? I want to say a few words about this matter.

Gage's 1863 Adaptation: Well, children, where there is so much racket there must be something out of kilter.

Note that Sojourner Truth was born into slavery and received no formal education. The diction of her 1851 speech was straightforward and conversational. Frances Gage imposed a Southern colloquial dialect, which resulted in an exaggerated, folksy voice.

STANDARDS

Language
• Apply the understanding that usage is a matter of convention, can change over time, and is sometimes contested.
• Apply knowledge of language to understand how language functions in different contexts, to make effective choices for meaning or style, and to comprehend more fully when reading or listening.

Read It

Work individually. Review the two versions of Truth's speech. Use a chart like the one shown to identify differences you notice in the two works. When you have completed the chart, meet with your group to discuss whether or not the colloquial diction changed the message of the original speech. Also, discuss the question: Was Gage justified in changing Truth's words? Why, or why not?

Ain't I a Woman?—Frances Gage	On Woman's Rights—Sojourner Truth

Write It

Notebook Write a paragraph that suggests the impact that Sojourner Truth may have had on her audience in 1851. Try to use a mix of formal and informal diction in your paragraph.

Writing to Sources

Assignment

With your group, prepare an **informative text** that presents facts about a topic. Choose from the following options:

- [ ] a **biographical sketch** about Sojourner Truth that expands upon the brief biography that accompanies this selection and that sheds light upon some of the references in "Ain't I a Woman?"

- [ ] an **extended definition** of *woman* as it would have been seen by many in Sojourner Truth's audience, focusing on the daily life of an ordinary woman in 1850s America

- [ ] a **cause-and-effect article** about the results of antislavery speeches by abolitionists in the 1850s

Project Plan Work with your group to divide the informative writing option that you chose into manageable sections or parts. Outline your ideas, and assign each member one part of the writing.

Working Title: _____

SECTION OR PART	ASSIGNED PERSON
Introduction	
Part I	
Part II	
Part III	
Part IV	
Part V	
Conclusion	

Tying It Together Work together to draft an introduction that touches on all the sections or parts that you plan to write. Once everyone has written his or her part of the project, get together again to read the parts aloud, suggest revisions, and draft a conclusion that follows from those parts.

EVIDENCE LOG

Before moving on to a new selection, go to your Evidence Log and record what you learned from "Ain't I a Woman?"

STANDARDS

Writing
Write informative/explanatory texts to examine and convey complex ideas, concepts, and information clearly and accurately through the effective selection, organization, and analysis of content.

Copyright © SAVVAS Learning Company LLC. All Rights Reserved.

DECLARATION OF
SENTIMENTS

Comparing Text to Media

In this lesson, you will compare the Declaration of Sentiments, a public document related to the campaign for women's suffrage, and a podcast called "Giving Women the Vote." First, you will complete the first-read and close-read activities for the Declaration of Sentiments.

GIVING WOMEN THE VOTE

About the Author

Elizabeth Cady Stanton
(1815–1902) became interested in reform movements through a cousin, who introduced her to Henry Brewster Stanton, an abolitionist. Cady and Stanton married in 1840—agreeing that the bride's promise to obey her husband would be omitted from their vows. Stanton was the primary writer of the Declaration of Sentiments, adopted at the 1848 Seneca Falls Convention. Later, Stanton and Susan B. Anthony founded the National Woman Suffrage Association.

☰ STANDARDS

Reading Informational Text
By the end of grade 11, read and comprehend literary nonfiction in the grades 11–CCR text complexity band proficiently, with scaffolding as needed at the high end of the range.

Language
• Use context as a clue to the meaning of a word or phrase.
• Verify the preliminary determination of the meaning of a word or phrase.

Declaration of Sentiments

Concept Vocabulary

As you perform your first read, you will encounter these words.

degraded	oppressed	subordinate

Context Clues If these words are unfamiliar to you, try using **context clues**—other words and phrases that appear in a text—to help you determine their meanings. There are various kinds of context clues. Some provide details that help you infer the word's meaning. You can then use a dictionary to confirm your inference.

> **Elaborating Details:** Even when the terrifying storm was at its worst, my cousin maintained her usual <u>calm and cheerful</u> **demeanor**.
>
> **Inference:** *Calm* and *cheerful* relate to a person's behavior. *Demeanor* must mean "how someone behaves."
>
> **Dictionary Meaning:** "outward behavior or bearing"

Apply your knowledge of context clues and other vocabulary strategies to determine the meanings of unfamiliar words you encounter during your first read.

First Read NONFICTION

Apply these strategies as you conduct your first read. You will have an opportunity to complete a close read after your first read.

NOTICE the general ideas of the text. *What* is it about? *Who* is involved?

ANNOTATE by marking vocabulary and key passages you want to revisit.

First Read

CONNECT ideas within the selection to what you already know and what you have already read.

RESPOND by completing the Comprehension Check and by writing a brief summary of the selection.

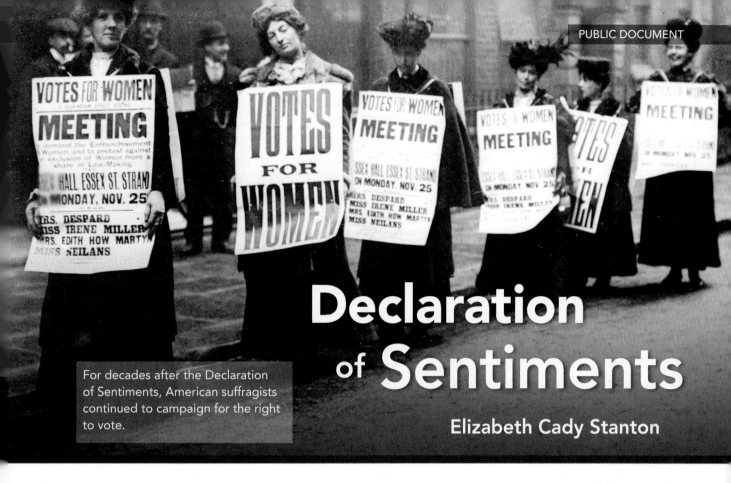

Declaration of Sentiments

Elizabeth Cady Stanton

For decades after the Declaration of Sentiments, American suffragists continued to campaign for the right to vote.

BACKGROUND

In 1848, Elizabeth Cady Stanton and Lucretia Mott convened the first women's rights conference to demand that women be given basic human rights, including the right to vote, to own property, and to have equal status under the law. Of those who attended the conference in Seneca Falls, New York, about a third—32 men and 68 women—signed the Declaration of Sentiments. The document was highly controversial. An article published shortly after the convention described it as "the most shocking and unnatural event ever recorded in the history of womanity."

1   When, in the course of human events, it becomes necessary for one portion of the family of man to assume among the people of the earth a position different from that which they have hitherto occupied, but one to which the laws of nature and of nature's God entitle them, a decent respect to the opinions of mankind requires that they should declare the causes that impel them to such a course.

2   We hold these truths to be self-evident: that all men and women are created equal; that they are endowed by their Creator with certain inalienable[1] rights; that among these are life, liberty, and the pursuit of happiness; that to secure these rights governments are instituted, deriving their just powers from the consent of the governed. Whenever any form of government becomes destructive of these ends, it is the right of those who suffer from it to refuse allegiance to it, and to insist upon the institution of a new government, laying its foundation on such principles, and organizing its powers in such

NOTES

1. **inalienable** (ihn AYL yuh nuh buhl) *adj.* absolute; not able to be taken or given away.

form, as to them shall seem most likely to effect their safety and happiness. Prudence, indeed, will dictate that governments long established should not be changed for light and transient[2] causes; and accordingly all experience hath shown that mankind are more disposed to suffer, while evils are sufferable, than to right themselves by abolishing the forms to which they are accustomed. But when a long train of abuses and usurpations[3] pursuing invariably the same object, evinces a design to reduce them under absolute despotism,[4] it is their duty to throw off such government, and to provide new guards for their future security. Such has been the patient sufferance of the women under this government, and such is now the necessity which constrains them to demand the equal station to which they are entitled. The history of mankind is a history of repeated injuries and usurpations on the part of man toward woman, having in direct object the establishment of an absolute tyranny over her. To prove this, let facts be submitted to a candid world.

3   He has never permitted her to exercise her inalienable right to the elective franchise.[5]

4   He has compelled her to submit to laws, in the formation of which she had no voice.

5   He has withheld from her rights which are given to the most ignorant and **degraded** men—both natives and foreigners.

6   Having deprived her of this first right of a citizen, the elective franchise, thereby leaving her without representation in the halls of legislation, he has **oppressed** her on all sides.

7   He has made her, if married, in the eye of the law, civilly dead.

8   He has taken from her all right in property, even to the wages she earns.

9   He has made her, morally, an irresponsible being, as she can commit many crimes with impunity,[6] provided they be done in the presence of her husband. In the covenant of marriage, she is compelled to promise obedience to her husband, he becoming, to all intents and purposes, her master—the law giving him power to deprive her of her liberty, and to administer chastisement.[7]

10   He has so framed the laws of divorce, as to what shall be the proper causes, and in case of separation, to whom the guardianship of the children shall be given, as to be wholly regardless of the happiness of women—the law, in all cases, going upon a false supposition of the supremacy of man, and giving all power into his hands.

11   After depriving her of all rights as a married woman, if single, and the owner of property, he has taxed her to support a government which recognizes her only when her property can be made profitable to it.

---

2. **transient** (TRAN see uhnt) *adj.* not lasting.
3. **usurpations** (yoo suhr PAY shuhnz) *n.* illegal seizures.
4. **evinces a design . . . despotism** shows an intent to submit women to a situation of total control.
5. **elective franchise** right to vote.
6. **impunity** (ihm PYOO nih tee) *n.* total freedom from punishment.
7. **chastisement** (CHAS tyz muhnt) *n.* strong, punishing criticism.

The demands of suffragist leaders aroused intense passions. In this artist's interpretation of a real event, suffragist Lucretia Mott is attacked by a mob when she appears in public.

12   He has monopolized nearly all the profitable employments, and from those she is permitted to follow, she receives but a scanty remuneration. He closes against her all the avenues to wealth and distinction which he considers most honorable to himself. As a teacher of theology, medicine, or law, she is not known.

13   He has denied her the facilities for obtaining a thorough education, all colleges being closed against her.

14   He allows her in church, as well as state, but a **subordinate** position, claiming apostolic[8] authority for her exclusion from the ministry, and, with some exceptions, from any public participation in the affairs of the church.

15   He has created a false public sentiment by giving to the world a different code of morals for men and women, by which moral delinquencies which exclude women from society, are not only tolerated, but deemed of little account in man.

16   He has usurped the prerogative of Jehovah himself, claiming it as his right to assign for her a sphere of action, when that belongs to her conscience and to her God.

17   He has endeavored, in every way that he could, to destroy her confidence in her own powers, to lessen her self-respect, and to make her willing to lead a dependent and abject life.

Mark context clues or indicate another strategy you used that helped you determine meaning.

subordinate (suh BAWR duh niht) *adj.*

MEANING:

---

8. **apostolic** (ap uh STOL ihk) *adj.* derived from the Bible (specifically, from the apostles appointed by Jesus to spread the gospel).

18   Now, in view of this entire disfranchisement of one-half the people of this country, their social and religious degradation—in view of the unjust laws above mentioned, and because women do feel themselves aggrieved, oppressed, and fraudulently deprived of their most sacred rights, we insist that they have immediate admission to all the rights and privileges which belong to them as citizens of the United States.

19   In entering upon the great work before us, we anticipate no small amount of misconception, misrepresentation, and ridicule; but we shall use every instrumentality within our power to effect our object. We shall employ agents, circulate tracts, petition the state and national legislatures, and endeavor to enlist the pulpit and the press in our behalf. We hope this convention will be followed by a series of conventions, embracing every part of the country.

20   Firmly relying upon the final triumph of the right and the true, we do this day affix our signatures to this declaration. ❧

Comprehension Check

Complete the following items after you finish your first read. Review and clarify details with your group.

1. According to this document, which truths are self-evident?

2. According to Stanton, why do women have a duty to throw off the government?

3. What does Stanton say is the result of denying women the right to vote?

4. What governmental action does the Declaration of Sentiments demand?

5. 📝 **Notebook** Confirm your understanding of the text by writing a summary.

- -

RESEARCH

Research to Explore This public document may spark your curiosity to learn more about this topic, author, or era. Briefly research a topic that interests you. You may wish to share what you discover with your group.

Close Read the Text

With your group, revisit sections of the text you marked during your first read. **Annotate** details that you notice. What **questions** do you have? What can you **conclude**?

ANNOTATE · QUESTION · **Close Read** · CONCLUDE

DECLARATION OF SENTIMENTS

Analyze the Text

> **CITE TEXTUAL EVIDENCE**
> to support your answers.

Complete the activities.

1. **Review and Clarify** With your group, discuss the "long train of abuses and usurpations" that are listed in the document. If you were to categorize them, what headings would you use? Explain.

2. **Present and Discuss** Now, work with your group to share the passages from the selection that you found especially important. Take turns presenting your passages. Discuss what you noticed in the selection, the questions you asked, and the conclusions you reached.

3. **Essential Question:** *In what ways does the struggle for freedom change with history?* What have you learned about the struggle for freedom from reading this text?

TIP

GROUP DISCUSSION

Give everyone a chance to contribute to the discussion. If you notice that someone is not participating, encourage him or her to join in.

LANGUAGE DEVELOPMENT

Concept Vocabulary

| degraded | oppressed | subordinate |

Why These Words? The three concept vocabulary words are related. With your group, discuss the words, and determine a concept that the words, have in common. How do these word choices enhance the text's impact?

Practice

Notebook Confirm your understanding of the concept vocabulary words by using them in sentences. Be sure to use context clues that hint at each word's meaning.

Word Study

Latin Prefix: *sub-* According to the Declaration of Sentiments, the document should tell the world that American women are in a *subordinate* position. The word *subordinate* begins with the Latin prefix *sub-*, which means "under." Find several other words that begin with this prefix. Use etymological information from the dictionary to verify your choices. Then, write the words and their meanings.

WORD NETWORK

Add words related to struggle from the text to your Word Network.

STANDARDS

Language
Consult general and specialized reference materials, both print and digital, to find the pronunciation of a word or determine or clarify its precise meaning, its part of speech, its etymology, or its standard usage.

TIP

CLARIFICATION

An **extended allusion** may imitate or borrow the structure of the text after which it is modeled, the wording of that text, or both.

Analyze Craft and Structure

Author's Choices: Allusions An **allusion** is an unexplained reference within a literary work to a well-known person, place, event, text, or work of art. An allusion adds meaning to a text by offering a point of similarity or comparison to the ideas the author is presenting. Authors assume that readers understand both the reference and the layer of meaning it adds.

Although most allusions are conveyed in a word or a phrase, some provide structure for an entire piece of writing. In the Declaration of Sentiments, Elizabeth Cady Stanton creates an extended allusion by modeling her argument after the Declaration of Independence.

Practice

CITE TEXTUAL EVIDENCE to support your answers.

Use this chart to analyze how the extended allusion to the Declaration of Independence helps introduce, develop, and conclude the argument made in the Declaration of Sentiments. A first example has been done for you. Gather your notes, and then share your responses with your group.

DECLARATION OF SENTIMENTS	ALLUSION TO THE DECLARATION OF INDEPENDENCE	DEVELOPMENT OF IDEAS
Paragraphs 1–2	The Declaration of Independence reads: "We hold these truths to be self-evident: that all men are created equal. . . . " Stanton revises this to read:". . . all men and women are created equal."	The allusion suggests that the Declaration of Sentiments is equal in importance to—and perhaps even goes beyond— the Declaration of Independence.
Paragraphs 3–17		
Paragraphs 18–20		

Conventions and Style

Types of Clauses A **clause** is a group of words that has a subject and a predicate. An **independent clause** can stand on its own as a complete sentence. A **subordinate** (also called **dependent**) **clause** is unable to stand alone because it does not express a complete thought. Writers use a variety of subordinate clauses to add information, to clarify meaning, and to link related ideas.

DECLARATION OF SENTIMENTS

TYPE OF CLAUSE	COMPOSITION	EXAMPLES
Independent	subject, predicate; expresses a complete thought	*We hold these truths to be self-evident . . . (paragraph 2)* *. . . it is their duty to throw off such government . . . (paragraph 2)*
Subordinate	subject, predicate; does not express a complete thought; begins with a word such as *which, who, that, since, when, if, as, although,* or *because*	*. . . that they should declare the causes . . . (paragraph 1)* *. . . as she can commit many crimes with impunity . . . (paragraph 9)*

Read It

1. Each example contains one independent clause and one subordinate clause. Mark independent clauses once and subordinate clauses twice.

   a. Although some proponents of women's rights supported the Declaration of Sentiments, others considered it too radical.

   b. It was no secret that the work entailed danger and public censure.

   c. Because suffrage is such a precious right, Americans should vote in all elections.

2. **Connect to Style** Reread this excerpt from Declaration of Sentiments. Mark independent clauses once and subordinate clauses twice.

   We hold these truths to be self-evident: that all men and women are created equal; that they are endowed by their Creator with certain inalienable rights. . . .

📝 **Notebook** Explain how the use of these clauses helps the writer show a main idea and the details that support it.

Write It

📝 **Notebook** Complete this paragraph by adding a clause to each sentence as directed.

   If I had been working alongside Elizabeth Cady Stanton, [independent clause]. I also would have marched for female suffrage, [subordinate clause]. Many people fought against giving women the vote [subordinate clause]. The work was important, however, so [independent clause].

📝 EVIDENCE LOG

Before moving on to a new selection, go to your Evidence Log and record what you learned from "Declaration of Sentiments."

☰ STANDARDS

Reading Informational Text
Analyze seventeenth-, eighteenth-, and nineteenth-century foundational U.S. documents of historical and literary significance for their themes, purposes, and rhetorical features.

Language
Demonstrate command of the conventions of standard English grammar and usage when writing or speaking.

Declaration of Sentiments **345**

DECLARATION OF SENTIMENTS

Comparing Text to Media

This podcast discusses the final steps that made women's suffrage a reality. After listening to it, you will compare how broadcast media can provide information in a way that differs from the way information is conveyed in a text.

GIVING WOMEN THE VOTE

About the Producer

Sandra Sleight-Brennan (b. 1951) is an award-winning scriptwriter and media producer. She is the driving force behind many audio and video projects, Web-based documentaries, and a variety of multimedia efforts. Although she has covered a wide range of topics, she has a special interest in projects that show societal change and that reflect the struggles of minorities. Sleight-Brennan's work has been broadcast on radio stations across the country.

Giving Women the Vote

Media Vocabulary

These words or concepts will be useful to you as you analyze, discuss, and write about podcasts.

Frame: main spoken narrative of a production	• A frame has a clear beginning, middle, and end. • Usually, one narrator or host presents the frame.
Special Elements: features that provide points of emphasis in a production	• Sound effects can add realism. Background music can highlight the emotion connected with an event. Either element can set a mood. • Interview segments can add information and insights. Dramatic reenactments can bring events to life.
Tone: production's attitude toward a subject or audience	• In a podcast, tone is created through the narrator or host's word choice and vocal qualities, as well as the use of special elements.

First Review MEDIA: AUDIO

Apply these strategies as you listen to the podcast.

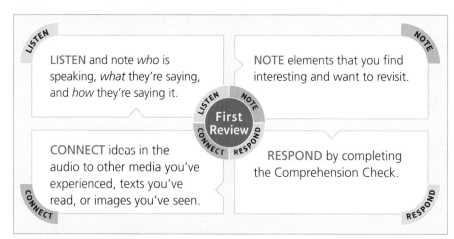

LISTEN and note *who* is speaking, *what* they're saying, and *how* they're saying it.

NOTE elements that you find interesting and want to revisit.

CONNECT ideas in the audio to other media you've experienced, texts you've read, or images you've seen.

RESPOND by completing the Comprehension Check.

First Review

Listening Strategy: Take Notes

Notebook As you listen, record your observations and questions, making sure to note time codes for later reference.

STANDARDS

Reading Informational Text
By the end of grade 11, read and comprehend literary nonfiction in the grades 11–CCR text complexity band proficiently, with scaffolding as needed at the high end of the range.

Giving Women the Vote

Sandra Sleight-Brennan

BACKGROUND

The campaign to give the vote to all American women faced many disappointments in the decades following the Seneca Falls Convention. Finally, however, in June 1919, Congress passed a women's suffrage amendment to the United States Constitution and sent it to the states for ratification. Nine months later, 35 states had ratified the amendment. Only one more state's ratification was needed, but the deadline for ratification was drawing near. "Giving Women the Vote," which Sandra Sleight-Brennan produced in 2010 to commemorate the ninetieth anniversary of the Nineteenth Amendment, tells the story of that final state's ratification—and the surprising way in which it happened.

NOTES

Comprehension Check

Complete the following items after you finish your first review. Review and clarify details with your group.

1. According to the interview with the reporter from the Cleveland *Plain Dealer*, what was the result of the campaign for women's suffrage in the years just prior to 1920?

2. Which state became the final battleground for making the Nineteenth Amendment the law of the land?

3. What was the significance of the red or yellow roses worn by people on the scene?

4. According to the dramatic reenactment, why did Harry Burn change his vote?

5. 🗐 **Notebook** Write a summary to confirm your understanding of the ratification of the Nineteenth Amendment, as presented in the podcast.

- -

RESEARCH

Research to Clarify Choose at least one unfamiliar detail from the podcast. Briefly research that detail. In what way does the information you learned shed light upon an aspect of the podcast? Share your findings with your group.

Close Review

With your group, review your notes. If necessary, listen to the podcast again. Record any new observations that seem important. What **questions** do you have? What can you **conclude**?

GIVING WOMEN THE VOTE

Analyze the Media

> **CITE TEXTUAL EVIDENCE**
> to support your answers.

Complete the activities.

1. **Present and Discuss** Choose the part of the podcast you find most interesting or powerful. Share your choice with your group, and discuss why you chose it. Explain what you noticed about that section, what questions it raised for you, and what conclusions you reached about it.

2. **Synthesize** With your group, review the entire podcast. Do the frame and the special elements work together to inform listeners? Are they examples of information, of entertainment, or of both? Explain.

3. **Essential Question:** *In what ways does the struggle for freedom change with history?* What have you learned about the struggle for freedom from listening to this podcast? Discuss with your group.

LANGUAGE DEVELOPMENT

Media Vocabulary

frame	special elements	tone

Use these vocabulary words in your responses to the following questions.

1. **(a)** What do listeners learn from the narrator about the ratification process? **(b)** Why might Sleight-Brennan have wanted to include this information?

2. How do the comments dramatized by the characters of Harry Burn and his mother help to show the tensions surrounding this final vote for ratification?

3. This podcast was produced in recognition of the ninetieth anniversary of the Nineteenth Amendment. What attitude toward the event do you think it was meant to encourage in listeners? Explain.

STANDARDS
Speaking and Listening
Evaluate a speaker's point of view, reasoning, and use of evidence and rhetoric, assessing the stance, premises, links among ideas, word choice, points of emphasis, and tone used.

DECLARATION OF SENTIMENTS

GIVING WOMEN THE VOTE

STANDARDS

Reading Informational Text
• Analyze and evaluate the effectiveness of the structure an author uses in his or her exposition or argument, including whether the structure makes points clear, convincing, and engaging.
• Determine an author's point of view or purpose in a text in which the rhetoric is particularly effective, analyzing how style and content contribute to the power, persuasiveness or beauty of the text.
• Integrate and evaluate multiple sources of information presented in different media or formats as well as in words in order to address a question or solve a problem.

Writing to Compare

You have read a document that launched the women's suffrage movement— Elizabeth Cady Stanton's Declaration of Sentiments. You have also listened to a podcast about the ratification of the nineteenth amendment in 1920. Now, deepen your understanding of the issue of women's suffrage by comparing and contrasting elements of the two selections and putting your ideas in writing.

Assignment

Both the document and the podcast illustrate the methods suffragists and politicians used to convince people that granting women the vote was the right course of action. Write a **compare-and-contrast essay** in which you analyze how each selection shows persuasion at work. Focus on the arguments and rhetorical strategies used by the people involved in the campaign. How did they seek to communicate key ideas in powerful, convincing ways?

Prewriting

Analyze the Texts **Persuasion** involves communicating a point of view and convincing others to adopt it. Persuasion is accomplished through effective **rhetoric,** or the use of stylistic elements to build meaning in a powerful way. The elements of rhetoric include:

• strong arguments—clearly stated claims supported by compelling evidence
• a lofty or passionate tone
• the repetition of words, phrases, or ideas
• the use of striking images
• allusions to established or respected ideas or texts
• the use of analogies, or comparisons.

📓 **Notebook** Complete the activity, and answer the questions.

1. Analyze elements of rhetoric used by suffragists and their supporters in each selection. Assign each group member one element to look for in either one or both selections. Then, discuss and analyze your findings.

Rhetorical Element	Declaration of Sentiments	Giving Women the Vote
Argument		
Tone		
Repetition		
Imagery		
Allusion		
Analogy		

2. Which elements of persuasion are showcased in both selections?
3. These two selections focus on events 70 years apart. How did the suffragists' arguments or strategies change over time?

Drafting

Draw Conclusions As a group, review and discuss your Prewriting notes. Based on those notes, what can you conclude about the use of rhetoric in the suffrage movement, as illustrated by these two selections? Which elements carried the movement to its successful conclusion?

Thesis/central idea: _____

_____

_____

Develop a Project Plan Work with your group to outline the body of your essay and divide the writing task into manageable parts. Use a chart like this one to assign parts. Write a description of each part in the left column, and the name of the person assigned to it in the right. Discuss and note key pieces of evidence to use in each section.

SECTIONS OR PARTS	PERSON ASSIGNED
Part I: Evidence:	
Part II: Evidence:	
Part III: Evidence:	
Part IV: Evidence:	
Part V: Evidence:	

Write a Draft Work as a group to draft an introduction that includes your working thesis and touches on all the sections or parts the body of the essay will include. Then, work independently to draft the body sections. When everyone is finished, share your drafts aloud. Discuss revisions that will make each section stronger. Tie the parts of your essay together with effective transitions. Finally, draft a conclusion that follows logically from all sections of the essay.

Reviewing, Revising, and Editing

Have each group member edit and proofread the text independently. Apply all your changes to the draft. Then, have one person read the finished essay aloud. What last small changes need to be made to finalize your work?

✏ EVIDENCE LOG

Before moving on to a new selection, go to your Evidence Log and record what you've learned from the Declaration of Sentiments and "Giving Women the Vote."

Kate Chopin (1850–1904) was born Kate O'Flaherty in St. Louis, Missouri. At the age of 20, she married Louisiana cotton trader Oscar Chopin. The couple lived in New Orleans before moving to a rural Louisiana plantation. Chopin briefly ran the plantation after her husband's death but then returned to St. Louis with their six children. There, she began writing fiction. In the portraits of Louisiana that she created from that point forward, Chopin often addressed women's rights and racial prejudice.

STANDARDS

Reading Literature
By the end of grade 11, read and comprehend literature, including stories, dramas, and poems, in the grades 11–CCR text complexity band proficiently, with scaffolding as needed at the high end of the range.

Language
Identify and correctly use patterns of word changes that indicate different meanings or parts of speech.

The Story of an Hour

Concept Vocabulary

As you perform your first read of "The Story of an Hour," you will encounter these words.

persistence	imploring	importunities

Familiar Word Parts Separating a word into its parts can often help you identify its meaning. Those parts might include familiar prefixes.

Some prefixes, such as *im-*, have more than one meaning. When you come across an unfamiliar word, consider all the meanings of the prefix.

- For example, in the word *immobile, im-* means "not." Added to the base word *mobile,* which means "in motion," *im-* creates a new word that means "not mobile," or "still."

- In the word *immigrate, im-* means "into" or "toward." Added to the base word *migrate,* which means "move from one region to another," *im-* creates a new word that means "move into a new place."

When you read an unfamiliar word that has a prefix, think about other words with the same prefix. Consider which meaning makes the most sense with the base word. If a prefix has more than one meaning, try out both to determine the meaning of the unfamiliar word.

Apply your knowledge of familiar word parts and other vocabulary strategies to determine the meanings of unfamiliar words you encounter during your first read.

First Read FICTION

Apply these strategies as you conduct your first read. You will have an opportunity to complete a close read after your first read.

NOTICE *whom* the story is about, *what* happened, *where* and *when* it happened, and *why* those involved reacted as they did.

ANNOTATE by marking vocabulary and key passages you want to revisit.

First Read

CONNECT ideas within the selection to what you already know and what you have already read.

RESPOND by completing the Comprehension Check and by writing a summary of the selection.

The Story of an Hour

Kate Chopin

BACKGROUND

"The Story of an Hour" was considered daring in its time. The editors of at least two magazines refused the story, calling it immoral. They wanted Chopin to soften her female character and to make her less independent and less unhappy in her marriage. Undaunted, Chopin continued to deal with issues of women's growth and emancipation in her writing, advancing ideas that are widely accepted today.

1   Knowing that Mrs. Mallard was afflicted with a heart trouble, great care was taken to break to her as gently as possible the news of her husband's death.

2   It was her sister Josephine who told her, in broken sentences; veiled hints that revealed in half concealing. Her husband's friend Richards was there, too, near her. It was he who had been in the newspaper office when intelligence of the railroad disaster was received, with Brently Mallard's name leading the list of "killed." He had only taken the time to assure himself of its truth by a second telegram, and had hastened to forestall any less careful, less tender friend in bearing the sad message.

3   She did not hear the story as many women have heard the same, with a paralyzed inability to accept its significance. She wept at once, with sudden, wild abandonment, in her sister's arms. When the storm of grief had spent itself she went away to her room alone. She would have no one follow her.

4   There stood, facing the open window, a comfortable, roomy armchair. Into this she sank, pressed down by a physical exhaustion that haunted her body and seemed to reach into her soul.

5   She could see in the open square before her house the tops of trees that were all aquiver with the new spring life. The delicious breath of rain was in the air. In the street below a peddler was crying his wares. The notes of a distant song which someone was singing reached her faintly, and countless sparrows were twittering in the eaves.

NOTES

6   There were patches of blue sky showing here and there through the clouds that had met and piled one above the other in the west facing her window.

7   She sat with her head thrown back upon the cushion of the chair, quite motionless, except when a sob came up into her throat and shook her, as a child who has cried itself to sleep continues to sob in its dreams.

8   She was young, with a fair, calm face, whose lines bespoke repression and even a certain strength. But now there was a dull stare in her eyes, whose gaze was fixed away off yonder on one of those patches of blue sky. It was not a glance of reflection, but rather indicated a suspension of intelligent thought.

9   There was something coming to her and she was waiting for it, fearfully. What was it? She did not know; it was too subtle and elusive to name. But she felt it, creeping out of the sky, reaching toward her through the sounds, the scents, the color that filled the air.

10   Now her bosom rose and fell tumultuously. She was beginning to recognize this thing that was approaching to possess her, and she was striving to beat it back with her will—as powerless as her two white slender hands would have been. When she abandoned herself a little whispered word escaped her slightly parted lips. She said it over and over under her breath: "free, free, free!" The vacant stare and the look of terror that had followed it went from her eyes. They stayed keen and bright. Her pulses beat fast, and the coursing blood warmed and relaxed every inch of her body.

11   She did not stop to ask if it were or were not a monstrous joy that held her. A clear and exalted perception enabled her to dismiss the suggestion as trivial. She knew that she would weep again when she saw the kind, tender hands folded in death; the face that had never looked save with love upon her, fixed and gray and dead. But she saw beyond that bitter moment a long procession of years to come that would belong to her absolutely. And she opened and spread her arms out to them in welcome.

12   There would be no one to live for during those coming years; she would live for herself. There would be no powerful will bending hers in that blind **persistence** with which men and women believe they have a right to impose a private will upon a fellow creature. A kind intention or a cruel intention made the act seem no less a crime as she looked upon it in that brief moment of illumination.

13   And yet she had loved him—sometimes. Often she had not. What did it matter! What could love, the unsolved mystery, count for in the face of this possession of self-assertion which she suddenly recognized as the strongest impulse of her being!

14   "Free! Body and soul free!" she kept whispering.

15   Josephine was kneeling before the closed door with her lips to the keyhole, **imploring** for admission. "Louise, open the door! I beg; open the door—you will make yourself ill. What are you doing, Louise? For heaven's sake open the door."

Mark familiar word parts or indicate another strategy you used that helped you determine meaning.

persistence (puhr SIHS tuhns) *n.*

MEANING:

imploring (ihm PLAWR ihng) *v.*

MEANING:

16   "Go away. I am not making myself ill." No; she was drinking in a very elixir of life[1] through that open window.

17   Her fancy was running riot along those days ahead of her. Spring days, and summer days, and all sorts of days that would be her own. She breathed a quick prayer that life might be long. It was only yesterday she had thought with a shudder that life might be long.

18   She arose at length and opened the door to her sister's **importunities**. There was a feverish triumph in her eyes, and she carried herself unwittingly like a goddess of Victory. She clasped her sister's waist, and together they descended the stairs. Richards stood waiting for them at the bottom.

19   Someone was opening the front door with a latchkey. It was Brently Mallard who entered, a little travel-stained, composedly carrying his gripsack[2] and umbrella. He had been far from the scene of the accident, and did not even know there had been one. He stood amazed at Josephine's piercing cry; at Richards' quick motion to screen him from the view of his wife.

20   But Richards was too late.

21   When the doctors came they said she had died of heart disease—of the joy that kills. ✿

---

1. **elixir of life** mythical liquid believed to prolong a person's life indefinitely.
2. **gripsack** small bag for holding clothes; suitcase.

NOTES

Mark familiar word parts or indicate another strategy you used that helped you determine meaning.

importunities (ihm pawr TOO nuh teez) *n.*

MEANING:

Comprehension Check

Complete the following items after you finish your first read. Review and clarify details with your group.

1. What medical problem afflicts Mrs. Mallard?

2. What news does Mrs. Mallard receive as the story opens?

3. As Mrs. Mallard sits alone in her room, what word does she keep whispering to herself?

4. What happens when Brently Mallard turns up, alive?

5. 📓 **Notebook** Write a summary of the story to confirm your understanding.

- -

RESEARCH

Research to Explore This story may spark your curiosity to learn more. Briefly research a relevant topic that interests you. You may want to share what you discover with your group.

THE STORY OF AN HOUR

Close Read the Text

With your group, revisit sections of the text you marked during your first read. **Annotate** details that you notice. What **questions** do you have? What can you **conclude**?

Analyze the Text

> **CITE TEXTUAL EVIDENCE**
> to support your answers.

📑 **Notebook** Complete the activities.

1. **Review and Clarify** With your group, discuss the ending of the story. Do you agree with the doctors' evaluation? Why, or why not?

2. **Present and Discuss** Now, work with your group to share the passages from the selection that you found especially important. Take turns presenting your passages. Discuss what you noticed in the selection, the questions you asked, and the conclusions you reached.

3. **Essential Question:** *In what ways does the struggle for freedom change with history?* What has this text taught you about the struggle for freedom? Discuss with your group.

LANGUAGE DEVELOPMENT

Concept Vocabulary

persistence	imploring	importunities

Why These Words? The three concept vocabulary words from the text are related. With your group, discuss the words, and determine what the words have in common. How do these word choices enhance the text?

Practice

📑 **Notebook** Use a dictionary or thesaurus to find and record two synonyms for each of the concept vocabulary words. Then, write a sentence that explains how you think Chopin's word choices affect readers' understanding of the story. Share your sentences with your group.

Word Study

📑 **Notebook** **Denotation and Connotation** The **denotation** of a word is its dictionary meaning. **Connotation** refers to the shades of meaning a word conveys. As Mrs. Mallard sits in her room, she hears Josephine's *importunities* for her to open the door. The denotation of the word is "instances of persistent begging." The connotation, however, suggests that such begging is especially annoying. Use a thesaurus to find four other words that mean "to beg," and think about their connotations. Then, list the words in order—from least to most forceful, or from most negative to most positive.

TIP

GROUP DISCUSSION
Listen carefully as others present their ideas so that you do not simply repeat their words when your turn comes. Try to add something new to the discussion.

🔗 WORD NETWORK

Add words related to struggle from the text to your Word Network.

☰ STANDARDS

Reading Literature
• Determine two or more themes or central ideas of a text and analyze their development over the course of the text, including how they interact and build on one another to produce a complex account; provide an objective summary of the text.

• Analyze the impact of the author's choices regarding how to develop and relate elements of a story or drama.

Language
• Analyze nuances in the meaning of words with similar denotations.

Analyze Craft and Structure

Development of Theme In this story, the author develops a central idea, or **theme**, about the ways in which the society of her time constrains women. To develop that thematic insight, Chopin focuses on the contrast between Mrs. Mallard's **internal monologue**—her main character's thoughts and conversation with herself—and the external situation in which Mrs. Mallard finds herself.

Practice

CITE TEXTUAL EVIDENCE to support your answers.

Use the chart to track Mrs. Mallard's actions and the emotional journey she undergoes. Then, explain how Mrs. Mallard's actions and feelings suggest Chopin's theme about the status of women in the society of her era. Note that there may be more than one theme. Complete this chart independently, and then share your responses with your group.

PARAGRAPH	WHAT MRS. MALLARD DOES	WHAT MRS. MALLARD FEELS	THEMATIC MEANING
3			
9			
10			
17			

Conventions and Style

Author's Choices: Irony "The Story of an Hour" is an ironic tale. **Irony** is a contradiction between appearance and reality, between expectation and outcome, or between meaning and intention. In literature, readers frequently encounter three types of irony.

Situational Irony: Something happens that contradicts readers' expectations.
Example: In the story "The Necklace," a couple must replace a diamond necklace that the wife borrowed from a friend and lost. Years later, after falling into poverty in order to pay for the replacement necklace, the couple discover the original was a fake.

Dramatic Irony: Readers or viewers are aware of something that a character does not know.
Example: In *Romeo and Juliet*, characters believe that Juliet is dead, but the audience knows that she is simply in a drugged sleep.

Verbal Irony: Someone says something that deliberately contradicts what that person actually means.
Example: In *Julius Caesar*, Marc Antony refers to Brutus as "an honorable man" when he means to prove that Brutus, Caesar's killer, is extremely dishonorable.

Read It

Work individually. Complete each situation below, and write your response to it based on the story. Then, reconvene with your group to compare and contrast your responses.

PARAGRAPHS	SITUATION	WHY IS THIS IRONIC?
5–6	Mrs. Mallard has just learned about her husband's death, but now she notices . . .	
20–21	Mrs. Mallard has reconciled herself to her newfound freedom, but now she discovers . . .	

Write It

Notebook Choose a favorite movie with a classic, expected ending. Write a paragraph that changes the ending so that it becomes ironic. Explain how your new ending is an example of situational irony.

STANDARDS

Reading Literature
Analyze a case in which grasping point of view requires distinguishing what is directly stated in a text from what is really meant.

Speaking and Listening
• Propel conversations by posing and responding to questions that probe reasoning and evidence; ensure a hearing for a full range of positions on a topic or issue; clarify, verify, or challenge ideas and conclusions; and promote divergent and creative perspectives.
• Respond thoughtfully to diverse perspectives; synthesize comments, claims, and evidence made on all sides of an issue; resolve contradictions when possible; and determine what additional information or research is required to deepen the investigation or complete the task.

Speaking and Listening

Assignment

Hold a **group discussion** to consider how readers of Chopin's time might have responded to "The Story of an Hour." Use what you know about the history of the era. Choose one of these social groups as the focus for your discussion.

☐ How might women in various social roles have responded to the story?

☐ How might other writers or artists have responded to the story?

☐ How might social critics or activists have responded to the story?

Preparing for the Discussion Locate areas of the text that support your ideas about how the social group you selected might respond to the story. Record your best examples here. Then, join up with others who chose the same perspective, and compare notes as a group.

Perspective: _____

SECTION OF TEXT	POSSIBLE RESPONSE / EXPLANATION

Holding the Discussion Decide as a group whether you want to go through the story section by section and have each person respond from his or her chosen perspective, or whether you prefer to look at the whole text through one perspective at a time. Either way, make sure that everyone has a chance to speak and to express opinions that are supported with evidence from the text and knowledge about 1890s America. If questions emerge from your discussion, decide together how you will locate the answers.

📝 **EVIDENCE LOG**

Before moving on to a new selection, go to your Evidence Log and record what you learned from "The Story of an Hour."

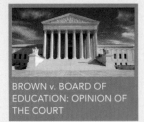

BROWN v. BOARD OF EDUCATION: OPINION OF THE COURT

Comparing Texts

In this lesson, you will read and compare the decision of the Supreme Court in the case *Brown v. Board of Education* and the magazine article "Was *Brown v. Board* a Failure?" First, you will complete the first-read and close-read activities for the Supreme Court decision. The work you do with your group on this title will help prepare you for your final comparison.

WAS *BROWN v. BOARD* A FAILURE?

About the Author

Earl Warren (1891–1974), a lawyer and three-time governor of California, served as the fourteenth Chief Justice of the United States, from 1953 to 1969. Warren's time on the Court was an active one, with landmark decisions in race relations, criminal procedure, and legislative apportionment. After the assassination of President John F. Kennedy in 1963, Warren headed a federal commission that investigated the murder.

STANDARDS

Reading Informational Text
By the end of grade 11, read and comprehend literary nonfiction in the grades 11–CCR text complexity band proficiently, with scaffolding as needed at the high end of the range.

Language
Identify and correctly use patterns of word changes that indicate different meanings or parts of speech.

Brown v. Board of Education: Opinion of the Court

Concept Vocabulary

As you read the Supreme Court's opinion in *Brown v. Board of Education*, you will encounter these words.

plaintiffs	jurisdiction	disposition

Familiar Word Parts In your reading, you may encounter words that are a bit unfamiliar but that seem to have word parts that you recognize. As this example shows, the word part that you recognize can help you determine the meaning of the unfamiliar word.

> **Sentence:** A sense of possibilities can **embolden** children to learn.
>
> **Familiar Word Part:** *bold,* which means "without fear" or "courageous"
>
> **Conclusion:** Since *bold* involves a lack of fear, *embolden* must have something to do with instilling fearlessness in someone.

First Read NONFICTION

Apply these strategies as you conduct your first read. You will have an opportunity to complete a close read after your first read.

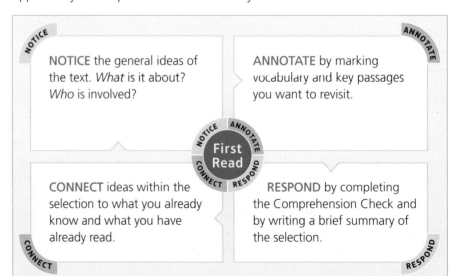

NOTICE the general ideas of the text. *What* is it about? *Who* is involved?

ANNOTATE by marking vocabulary and key passages you want to revisit.

CONNECT ideas within the selection to what you already know and what you have already read.

RESPOND by completing the Comprehension Check and by writing a brief summary of the selection.

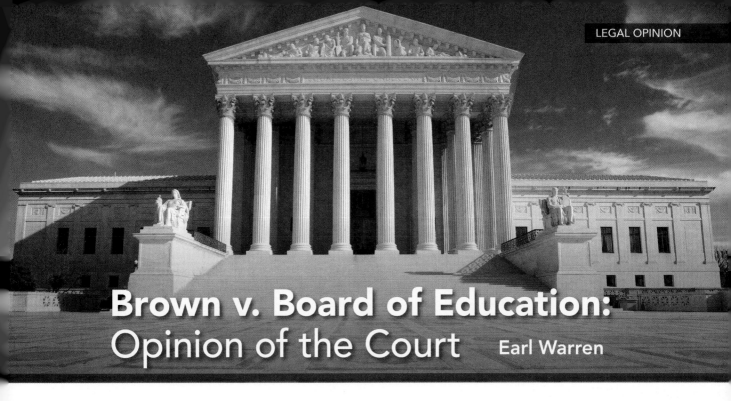

Brown v. Board of Education: Opinion of the Court
Earl Warren

BACKGROUND

In 1951, when 17 states required schools to be segregated by race, 13 parents brought a lawsuit against the Board of Education of Topeka, Kansas. At the forefront of the case was the Brown family. Linda Brown, an African American third-grader, was not allowed to attend the elementary school seven blocks from her house. Instead, she was required to take a bus to a school across town. Since the United States Supreme Court decision in the 1896 case *Plessy v. Ferguson*, racial segregation of schools had been allowed so long as the schools were "separate but equal." In the landmark case of *Brown v. Board of Education*, the Supreme Court ruled unanimously (9–0) to overrule *Plessy*.

> SUPREME COURT OF THE UNITED STATES
>
> Brown v. Board of Education,
> 347 U.S. 483 (1954) (USSC+)
> 347 U.S. 483
> Argued December 9, 1952
> Reargued December 8, 1953
> Decided May 17, 1954
>
> APPEAL FROM THE UNITED STATES DISTRICT COURT
> FOR THE DISTRICT OF KANSAS*

NOTES

Syllabus

1   Segregation of white and Negro children in the public schools of a State solely on the basis of race, pursuant to[1] state laws permitting or requiring such segregation, denies to Negro children the equal protection of the laws guaranteed by the Fourteenth Amendment— even though the physical facilities and other "tangible" factors of white and Negro schools may be equal.

---

1. **pursuant to** in a way that agrees with or follows.

2   (a) The history of the Fourteenth Amendment is inconclusive[2] as to its intended effect on public education.

3   (b) The question presented in these cases must be determined not on the basis of conditions existing when the Fourteenth Amendment was adopted, but in the light of the full development of public education and its present place in American life throughout the Nation.

4   (c) Where a State has undertaken to provide an opportunity for an education in its public schools, such an opportunity is a right which must be made available to all on equal terms.

5   (d) Segregation of children in public schools solely on the basis of race deprives children of the minority group of equal educational opportunities, even though the physical facilities and other "tangible" factors may be equal.

6   (e) The "separate but equal" doctrine adopted in *Plessy v. Ferguson*, 163 U.S. 537, has no place in the field of public education.

7   (f) The cases are restored to the docket[3] for further argument on specified questions relating to the forms of the decrees.

Opinion

8   MR. CHIEF JUSTICE WARREN delivered the opinion of the Court.

9   These cases come to us from the States of Kansas, South Carolina, Virginia, and Delaware. They are premised on[4] different facts and different local conditions, but a common legal question justifies their consideration together in this consolidated opinion.

10   In each of the cases, minors of the Negro race, through their legal representatives, seek the aid of the courts in obtaining admission to the public schools of their community on a nonsegregated basis. In each instance, they had been denied admission to schools attended by white children under laws requiring or permitting segregation according to race. This segregation was alleged to deprive the **plaintiffs** of the equal protection of the laws under the Fourteenth Amendment. In each of the cases other than the Delaware case, a three-judge federal district court denied relief to the plaintiffs on the so-called "separate but equal" doctrine announced by this Court in *Plessy v. Fergson*, 163 U.S. 537. Under that doctrine, equality of treatment is accorded when the races are provided substantially equal facilities, even though these facilities be separate. In the Delaware case, the Supreme Court of Delaware adhered to that doctrine, but ordered that the plaintiffs be admitted to the white schools because of their superiority to the Negro schools.

11   The plaintiffs contend that segregated public schools are not "equal" and cannot be made "equal," and that hence they are deprived of the equal protection of the laws. Because of the obvious importance of the question presented, the Court took **jurisdiction**.

Mark familiar word parts or indicate another strategy you used that helped you determine meaning.

plaintiffs (PLAYN tihfs) *n.*

MEANING:

Mark familiar word parts or indicate another strategy you used that helped you determine meaning.

jurisdiction (jur ihs DIHK shuhn) *n.*

MEANING:

---

2. **inconclusive** *adj.* not fully resolving all doubts or questions.
3. **docket** *n.* list of the legal cases that will be tried in a court of law.
4. **premised on** based on.

Argument was heard in the 1952 Term, and reargument was heard this Term on certain questions propounded[5] by the Court.

12   Reargument was largely devoted to the circumstances surrounding the adoption of the Fourteenth Amendment in 1868. It covered exhaustively consideration of the Amendment in Congress, ratification[6] by the states, then-existing practices in racial segregation, and the views of proponents and opponents of the Amendment. This discussion and our own investigation convince us that, although these sources cast some light, it is not enough to resolve the problem with which we are faced. At best, they are inconclusive. The most avid proponents of the post-War Amendments undoubtedly intended them to remove all legal distinctions among "all persons born or naturalized in the United States." Their opponents, just as certainly, were antagonistic to both the letter and the spirit of the Amendments and wished them to have the most limited effect. What others in Congress and the state legislatures had in mind cannot be determined with any degree of certainty.

13   An additional reason for the inconclusive nature of the Amendment's history with respect to segregated schools is the status of public education at that time. In the South, the movement toward free common schools, supported by general taxation, had not yet taken hold. Education of white children was largely in the hands of private groups. Education of Negroes was almost nonexistent, and practically all of the race were illiterate. In fact, any education of Negroes was forbidden by law in some states. Today, in contrast, many Negroes have achieved outstanding success in the arts and sciences, as well as in the business and professional world. It is true that public school education at the time of the Amendment had advanced further in the North, but the effect of the Amendment on Northern States was generally ignored in the congressional debates. Even in the North, the conditions of public education did not approximate those existing today. The curriculum was usually rudimentary; ungraded schools were common in rural areas; the school term was but three months a year in many states, and compulsory school attendance was virtually unknown. As a consequence, it is not surprising that there should be so little in the history of the Fourteenth Amendment relating to its intended effect on public education.

14   In the first cases in this Court construing the Fourteenth Amendment, decided shortly after its adoption, the Court interpreted it as proscribing all state-imposed discriminations against the Negro race. The doctrine of "separate but equal" did not make its appearance in this Court until 1896 in the case of *Plessy v. Ferguson*, supra,[7] involving not education but transportation. American courts have since labored with the doctrine for over half a century. In this

---

5. **propounded** *v.* suggested for consideration.
6. **ratification** *n.* process of officially approving and accepting an agreement.
7. **supra** mentioned earlier in this writing.

Court, there have been six cases involving the "separate but equal" doctrine in the field of public education. In *Cumming v. County Board of Education*, 175 U.S. 528, and *Gong Lum v. Rice*, 275 U.S. 78, the validity of the doctrine itself was not challenged. In more recent cases, all on the graduate school level, inequality was found in that specific benefits enjoyed by white students were denied to Negro students of the same educational qualifications. *Missouri ex rel. Gaines v. Canada*, 305 U.S. 337; *Sipuel v. Oklahoma*, 332 U.S. 631; *Sweatt v. Painter*, 339 U.S. 629; *McLaurin v. Oklahoma State Regents*, 339 U.S. 637. In none of these cases was it necessary to reexamine the doctrine to grant relief to the Negro plaintiff. And in *Sweatt v. Painter*, supra, the Court expressly reserved decision on the question whether *Plessy v. Ferguson* should be held inapplicable to public education.

15   In the instant cases, that question is directly presented. Here, unlike *Sweatt v. Painter*, there are findings below that the Negro and white schools involved have been equalized, or are being equalized, with respect to buildings, curricula, qualifications and salaries of teachers, and other "tangible" factors. Our decision, therefore, cannot turn on merely a comparison of these tangible factors in the Negro and white schools involved in each of the cases. We must look instead to the effect of segregation itself on public education.

16   In approaching this problem, we cannot turn the clock back to 1868, when the Amendment was adopted, or even to 1896, when *Plessy v. Ferguson* was written. We must consider public education in the light of its full development and its present place in American life throughout the Nation. Only in this way can it be determined if segregation in public schools deprives these plaintiffs of the equal protection of the laws.

17   Today, education is perhaps the most important function of state and local governments. Compulsory school attendance laws and the great expenditures for education both demonstrate our recognition of the importance of education to our democratic society. It is required in the performance of our most basic public responsibilities, even service in the armed forces. It is the very foundation of good citizenship. Today it is a principal instrument in awakening the child to cultural values, in preparing him for later professional training, and in helping him to adjust normally to his environment. In these days, it is doubtful that any child may reasonably be expected to succeed in life if he is denied the opportunity of an education. Such an opportunity, where the state has undertaken to provide it, is a right which must be made available to all on equal terms.

18   We come then to the question presented: Does segregation of children in public schools solely on the basis of race, even though the physical facilities and other "tangible" factors may be equal, deprive the children of the minority group of equal educational opportunities? We believe that it does.

19   In *Sweatt v. Painter*, supra, in finding that a segregated law school for Negroes could not provide them equal educational opportunities,

this Court relied in large part on "those qualities which are incapable of objective measurement but which make for greatness in a law school." In *McLaurin v. Oklahoma State Regents,* supra, the Court, in requiring that a Negro admitted to a white graduate school be treated like all other students, again resorted to intangible considerations: ". . . his ability to study, to engage in discussions and exchange views with other students, and, in general, to learn his profession." Such considerations apply with added force to children in grade and high schools. To separate them from others of similar age and qualifications solely because of their race generates a feeling of inferiority as to their status in the community that may affect their hearts and minds in a way unlikely ever to be undone. The effect of this separation on their educational opportunities was well stated by a finding in the Kansas case by a court which nevertheless felt compelled to rule against the Negro plaintiffs:

> Segregation of white and colored children in public schools has a detrimental effect upon the colored children. The impact is greater when it has the sanction[8] of the law, for the policy of separating the races is usually interpreted as denoting the inferiority of the negro group. A sense of inferiority affects the motivation of a child to learn. Segregation with the sanction of law, therefore, has a tendency to [retard] the educational and mental development of negro children and to deprive them of some of the benefits they would receive in a racial[ly] integrated school system.

20 Whatever may have been the extent of psychological knowledge at the time of *Plessy v. Ferguson,* this finding is amply supported by modern authority. Any language in *Plessy v. Ferguson* contrary to this finding is rejected.

21 We conclude that, in the field of public education, the doctrine of "separate but equal" has no place. Separate educational facilities are inherently unequal. Therefore, we hold that the plaintiffs and others similarly situated for whom the actions have been brought are, by reason of the segregation complained of, deprived of the equal protection of the laws guaranteed by the Fourteenth Amendment. This **disposition** makes unnecessary any discussion whether such segregation also violates the Due Process Clause of the Fourteenth Amendment.

22 Because these are class actions, because of the wide applicability of this decision, and because of the great variety of local conditions, the formulation of decrees in these cases presents problems of considerable complexity. On reargument, the consideration of appropriate relief was necessarily subordinated to the primary question—the constitutionality of segregation in public education. We have now announced that such segregation is a denial of the equal

Mark familiar word parts or indicate another strategy you used that helped you determine meaning.

disposition (dihs puh ZIHSH uhn) *n.*

MEANING:

---

8. **sanction** *n.* official permission or approval.

protection of the laws. In order that we may have the full assistance of the parties in formulating decrees, the cases will be restored to the docket, and the parties are requested to present further argument on Questions 4 and 5 previously propounded by the Court for the reargument this Term. The Attorney General of the United States is again invited to participate. The Attorneys General of the states requiring or permitting segregation in public education will also be permitted to appear as amici curiae upon request to do so by September 15, 1954, and submission of briefs by October 1, 1954.

23   *It is so ordered.* 🙜

Comprehension Check

Complete the following items after you finish your first read. Review and clarify details with your group.

1. What change are the plaintiffs in this case seeking?

2. What standard had been set earlier by the *Plessy v. Ferguson* decision?

3. According to the opinion of the Court, what fundamental conflict exists between segregation and the Fourteenth Amendment?

4. 📖 **Notebook** Write a summary of *Brown v. Board of Education*.

- -

RESEARCH

Research to Clarify Choose at least one unfamiliar detail from the text. Briefly research that detail. In what way does the information you learned shed light on an aspect of the Supreme Court's opinion? Share your findings with your group.

Close Read the Text

With your group, revisit sections of the text you marked during your first read. **Annotate** details that you notice. What **questions** do you have? What can you **conclude?**

BROWN v. BOARD OF EDUCATION: OPINION OF THE COURT

Analyze the Text

CITE TEXTUAL EVIDENCE to support your answers.

Complete the activities.

1. **Review and Clarify** With your group, review paragraphs 15–19. Then, discuss the justices' argument about why "separate but equal" is inherently unequal.

2. **Present and Discuss** Share with your group the passages from the text that you found especially significant, taking turns with others. Discuss what you noticed in the text, what questions you asked, and what conclusions you reached.

3. **Essential Question:** *In what ways does the struggle for freedom change with history?* What has this text taught you about the struggle for freedom? Discuss with your group.

LANGUAGE DEVELOPMENT

Concept Vocabulary

| plaintiffs | jurisdiction | disposition |

Why These Words? The three concept vocabulary words from the text are related. With your group, discuss the words, and determine what the words have in common. How do these word choices enhance the text?

Practice Use each concept vocabulary word in a sentence. Make sure to include context clues that hint at the word's meaning.

Word Study

Technical Words Most professions, including such fields as medicine and law, have their own technical language, often called **jargon**. In writing the Court's opinion in *Brown v. Board of Education*, Chief Justice Earl Warren uses technical legal words such as *plaintiffs*, *jurisdiction*, and *disposition*. Find four other words in the selection that could be classified as legal jargon. Write the words and their meanings.

TIP

GROUP DISCUSSION
If you do not fully understand a classmate's comment, ask for clarification. Using a respectful tone, state exactly what you don't understand.

WORD NETWORK

Add words related to struggle from the text to your Word Network.

STANDARDS

Reading Informational Text
Determine the meaning of words and phrases as they are used in a text, including figurative, connotative, and technical meanings; analyze how an author uses and refines the meaning of a key term or terms over the course of a text.

Language
Acquire and use accurately general academic and domain-specific words and phrases, sufficient for reading, writing, speaking, and listening at the college and career readiness level; demonstrate independence in gathering vocabulary knowledge when considering a word or phrase important to comprehension or expression.

BROWN v. BOARD OF EDUCATION:
OPINION OF THE COURT

Analyze Craft and Structure

Author's Choices: Structure In *Brown v. Board of Education*, Chief Justice Earl Warren delivers the **opinion**, or legal judgment, of the Court. He defends the Court's position in the form of an analytical argument. In an **analytical argument**, a writer or speaker uses logical reasoning and persuasive evidence to examine an issue and to support a particular conclusion, called a **claim**. In legal opinions, the writer presenting the argument anticipates and considers objections and challenges, or **counterclaims.**

Practice

CITE TEXTUAL EVIDENCE to support your answers.

Work with your group to analyze the structure of the Court's opinion. Review the text, and complete the chart. Notice the order of topics: Warren proceeds from historical to legal to social considerations before arriving at a conclusion. Identify specific details from each section of the opinion, and explain the main idea they develop. Then, explain how each section adds to the line of reasoning that results in the Court's decision.

TOPIC	DETAILS IN THE TEXT	MAIN IDEA
Fourteenth Amendment (historical considerations)		
Plessy v. Ferguson (legal considerations)		
Importance of education (social considerations)		
Conclusions reached by the Court		

Conventions and Style

Coordinating Conjunctions A **coordinating conjunction** connects words, phrases, or clauses of equal rank. You can improve your sentence variety by using coordinating conjunctions to combine short, simple sentences into compound sentences.

> **Original:** These cases are premised on different facts. A common legal question justifies their consideration together.
>
> **Revision:** These cases are premised on different facts, *but* a common legal question justifies their consideration together.

Coordinating conjunctions show different relationships between the words or ideas that they connect. Study this chart.

COORDINATING CONJUNCTION	RELATIONSHIP
and	addition or similarity
but, yet	contrast
so	result or effect
for	reason or cause
or, nor	choice

Read It

In each item from or about the Supreme Court's opinion in *Brown v. Board of Education*, mark the coordinating conjunction and the words or groups of words that it connects.

1. Compulsory attendance laws and the great expenditures for education demonstrate our recognition of its importance.

2. Education is a principal instrument in awakening the child to cultural values, but success in life without the opportunity of an education is doubtful.

3. The state undertakes to make education available, yet it must be available to all on equal terms.

4. Education is a key function of government, for it is the very foundation of good citizenship.

Write It

📓 **Notebook** Use a coordinating conjunction to combine each pair of sentences. Write the new sentence.

1. According to the plaintiffs, public schools are not "equal." The schools cannot be made "equal."

2. Schools may have equal physical facilities. That fact doesn't guarantee equal educational opportunities.

3. Minority children in segregated schools may lack motivation to learn. By their very nature, such schools tend to instill a sense of inferiority.

4. The Court agreed. Segregation in public schools was struck down.

TIP

PUNCTUATION

If you use a coordinating conjunction to join two independent clauses, place a comma before the coordinating conjunction.

📝 **EVIDENCE LOG**

Before moving on to a new selection, go to your Evidence Log and record what you learned from the Supreme Court's opinion in *Brown v. Board of Education*.

STANDARDS

Reading Informational Text
Analyze and evaluate the effectiveness of the structure an author uses in his or her exposition or argument, including whether the structure makes points clear, convincing, and engaging.

Language
• Demonstrate command of the conventions of standard English grammar and usage when writing or speaking.

• Apply knowledge of language to understand how language functions in different contexts, to make effective choices for meaning or style, and to comprehend more fully when reading or listening.

BROWN V BOARD OF EDUCATION:
OPINION OF THE COURT

Writing to Sources

News articles inform the public about major events taking place in the world. They often summarize and explain complex happenings in a way that is easily understood.

Assignment

With your group, analyze the Supreme Court's opinion in *Brown v. Board of Education*. Then, write a **news article** in which you summarize and explain the Court's historic decision.

- Outline the essay, and take note of the key ideas you will include in your article.
- Provide an accurate summarization of the opinion.
- Use precise words to ensure your reporting is factual.
- Avoid injecting your own group's opinions or commentary.
- Title your article and list its contributors.

Vocabulary and Conventions Connection Consider including some of the concept vocabulary words. Also, consider using coordinating conjunctions to link ideas and to combine short sentences.

plaintiffs	jurisdiction	disposition

- -

Reflect on Your Writing

After you have drafted your news article answer these questions.

1. In what ways is your writing suited to a general audience?

2. Are your summarizations and explanations an accurate reflection of the original text?

3. **Why These Words?** The words you choose can greatly increase the effect of your writing. To what extent are your word choices precise and clear?

Speaking and Listening

Assignment
Chief Justice Warren's Court tried several cases concerning civil rights. Choose one of the following cases to research. Then, hold a **group discussion** in which you share your findings.

- *Bolling v. Sharpe*
- *Cooper v. Aaron*
- *Lucy v. Adams*
- *Loving v. Virginia*

1. **Perform Research** As a group, decide which case to research, and then, working individually, find 2-3 reputable sources to consult. Keep the following in mind as you conduct research:

   - Internet sources that contain *.gov* or *.edu* are generally more reliable than sites containing *.com* or *.org*.
   - Be sure to verify evidence by cross-checking with another source.

2. **Take Notes** As you research, take careful, accurate notes and be sure to indicate which sources you used. At the end of your notes document, create a set of "talking points" to bring up during your group's discussion.

3. **Hold the Discussion** When all group members have completed their research, come together to discuss your findings.

   - Appoint a facilitator, who will lead the discussion and ensure that the group stays on topic and follows ground rules for discussion.
   - When it is your turn to share your research, refer to your talking points. Be brief and to the point, but try to make your research findings interesting to listeners. When you have finished presenting, invite questions from listeners.
   - When you are listening to others present, be respectful and attentive. When invited to do so, ask questions that are relevant to the topic.

4. **Summarize Findings** At the conclusion of your group discussion, work with your group's facilitator to summarize the work of Earl Warren's Court as it relates to civil rights. Share your findings with other groups, and invite questions from your audience.

EVIDENCE LOG

Before moving on to a new selection, go to your Evidence Log and record what you learned from the Supreme Court's opinion in *Brown v. Board of Education*.

SOURCES

• AIN'T I A WOMAN?

• DECLARATION OF SENTIMENTS

• GIVING WOMEN THE VOTE

• THE STORY OF AN HOUR

• BROWN v. BOARD OF EDUCATION: OPINION OF THE COURT

Panel Discussion

Assignment

You have read a variety of texts by people who sought to protest social ills and encourage change. Work with your group to hold an informative **panel discussion** that addresses these questions:

> What were the goals of these reformers?
>
> Why did they want to achieve those goals?

Make a video recording of your discussion to share with others.

Plan With Your Group

Analyze the Texts There are four texts in the chart. If there are four members in your group, have each member choose one text as his or her area of expertise. If there are more than four members, form partnerships to choose texts. Use the chart headings to formulate key ideas about the particular text you or your partnership has chosen.

TITLE	GOAL OF REFORMER	REASONS FOR GOAL
Ain't I a Woman?		
Declaration of Sentiments		
Giving Women the Vote		
The Story of an Hour		
Brown v. Board of Education: Opinion of the Court		

Gather Evidence Find specific details from your text to support your ideas. Take notes or use note cards to list quotations from the text that support your understanding of the reformer's goal. If necessary, conduct research to locate evidence that supports your understanding of why that goal was important to the reformer.

⊞ STANDARDS

Speaking and Listening
Come to discussions prepared, having read and researched material under study; explicitly draw on that preparation by referring to evidence from texts and other research on the topic or issue to stimulate a thoughtful, well-reasoned exchange of ideas.

Organize Your Presentation Choose a moderator to present the assignment questions, which each panel member will answer in turn. The moderator should also make sure that each speaker keeps to agreed-upon time limits and doesn't speak out of turn. Decide on the order in which presenters will speak. Ask a classmate from another group to make a video recording of your discussion.

Rehearse With Your Group

Practice With Your Group Use this checklist to evaluate the effectiveness of your group's first run-through. Then, use your evaluation and these instructions to guide your revision.

CONTENT	USE OF MEDIA	PRESENTATION TECHNIQUES
☐ Each speaker clearly answers the questions asked. ☐ Each speaker supports ideas with evidence from the texts or additional research.	☐ The equipment functions properly. ☐ The focus moves smoothly from speaker to speaker.	☐ The speakers use formal language appropriately. ☐ The speakers make eye contact and speak clearly. ☐ Interactions between speakers and the moderator are civil and smooth.

Fine-Tune the Content If necessary, find additional examples from your chosen text to support your ideas. Make sure that you have incorporated all of the outside research you did as you respond to the moderator's questions.

Improve Your Use of Media Watch a playback of your recording, and give feedback to your recorder. In particular, make sure that the sound is audible so that viewers can easily hear what is being asked and answered.

Brush-Up on Your Presentation Techniques Listen for places where you may revert to language that is more informal or less polished. Try to speak as though you are educating an audience that is eager to learn about these reformers.

Present and Evaluate

As you record your final panel discussion, give all speakers equal time to share their ideas. As you watch the videos made by other groups, evaluate the presentations based on the evaluation checklist.

STANDARDS

Speaking and Listening
• Present information, findings, and supporting evidence, conveying a clear and distinct perspective, such that listeners can follow the line of reasoning, alternative or opposing perspectives are addressed, and the organization, development, substance, and style are appropriate to purpose, audience, and a range of formal and informal tasks.
• Adapt speech to a variety of contexts and tasks, demonstrating a command of formal English when indicated or appropriate.

PRIMARY SOURCES

- MARY CHESNUT'S CIVIL WAR

- BOMBARDMENT OF SUMTER (ART)

- RECOLLECTIONS OF A PRIVATE

- CIVIL WAR SOLDIER (ART)

Research Presentation

Assignment

You have explored ways in which people across history have struggled for freedom. Now, expand your knowledge by researching how individuals in the Civil War period dealt with realities of war. With your group, read the primary sources that have been provided. Then, form additional research questions based on your reading and locate another source to explore. Synthesize your learning to answer this question:

> What can we learn from ordinary people about extraordinary wartime events?

Share your learning in a **research presentation.**

Plan With Your Group

Analyze the Texts As a group, analyze and discuss each primary source listed here. Remember that a primary source is a document, image, or artifact that provides information about a historical topic. As you study each source, note what information it conveys and also note what further questions the source raises. Perform additional research as needed to find additional information on events, authors, or artists.

TITLE	WHAT WE LEARNED	QUESTIONS WE HAVE
Mary Chesnut's Civil War		
Bombardment of Sumter (art)		
Recollections of a Private		
Civil War Soldier (art)		

Formulate a Research Question Once you have studied the sources that have been provided, formulate a research question that arises from your reading. With your group, locate and analyze a source that will provide the information you seek, and take notes on your learning.

Synthesize Your Findings Review what you've learned from the primary sources you consulted. Then, with your group, answer the question posed in the assignment.

from Mary Chesnut's
Civil War

Mary Chesnut

BACKGROUND

The excerpts are from the diary of Mary Chestnut, who provides an eyewitness account of events leading to and following an attack on Fort Sumter.

APRIL 7, 1861. Today things seem to have settled down a little.

One can but hope still. Lincoln or Seward have made such silly advances and then far sillier drawings back. There may be a chance for peace, after all.

Things are happening so fast.

My husband has been made an aide-de-camp of General Beauregard.

Three hours ago we were quietly packing to go home. The convention has adjourned.

Now he tells me the attack upon Fort Sumter may begin tonight. Depends upon Anderson and the fleet outside. The Herald says that this show of war outside of the bar is intended for Texas.

John Manning came in with his sword and red sash. Pleased as a boy to be on Beauregard's staff while the row goes on. He has gone with Wigfall to Captain Hartstene with instructions.

Mr. Chesnut is finishing a report he had to make to the convention.

Mrs. Hayne called. She had, she said, "but one feeling, pity for those who are not here."

Jack Preston, Willie Alston—"the take-life-easys," as they are called—with John Green, "the big brave," have gone down to the island—volunteered as privates.

Seven hundred men were sent over. Ammunition wagons rumbling along the streets all night. Anderson burning blue lights— signs and signals for the fleet outside, I suppose.

Today at dinner there was no allusion to things as they stand in Charleston Harbor. There was an undercurrent of intense excitement. There could not have been a more brilliant circle. In addition to our usual quartet (Judge Withers, Langdon Cheves, and Trescot) our two governors dined with us, Means and Manning.

Primary Sources
Diaries and Journals What details of style and form tell you that you are reading a diary or journal entry?

Primary Sources
Diaries and Journals Judging from her list of dinner guests, what can you infer about Mary Chesnut's social circumstances?

Bombardment of Sumter, Harper's Weekly, 1861

> **Primary Source: Art**
Describe the spectators' differing reactions to the attack on Fort Sumter as shown in this illustration.

These men all talked so delightfully. For once in my life I listened. That over, business began. In earnest, Governor Means rummaged a sword and red sash from somewhere and brought it for Colonel Chesnut, who has gone to demand the surrender of Fort Sumter.

And now, patience—we must wait.

Why did that green goose Anderson go into Fort Sumter? Then everything began to go wrong.

Now they have intercepted a letter from him, urging them to let him surrender. He paints the horrors likely to ensue if they will not.

He ought to have thought of all that before he put his head in the hole.

APRIL 12, 1861. Anderson will not capitulate.

Yesterday was the merriest, maddest dinner we have had yet. Men were more audaciously wise and witty. We had an unspoken foreboding it was to be our last pleasant meeting. Mr. Miles dined with us today. Mrs. Henry King rushed in: "The news, I come for the latest news—all of the men of the King family are on the island"—of which fact she seemed proud.

While she was here, our peace negotiator—or envoy—came in. That is, Mr. Chesnut returned—his interview with Colonel Anderson had been deeply interesting—but was not inclined to be communicative, wanted his dinner. Felt for Anderson. Had telegraphed to President Davis for instructions. . . .

I do not pretend to go to sleep. How can I? If Anderson does not accept terms—at four—the orders are—he shall be fired upon.

I count four—St. Michael chimes. I begin to hope. At half-past four, the heavy booming of a cannon.

I sprang out of bed. And on my knees—prostrate—I prayed as I never prayed before.

There was a sound of stir all over the house—pattering of feet in the corridor—all seemed hurrying one way. I put on my double gown and a shawl and went, too. It was to the housetop.

The shells were bursting. In the dark I heard a man say "waste of ammunition."

I knew my husband was rowing about in a boat somewhere in that dark bay. And that the shells were roofing it over—bursting toward the fort. If Anderson was obstinate—he was to order the forts on our side to open fire. Certainly fire had begun. The regular roar of the cannon—there it was. And who could tell what each volley accomplished of death and destruction.

The women were wild, there on the housetop. Prayers from the women and imprecations from the men, and then a shell would light up the scene. Tonight, they say, the forces are to attempt to land.

The *Harriet Lane* had her wheelhouse smashed and put back to sea.

We watched up there—everybody wondered. Fort Sumter did not fire a shot.

Today Miles and Manning, colonels now—aides to Beauregard—dined with us. The latter hoped I would keep the peace. I give him only good words, for he was to be under fire all day and night, in the bay carrying orders, etc.

Last night—or this morning truly—up on the housetop I was so weak and weary I sat down on something that looked like a black stool.

Primary Sources
Diaries and Journals
What seems to be Chesnut's emotional state as she writes this entry? What clues in the text support your analysis?

"Get up, you foolish woman—your dress is on fire," cried a man. And he put me out.

It was a chimney, and the sparks caught my clothes. Susan Preston and Mr. Venable then came up. But my fire had been extinguished before it broke out into a regular blaze. . . .

APRIL 13, 1861. Nobody hurt, after all. How gay we were last night.

Reaction after the dread of all the slaughter we thought those dreadful cannons were making such a noise in doing.

Not even a battery the worse for wear.

Fort Sumter has been on fire. He has not yet silenced any of our guns. So the aides—still with swords and red sashes by way of uniform—tell us.

But the sound of those guns makes regular meals impossible. None of us go to table. But tea trays pervade the corridors, going everywhere.

Some of the anxious hearts lie on their beds and moan in solitary misery. Mrs. Wigfall and I solace ourselves with tea in my room.

These women have all a satisfying faith.

APRIL 15, 1861. I did not know that one could live such days of excitement.

They called, "Come out—there is a crowd coming."

A mob indeed, but it was headed by Colonels Chesnut and Manning.

The crowd was shouting and showing these two as messengers of good news. They were escorted to Beauregard's headquarters. Fort Sumter had surrendered.

Those up on the housetop shouted to us, "The fort is on fire." That had been the story once or twice before.

When we had calmed down, Colonel Chesnut, who had taken it all quietly enough—if anything, more unruffled than usual in his serenity—told us how the surrender came about.

Wigfall was with them on Morris Island when he saw the fire in the fort, jumped in a little boat and, with his handkerchief as a white flag, rowed over to Fort Sumter. Wigfall went in through a porthole.

When Colonel Chesnut arrived shortly after and was received by the regular entrance, Colonel Anderson told him he had need to pick his way warily, for it was all mined.

As far as I can make out, the fort surrendered to Wigfall.

But it is all confusion. Our flag is flying there. Fire engines have been sent to put out the fire.

Everybody tells you half of something and then rushes off to tell something else or to hear the last news. . . . ❧

Primary Sources
Diaries and Journals
What do you learn from the entry of April 13, 1861, that you would probably not learn from a textbook?

Recollections of a Private

Warren Lee Goss

In the weeks that followed the attack on Fort Sumter, thousands of men on both sides volunteered to fight. Among the early enlistees was Warren Lee Goss of Massachusetts.

"Cold chills" ran up and down my back as I got out of bed after the sleepless night, and shaved preparatory to other desperate deeds of valor. I was twenty years of age, and when anything unusual was to be done, like fighting or courting, I shaved.

With a nervous tremor convulsing my system, and my heart thumping like muffled drumbeats, I stood before the door of the recruiting office, and before turning the knob to enter read and reread the advertisement for recruits posted thereon, until I knew all its peculiarities. The promised chances for "travel and promotion" seemed good, and I thought I might have made a mistake in considering war so serious after all. "Chances for travel!" I must confess now, after four years of soldiering, that the "chances for travel" were no myth; but "promotion" was a little uncertain and slow.

I was in no hurry to open the door. Though determined to enlist, I was half inclined to put it off awhile; I had a fluctuation of desires; I was fainthearted and brave; I wanted to enlist, and yet—Here I turned the knob, and was relieved. . . .

My first uniform was a bad fit: My trousers were too long by three or four inches; the flannel shirt was coarse and unpleasant, too large at the neck and too short elsewhere. The forage cap was an ungainly bag with pasteboard top and leather visor; the blouse was the only part which seemed decent; while the overcoat made me feel like a little nubbin of corn in a large preponderance of husk. Nothing except "Virginia mud" ever took down my ideas of military pomp quite so low.

^ **Primary Source: Art**
What attitude toward war does this 1861 painting of a young Civil War soldier convey? Explain.

Primary Sources
Diaries and Journals
What does this account reveal about experiences of new soldiers?

After enlisting I did not seem of so much consequence as I had expected. There was not so much excitement on account of my military appearance as I deemed justly my due. I was taught my facings, and at the time I thought the drillmaster needlessly fussy about shouldering, ordering, and presenting arms. At this time men were often drilled in company and regimental evolutions long before they learned the manual of arms, because of the difficulty of obtaining muskets. These we obtained at an early day, but we would willingly have resigned them after carrying them a few hours. The musket, after an hour's drill, seemed heavier and less ornamental than it had looked to be.

The first day I went out to drill, getting tired of doing the same things over and over, I said to the drill sergeant: "Let's stop this fooling and go over to the grocery." His only reply was addressed to a corporal: "Corporal, take this man out and drill him"; and the corporal did! I found that suggestions were not so well appreciated in the army as in private life, and that no wisdom was equal to a drillmaster's "Right face," "Left wheel," and "Right, oblique, march." It takes a raw recruit some time to learn that he is not to think or suggest, but obey. Some never do learn. I acquired it at last, in humility and mud, but it was tough. Yet I doubt if my patriotism, during my first three weeks' drill, was quite knee high. Drilling looks easy to a spectator, but it isn't. After a time I had cut down my uniform so that I could see out of it, and had conquered the drill sufficiently to see through it. Then the word came: on to Washington! . . . ❧

Develop Your Script

Plan Your Presentation Now that you have gathered information, create an outline and script for your group to follow during your research presentation.

- Be sure your presentation provides a response to the Assignment prompt: *What can we learn from ordinary people about extraordinary wartime events?*

- Develop a working script in which you decide which group member will deliver what information. For example, you may want each group member to discuss findings from one particular primary source.

- Be sure to include information about your additional research question and how you went about finding answers to it.

- Conclude with a summary of your findings.

Rehearse With Your Group

Practice With Your Group Rehearse your presentation with your group. Use this checklist to evaluate the effectiveness of your group's first run-through. Then, use your evaluation and these instructions to guide your revision.

CONTENT	PRESENTATION TECHNIQUES
☐ Each speaker clearly identifies the topic of his or her portion of the presentation.	☐ The focus moves smoothly from speaker to speaker.
☐ Each speaker supports ideas with evidence from the texts or additional research.	☐ The speakers use formal language appropriately.
	☐ The speakers make eye contact and speak clearly.

Fine-Tune the Content If necessary, find additional examples from your source materials to support your ideas. Consider switching the order of presenters, if necessary, for flow and logic. You may also want to include visuals to add interest to your presentation.

Brush-Up on Your Presentation Techniques Adapt your word choice if you find your presentation seems too informal. Make eye contact with your audience when it is your turn to speak. When others in your group are presenting, keep your focus on them.

Present and Evaluate

Once you have finished your presentation, invite comments and feedback from your audience. As you watch and listen to presentations of other groups, take notes and offer feedback based on the evaluation checklist.

ESSENTIAL QUESTION:

In what ways does the struggle for freedom change with history?

Freedom is a concept that means so many things, including the right to choose your path in life and to follow your ambitions wherever they may take you. In this section, you will complete your study of the struggle for freedom by exploring an additional selection related to the topic. You'll then share what you learn with classmates. To choose a text, follow these steps.

Look Back Think about the selections you have already studied. What more do you want to know about the topic of the struggle for freedom?

Look Ahead Preview the texts by reading the descriptions. Which one seems most interesting and appealing to you?

Look Inside Take a few minutes to scan the text you chose. Choose a different one if this text doesn't meet your needs.

Independent Learning Strategies

Throughout your life, in school, in your community, and in your career, you will need to rely on yourself to learn and work on your own. Review these strategies and the actions you can take to practice them during Independent Learning. Add ideas of your own for each category.

STRATEGY	ACTION PLAN
Create a schedule	• Understand your goals and deadlines. • Make a plan for what to do each day. •
Practice what you have learned	• Use first-read and close-read strategies to deepen your understanding. • After you read, evaluate the usefulness of the evidence to help you understand the topic. • After reading, consult reference sources for background information that can help you clarify meaning. •
Take notes	• Record important ideas and information. • Review your notes before preparing to share with a group. •

CONTENTS

Choose one selection. Selections are available online only.

POETRY COLLECTION 1

The Poetry of Langston Hughes

Langston Hughes

How does it feel to grow up an outsider in the land of the free?

POETRY COLLECTION 2

Douglass   *Paul Laurence Dunbar*

The Fifth Fact   *Sarah Browning*

Who Burns for the Perfection of Paper   *Martín Espada*

How does the past affect our present view of change?

HISTORY

from The Warmth of Other Suns

Isabel Wilkerson

How far will people travel to find the freedom that they desire?

ESSAY

What a Factory Can Teach a Housewife

Ida Tarbell

Why might factory work be more freeing than a life of service?

PERSUASIVE ESSAY

from Books as Bombs

Louis Menand

How can one book change the world?

MEDIA: PODCAST

A Balance Between Nature and Nurture

Gloria Steinem

Are humans born unequal, or is inequality learned?

PERFORMANCE-BASED ASSESSMENT PREP

Review Evidence for an Informative Essay

Complete your Evidence Log for the unit by evaluating what you've learned and synthesizing the information you have recorded.

First-Read Guide

Use this page to record your first-read ideas.

🔧 **Tool Kit**
First-Read Guide and
Model Annotation

Selection Title: _____

NOTICE new information or ideas you learn about the unit topic as you first read this text.

ANNOTATE by marking vocabulary and key passages you want to revisit.

First
Read

CONNECT ideas within the selection to other knowledge and the selections you have read.

RESPOND by writing a brief summary of the selection.

≡ STANDARD

Reading Read and comprehend complex literary and informational texts independently and proficiently.

Close-Read Guide

Use this page to record your close-read ideas.

Selection Title: _____

Tool Kit
Close-Read Guide and
Model Annotation

Close Read the Text

Revisit sections of the text you marked during your first read. Read these sections closely and **annotate** what you notice. Ask yourself **questions** about the text. What can you **conclude**? Write down your ideas.

Analyze the Text

Think about the author's choices of patterns, structure, techniques, and ideas included in the text. Select one and record your thoughts about what this choice conveys.

QuickWrite

Pick a paragraph from the text that grabbed your interest. Explain the power of this passage.

_____
_____
_____
_____
_____
_____
_____
_____
_____
_____

▤ STANDARD
Reading Read and comprehend complex literary and informational texts independently and proficiently.

Share Your Independent Learning

Prepare to Share

In what ways does the struggle for freedom change with history?

Even when you read or learn something independently, your understanding continues to grow when you share what you have learned with others. Reflect on the text you explored independently, and write notes about its connection to the unit. In your notes, consider why this text belongs in this unit.

Learn From Your Classmates

Discuss It Share your ideas about the text you explored on your own. As you talk with your classmates, jot down ideas that you learn from them.

Reflect

Review your notes, and mark the most important insight you gained from these writing and discussion activities. Explain how this idea adds to your understanding of the meaning of freedom.

STANDARDS
Speaking and Listening
Initiate and participate effectively in a range of collaborative discussions with diverse partners on *grades 11–12 topics, texts, and issues,* building on others' ideas and expressing their own clearly and persuasively.

Review Evidence for an Informative Essay

At the beginning of this unit, you took a position on the following question:

What motivates people to struggle for change?

Review your Evidence Log and your QuickWrite from the beginning of the unit. Have your ideas changed?

☐ YES	☐ NO
Identify at least three pieces of evidence that have caused you to reevaluate your ideas.	Identify at least three pieces of evidence that reinforced your original ideas.
1.	**1.**
2.	**2.**
3.	**3.**

Develop your thoughts into a topic sentence: *One significant motivation that may inspire people to struggle for change is*: _____

_____

_____

Identify a historical example of the motivation you identified: _____

_____

_____

Evaluate the Strength of Your Evidence Which two texts that you read in this unit offer the strongest support for your topic sentence?

1. _____

2. _____

What are some other resources you might use to locate information about the topic?

1. _____ 2. _____

▤ STANDARDS

Writing
Introduce a topic; organize complex ideas, concepts, and information so that each new element builds on that which precedes it to create a unified whole; include formatting, graphics, and multimedia when useful to aiding comprehension.

SOURCES

• WHOLE-CLASS SELECTIONS

• SMALL-GROUP SELECTIONS

• INDEPENDENT-LEARNING SELECTION

PART 1
Writing to Sources: Informative Essay

In this unit, you read a variety of texts by reformers whose goal was to initiate change. Not all struggles were alike: The writers faced various obstacles in their quests for reform.

Assignment

Write an **informative essay** in which you explore this question:

What motivates people to struggle for change?

Begin by defining the various reasons people decide to fight for change. Identify two or three texts from this unit that you feel most clearly show the connections between motivation and action. Use specific examples from each text to support your analysis and deductions.

Reread the Assignment Review the assignment to be sure you fully understand it. The assignment may reference some of the academic words presented at the beginning of the unit. Be sure you understand each of the words given below in order to complete the assignment correctly.

Academic Vocabulary

informational	verbatim	specific
inquire	deduction	

Review the Elements of an Informative Essay Before you begin writing, read the Informative Text Rubric. Once you have completed your first draft, check it against the rubric. If one or more of the elements are missing or not as strong as they could be, revise your text to add or strengthen those components.

🔗 **WORD NETWORK**

As you write and revise your text, use your Word Network to help vary your word choices.

☰ **STANDARDS**

Writing
• Write informative/explanatory texts to examine and convey complex ideas, concepts, and information clearly and accurately through the effective selection, organization, and analysis of content.
• Draw evidence from literary or informational texts to support analysis, reflection, and research.
• Write routinely over extended time frames and shorter time frames for a range of tasks, purposes, and audiences.

Informative Text Rubric

	Focus and Organization	Evidence and Elaboration	Language Conventions
4	The introduction is engaging and reveals the topic in a way that appeals to a reader. Facts, details, and examples progress logically, and transition words and phrases link and separate ideas. The conclusion leaves a strong impression on the reader.	Ideas are supported with specific and relevant examples from research and the texts. The style of the essay is formal, and the tone is objective. Vocabulary is used strategically and appropriately for the audience and purpose.	The essay demonstrates a clear command of standard English conventions of usage and mechanics.
3	The introduction is engaging and clearly reveals the topic. Facts, details, and examples progress logically, and transition words appear frequently. The conclusion follows from the rest of the essay.	Ideas are supported with relevant examples from research and the texts. The style of the essay is mostly formal, and the tone tends to be objective. Vocabulary is generally appropriate for the audience and purpose.	The essay demonstrates accuracy in standard English conventions of usage and mechanics.
2	The introduction states the topic. Facts, details and examples progress somewhat logically, and transition words may be used. The conclusion restates the main ideas.	Many ideas are supported with examples from research and the texts. The style of the essay is occasionally formal, and the tone is at times objective. Vocabulary is somewhat appropriate for the audience and purpose.	The essay demonstrates some accuracy in standard English conventions of usage and mechanics.
1	The introduction does not clearly state the topic, or there is no introduction. Facts, details, and examples do not progress logically, and sentences seem disconnected. The conclusion does not follow from the essay, or there is no conclusion.	Ideas are not supported with examples from research and the texts, or examples are irrelevant. The style of the essay is informal, and the tone frequently reveals biases. Vocabulary is limited, ineffective, or inappropriate.	The essay contains mistakes in standard English conventions of usage and mechanics.

PART 2
Speaking and Listening: Podcast

Assignment
After completing the final draft of your informative essay, make a **podcast** or audio recording that could be uploaded for listeners. Then, share your recording, so that your classmates can listen to your work.

Follow these steps to make your podcast both informative and interesting.

- Give your podcast a title, and provide your name.
- Mark key examples in your informative essay that answer this question: *How does the motivator I analyzed encourage people to struggle for change?* These are the key points you will want to emphasize in your delivery.
- Practice your delivery, keeping in mind that you will be heard but not seen. You will need to vary your voice accordingly. Also, take care to eliminate distracting background noises.
- Deliver your podcast, being sure to maintain an even distance from the recording device. Focus on speaking clearly, and build in pauses so that listeners can follow and digest your ideas.

Review the Rubric The criteria by which your podcast will be evaluated appear in the rubric below. Review the criteria before recording to ensure that you are prepared.

	Content	Use of Media	Presentation Technique
3	The podcast focuses on the question. The flow of ideas is logical, clear, and easy to follow.	The voice on the recording is consistent and audible. The podcast file has a title that clearly illustrates the focus.	The speaker's voice is consistently clear and appropriately loud for the recording. The speaker varies tone and pace consistently and effectively.
2	The podcast mostly focuses on the question. The flow of ideas is fairly logical and mostly easy to follow.	The voice on the recording may vary but is mostly audible. The podcast file has a logical title.	The speaker's voice is mostly clear and sufficiently loud for the recording. The speaker varies tone and pace to some extent.
1	The podcast has no clear focus. The flow of ideas is illogical and difficult to follow.	The voice on the recording sometimes fades in and out. The podcast file lacks a meaningful title.	The speaker mumbles or speaks too quickly or quietly. The speaker does not vary tone and pace.

Reflect on the Unit

Now that you've completed the unit, take a few moments to reflect on your learning. Use the questions below to think about where you succeeded, what skills and strategies helped you, and where you can continue to grow in the future.

Reflect on the Unit Goals

Look back at the goals at the beginning of the unit. Use a different colored pen to rate yourself again. Think about readings and activities that contributed the most to the growth of your understanding. Record your thoughts.

Reflect on the Learning Strategies

💬 Discuss It Write a reflection on whether you were able to improve your learning based on your Action Plans. Think about what worked, what didn't, and what you might do to keep working on these strategies. Record your ideas before a class discussion.

Reflect on the Text

Choose a selection that you found challenging, and explain what made it difficult.

Explain something that surprised you about a text in the unit.

STANDARDS
Speaking and Listening
Come to discussions prepared, having read and researched material under study; explicitly draw on that preparation by referring to evidence from texts and other research on the topic or issue to stimulate a thoughtful, well-reasoned exchange of ideas.

Which activity taught you the most about power, protest, and change? What did you learn?

RESOURCES

CONTENTS

TOOL KIT

Close Reading R1
Marking the Text
First-Read Model and Guide
Close-Read Model and Guide
Analyzing Legal Meanings and Reasoning

Writing R8
Argument Model
Informative/Explanatory Model
Narrative Model

Research R26
Conducting Research
Reviewing Research Findings
Incorporating Research Into Writing
MLA Style for Listing Sources

Program Resources R36
Evidence Log Model
Word Network Model

GLOSSARY

Academic/
Concept Vocabulary R38
Vocabulario académicos/
Vocabulario de conceptos

Literary Terms Handbook R47
Manual de términos literarios

Grammar Handbook R59

INDEXES

Index of Skills R69

Index of Authors
and Titles. R78

ACKNOWLEDGMENTS

Acknowledgments
and Credits. R81

Marking the Text: Strategies and Tips for Annotation

When you close read a text, you read for comprehension and then reread to unlock layers of meaning and to analyze a writer's style and techniques. Marking a text as you read it enables you to participate more fully in the close-reading process.

Following are some strategies for text mark-ups, along with samples of how the strategies can be applied. These mark-ups are suggestions; you and your teacher may want to use other mark-up strategies.

* Key Idea
! I love it!
? I have questions
◯ Unfamiliar or important word
---- Context Clues

Suggested Mark-Up Notations

WHAT I NOTICE	HOW TO MARK UP	QUESTIONS TO ASK
Key Ideas and Details	• Highlight key ideas or claims. • Underline supporting details or evidence.	• What does the text say? What does it leave unsaid? • What inferences do you need to make? • What details lead you to make your inferences?
Word Choice	• Circle unfamiliar words. • Put a dotted line under context clues, if any exist. • Put an exclamation point beside especially rich or poetic passages.	• What inferences about word meaning can you make? • What tone and mood are created by word choice? • What alternate word choices might the author have made?
Text Structure	• Highlight passages that show key details supporting the main idea. • Use arrows to indicate how sentences and paragraphs work together to build ideas. • Use a right-facing arrow to indicate foreshadowing. • Use a left-facing arrow to indicate flashback.	• Is the text logically structured? • What emotional impact do the structural choices create?
Author's Craft	• Circle or highlight instances of repetition, either of words, phrases, consonants, or vowel sounds. • Mark rhythmic beats in poetry using checkmarks and slashes. • Underline instances of symbolism or figurative language.	• Does the author's style enrich or detract from the reading experience? • What levels of meaning are created by the author's techniques?

CLOSE READING

* Key Idea
! I love it!
? I have questions
◯ Unfamiliar or important word
---- Context Clues

NOTES

In a first read, work to get a sense of the main idea of a text. Look for key details and ideas that help you understand what the author conveys to you. Mark passages which prompt a strong response from you.

Here is how one reader marked up this text.

MODEL

INFORMATIONAL TEXT

from Classifying the Stars
Cecilia H. Payne

1   Sunlight and starlight are composed of waves of various lengths, * which the eye, even aided by a telescope, is unable to separate. We must use more than a telescope. In order to sort out the ? component colors, the light must be dispersed by a prism, or split up by some other means. For instance, sunbeams passing through rain drops, are transformed into the ◯myriad◯ tinted rainbow. The familiar rainbow spanning the sky is Nature's most ! glorious demonstration that light is composed of many colors.

2   The very beginning of our knowledge * of the nature of a star dates back to 1672, when Isaac Newton gave to the world the results of his experiments on passing sunlight through a prism. To describe the beautiful band of rainbow tints, produced when sunlight was dispersed by his three-cornered piece of glass, he took from the Latin the word *spectrum*, meaning an appearance. The rainbow is the ◯spectrum◯ of the Sun. . . .

3   In 1814, more than a century after Newton, the spectrum of the * Sun was obtained in such purity that an amazing detail was seen and studied by the German optician, Fraunhofer. He saw that the multiple spectral tints, ranging from delicate violet to deep red, were crossed by hundreds of fine dark lines. In other words, there were narrow gaps in the spectrum where certain shades were wholly blotted out. We must remember that the word spectrum is applied not only to sunlight, but also to the light of any glowing substance when its rays are sorted out by a prism or a ◯grating.◯

First-Read Guide

Use this page to record your first-read ideas.

You may want to use a guide like this to organize your thoughts after you read. Here is how a reader completed a First-Read Guide.

Selection Title: _Classifying the Stars_

NOTICE

NOTICE new information or ideas you learned about the unit topic as you first read this text.

Light = different waves of colors. (Spectrum)

Newton - the first person to observe these waves using a prism.

Faunhofer saw gaps in the spectrum.

ANNOTATE

ANNOTATE by marking vocabulary and key passages you want to revisit.

Vocabulary
   myriad
   grating
   component colors

Different light types = different lengths

Isaac Newton also worked theories of gravity.

<u>Multiple spectral tints?</u> "colors of various appearance"

Key Passage:
Paragraph 3 shows that Fraunhofer discovered more about the nature of light spectrums: he saw the spaces in between the tints.

First Read

CONNECT

CONNECT ideas within the selection to other knowledge and the selections you have read.

I remember learning about prisms in science class.

Double rainbows! My favorite. How are they made?

RESPOND

RESPOND by writing a brief summary of the selection.

Science allows us to see things not visible to the naked eye. What we see as sunlight is really a spectrum of colors. By using tools, such as prisms, we can see the components of sunlight and other light. They appear as single colors or as multiple colors separated by gaps of no color. White light contains a rainbow of colors.

TOOL KIT: CLOSE READING

CLOSE READING

✳ Key Idea

! I love it!

? I have questions

◯ Unfamiliar or important word

---- Context Clues

In a close read, go back into the text to study it in greater detail. Take the time to analyze not only the author's ideas but the way that those ideas are conveyed. Consider the genre of the text, the author's word choice, the writer's unique style, and the message of the text.

Here is how one reader close read this text.

MODEL

from **Classifying the Stars**

Cecilia H. Payne

NOTES

explanation of sunlight and starlight

What is light and where do the colors come from?

✳

1 Sunlight and starlight are composed of waves of various lengths, which the eye, even aided by a telescope, is unable to separate. We must use more than a telescope. In order to sort out the **?** component colors, the light must be dispersed by a prism, or split up by some other means. For instance, sunbeams passing through rain drops, are transformed into the myriad-tinted rainbow. The familiar rainbow spanning the sky is Nature's most **!** glorious demonstration that light is composed of many colors.

This paragraph is about Newton and the prism.

What discoveries helped us understand light?

✳

2 The very beginning of our knowledge of the nature of a star dates back to 1672, when Isaac Newton gave to the world the results of his experiments on passing sunlight through a prism. To describe the beautiful band of rainbow tints, produced when sunlight was dispersed by his three-cornered piece of glass, he took from the Latin the word *spectrum*, meaning an appearance. The rainbow is the spectrum of the Sun. . . .

Fraunhofer and gaps in spectrum

✳

3 In 1814, more than a century after Newton, the spectrum of the Sun was obtained in such purity that an amazing detail was seen and studied by the German optician, Fraunhofer. He saw that the multiple spectral tints, ranging from delicate violet to deep red, were crossed by hundreds of fine dark lines. In other words, there were narrow gaps in the spectrum where certain shades were wholly blotted out. We must remember that the word spectrum is applied not only to sunlight, but also to the light of any glowing substance when its rays are sorted out by a prism or a grating.

Close-Read Guide

Use this page to record your close-read ideas.

Selection Title: ___Classifying the Stars___

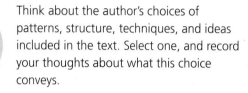

You can use the Close-Read Guide to help you dig deeper into the text. Here is how a reader completed a Close-Read Guide.

Close Read the Text

Revisit sections of the text you marked during your first read. Read these sections closely and **annotate** what you notice. Ask yourself **questions** about the text. What can you **conclude?** Write down your ideas.

Paragraph 3: Light is composed of waves of various lengths. Prisms let us see different colors in light. This is called the spectrum. Fraunhofer proved that there are gaps in the spectrum, where certain shades are blotted out.

More than one researcher studied this and each built off the ideas that were already discovered.

Analyze the Text

Think about the author's choices of patterns, structure, techniques, and ideas included in the text. Select one, and record your thoughts about what this choice conveys.

The author showed the development of human knowledge of the spectrum chronologically. Helped me see how ideas were built upon earlier understandings. Used dates and "more than a century after Newton" to show time.

QuickWrite

Pick a paragraph from the text that grabbed your interest. Explain the power of this passage.

The first paragraph grabbed my attention, specifically the sentence "The familiar rainbow spanning the sky is Nature's most glorious demonstration that light is composed of many colors." The paragraph began as a straightforward scientific explanation. When I read the word "glorious," I had to stop and deeply consider what was being said. It is a word loaded with personal feelings. With that one word, the author let the reader know what was important to her.

CLOSE READING

Analyzing Legal Meanings and Reasoning

Reading historical and legal texts requires careful analysis of both the vocabulary and the logical flow of ideas that support a conclusion.

Understanding Legal Meanings

The language of historical and legal documents is formal, precise, and technical. Many words in these texts have specific meanings that you need to understand in order to follow the flow of ideas. For example, the second amendment to the U.S. Constitution states that "A well regulated Militia being necessary to the security of a free State, the right of the people to keep and bear Arms shall not be infringed." To understand this amendment, it is important to know that in this context *militia* means "armed forces," *bear* means "carry," and *infringed* means "denied." To understand legal meanings:

- Use your knowledge of word roots to help you understand unfamiliar words. Many legal terms use familiar Greek or Latin roots, prefixes, or suffixes.

- Do not assume that you know a word's legal meaning: Use a dictionary to check the meanings of key words to be certain that you are applying the correct meaning.

- Paraphrase the text to aid comprehension. Replace difficult words with synonyms to make sure you follow the logic of the argument.

Delineating Legal Reasoning

Works of public advocacy, such as court decisions, political proclamations, proposed laws, or constitutional amendments, use careful reasoning to support conclusions. These strategies can help you understand the legal reasoning in an argument:

- State the **purpose** of the document in your own words to help you focus on the writer's primary goal.

- Look for the line of reasoning that supports the **arguments** presented. To be valid and persuasive, key arguments should be backed up by clearly stated logical analysis. Be aware of persuasive techniques, such as citing facts and statistics, referring to expert testimonials, and using emotional language with strong connotations.

- Identify the **premises,** or evidence, upon which a decision rests. In legal texts, premises often include **precedents,** which are earlier examples that must be followed or specifically overturned. Legal reasoning is usually based on the decisions of earlier trials. Be sure you understand precedents in order to identify how the court arrived at the current decision.

TOOL KIT: CLOSE READING

Note the strategies used to evaluate legal meanings and reasoning in this Supreme Court decision from 1954 regarding the legality of segregated, "separate but equal" schools for students of different races.

LEGAL TEXT

from *Brown v. Board of Education of Topeka*, Opinion of the Supreme Court by Chief Justice Earl Warren

We come then to the question presented: Does segregation of children in public schools solely on the basis of race, even though the physical facilities and other "tangible" factors may be equal, deprive the children of the minority group of equal educational opportunities? We believe that it does.

In *Sweatt v. Painter*, in finding that a segregated law school for Negroes could not provide them equal educational opportunities, this Court relied in large part on "those qualities which are incapable of objective measurement but which make for greatness in a law school." In *McLaurin v. Oklahoma State Regents*, the Court, in requiring that a Negro admitted to a white graduate school be treated like all other students, again resorted to intangible considerations: ". . . his ability to study, to engage in discussions and exchange views with other students, and, in general, to learn his profession." Such considerations apply with added force to children in grade and high schools. To separate them from others of similar age and qualifications solely because of their race generates a feeling of inferiority as to their status in the community that may affect their hearts and minds in a way unlikely ever to be undone. The effect of this separation on their educational opportunities was well stated by a finding in the Kansas case by a court which nevertheless felt compelled to rule against the Negro plaintiffs: Segregation of white and colored children in public schools has a detrimental effect upon the colored children. The impact is greater when it has the sanction of the law, for the policy of separating the races is usually interpreted as denoting the inferiority of the negro group. A sense of inferiority affects the motivation of a child to learn. Segregation with the sanction of law, therefore, has a tendency to [retard] the educational and mental development of negro children and to deprive them of some of the benefits they would receive in a racially integrated school system. Whatever may have been the extent of psychological knowledge at the time of *Plessy v. Ferguson*, this finding is amply supported by modern authority. Any language in *Plessy v. Ferguson* contrary to this finding is rejected.

We conclude that, in the field of public education, the doctrine of "separate but equal" has no place. Separate educational facilities are inherently unequal.

Use Word Roots The word *tangible* comes from the Latin root meaning "to touch." In this decision, the court contrasts tangible, measurable features with intangible features that are difficult to measure.

Identify the Premises The court cites two precedents: earlier cases relating to unequal education opportunities for black students.

Paraphrase the Text Here's one way you might break down the ideas in this sentence when you paraphrase: Segregating students just because of their race makes them feel as if they are less valued by our society. This separation can have a permanent negative influence on their character.

Line of Reasoning The conclusion makes the **purpose** of the decision clear: to overturn the precedent established by *Plessy v.* Ferguson. The **argument** describes the reasons the Court no longer considers the reasoning in that earlier case to be valid.

TOOL KIT: CLOSE READING

Argument

When you think of the word *argument*, you might think of a disagreement between two people, but an argument is more than that. An argument is a logical way of presenting a belief, conclusion, or stance. A good argument is supported with reasoning and evidence.

Argument writing can be used for many purposes, such as to change a reader's point of view or opinion or to bring about an action or a response from a reader.

Elements of an Argumentative Text

An **argument** is a logical way of presenting a viewpoint, belief, or stand on an issue. A well-written argument may convince the reader, change the reader's mind, or motivate the reader to take a certain action.

An effective argument contains these elements:

- a precise claim
- consideration of counterclaims, or opposing positions, and a discussion of their strengths and weaknesses
- logical organization that makes clear connections among claim, counterclaim, reasons, and evidence
- valid reasoning and evidence
- a concluding statement or section that logically completes the argument
- formal and objective language and tone
- error-free grammar, including accurate use of transitions

ARGUMENT: SCORE 1

Community Service Should be a Requirement for High School Graduation

Volunteering is a great idea for high school students. Those who don't volunteer are missing out.

You can learn a lot at your volunteer job. It might not seem like a big deal at the time, but the things you learn and do can be useful. You might volunteer somewhere with a spreadsheet. Everyone needs to know how to use a spreadsheet! That's going to be a useful again really soon.

Their lots of reasons to get involved. One of them is to become a better student in school. Also, to feel better about yourself and not act out so much.

So, volunteering helps you learn and get better at lots of things, not just what you are doing at your volunteer job. It's good not just to learn reading and writing and math and science all the time—the usual stuff we study in school. That's how volunteering can help you out.

Students today are really busy and they can't add anything more to they're busy schedules. But I think they can add a little more if it doesn't take too much time. Especially if it is important like volunteering.

High school students who volunteer get involved with the real world outside school, and that means a lot. They have a chance to do something that can make a difference in the world. This helps them learn things that maybe they can't learn in school, like, how to be kind and jenerous and care about making the world a better place.

Volunteering in high school is a great idea. Everybody should do it. There are lots of different ways to volunteer. You can even do it on weekends with your friends.

The claim is not clearly stated in the introduction.

The argument contains mistakes in standard English conventions of usage and mechanics.

The vocabulary used is limited and ineffective, and the tone is informal.

The writer does not acknowledge counterclaims.

TOOL KIT: WRITING

WRITING

ARGUMENT: SCORE 2

Community Service Should be a Requirement for High School Graduation

High school students should have to volunteer before they can graduate. It makes sense because it is helpful to them and others. Some students would volunteer anyway even if it wasn't required, but some wouldn't. If they have to do it for graduation then they won't miss out.

Their lots of reasons to get involved. One is to be a better student in school. Researchers have done studies to see the connection between community service and doing well in school. One study showed that most schools with programs said grades went up most of the time for kids that volunteered. Another study said elementary and middle school kids got better at problem-solving and were more interested in school. One study said students showed more responsibility. Another researcher discovered that kids who been volunteering have better self-esteem. They also have fewer problems.

Volunteering helps you learn and improve at lots of things, not just what you are doing at your volunteer job. One thing you might get better at is being a nicer person, like having more patience and listening well to others. Because you might need those skills when you are volunteering at a senior center or a preschool.

Some people say that volunteering in high school should NOT be required for graduation. They say students already have too much to do and they can't add anything more to they're schedules. But they can add a little more if it doesn't take too much time. Especially if it is important like volunteering.

Why should students be forced to do something, even if it is good? Well, that's just the way it is. When you force students to do something that is good, you are doing them a favor. Like forcing them to eat their vegetables or do their homework. The kids might not like it at first but what do you want to bet they are happy about it later on. That's the point.

Volunteering should be required for all high school students before they graduate. That's not just because they can do a lot of good in the world, but also because doing community service will help them in lots of ways.

The introduction establishes the claim.

The tone of the argument is occasionally formal and objective.

The writer briefly acknowledges and refutes counterclaims.

The writers relies too much on weak anecdotal evidence.

The conclusion offers some insight into the claim and restates some information.

ARGUMENT: SCORE 3

Community Service Should be a Requirement for High School Graduation

Requiring community service for high school graduation is an excellent idea that offers benefits not only to the community but to the student as well. Making it a requirement ensures that all students will be able to get in on the act.

Volunteering is a great way to build skills. It might not seem like a big deal at the time, but the experience you gain is very likely to be useful in the future. For example, while tracking, sorting, and distributing donations at an afterschool program, a volunteer might learn how to use a spreadsheet. That's going to come in handy very quickly, both in and out of school.

Participating in service learning can help you do better in school. ("Service learning" is when community service is part of a class curriculum.) For example, one study found that most schools with service learning programs reported grade point averages of participating students improved 76 percent of the time. Another study showed improved problem-solving skills and increased interest in academics among elementary and middle school students.

A study showed that middle and high school students who participated in quality service learning projects showed more personal and social responsibility. Another study found that students were more likely to help each other and be kind to each other, and care about doing their best. Studies also show better self-esteem and fewer behavioral problems in students who have been involved with service learning.

Despite all this, many people say that volunteering in high school should NOT be a requirement for graduation. They point out that students today are already over-stressed and over-scheduled. There simply isn't room for anything more.

True! But community service doesn't have to take up a lot of time. It might be possible for a group of time-stressed students to use class-time to organize a fundraiser, or to squeeze their service into a single "marathon" weekend. It's all a question of priorities.

In short, volunteering is a great way for students to help others, and reap benefits for themselves as well. Making it a requirement ensures that all students have the chance to grow through involvement with their communities. Volunteering opens doors and offers life-long benefits, and high school is the perfect time to get started!

> The claim is established in the introduction but is not as clear as it could be.

> The tone of the argument is mostly formal and objective.

> The writer does not transition very well into new topics.

> The writer uses some transitional phrases.

> The writer gives a reason for the counterclaim, but does not provide firm examples.

> The conclusion restates the claim and provides additional detail.

TOOL KIT: WRITING

WRITING

ARGUMENT: SCORE 4

Community Service Should be a Requirement for High School Graduation

Every high school student should be required to do community service in order to graduate. Volunteering offers life-long benefits that will prepare all students for adulthood.

First and foremost, studies show that participating in service learning —when community service is part of a class curriculum—often helps students do better in school. For example, a study conducted by Leeward County found that 83 percent of schools with service learning programs reported grade point averages of participating students improved 76 percent of the time. Another study, conducted by Hilliard Research, showed improved problem-solving skills and increased interest in academics among elementary and middle school students who participated in service learning.

But it's not just academic performance that can improve through volunteering: There are social and psychological benefits as well. For example, a student survey showed that students who participated in quality service learning projects showed more personal and social responsibility. Another survey found that students involved in service learning were more likely to be kind to each other, and care about doing their best. Studies also show better self-esteem and fewer behavioral problems in students who have been involved with service learning.

Despite all this, there are still many who say that volunteering in high school should NOT be a requirement for graduation. They point out that students today are already over-stressed and over-scheduled. What's more, requiring community service for graduation would be particularly hard on athletes and low-income students who work after school to help their families make ends meet.

Good points, but community service does not have to take up vast quantities of time. It might be possible for a group of time-stressed students to use class-time to organize a fundraiser, or to compress their service into a single "marathon" weekend. Showing students that helping others is something to make time for is an important lesson.

In short, volunteering encourages engagement: It shows students that their actions matter, and that they have the power—and responsibility—to make the world a better place. What could be a more important lesson than that?

The introduction establishes the writer's claim in a clear and compelling way.

The writer uses a variety of sentence transitions.

Sources of evidence are comprehensive and contain relevant information.

Counterclaims are clearly acknowledged and refuted.

The conclusion offers fresh insight into the claim.

Argument Rubric

	Focus and Organization	Evidence and Elaboration	Conventions
4	The introduction engages the reader and establishes a claim in a compelling way. The argument includes valid reasons and evidence that address and support the claim while clearly acknowledging counterclaims. The ideas progress logically, and transitions make connections among ideas clear. The conclusion offers fresh insight into the claim.	The sources of evidence are comprehensive and specific and contain relevant information. The tone of the argument is always formal and objective. The vocabulary is always appropriate for the audience and purpose.	The argument intentionally uses standard English conventions of usage and mechanics.
3	The introduction engages the reader and establishes the claim. The argument includes reasons and evidence that address and support my claim while acknowledging counterclaims. The ideas progress logically, and some transitions are used to help make connections among ideas clear. The conclusion restates the claim and important information.	The sources of evidence contain relevant information. The tone of the argument is mostly formal and objective. The vocabulary is generally appropriate for the audience and purpose.	The argument demonstrates general accuracy in standard English conventions of usage and mechanics.
2	The introduction establishes a claim. The argument includes some reasons and evidence that address and support the claim while briefly acknowledging counterclaims. The ideas progress somewhat logically. A few sentence transitions are used that connect readers to the argument. The conclusion offers some insight into the claim and restates information.	The sources of evidence contain some relevant information. The tone of the argument is occasionally formal and objective. The vocabulary is somewhat appropriate for the audience and purpose.	The argument demonstrates some accuracy in standard English conventions of usage and mechanics.
1	The introduction does not clearly state the claim. The argument does not include reasons or evidence for the claim. No counterclaims are acknowledged. The ideas do not progress logically. Transitions are not included to connect ideas. The conclusion does not restate any information that is important.	Reliable and relevant evidence is not included. The vocabulary used is limited or ineffective. The tone of the argument is not objective or formal.	The argument contains mistakes in standard English conventions of usage and mechanics.

TOOL KIT: WRITING

Informative/Explanatory Texts

Informative and explanatory writing should rely on facts to inform or explain. Informative writing serves several purposes: to increase readers' knowledge of a subject, to help readers better understand a procedure or process, or to provide readers with an enhanced comprehension of a concept. It should also feature a clear introduction, body, and conclusion.

Elements of Informative/Explanatory Texts

Informative/explanatory texts present facts, details, data, and other kinds of evidence to give information about a topic. Readers turn to informational and explanatory texts when they wish to learn about a specific idea, concept, or subject area, or if they want to learn how to do something.

An effective informative/explanatory text contains these elements:

- a topic sentence or thesis statement that introduces the concept or subject
- relevant facts, examples, and details that expand upon a topic
- definitions, quotations, and/or graphics that support the information given
- headings (if desired) to separate sections of the essay
- a structure that presents information in a direct, clear manner
- clear transitions that link sections of the essay
- precise words and technical vocabulary where appropriate
- formal and object language and tone
- a conclusion that supports the information given and provides fresh insights

How Technology is Changing the Way We Work

Lot's of people work on computers. So, technology is everywhere. If you feel comfortable using computers and all kinds of other technology, your going to be a head at work, for sure.

They're new Devices and Apps out there every day. Each different job has its own gadgets and programs and apps that you have to learn. Every day their more new apps and devices, they can do all kinds of things.

In the past, people only worked at the office. They didn't get to work at home. Now, if you have a smart phone, you can check your email wherever. You can work at home on a computer. You can work in cafés or wherever. Also on a tablet. If you wanted to, you can be working all the time. But that will be a drag!

Technology is now an important part of almost every job. You also have to have a website. You have to have a social media page. Maybe if your business is doing really well you could afford to hire someone to take care of all that stuff—but it would be better if you knew how to do it yourself.

Technology brings people together and helps them work. It could be someone next to you or someone even on the other side of the world. You can connect with them using email. You can send a text. You could have a conference or video call.

Working from home is cheaper for the worker and boss. They can get stuff done during the day like going to the post office or the library, or picking up their kids at school. This is all thanks to technology.

Lots of jobs today are in technology. Way more than before! That's why it's a good idea to take classes and learn about something in technology, because then you will be able to find a job.

There are apps to find houses for sale, find restaurants, learn new recipes, keep track of how much you exercise, and all kinds of other things, like playing games and tuning your guitar. And there are apps to help you work. It's hard to imagine how people would manage to work now without this kind of technology to help them.

The writer's opening statement does not adequately introduce the thesis, and there are numerous spelling mistakes.

The writer's word choice often does not support the proper tone the essay ought to have.

The essay's sentences are often not purposeful, varied, or well-controlled.

The writer does not include a concluding statement.

TOOL KIT: WRITING

WRITING

INFORMATIVE: SCORE 2

How Technology is Changing the Way We Work

Technology affects the way we work, in every kind of job and industry. Each different job has its own gadgets and programs and apps that you have to learn. Every day there are more new apps and devices that can do all kinds of things.

> The writer's opening does not clearly introduce the thesis.

In the past, people went to the office to work. That's not always true today. Now if you have a smart phone, you can check your email wherever you are. You can work at home on a desktop computer. You can work on a laptop in a café or wherever. Or a tablet. Technology makes it so people can work all the time.

It doesn't matter whether the person is on the other side of the world—technology brings you together. Theirs email. Theirs text messaging. You have conference calls. You've got video calling. All these things let people work together wherever they are. And don't forget, today people can access files from the cloud. That helps them work from whatever device they want. More than one person can work on the same file.

> The essay is somewhat lacking in organizational structure.

Different kinds of work places and schedules are becoming more common and normal. Working from home has benefits businesses. It means cost savings. It means higher productivity. It means higher job satisfaction. They can get stuff done during the day like going to the post office or the bank, or picking up their kids at school. That is very convenient.

> The essay has many interesting details, but some do not relate specifically to the topic.

It's also true that lots and lots of jobs today are in technology, or related to technology in some way. Way more than before! That's why it's a good idea to get a degree or take classes and learn about something in technology, because it seems like that's where all the new jobs are. Software designers make a really good salary, and so do other tech-related jobs.

> The writer's word choice is overly informal.

Technology is now an important part of almost every job. It's no longer enough to be just a photographer or whatever. You have to get a social media page. You have to be able to use the latest tech gadgets. You can't just take pictures.

> The writer's sentences are disjointed and ineffective.

In todays world, technology is changing how we work. You have to be able to feel comfortable with technology in order to survive at work. Even if you really don't like technology, you don't really have a choice. So, get used to it!

> The conclusion follows logically but is not mature and is overly informal.

How Technology Is Changing the Way We Work

Technology has been changing how we work for a long time, but the pace of change has gotten dramatically faster. No industry or job is exempt. Powerful computing technology and Internet connectivity affects all sectors of the economy. It doesn't matter what job you're talking about: Technology is transforming the way people work. It's an exciting time to be entering the workforce!

> The thesis is introduced but is buried in the introduction.

The Office Is Everywhere

Technology is rapidly changing not just *how* but *where, when,* and *with whom* we work. It used to be that work was something that happened only at the office. All kinds of different work places and schedules are becoming much more common and normal. According to a study, telecommuting (working from home) rose 79 percent between 2005 and 2012. Working from home has benefits for both the employee and employer. It means cost savings for both, increased productivity, and higher job satisfaction.

> The writer uses headings to help make the organization of ideas clear.

> Statistics support the writer's claim.

The Cloud

Cloud and other data storage and sharing options mean that workers have access to information whenever they want, wherever they are. Whether it's one person who wants the convenience of being able to work on a file from several devices (and locations), or several people who are working on something together, the ability to store data in the cloud and access it from anywhere is a huge change in the way we work. It's almost like all being in the same office, working on the same computer.

Tech Industries and Jobs

Technology is changing the way we work in part by making technology itself such an important element in almost every profession. Therefore, you can see it's no longer good enough to be just a photographer or contractor. You have to know something about technology to do your job, market yourself, and track your performance. No matter what jobs someone does they have to be tech-savvy to be able to use their devices to connect and interact with each other across the globe.

> The writer uses some transitions and sentence connections, but more would be helpful.

Conclusion

In todays world, technology is quickly and continuously changing how we work, what we do, where and when we do it. In order to do well and thrive, everyone has to be a little bit of a tech geek. So, get used to technology being a part of your work life. And get used to change. Because, in a constantly changing technological world, change is going to be one of the few things that stays the same!

> There are a few errors in spelling and punctuation but they do not detract from the effectiveness of the essay.

> The conclusion sums up the main ideas of the essay and links to the opening statements.

TOOL KIT: WRITING

WRITING

MODEL

INFORMATIVE: SCORE 4

How Technology Is Changing the Way We Work

While advances in technology have been changing how we work for hundreds of years, the pace of change has accelerated dramatically in the past two decades. With powerful computing technology and Internet connectivity affecting all sectors of the economy, no industry or profession is exempt. It doesn't matter whether you're talking about financial advisors, architects, or farmers: Technology is transforming the way people work.

The opening paragraph ends with a thesis, which is strong and clear.

The Office Is Everywhere

Technology is rapidly revolutionizing not just *how* but *where, when,* and *with whom* we work. It used to be that work was something that happened strictly at the office. In fact, non-traditional work places are becoming much more common. According to one study, telecommuting rose 79 percent between 2005 and 2012. Working from home has proven benefits for both the employee and employer, including cost savings for both, increased productivity, and job satisfaction.

The writer makes an effort to be thoughtful and engage the reader.

Headings help ensure that the organizing structure of the essay is clear and effective.

Working with the Cloud

Another important technological advancement that is impacting how we work is the development of cloud computing. Whether it's one person who wants the convenience of being able to work from several devices, or several people who are working together from different locations, the ability to store data in the cloud and access it from anywhere is a huge change in the way we work. Over long distances, coworkers can not only *communicate* with each other, they can *collaborate*, in real time, by sharing and accessing files through the. Only five years ago, this kind of instant access was impossible.

The sentences in the essay are purposeful and varied.

Tech Industries and Jobs

Technology is changing the way we work is by making technology itself an important element in almost every job. It's no longer good enough to be just a photographer or contractor: you have to know something about technology to perform, market, and track your work. No matter what job someone is doing, he or she has to be tech-savvy to be able to use their devices to connect and interact.

The progression of ideas in the essay is logical and well-controlled.

Conclusion

In today's world, technology is quickly and continuously changing what work we do, and how, where, when, and with whom we do it. Comfort with new technology—and with rapid technological change—is a prerequisite for success, no matter where your interests lie, or what kind of job you are looking to find. It's a brave new technological world of work, and it's changing every day!

The writer's word choice contributes to the clarity of the essay and shows awareness of the essay's purpose and tone.

NARRATIVE: SCORE 1

Getting Away With It

That night, Luanne made two mistakes.

She ran in the house.

The McTweedys were rich and had a huge place and there was an expensive rug.

She was sad in her room remembering what happened:

She was carrying a tray of glasses back to the kitchen and spilled on the carpet. She tried to put furniture over it. Then she ran in the rain.

Luanne should have come clean. She would of said I'm sorry, Mrs. Mc Tweedy, I spilled punch on ur carpet.

She knew getting away with it felt crummy for some reason. it was wrong and she also didn't want to get in trouble.

The phone rings.

"Oh, hello?"

"It's Mrs. Tweedy's!" said her mom. "You forgot to get paid!"

Luanne felt relieve. She was going to do the right thing.

The introduction is interesting but is not built upon.

The chronology and situation are unclear.

The narrative contains mistakes in standard English conventions of usage and mechanics.

The name of the character does not remain consistent.

The conclusion reveals what will happen but is not interesting.

TOOL KIT: WRITING

WRITING

NARRATIVE: SCORE 2

Getting Away With It

That night, Luanne made two fatal mistakes: ruining a rug, and thinking she could get away with it.

> The introduction establishes a clear context.

She ran in the house.

The McTweedys hired her to be a waiter at their party. They were rich and had a huge place and there was an expensive rug.

She was sad in her room remembering what happened:

Luanne was wearing black pants and a white shirt. She was carrying a tray of glasses back to the kitchen. One spilled on the carpet. She tried to put furniture to cover up the stain. She ran away in the rain.

Luanne should have come clean right away. But what would she have said? I'm sorry, Mrs. McTweedy, but I spilled punch all over your expensive carpet.

> The writer has made some mistakes in spelling, grammar, and punctuation.

Luanne imagined getting away with it. But getting away with it felt crummy for some reason. She knew it was wrong somehow, but she also didn't want to get in trouble.

> The chronology is sometimes unclear.

The phone rang.

"Oh, hello, how was the party?"

Luanne felt like throwing up.

"Mrs. McTweedy's on the phone!" her mom sang out. "She said you forgot your check!"

> Narrative techniques, such as the use of dialogue, are used at times.

Luanne felt relieved. But she already made up her mind to do the right thing.

> The conclusion tells what will happen but is not interesting.

NARRATIVE: SCORE 3

Getting Away With It

That night, Luanne made two fatal mistakes: (1) ruining a priceless Persian rug, and (2) thinking she could get away with it.

She bursted in the front door breathless.

"How was it?" called her mom.

The McTweedys had hired her to serve drinks at their fundraiser. Henry and Estelle McTweedy loved having parties. They were rich and had a huge apartment filled with rare books, art, and tapestries from all over the world.

"Luanne? Are you alright?"

"Just tired, Mom."

Actually she was face-planted on her bed, replaying the scene over and over just in case she could change it.

It was like a movie: A girl in black trousers and a crisp white shirt carrying a tray of empty glasses back to the kitchen. Then the girl's horrified expression as she realizes that one of the glasses was not quite as empty as she'd thought and was dripping onto the carpet. The girl frantically moving furniture to cover up the stain. The girl running out of the apartment into the hard rain.

Luanne kicked herself. She should have come clean right away. But what would she have said? I'm sorry, Mrs. McTweedy, but I spilled punch all over your expensive carpet.

Luanne imagined getting away with it. But getting away with it felt crummy for some reason. She knew it was wrong somehow, but she also didn't want to get in trouble.

The phone was ringing. Luanne froze.

"Oh, hello there, Mrs. McTweedy! How was the party?"

Luanne felt felt like throwing up.

"Mrs. McTweedy's on the phone!" her mom sang out. "She said you forgot your check!"

Luanne felt relief. It was nothing at all! Although she'd already made up her mind to come clean. Because she had to do the right thing.

She walked into the kitchen. And then she explained the whole thing to both her mom and Mrs. McTweedy.

The story's introduction establishes a clear context and point of view.

Descriptive details, sensory language, and precise words and phrases help to bring the narrative to life.

The writer mostly attends to the norms and conventions of usage and punctuation, but sometimes makes mistakes.

The writer has effectively used dialogue in her story.

The conclusion follows logically but is not memorable.

TOOL KIT: WRITING

WRITING

NARRATIVE: SCORE 4

Getting Away With It

That night, Luanne made two fatal mistakes: (1) ruining a priceless Persian rug, and (2) thinking she could get away with it.

She'd burst in the front door breathless.

"How was it?" called her mother from the kitchen.

The McTweedys had hired Luanne to serve drinks at their fundraiser. Henry and Estelle McTweedy loved entertaining. They loved traveling, and the opera, and the finer things in life. They had a huge apartment filled with rare books, art, and tapestries from all over the world.

"Luanne? Are you alright?"

"Just tired, Mom."

Actually she was face-down on her bed, replaying the humiliating scene over and over just in case she could make it come out differently.

It was like a movie: A girl in black trousers and a crisp white shirt carrying a tray of empty glasses back to the kitchen. Cut to the girl's horrified expression as she realizes that one of the glasses —not quite as empty as she'd thought—was dripping its lurid contents onto the carpet. Close in on the girl's frantic attempts to move furniture over the stain. Montage of images showing the girl running out of the apartment into the pounding rain. Fade to Black.

Luanne could kick herself. She should have come clean right away. But what would she have said? *I'm sorry, Mrs. McTweedy, but I spilled punch all over your irreplaceable carpet.*

Luanne imagined getting away with it. If she got away with it, she'd be a person who got away with things. For the rest of her life, no matter what, she'd be a person who got away with things. And if something good happened to her, she'd feel like she didn't deserve it.

Somewhere in the house, a phone was ringing. Luanne froze and listened in.

"Oh, hello there, Estelle! How was the party?"

Luanne felt cold, then hot. Her skin prickled. She was sweating. She felt like throwing up.

"Mrs. McTweedy's on the phone!" Luanne's mother sang out. "She wants to tell you that you forgot your check!"

Luanne felt a surge a relief wash over her—it was nothing, nothing at all!—but she'd already made up her mind to come clean. Not because owning up to it was so Right, but because getting away with it was so wrong. Which made it right.

Luanne padded into the kitchen. "Don't hang up," she told her mother.

The writer provides an introduction that establishes a clear context and point of view.

The writer has used descriptive details, sensory language, and precise words and phrases.

The writer's use of movie terminology is clever and memorable.

The narrative presents a clear chronological sequence of events.

The writer effectively uses narrative techniques, such as dialogue.

The story's conclusion is abrupt but fitting. It reveals a critical decision that resolves the conflict.

TOOL KIT: WRITING

Narrative Rubric

	Focus and Organization	Development of Ideas/ Elaboration	Conventions
4	The introduction establishes a clear context and point of view. Events are presented in a clear sequence, building to a climax, then moving toward the conclusion. The conclusion follows from and reflects on the events and experiences in the narrative.	Narrative techniques such as dialogue, pacing, and description are used effectively to develop characters, events, and setting. Descriptive details, sensory language, and precise words and phrases are used to convey the experiences in the narrative and to help the reader imagine the characters and setting. Voice is established through word choice, sentence structure, and tone.	The narrative uses standard English conventions of usage and mechanics. Deviations from standard English are intentional and serve the purpose of the narrative. Rules of spelling and punctuation are followed.
3	The introduction gives the reader some context and sets the point of view. Events are presented logically, though there are some jumps in time. The conclusion logically ends the story, but provides only some reflection on the experiences related in the story.	Narrative techniques such as dialogue, pacing, and description are used occasionally. Descriptive details, sensory language, and precise words and phrases are used occasionally. Voice is established through word choice, sentence structure, and tone occasionally, though not evenly.	The narrative mostly uses standard English conventions of usage and mechanics, though there are some errors. There are few errors in spelling and punctuation.
2	The introduction provides some description of a place. The point of view can be unclear at times. Transitions between events are occasionally unclear. The conclusion comes abruptly and provides only a small amount of reflection on the experiences related in the narrative.	Narrative techniques such as dialogue, pacing, and description are used sparingly. The story contains few examples of descriptive details and sensory language. Voice is not established for characters, so that it becomes difficult to determine who is speaking.	The narrative contains some errors in standard English conventions of usage and mechanics. There are many errors in spelling and punctuation.
1	The introduction fails to set a scene or is omitted altogether. The point of view is not always clear. The events are not in a clear sequence, and events that would clarify the narrative may not appear. The conclusion does not follow from the narrative or is omitted altogether.	Narrative techniques such as dialogue, pacing, and description are not used. Descriptive details are vague or missing. No sensory language is included. Voice has not been developed.	The text contains mistakes in standard English conventions of usage and mechanics. Rules of spelling and punctuation have not been followed.

RESEARCH

Conducting Research

We are lucky to live in an age when information is accessible and plentiful. However, not all information is equally useful, or even accurate. Strong research skills will help you locate and evaluate information.

Narrowing or Broadening a Topic

The first step of any research project is determining your topic. Consider the scope of your project and choose a topic that is narrow enough to address completely and effectively. If you can name your topic in just one or two words, it is probably too broad. Topics such as Shakespeare, jazz, or science fiction are too broad to cover in a single report. Narrow a broad topic into smaller subcategories.

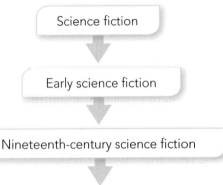

Science fiction

↓

Early science fiction

↓

Nineteenth-century science fiction

↓

Nineteenth-century science fiction that predicted the future accurately

When you begin to research a topic, pay attention to the amount of information available. If you feel overwhelmed by the number of relevant sources, you may need to narrow your topic further.

If there isn't enough information available as your research, you might need to broaden your topic. A topic is too narrow when it can be thoroughly presented in less space than the required size of your assignment. It might also be too narrow if you can find little or no information in library and media sources, so consider broadening your topic to include other related ideas.

Generating Research Questions

Use research questions to focus your research. Specific questions can help you avoid time-wasting digressions. For example, instead of simply hunting for information about Mark Twain, you might ask, "What jobs did Mark Twain have, other than being a writer?" or "Which of Twain's books was most popular during his lifetime?"

In a research report, your research question often becomes your thesis statement, or may lead up to it. The question will also help you focus your research into a comprehensive but flexible search plan, as well as prevent you from gathering unnecessary details. As your research teaches you more about your topic, you may find it necessary to refocus your original question.

Consulting Print and Digital Sources

Effective research combines information from several sources, and does not rely too heavily on a single source. The creativity and originality of your research depends on how you combine ideas from multiple sources. Plan to consult a variety of resources, such as the following:

- **Primary and Secondary Sources:** To get a thorough view of your topic, use primary sources (firsthand or original accounts, such as interview transcripts, eyewitness reports, and newspaper articles) and secondary sources (accounts, created after an event occurred, such as encyclopedia entries).

- **Print and Digital Resources:** The Internet allows fast access to data, but print resources are often edited more carefully. Use both print and digital resources in order to guarantee the accuracy of your findings.

- **Media Resources:** You can find valuable information in media resources such as documentaries, television programs, podcasts, and museum exhibitions. Consider attending public lectures given by experts to gain an even more in-depth view of your topic.

- **Original Research:** Depending on your topic, you may wish to conduct original research to include among your sources. For example, you might interview experts or eyewitnesses, or conduct a survey of people in your community.

> ### Using Online Encyclopedias
>
> Online encyclopedias are often written by anonymous contributors who are not required to fact-check information. These sites can be very useful as a launching point for research, but should not be considered accurate. Look for footnotes, endnotes, or hyperlinks that support facts with reliable sources that have been carefully checked by editors.

Evaluating Sources It is important to evaluate the credibility, validity, and accuracy of any information you find, as well as its appropriateness for your purpose and audience. You may find the information you need to answer your research question in specialized and authoritative sources, such as almanacs (for social, cultural, and natural statistics), government publications (for law, government programs, and subjects such as agriculture), and information services. Also, consider consumer, workplace, and public documents.

Ask yourself questions such as these to evaluate these additional sources:

- **Authority:** Is the author well known? What are the author's credentials? Does the source include references to other reliable sources? Does the author's tone win your confidence? Why or why not?

- **Bias:** Does the author have any obvious biases? What is the author's purpose for writing? Who is the target audience?

- **Currency:** When was the work created? Has it been revised? Is there more current information available?

Using Search Terms

Finding information on the Internet can be both easy and challenging. Type a word or phrase into a general search engine and you will probably get hundreds—or thousands—of results. However, those results are not guaranteed to be relevant or accurate.

These strategies can help you find information from the Internet:

- Create a list of keywords that apply to your topic before you begin using a search engine. Consult a thesaurus to expand your list.
- Enter six to eight keywords.
- Choose precise nouns. Most search engines ignore articles and prepositions. Verbs may be used in multiple contexts, leading to sources that are not relevant. Use modifiers, such as adjectives, when necessary to specify a category.
- Use quotation marks to focus a search. Place a phrase in quotation marks to find pages that include exactly that phrase. Add several phrases in quotation marks to narrow your results.
- Spell carefully. Many search engines autocorrect spelling, but they cannot produce accurate results for all spelling errors.
- Scan search results before you click them. The first result isn't always the most relevant. Read the text and consider the domain before make a choice.
- Utilize more than one search engine.

Evaluating Internet Domains

Not everything you read on the Internet is true, so you have to evaluate sources carefully. The last three letters of an Internet URL identify the Website's domain, which can help you evaluate the information of the site.

- **.gov**—Government sites are sponsored by a branch of the United States federal government, such as the Census Bureau, Supreme Court, or Congress. These sites are considered reliable.
- **.edu**—Education domains include schools from kindergartens to universities. Information from an educational research center or department is likely to be carefully checked. However, education domains can also include student pages that are not edited or monitored.
- **.org**—Organizations are nonprofit groups and usually maintain a high level of credibility. Keep in mind that some organizations may express strong biases.
- **.com** and **.net**—Commercial sites exist to make a profit. Information may be biased to show a product or service in a good light. The company may be providing information to encourage sales or promote a positive image.

Taking Notes

Take notes as you locate and connect useful information from multiple sources, and keep a reference list of every source you use. This will help you make distinctions between the relative value and significance of specific data, facts, and ideas.

For long-term research projects, create source cards and notecards to keep track of information gathered from multiple resources.

Source Cards
Create a card that identifies each source.

- For print materials, list the author, title, publisher, date of publication, and relevant page numbers.
- For Internet sources, record the name and Web address of the site, and the date you accessed the information.
- For media sources, list the title, person, or group credited with creating the media, and the year of production.

Notecards
Create a separate notecard for each item of information.

- Include the fact or idea, the letter of the related source card, and the specific page(s) on which the fact or idea appears.
- Use quotation marks around words and phrases taken directly from print or media resources.
- Mark particularly useful or relevant details using your own annotation method, such as stars, underlining, or colored highlighting.

Source Card	[A]

Marsh, Peter. *Eye to Eye: How People Interact*. Salem House Publishers, 1988.

Notecard

Gestures vary from culture to culture. The American "OK" symbol (thumb and forefinger) is considered insulting in Greece and Turkey.

Source Card: A, p. 54.

Quote Accurately Responsible research begins with the first note you take. Be sure to quote and paraphrase your sources accurately so you can identify these sources later. In your notes, circle all quotations and paraphrases to distinguish them from your own comments. When photocopying from a source, include the copyright information. When printing out information from an online source, include the Web address.

RESEARCH

Reviewing Research Findings

While conducting research, you will need to review your findings, checking that you have collected enough accurate and appropriate information.

Considering Audience and Purpose

Always keep your audience in mind as you gather information, since different audiences may have very different needs. For example, if you are writing an in-depth analysis of a text that your entire class has read together and you are writing for your audience, you will not need to gather background information that has been thoroughly discussed in class. However, if you are writing the same analysis for a national student magazine, you cannot assume that all of your readers have the same background information. You will need to provide facts from reliable sources to help orient these readers to your subject. When considering whether or not your research will satisfy your audience, ask yourself:

- Who am I writing for?
- Have I collected enough information to explain my topic to this audience?
- Are there details in my research that I can omit because they are already familiar to my audience?

Your purpose for writing will also influence your review of research. If you are researching a question to satisfy your own curiosity, you can stop researching when you feel you understand the answer completely. If you are writing a research report that will be graded, you need to consider the criteria of the assignment. When considering whether or not you have enough information, ask yourself:

- What is my purpose for writing?
- Will the information I have gathered be enough to achieve my purpose?
- If I need more information, where might I find it?

Synthesizing Sources

Effective research writing does not merely present facts and details; it synthesizes—gathers, orders, and interprets—them. These strategies will help you synthesize information effectively:

- Review your notes and look for connections and patterns among the details you have collected.
- Arrange notes or notecards in different ways to help you decide how to best combine related details and present them in a logical way.
- Pay close attention to details that support one other, emphasizing the same main idea.
- Also look for details that challenge each other, highlighting ideas about which there is no single, or consensus, opinion. You might decide to conduct additional research to help you decide which side of the issue has more support.

Types of Evidence

When reviewing your research, also consider the kinds of evidence you have collected. The strongest writing contains a variety of evidence effectively. This chart describes three of the most common types of evidence: statistical, testimonial, and anecdotal.

TYPE OF EVIDENCE	DESCRIPTION	EXAMPLE
Statistical evidence includes facts and other numerical data used to support a claim or explain a topic.	Examples of statistical evidence include historical dates and information, quantitative analyses, poll results, and quantitative descriptions.	"Although it went on to become a hugely popular novel, the first edition of William Goldman's book sold fewer than 3,000 copies."
Testimonial evidence includes any ideas or opinions presented by others, especially experts in a field.	Firsthand testimonies present ideas from eyewitnesses to events or subjects being discussed.	"The ground rose and fell like an ocean at ebb tide." —Fred J. Hewitt, eyewitness to the 1906 San Francisco earthquake
	Secondary testimonies include commentaries on events by people who were not involved. You might quote a well-known literary critic when discussing a writer's most famous novel, or a prominent historian when discussing the effects of an important event	Gladys Hansen insists that "there was plenty of water in hydrants throughout [San Francisco] . . . The problem was this fire got away."
Anecdotal evidence presents one person's view of the world, often by describing specific events or incidents.	Compelling research should not rely solely on this form of evidence, but it can be very useful for adding personal insights and refuting inaccurate generalizations. An individual's experience can be used with other forms of evidence to present complete and persuasive support.	Although many critics claim the novel is universally beloved, at least one reader "threw the book against a wall because it made me so angry."

Incorporating Research Into Writing

Avoiding Plagiarism

Plagiarism is the unethical presentation of someone else's ideas as your own. You must cite sources for direct quotations, paraphrased information, or facts that are specific to a single source. When you are drafting and revising, circle any words or ideas that are not your own. Follow the instructions on pages R34 and R35 to correctly cite those passages.

Review for Plagiarism Always take time to review your writing for unintentional plagiarism. Read what you have written and take note of any phrases or sentences that do not have your personal writing voice. Compare those passages with your resource materials. You might have copied them without remembering the exact source. Add a correct citation to give credit to the original author. If you cannot find the questionable phrase in your notes, revise it to ensure that your final report reflects your own thinking and not someone else's work.

Quoting and Paraphrasing

When including ideas from research into your writing, you will decide to quote directly or paraphrase.

Direct Quotation Use the author's exact words when they are interesting or persuasive. You might decide to include direct quotations for these reasons:

- to share an especially clear and relevant statement
- to reference a historically significant passage
- to show that an expert agrees with your position
- to present an argument that you will counter in your writing.

Include complete quotations, without deleting or changing words. If you need to omit words for space or clarity, use ellipsis points to indicate the omission. Enclose direct quotations in quotation marks and indicate the author's name.

Paraphrase A paraphrase restates an author's ideas in your own words. Be careful to paraphrase accurately. Beware of making sweeping generalizations in a paraphrase that were not made by the original author. You may use some words from the original source, but a legitimate paraphrase does more than simply rearrange an author's phrases, or replace a few words with synonyms.

Original Text	"*The Tempest* was written as a farewell to art and the artist's life, just before the completion of his forty-ninth year, and everything in the play bespeaks the touch of autumn." Brandes, Georg. "Analogies Between *The Tempest* and *A Midsummer Night's Dream.*" *The Tempest*, by William Shakespeare, William Heinemann, 1904, p. 668.
Patchwork Plagiarism phrases from the original are rearranged, but too closely follows the original text.	A farewell to art, Shakespeare's play, *The Tempest*, was finished just before the completion of his forty-ninth year. The artist's life was to end within three years. The touch of autumn is apparent in nearly everything in the play.
Good Paraphrase	Images of autumn occur throughout *The Tempest*, which Shakespeare wrote as a way of saying goodbye to both his craft and his own life.

Maintaining the Flow of Ideas

Effective research writing is much more that just a list of facts. Be sure to maintain the flow of ideas by connecting research information to your own ideas. Instead of simply stating a piece of evidence, use transition words and phrases to explain the connection between information you found from outside resources and your own ideas and purpose for writing. The following transitions can be used to introduce, compare, contrast, and clarify.

Useful Transitions

When providing examples:

for example   for instance   to illustrate   in [name of resource], [author]

When comparing and contrasting ideas or information:

in the same way   similarly   however   on the other hand

When clarifying ideas or opinions:

in other words   that is   to explain   to put it another way

Choosing an effective organizational structure for your writing will help you create a logical flow of ideas. Once you have established a clear organizational structure, insert facts and details from your research in appropriate places to provide evidence and support for your writing.

ORGANIZATIONAL STRUCTURE	USES
Chronological order presents information in the sequence in which it happens.	historical topics; science experiments; analysis of narratives
Part-to-whole order examines how several categories affect a larger subject.	analysis of social issues; historical topics
Order of importance presents information in order of increasing or decreasing importance.	persuasive arguments; supporting a bold or challenging thesis
Comparison-and-contrast organization outlines the similarities and differences of a given topic.	addressing two or more subjects

RESEARCH

Formats for Citing Sources

In research writing, cite your sources. In the body of your paper, provide a footnote, an endnote, or a parenthetical citation, identifying the sources of facts, opinions, or quotations. At the end of your paper, provide a bibliography or a Works Cited list, a list of all the sources referred to in your research. Follow an established format, such as Modern Language Association (MLA) style.

Parenthetical Citations (MLA Style)

A parenthetical citation briefly identifies the source from which you have taken a specific quotation, factual claim, or opinion. It refers readers to one of the entries on your Works Cited list. A parenthetical citation has the following features:

- It appears in parentheses.
- It identifies the source by the last name of the author, editor, or translator, or by the title (for a lengthy title, list the first word only).
- It provides a page reference, the page(s) of the source on which the information cited can be found.

A parenthetical citation generally falls outside a closing quotation mark but within the final punctuation of a clause or sentence. For a long quotation set off from the rest of your text, place the citation at the end of the excerpt without any punctuation following.

Sample Parenthetical Citations

It makes sense that baleen whales such as the blue whale, the bowhead whale, the humpback whale, and the sei whale (to name just a few) grow to immense sizes (Carwardine et al. 19–21). The blue whale has grooves running from under its chin to partway along the length of its underbelly. As in some other whales, these grooves expand and allow even more food and water to be taken in (Ellis 18–21).

Authors' last names

Page numbers where information can be found

Works Cited List (MLA Style)

A Works Cited list must contain accurate information to enable a reader to locate each source you cite. The basic components of an entry are as follows:

- name of the author, editor, translator, and/or group responsible for the work
- title of the work
- publisher
- date of publication

For print materials, the information for a citation generally appears on the copyright and title pages. For the format of a Works Cited list, consult the examples on this page and in the MLA Style for Listing Sources chart.

Sample Works Cited List (MLA 8th Edition)

Carwardine, Mark, et al. *The Nature Company Guides: Whales, Dolphins, and Porpoises.* Time-Life, 1998.

"Discovering Whales." *Whales on the Net.* Whales in Danger, 1998, www.whales.org.au/discover/index.html. Accessed 11 Apr. 2017.

Neruda, Pablo. "Ode to Spring." *Odes to Opposites,* translated by Ken Krabbenhoft, edited and illustrated by Ferris Cook, Little, 1995, p. 16.

The Saga of the Volsungs. Translated by Jesse L. Byock, Penguin, 1990.

List an anonymous work by title.

List both the title of the work and the collection in which it is found.

Works Cited List or Bibliography?

A Works Cited list includes only those sources you paraphrased or quoted directly in your research paper. By contrast, a bibliography lists all the sources you consulted during research—even those you did not cite.

MLA (8th Edition) Style for Listing Sources

Book with one author	Pyles, Thomas. *The Origins and Development of the English Language*. 2nd ed., Harcourt Brace Jovanovich, 1971. [Indicate the edition or version number when relevant.]
Book with two authors	Pyles, Thomas, and John Algeo. *The Origins and Development of the English Language*. 5th ed., Cengage Learning, 2004.
Book with three or more authors	Donald, Robert B., et al. *Writing Clear Essays*. Prentice Hall, 1983.
Book with an editor	Truth, Sojourner. *Narrative of Sojourner Truth*. Edited by Margaret Washington, Vintage Books, 1993.
Introduction to a work in a published edition	Washington, Margaret. Introduction. *Narrative of Sojourner Truth*, by Sojourner Truth, edited by Washington, Vintage Books, 1993, pp. v–xi.
Single work in an anthology	Hawthorne, Nathaniel. "Young Goodman Brown." *Literature: An Introduction to Reading and Writing*, edited by Edgar V. Roberts and Henry E. Jacobs, 5th ed., Prentice Hall, 1998, pp. 376–385. [Indicate pages for the entire selection.]
Signed article from an encyclopedia	Askeland, Donald R. "Welding." *World Book Encyclopedia*, vol. 21, World Book, 1991, p. 58.
Signed article in a weekly magazine	Wallace, Charles. "A Vodacious Deal." *Time*, 14 Feb. 2000, p. 63.
Signed article in a monthly magazine	Gustaitis, Joseph. "The Sticky History of Chewing Gum." *American History*, Oct. 1998, pp. 30–38.
Newspaper article	Thurow, Roger. "South Africans Who Fought for Sanctions Now Scrap for Investors." *Wall Street Journal*, 11 Feb. 2000, pp. A1+. [For a multipage article that does not appear on consecutive pages, write only the first page number on which it appears, followed by the plus sign.]
Unsigned editorial or story	"Selective Silence." Editorial. *Wall Street Journal*, 11 Feb. 2000, p. A14. [If the editorial or story is signed, begin with the author's name.]
Signed pamphlet or brochure	[Treat the pamphlet as though it were a book.]
Work from a library subscription service	Ertman, Earl L. "Nefertiti's Eyes." *Archaeology*, Mar.–Apr. 2008, pp. 28–32. *Kids Search*, EBSCO, New York Public Library. Accessed 7 Jan. 2017. [Indicating the date you accessed the information is optional but recommended.]
Filmstrips, slide programs, videocassettes, DVDs, and other audiovisual media	*The Diary of Anne Frank*. 1959. Directed by George Stevens, performances by Millie Perkins, Shelley Winters, Joseph Schildkraut, Lou Jacobi, and Richard Beymer, Twentieth Century Fox, 2004. [Indicating the original release date after the title is optional but recommended.]
CD-ROM (with multiple publishers)	Simms, James, editor. *Romeo and Juliet*. By William Shakespeare, Attica Cybernetics / BBC Education / Harper, 1995.
Radio or television program transcript	"Washington's Crossing of the Delaware." *Weekend Edition Sunday*, National Public Radio, 23 Dec. 2013. Transcript.
Web page	"Fun Facts About Gum." ICGA, 2005–2017, www.gumassociation.org/index.cfm/facts-figures/fun-facts-about-gum. Accessed 19 Feb. 2017. [Indicating the date you accessed the information is optional but recommended.]
Personal interview	Smith, Jane. Personal interview, 10 Feb. 2017.

All examples follow the style given in the MLA Handbook, 8th edition, published in 2016.

MODEL

Evidence Log

Unit Title: _Discovery_

Perfomance-Based Assessment Prompt:
Do all discoveries benefit humanity?

My initial thoughts:
Yes - all knowledge moves us forward.

As you read multiple texts about a topic, your thinking may change. Use an Evidence Log like this one to record your thoughts, to track details you might use in later writing or discussion, and to make further connections.

Here is a sample to show how one reader's ideas deepened as she read two texts.

Title of Text: _Classifying the Stars_   Date: _Sept. 17_

CONNECTION TO THE PROMPT	TEXT EVIDENCE/DETAILS	ADDITIONAL NOTES/IDEAS
Newton shared his discoveries and then other scientists built on his discoveries.	Paragraph 2: "Isaac Newton gave to the world the results of his experiments on passing sunlight through a prism." Paragraph 3: "In 1814 . . . the German optician, Fraunhofer . . . saw that the multiple spectral tints . . . were crossed by hundreds of fine dark lines."	It's not always clear how a discovery might benefit humanity in the future.

How does this text change or add to my thinking? This confirms what I think.   Date: _Sept. 20_

Title of Text: _Cell Phone Mania_   Date: _Sept. 21_

CONNECTION TO THE PROMPT	TEXT EVIDENCE/DETAILS	ADDITIONAL NOTES/IDEAS
Cell phones have made some forms of communication easier, but people don't talk to each other as much as they did in the past.	Paragraph 7: "Over 80% of young adults state that texting is their primary method of communicating with friends. This contrasts with older adults who state that they prefer a phone call."	Is it good that we don't talk to each other as much? Look for article about social media to learn more about this question.

How does this text change or add to my thinking?
Maybe there are some downsides to discoveries. I still think that knowledge moves us forward, but there are sometimes unintended negative effects.   Date: _Sept. 25_

Word Network

A word network is a collection of words related to a topic. As you read the selections in a unit, identify interesting theme-related words and build your vocabulary by adding them to your Word Network.

Use your Word Network as a resource for your discussions and writings. Here is an example:

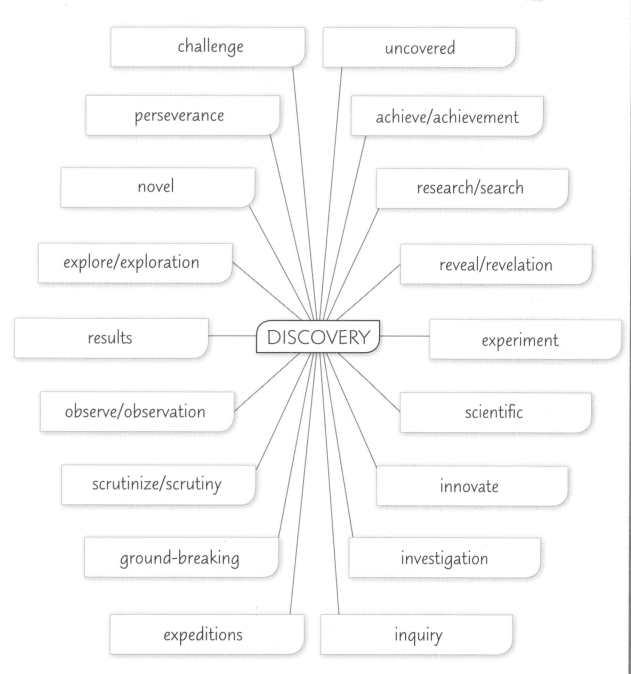

challenge

uncovered

perseverance

achieve/achievement

novel

research/search

explore/exploration

reveal/revelation

results

DISCOVERY

experiment

observe/observation

scientific

scrutinize/scrutiny

innovate

ground-breaking

investigation

expeditions

inquiry

ACADEMIC / CONCEPT VOCABULARY

Academic vocabulary appears in **blue type**.

Pronunciation Key

Symbol	Sample Words	Symbol	Sample Words
a	*at, catapult, Alabama*	oo	*boot, soup, crucial*
ah	*father, charms, argue*	ow	*now, stout, flounder*
ai	*care, various, hair*	oy	*boy, toil, oyster*
aw	*law, maraud, caution*	s	*say, nice, press*
awr	*pour, organism, forewarn*	sh	*she, abolition, motion*
ay	*ape, sails, implication*	u	*full, put, book*
ee	*even, teeth, really*	uh	*ago, focus, contemplation*
eh	*ten, repel, elephant*	ur	*bird, urgent. perforation*
ehr	*merry, verify, terribly*	y	*by, delight, identify*
ih	*it, pin, hymn*	yoo	*music, confuse, few*
o	*shot, hopscotch, condo*	zh	*pleasure, treasure, vision*
oh	*own, parole, rowboat*		

A

abridging (uh BRIHJ ihng) *adj.* limiting

acquiesce (ak wee EHS) *v.* accept something reluctantly but without protest

adamant (AD uh muhnt) *adj.* unrelenting; refusing to be persuaded

ampler (AM pluhr) *adj.* more abundant

analyze (AN uh lyz) *v.* examine carefully and in detail

anticipation (an tihs uh PAY shuhn) *n.* eager expectation

appeal (uh PEEL) *n.* ability to attract and engage an audience's mind or emotions

ascendant (uh SEHN duhnt) *adj.* moving upward; rising

assent (uh SEHNT) *n.* approval or agreement

assert (uh SURT) *v.* declare firmly; insist upon; claim to be true

audio play (AW dee oh) (play) *n.* theatrical performance of a drama produced for radio, podcast, or another non-visual and non-print recorded form

awkward (AWK wuhrd) *adj.* not graceful or skillful in movement or shape; clumsy

B

background (BAK grownd) *n.* more distant objects in a photograph

brawling (BRAWL ihng) *adj.* fighting noisily

brazenness (BRAY zuhn nuhs) *n.* act of being shameless; boldness

breadth (brehdth) *n.* wide range; expansive extent

buttonholed (BUHT uhn hohld) *v.* held in conversation

C

cabana (kuh BAN uh) *n.* small tent or cabin

callously (KAL uhs lee) *adv.* without sympathy; coldly

calumny (KAL uhm nee) *n.* the making of false statements with the intent to harm

cantina (kan TEE nuh) *n.* tavern

caption (KAP shuhn) *n.* in graphic novels, separate text that presents information that cannot be expressed quickly and easily in dialogue

captivity (kap TIHV ih tee) *n.* condition of being held prisoner

caricature (KAIR ih kuh chuhr) *n.* exaggeration of details relating to people or events, often for humorous effect, in a cartoon or other created image

certify (SUR tuh fy) *v.* declare something is true; verify that something is true

clammy (KLAM ee) *adj.* cold and damp

collaborator (kuh LAB uh ray tuhr) *n.* person who helps the enemy

colloquial (kuh LOH kwee uhl) *adj.* written or spoken in informal language used in everyday conversation

commentary (KOM uhn tehr ee) *n.* remarks that illustrate a point, prompt a realization, or explain something

composition (kom puh ZIH shuhn) *n.* arrangement of the parts of an image, whether drawn or recorded in some other visual format

conceded (kuhn SEED ihd) *v.* admitted

conciliatory (kuhn SIHL ee uh tawr ee) *adj.* in a manner intended to make peace and bring about agreement

conclave (KON klayv) *n.* private meeting

condemnation (kon dehm NAY shuhn) *n.* very strong disapproval

confirm (kuhn FURM) *v.* prove the truth of; verify

consecrate (KON sih krayt) *v.* set apart as holy; dedicate

conspirators (kuhn SPIHR uh tuhrz) *n.* people who join in a secret plan

constrains (kuhn STRAYNZ) *v.* requires or forces

constricting (kuhn STRIHKT ihng) *adj.* limiting; tightening

conviction (kuhn VIHK shuhn) *n.* strong belief; certainty

corrupted (kuh RUHPT ihd) *adj.* dishonest

cowering (KOW uhr ihng) *adj.* crouching or drawing back in fear or shame

cross-section (KRAWS sehk shuhn) *n.* view of a three-dimensional object that shows the interior as if a cut has been made across the object

cunning (KUHN ihng) *adj.* done with skill or cleverness

D

dedicated (DEHD uh kayt ihd) *adj.* committed; devoted

deduction (dih DUHK shuhn) *n.* the process of using reason or logic to come to a conclusion or form an opinion

defamation (dehf uh MAY shuhn) *n.* unjust injury to someone's good reputation through the making of false statements

deference (DEHF uhr uhns) *n.* great respect

definitive (dih FIHN uh tihv) *adj.* deciding or settling a question; final

degraded (dih GRAYD ihd) *adj.* reduced in respectablility; disgraced

deicide (DEE uh syd) *n.* killing of a god

dejected (dee JEHK tihd) *adj.* depressed; sad

demonstrate (DEHM uhn strayt) *v.* show how to do something

denounce (dih NOWNS) *v.* criticize harshly

depth of field (dehpth) (uhv) (feeld) *n.* distance between the closest and most distant objects that are in focus

despotism (DEHS puh tihz uhm) *n.* absolute rule; tyranny

determine (dih TUR muhn) *v.* decide; find out, as the exact cause or reason

dictum (DIHK tuhm) *n.* short statement that expresses a general truth; saying or proverb

digress (dih GREHS) *v.* go off topic in speaking or writing

dilatory (dihl uh TAWR ee) *adj.* inclined to delay; slow

discern (dih SURN) *v.* recognize as different

disparity (dihs PAR uh tee) *n.* great difference or inequality

disposition (DIHS puh ZIHSH uhn) *n.* act of settling a case or argument; decision

disputation (dihs pyu TAY shuhn) *n.* debate or argument

dissented (dih SENT ihd) *v.* rejected an official opinion; disagreed

documentary (dok yuh MEHN tuhr ee) *n.* program or film that provides a factual record or report of real events

dyspepsia (dihs PEHP see uh) *n.* indigestion

E

effrontery (ih FRUHN tuh ree) *n.* shameless boldness

eminence (EHM uh nuhns) *n.* position of great importance or superiority

eminent (EHM uh nuhnt) *adj.* distinguished; famous; noteworthy

emperor (EHM puhr uhr) *n.* ruler of highest rank and authority, especially of an empire

encroaching (ehn KROHCH ihng) *adj.* intruding; steadily advancing

epiphany (ih PIHF uh nee) *n.* flash of insight and understanding

equivocate (ih KWIHV uh kayt) *v.* use unclear language to avoid committing oneself to something

espionage (EHS pee uh nozh) *n.* use of spies to obtain secret information

establish (ehs TAB lihsh) *v.* set up; prove; demonstrate

etiquette (EHT uh kiht) *n.* proper manners

exalted (ehg ZAWLT ihd) *adj.* of high rank

exasperating (ehg ZAS puh rayt ihng) *adj.* annoying

exercise (EHK suhr syz) *n.* implementation; state of putting something into action

expression (ehk SPREHSH uhn) *n.* tone of voice that indicates specific emotion

eyewitness account (Y WIHT nihs) (uh KOWNT) n. description given by someone who was present at an event

F

figure (FIHG yuhr) *n.* one of a set of drawings or illustrations

fix (fihks) *n.* difficult or awkward situation

focal point (FOH kuhl) (poynt) *n.* center of activity or attention in a photograph

foment (foh MEHNT) *v.* stir up; agitate

foreground (FAWR grownd) *n.* nearer or closer objects in a photograph

forward (FAWR wuhrd) *adj.* bold; brazen; shameless

frame (fraym) *n.* main spoken narrative of a production

framing (FRAYM ihng) *n.* composing a visual so that an enclosing border surrounds the image in the foreground

furtive (FUR tihv) *adj.* done or acting in a stealthy way to avoid being noticed; secret

G

garrulous (GAR uh luhs) *adj.* very talkative

gilded (GIHLD ihd) *adj.* covered with a thin layer of gold

grandeur (GRAN juhr) *n.* state of being impressive; magnificence

H

hallow (HAL oh) *v.* make sacred; consecrate

hangdog (HANG dawg) *adj.* sad; ashamed; guilty

hermitage (HUR muh tihj) *n.* secluded retreat

hospitality (hos puh TAL uh tee) *n.* warm, welcoming attitude toward guests

host (hohst) *n.* master of ceremonies, moderator, or interviewer on a broadcast

hypodermic (hy puh DUR mihk) *n.* injection of medicine

I

immutable (ih MYOO tuh buhl) *adj.* never changing; not changeable

impact (IHM pakt) *n.* collision; powerful or lasting effect

imperial (ihm PEER ee uhl) *adj.* like something associated with an empire; magnificent or majestic

imploring (ihm PLAWR ihng) *v.* asking or begging someone for something

importunities (ihm pawr TOO nuh teez) *n.* annoyingly urgent requests

impressionism (ihm PREHSH uh nihz uhm) *n.* style of art where mood, color, and light matter more than details

incident (IHN suh duhnt) *n.* event; occurrence

indecisions (ihn dih SIHZH uhnz) *n.* things not decided or finalized

infallibility (ihn fal uh BIHL uh tee) *n.* inability to be in error

inflection (ihn FLEHK shuhn) *n.* rise and fall of pitch and tone in a person's voice

informational (ihn fuhr MAY shuh nuhl) *adj.* giving knowledge and facts

infringed (ihn FRIHNJD) *v.* violated

inquire (ihn KWYR) *v.* ask for information

instantaneously (ihn stuhn TAY nee uhs lee) *adv.* immediately

insurgent (ihn SUR juhnt) *adj.* rebellious or in revolt against a government in power

integrity (in TEHG rih tee) *n.* virtue of following moral or ethical principles

interminable (ihn TUR muh nuh buhl) *adj.* seemingly unending

interview (IHN tuhr vyoo) *n.* conversation in which a host asks questions of one or more guests

J

jurisdiction (juhr ihs DIHK shuhn) *n.* legal power to hear and decide cases

L

labeling and **captions** (LAY buhl ihng) (KAP shuhnz) *n.* written labels and other text that often accompany politically charged images to clarify their meanings

layout (LAY owt) *n.* overall design and look of a graphic presentation

legacy (LEHG uh see) *n.* anything handed down from someone

letterhead (LEHT uhr hehd) *n.* personalized stationery

literal (LIHT uhr uhl) *adj.* true to fact; not exaggerated

loathsome (LOHTH suhm) *adj.* causing disgust

loitered (LOY tuhrd) *v.* lingered; moved slowly

M

machetes (muh SHEHT eez) *n.* knives

magistrates (MAJ uh strayts) *n.* officials who have some of the powers of a judge

malice (MAL ihs) *n.* desire to harm or inflict injury

mission (MIHSH uhn) *n.* goal or ambition

monotonous (muh NOT uh nuhs) *adj.* boring due to a lack of variety

motifs (moh TEEFS) *n.* major themes, features, or elements

multitudes (MUHL tuh toodz) *n.* large number of people or things; masses

O

obdurate (OB duhr iht) *adj.* resistant to persuasion

obliged (uh BLYJD) *adj.* grateful

oppressed (uh PREHST) *v.* deprived of rights or power

ornamented (AWR nuh mehnt ihd) *adj.* decorated; adorned

overcast (OH vuhr kast) *adj.* covered with clouds, as a gray sky

overture (OH vuhr chuhr) *n.* musical introduction to an opera or symphony

P

palette (PAL iht) *n.* range of colors used in a particular work

perish (PEH rihsh) *v.* die

perpetually (puhr PEHCH oo uh lee) *adv.* happening all the time

persistence (puhr SIHS tuhns) *n.* act of not giving up

perspective (puhr SPEHK tihv) *n.* method of giving a sense of depth on a flat or shallow surface

petition (puh TIHSH uhn) *v.* formally request; seek help from

picturesquely (pihk chuh REHSK lee) *adv.* in a way that resembles a picture; in a way that is striking or interesting

plaintiffs (PLAYN tihfs) *n.* people who bring a lawsuit to court

policy (POL uh see) *n.* particular course of action by a person, government, organization

populist (POP yuh lihst) *adj.* related to serving the needs of common people

prejudices (PREHJ uh dihs ihz) *n.* unfavorable opinions or feelings formed beforehand or without factual support

prelude (PRAY lood) *n.* introduction to a musical work; overture

prescribed (prih SKRYBD) *v.* stated in writing; set down as a rule

proceedings (pruh SEE dihngz) *n.* events in a court of law

prolific (pruh LIHF ihk) *adj.* fruitful; abundant

propaganda (prop uh GAN duh) *n.* information, ideas, or rumors spread widely and deliberately to help or harm a person, group, movement, cause, or nation

protagonist (proh TAG uh nihst) *n.* main character in a play, story, or novel

Q

quaint (kwaynt) *adj.* unusual; curious; singular

R

racket (RAK iht) *n.* noisy confusion; uproar

realism (REE uh lihz uhm) *n.* style of art closely resembling reality

rectitude (REHK tuh tood) *n.* morally correct behavior or thinking; uprightness

redeemers (rih DEE muhrz) *n.* people who pay for the wrongdoing of others

redress (rih DREHS) *n.* correction; setting right of some wrong

relevant (REHL uh vuhnt) *adj.* puposeful; meaningful

remorseless (rih MAWRS lihs) *adj.* relentless; cruel

renaissance (REHN uh sons) *n.* revival; period of cultural importance

rend (rehnd) *v.* tear apart with violent force

resolution (rehz uh LOO shuhn) *n.* act of coming to a decision; the part of a story in which the plot is made clear

reverence (REHV uhr uhns) *n.* feeling of deep respect

rites (ryts) *n.* ceremonies

romanticism (roh MAN tuh sihz uhm) *n.* style of art evoking emotion by idealizing subjects

S

salutary (SAL yuh tehr ee) *adj.* beneficial; promoting a positive purpose

sanctity (SANGK tuh tee) *n.* fact of being sacred; holiness

scourge (skurj) *n.* cause of serious trouble or suffering

self-assurance (sehlf uh SHUR uhns) *n.* self-confidence

sequence (SEE kwuhns) *n.* particular order

shotgun (SHOT guhn) *n.* gun with a long, smooth barrel, that is often used to fire "shot," or small, pellet-like ammunition

shuffle (SHUHF uhl) *n.* dragging movement of the feet over the ground or floor without lifting them

sidle (SY duhl) *v.* move sideways, as in an unobtrusive, stealthy, or shy manner

significant (sihg NIHF uh kuhnt) *adj.* full of meaning; important

sinister (SIHN uh stuhr) *adj.* evil; threatening

sovereign (SOV ruhn) *n.* monarch or ruler

spatial (SPAY shuhl) *adj.* existing in space

special elements (SPEHSH uhl) (EHL uh muhnts) *n.* features that provide points of emphasis in a production

specific (spih SIHF ihk) *adj.* definite; precise; particular

specifications (spehs uh fuh KAY shuhnz) *n.* section of a patent application in which the inventor fully describes the invention

speech balloon (speech) (buh LOON) *n.* shape used in graphic novels and comic books to show what a character says

squalor (SKWOL uhr) *n.* filth; wretchedness

stolid (STOL ihd) *adj.* feeling little or no emotion

strife (stryf) *n.* act of fighting

subordinate (suh BAWR duh niht) *adj.* having less importance

sufficed (suh FYST) *v.* was adequate

superannuated (soo puhr AN yu ayt uhd) *adj.* too old to be usable; obsolete

superfluous (suh PUR floo uhs) *adj.* more than is needed or wanted; unnecessary

supplanted (suh PLANT ihd) *v.* took the place of; removed

supplement (SUHP luh muhnt) *n.* something added; *v.* add to

symbolism (SIHM buh lihz uhm) *n.* use of images or objects to represent ideas or qualities

T

tedious (TEE dee uhs) *adj.* boring; dull

teeming (TEE mihng) *adj.* full

temporal (TEHM puhr uhl) *adj.* not eternal; limited by time

tension (TEHN shuhn) *n.* mental or nervous stress; uneasiness; state of strained relations

tone (tohn) *n.* production's attitude toward a subject or audience

transcendent (tran SEHN duhnt) *adj.* beyond the limits of possible experience

treason (TREE zuhn) *n.* betrayal of trust or faith, especially against one's country

trivialize (TRIHV ee uhl yz) *v.* treat as not important; make trivial

tyranny (TIHR uh nee) *n.* oppressive power

U

unalienable (un AYL yuh nuh buhl) *adj.* impossible to take away or give up

unique (yoo NEEK) *adj.* being the only one of its kind

unrequited (uhn rih KWY tihd) *adj.* not repaid or avenged

V

vassals (VAS uhlz) *n.* subjects of a kingdom; servants

vast (vast) *adj.* very great in size

verbatim (vuhr BAY tihm) *adv.* in exactly the same words; *adj.* repeating the original word for word

vigilant (VIHJ uh luhnt) *adj.* on the alert; watchful

vindictive (vihn DIHK tihv) *adj.* characterized by an intense, unreasoning desire for revenge

vital (VY tuhl) *adj.* necessary or important

W

wanton (WON tuhn) *adj.* unrestrained; wild

waterfowl (WAWT uhr fowl) *n.* birds that live in or near water

wretched (REHCH ihd) *adj.* very unhappy; miserable

VOCABULARIO ACADÉMICO/ VOCABULARIO DE CONCEPTOS

abridging: abreviar *v.* limitar

acquiesce: consentir *v.* aceptar algo con pocas ganas pero sin protestar

adamant: terco/a *adj.* que no se deja convencer; inflexible

ampler: más copioso/a *adj.* más abundante

analyze: analizar *v.* examinar detalladamente y en profundidad

anticipation: anticipación *s.* expectación; espera ansiosa

appeal: cautivar *v.* capacidad de atraer e involucrar al público, sus pensamientos o emociones

ascendant: ascendente *adj.* que se mueve hacia arriba; que se eleva

assent: consentimiento *s.* aprobación o acuerdo

assert: aseverar *v.* afirmar; insistir

audio play: radioteatro *s.* obra de teatro producida para la radio, para un *podcast* o para otro tipo de grabación no visual ni impresa

awkward: torpe *adj.* desmañado/a; sin gracia, patoso

B

backdrop: fondo *s.* escena o decorado detrás de fotografías y retratos

background: fondo *s.* objetos lejanos en una fotografía

brawling: pendenciero/a *adj.* que se pelea ruidosamente; alborotador/a

brazenness: descaro *s.* no tener vergüenza; atrevimiento

breadth: anchura *s.* amplitud

buttonholed: acorraló *v.* detuvo a alguien en una conversación

C

cabana: cabaña *s.* tienda pequeña, choza

callously: despiadadamente *adv.* sin compasión; fríamente

calumny: calumnia *s.* afirmación falsa que intenta herir o dañar

cantina: cantina *s.* taberna

caption: leyenda *s.* en las novelas gráficas, texto en un recuadro que presenta información que no puede expresarse rápida y fácilmente en el diálogo

captivity: cautividad *s.* estado de privación de libertad; ser prisionero

caricature: caricatura *s.* exageración, generalmente con efecto humorístico, de detalles relacionados con personas o sucesos en una tira cómica u otra imagen creada

certify: certificar *v.* declarar que algo es cierto

clammy: sudado/a *adj.* frío y húmedo

collaborator: colaboracionista *s.* persona que colabora con o ayuda al enemigo

colloquial: coloquial *adj.* lenguaje informal que se usa en las conversaciones diarias

commentary: comentario *s.* observación o ejemplo que ilustra una idea, una opinión o explica algo

composition: composición *s.* disposición de las partes de una imagen, ya sea de un dibujo o de cualquier otro formato visual

conceded: concedió *v.* admitió

conciliatory: conciliador/a *adj.* que tiene la intención de hacer las paces y llegar a un acuerdo

conclave: cónclave *s.* reunión privada

condemnation: condena *s.* fuerte desaprobación; repulsa

confirm: confirmar *v.* probar la certeza de algo; verificar

consecrate: consagrar *v.* declarar algo como sagrado; dedicar

conspirators: conspiradores *s.* personas que se unen a un plan secreto

constrains: constriñe *v.* requiere, obliga

constricting: estrecho/a *adj.* limitado/a

conviction: condena *s.* acto de dar a alguien un veredicto de culpabilidad

conviction: convicción *s.* creencia firme

correlate: correlacionar *v.* mostrar la conexión entre dos elementos

corrupted: corrupto/a *adj.* deshonesto/a

cowering: achicarse *v.* encogerse de miedo

cross-section: sección transversal *s.* imagen de un objeto tridimensional que muestra su interior como si se hubiera hecho un corte transversal del objeto

cunning: astuto/a *adj.* con ingenio y astucia

D

dedicate: dedicar *v.* apartar para un objetivo especial

deduction: deducción *s.* el proceso de usar la razón o la lógica para llegar a una conclusión o formar una opinion

defamation: difamación *s.* dañar la reputación de alguien injustamente mediante afirmaciones falsas

deference: deferencia *s.* gran respeto

defining: definir *v.* aclarar el significado; explicar

definitive: definitivo *adj.* que decide y resuelve una cuestión

degraded: degradado *adj.* con respetabilidad reducida; desgraciado

deicide: deicidio *s.* matar a un dios

dejected: abatido/a *adj.* deprimido/a; triste

demonstrate: demostrar *v.* enseñar cómo hacer algo

denounce: denunciar *v.* criticar duramente

depth of field: profundidad de campo *s.* la distancia entre los objetos más cercanos y los más lejanos que enfoca una cámara

despotism: despotismo *s.* ejercicio de autoridad absoluta

determine: determinar *v.* decidir; buscar la causa o la razón exacta

dictum: dicho *s.* un enunciado corto que expresa una verdad general; un refrán o proverbio

digress: divagar *v.* desviarse del tema al hablar o escribir

dilatory: dilatorio/a *adj.* inclinado a retrasarse; lento/a

discern: discernir *v.* reconocer como diferente

disparity: disparidad *s.* gran diferencia o desigualdad

disposition: disposición *s.* el acto de llegar a un acuerdo en un caso o discusión; predisposición

disputation: disputa *s.* debate o discusión

dissented: disintió *v.* rechazó una opinion oficial; estuvo en desacuerdo

documentary: documental *s.* programa o película que ofrece datos o un informe sobre hechos reales

dyspepsia: dispepsia *s.* indigestión

E

effrontery: desfachatez *s.* descaro; desvergüenza

eminence: eminencia *s.* persona con un cargo de gran importancia o superioridad

eminent: eminente *adj.* distinguido; famoso; notorio

emperor: emperador *s.* gobernante supremo de un imperio

encroaching: traspasar *v.* infringir; meterse; avanzar continuamente

epiphany: epifanía *s.* sensación súbita de comprensión o entendimiento

equivocate: usar equívocos *v.* usar un lenguaje ambiguo para evitar comprometerse a algo

espionage: espionaje *s.* uso de espías para obtener información secreta

establish: establecer *v.* instituir, crear, montar

etiquette: etiqueta *s.* buenos modales

exalted: elevado/a *adj.* de alto rango

exasperating: exasperante *adj.* molesto

exercise: ejercicio *s.* implementación; puesta en práctica

expression: expresión *s.* tono de voz que indica una emoción específica

eyewitness account: declaración de un testigo *s.* descripción hecha por alguien que estuvo presente en un suceso

F

faultfinder: criticón/a *adj.* persona que critica con frecuencia; un quejica

figure: figura *s.* grupo de dibujos o ilustraciones

fix: momento difícil *s.* una situación complicada

focal point: punto de enfoque *s.* el centro de actividad o de atención de una fotografía

foment: fomentar *v.* suscitar, promover; agitar

foreground: primer plano *s.* objetos más cercanos en una fotografía

forward: atrevido/a *adj.* audaz; descarado/a

frame: prototipo *s.* la narrativa oral principal de una producción

framing: composición *s.* creación visual de forma que el marco rodee la imagen del primer plano

furtive: furtivo/a *adj.* hecho de forma sigilosa, a escondidas, para evitar ser descubierto: secreto/a

G

garrulous: charlatán/a *adj.* que habla mucho; parlanchín/a

gilded: bañado en oro *adj.* cubierto con una capa fina de oro

grandeur: esplendor *s.* magnificencia; grandeza; majestuosidad

H

hallow: santificar *v.* hacer sagrado; consagrar

hangdog: abatido/a *adj.* avergonzado/a; triste; culpable

heedless: ignorando *adj.* sin escuchar el consejo; imprudente

hermitage: retiro *s.* lugar apartado, solitario

hospitality: hospitalidad *s.* actitud cálida de bienvenida hacia los invitados

host: anfitrión *s.* maestro de ceremonia, moderador o presentador de un programa

hypodermic: inyección hipodérmica *s.* inyección de un medicamento

I

immutable: inmutable *adj.* que no cambia nunca

impact: colisión *s.* choque; *v.* colisionar, chocar

imperial: imperial *adj.* de calidad superior

imploring: implorar *v.* pedir algo a alguien o suplicar

importunities: importunidades *s.* peticiones urgentes molestas

impressionism: impresionismo *s.* estilo artístico en el que el estado de ánimo, el color y la luz importan más que los detalles

incident: incidente *s.* suceso

indecisions: indecisiones *s.* cosas que no están decididas o finalizadas

infallibility: infalibilidad *s.* imposibilidad de equivocarse

inflection: inflexión *s.* subidas y bajadas en el tono de voz de una persona

informational: informativo/a *adj.* que proporciona conocimientos y hechos

infringed: infringió *v.* violó la ley

instantaneously: instantáneamente *adv.* inmediatamente

insurgent: insurgente *adj.* rebelde o que se rebela contra el gobierno en el poder

integrity: integridad *s.* la virtud de seguir principios morales o éticos

interminable: interminable *adj.* que parece que no tiene fin

interview: entrevista *s.* conversación en la que un presentador hace preguntas a uno o más invitados

inquire: inquirir *v.* solicitar información; indagar

investigate: investigar *v.* indagar a fondo

J

jurisdiction: jurisdicción *s.* poder legal para escuchar una causa y dictar sentencia

L

labeling and **captions: rótulos** y **leyendas** *s.* etiquetas y texto que suelen acompañar las imágenes de contenido político para clarificar su significado

layout: diseño *s.* la disposición gráfica de una presentación

legacy: legado *s.* algo heredado, que se traspasa

letterhead: membrete *s.* papelería personalizada

literal: literal *adj.* acorde a los hechos; sin exagerar

loathsome: repugnante *adj.* que causa gran desagrado

loitered: deambuló *v.* holgazaneó; que se movió despacio

M

machetes: machetes *s.* cuchillos

magistrates: magistrados *s.* cargos públicos que tienen el poder de un juez

majority: mayoría *s.* más de la mitad

malice: malicia *s.* deseo de herir a alguien

mission: misión *s.* objetivo o ambición

monotonous: monótono/a *adj.* aburrido/a debido a la falta de variación

motifs: motivos *s.* temas, características o elementos principales

multitudes: multitudes *s.* gran número de personas

O

obdurate: obstinado/a *adj.* resistente a la persuasión

obliged: agradecido/a *adj.* que da las gracias

oppressed: oprimidos/as *s.* personas cuyos derechos son pisoteados por otros

ornamented: ornamentado *adj.* decorado; adornado

overcast: nublado *adj.* cubierto de nubes

overture: obertura *s.* introducción musical de un ópera o sinfonía

P

palette: paleta *s.* rango de colores usados en una obra determinada

perish: perecer *v.* morir; ser matado

perpetually: perpetuamente *adv.* que sucede todo el tiempo

persistence: persistencia *s.* acción de no darse por vencido

perspective: perspectiva *s.* método mediante el cual se le da sentido de profundidad a una superficie plana

petition: petición *s.* hacer una solicitud formal; buscar la ayuda de alguien

picturesquely: de modo pintoresco *adv.* de manera que parece un cuadro; de manera sorprendente o interesante

plaintiffs: demandantes *s.* las personas que interponen una demanda en un juicio

policy: política *s.* acciones específicas de una persona, gobierno u organización

populist: populista *adj.* persona que cree servir las necesidades del pueblo

prejudices: prejuicios *s.* sentimientos u opiniones desfavorables formados con anterioridad o sin apoyarse en los hechos

prelude: preludio *s.* introducción de una obra musical; obertura

prescribed: prescrito *v.* manifestado por escrito; mandado

proceedings: pleito *s.* proceso judicial, los sucesos de un juzgado

prolific: prolífico *adj.* fructífero

propaganda: propaganda *s.* información, ideas o rumores que se divulgan amplia y deliberadamente para hacerle daño a una persona, grupo, movimiento, causa o nación

protagonist: protagonista *s.* el personaje principal de una obra de teatro, cuento o novela

Q

quaint: singular *adj.* inusual; curioso

R

racket: barullo *s.* confusión ruidosa; jaleo

realism: realismo *s.* estilo artístico que se parece mucho a la realidad

rectitude: rectitud *s.* comportamiento o pensamiento moralmente correcto; integridad

redeemers: redentores *s.* personas que pagan por las malas acciones de otros

redress: rectificación *s.* corrección reparación de un daño

relevant: relevante *adj.* pertinente

remorseless: despiadado/a *adj.* que no tiene remordimientos; cruel

renaissance: renacimiento *s.* resurgimiento; periodo de importancia cultural

rend: rasgar *v.* hacer pedazos con fuerza

resolution: resolución *s.* acción de resolver o decidir; expresión formal de una opinión

reverence: reverencia *s.* sentimiento de profundo respeto

rites: ritos *s.* ceremonias

romanticism: romanticismo *s.* estilo artístico que evoca la emoción idealizando los sujetos

S

salutary: saludable *adj.* beneficioso/a

sanctity: santidad *s.* hecho de ser sagrado

scourge: azote *s.* causa de serios problemas o sufrimiento

self-assurance: autoconfianza *s.* seguridad en uno mismo

sequence: secuencia *s.* en un orden particular; *v.* (secuenciar) poner en orden

sequence photography: secuencia fotográfica *n.* una serie de imágenes en las que se ve el sujeto en instantes sucesivos

shotgun: escopeta *s.* arma de cañón largo, con frecuencia usada para disparar perdigones

shuffle: arrastrar los pies *v.* caminar sin levantar los pies

sidle: caminar de lado *v.* moverse de costado furtiva o tímidamente

significant: significativo/a *adj.* lleno/a de significado; importante

sinister: siniestro *adj.* malvado; amenazador

sovereign: soberano *s.* un monarca o gobernante

spatial: espacial *adj.* que existe en el espacio

special elements: elementos especiales *s.* características que dan puntos de énfasis en una producción

specific: específico/a *adj.* definido/a; preciso/a; particular

specifications: especificaciones *s.* apartado de una patente en que el inventor describe con detalle el invento

speech balloon: bocadillo *s.* el modo en que se representa lo que dice cada personaje en las novelas gráficas

squalor: mugre *s.* suciedad; estado lamentable

stolid: impasible *adj.* imperturbable; que no siente emoción alguna

strife: lucha *s.* acción de luchar; conflicto

subordinate: subordinado/a *adj.* que tiene menos importancia

subordinate: subordinado/a *s.* una persona de menor rango o clase

superannuated: viejo/a *adj.* demasiado viejo/a para usarse; obsoleto/a

superfluous: superfluo/a *adj.* más de lo necesario o deseado; innecesario/a

supplanted: suplantó *v.* tomó el lugar de; quitó a

supplement: suplemento *s.* algo añadido

surrealism: surrealismo *s.* uso intencional de detalles imaginativos y hasta extraños en el arte

symbolism: simbolismo *s.* uso de imágenes u objetos para representar ideas o cualidades

T

tedious: tedioso/a *adj.* aburrido/a, soso/a

teeming: repleto/a *adj.* lleno/a

temporal: temporal *adj.* no eterno, limitado por el tiempo

tension: tensión *s.* estrés causado al tirar

tone: tono *s.* la actitud de una producción hacia un tema o el público

transcendent: trascendente *adj.* más allá de los límites de la experiencia posible

treason: traición *s.* deslealtad hacia la confianza o la fe

trivialize: trivializar *v.* quitar importancia; hacer trivial

tyranny: tiranía *s.* poder opresivo

U

unalienable: inalienable *adj.* imposible de quitar o de abandonar

unique: único/a *adj.* que es el único de su especie o tipo

unrequited: no correspondido *adj.* que no se ha liquidado o vengado

V

vassals: vasallos *s.* sujetos de un reino; siervos

vast: vasto/a *adj.* de gran tamaño

verbatim: textualmente *adv.* palabra por palabra

vigilant: vigilante *adj.* en alerta, atento/a

vindictive: vengativo/a *adj.* lleno/a de un deseo intenso e irracional de venganza

W

wanton: excesivo/a *adj.* descontrolado/a; sin ley

waterfowl: ave acuática *s.* relativo a las aves acuáticas

wretched: desdichado/a *adj.* muy infeliz; desgraciado/a

ALLEGORY An *allegory* is a story or tale with two or more levels of meaning—a literal level and one or more symbolic levels. The events, setting, and characters in an allegory are symbols for ideas and qualities.

ALLUSION An *allusion* is a reference to a well-known person, place, event, literary work, or work of art. Writers often make allusions to stories from the Bible, to Greek and Roman myths, to plays by Shakespeare, to political and historical events, and to other materials with which they can expect their readers to be familiar.

ANALOGY An *analogy* is an extended comparison of relationships. It is based on the idea that the relationship between one pair of things is like the relationship between another pair. Unlike a metaphor, an analogy involves an explicit comparison, often using the words *like* or *as*.

ANAPHORA *Anaphora* is a type of parallel structure in which a word or phrase is repeated at the beginning of successive clauses for emphasis.

ANECDOTE An *anecdote* is a brief story about an interesting, amusing, or strange event. An anecdote is told to entertain or to make a point.

APPEAL An *appeal* is a rhetorical device used in argumentative writing to persuade an audience.

An appeal to ethics (Ethos) shows that an argument is just or fair.

An appeal to logic (Logos) shows that an argument is well reasoned.

An appeal to authority shows that a higher power supports the ideas.

An appeal to emotion (Pathos) is designed to influence readers' feelings.

ARGUMENT An *argument* is writing or speech that attempts to convince a reader to think or act in a particular way. An argument is a logical way of presenting a belief, conclusion, or stance. A good argument is supported with reasoning and evidence.

AUTOBIOGRAPHY An *autobiography* is a form of nonfiction in which a person tells his or her own life story. *Memoirs*, first-person accounts of personally or historically significant events in which the writer was a participant or an eyewitness, are a form of autobiographical writing.

BIOGRAPHY A *biography* is a form of nonfiction in which a writer tells the life story of another person.

CATALOGUE A *catalogue* in poetry is a list of people, objects, or situations, used to evoke a range of experience and/or emotion.

CHARACTER A *character* is a person or an animal that takes part in the action of a literary work. The following are some terms used to describe various types of characters:

The *main character* in a literary work is the one on whom the work focuses. *Major characters* in a literary work include the main character and any other characters who play significant roles. A *minor character* is one who does not play a significant role. A *round character* is one who is complex and multifaceted, like a real person. A *flat character* is one who is one-dimensional. A *dynamic character* is one who changes in the course of a work. A *static character* is one who does not change in the course of a work.

CHARACTERIZATION *Characterization* is the act of creating and developing a character. In **direct characterization,** a writer simply states a character's traits. In *indirect characterization,* character is revealed through one of the following means:

1. words, thoughts, or actions of the character
2. descriptions of the character's appearance or background
3. what other characters say about the character
4. the ways in which other characters react to the character

CLAIM A *claim* is a particular belief, conclusion, or point of view that a writer presents in an *argument.*

CONCESSION *Concession* is a rhetorical device that acknowledges the opposition's arguments.

CONFLICT A *conflict* is a struggle between opposing forces. Sometimes this struggle is internal, or within a character. At other times, this struggle is external, or between a character and an outside force. Conflict is one of the primary elements of narrative literature because most plots develop from conflicts.

CONNOTATION The *connotation* is an association that a word calls to mind in addition to the dictionary meaning of the word. Many words that are similar in their dictionary meanings, or denotations, are quite different in their connotations. Poets and other writers choose their words carefully so that the connotations of those words will be appropriate.

COUNTERCLAIM A *counterclaim* is an objection or challange to the *claim*—or particular belief, conclusion, or point of view—that a writer presents in an *argument.* Counterclaims are often brought up by the writer of the argument in anticipation of challenges.

DENOTATION The *denotation* of a word is its objective meaning, independent of other associations that the word brings to mind.

DESCRIPTION A *description* is a portrayal, in words, of something that can be perceived by the senses. Writers create descriptions by using images.

DIALECT A *dialect* is the form of a language spoken by people in a particular region or group. Writers often use dialect to make their characters seem realistic and to create local color.

DIALOGUE A *dialogue* is a conversation between characters. Writers use dialogue to reveal character, to present events, to add variety to narratives, and to arouse their readers' interest.

DICTION *Diction* is a writer's or speaker's word choice. Diction is part of a writer's style and may be described as formal or informal, plain or ornate, common or technical, abstract or concrete.

DRAMA A *drama* is a story written to be performed by actors. The playwright supplies dialogue for the characters to speak, as well as *stage directions* that give information about costumes, lighting, scenery, properties, the setting, and the characters' movements and ways of speaking. Dramatic conventions include soliloquies, asides, or the passage of time between acts or scenes. *Dramatic exposition* is a brief essay, or prose commentary, inserted by the writer to help readers and producers understand the characters and past conflicts. *Background knowledge* includes information about the period during which the action takes place.

DRAMATIC MONOLOGUE A *dramatic monologue* is a poem or speech in which an imaginary character speaks to a silent listener.

DRAMATIC POEM A *dramatic poem* is one that makes use of the conventions of drama. Such poems may be monologues or dialogues or may present the speech of many characters. Robert Frost's "The Death of the Hired Man" is a famous example of a dramatic poem.

See also *Dramatic Monologue.*

EPIC THEME An *epic theme* is an underlying message that all people of all times are connected by their shared experiences.

EDITORIAL An *editorial* is a form of persuasive writing or argument. Editorials must have a clear position, be supported by reasons, and include an appeal to ethics, logic, authority, and/or emotion.

ELLIPTICAL PHRASING *Elliptical phrasing* is a style of poetry in which the poet omits words that are expected to be understood by the reader.

ENUMERATION *Enumeration* is a document style in which the major ideas are listed in numerical order.

ESSAY An *essay* is a short nonfiction work about a particular subject. Essays can be classified as *formal* or *informal*, *personal*, or *impersonal*. They can also be classified according to purpose, such as *cause-and-effect*, *satirical*, or *reflective.* Modes of discourse, such as *expository*, *descriptive*, *persuasive*, or *narrative*, are other means of classifying essays.

EXPLANATORY ESSAY An *explanatory essay* describes and summarizes information gathered from a number of sources on a concept.

FICTION *Fiction* is prose writing that tells about imaginary characters and events. Short stories and novels are works of fiction.

FIGURATIVE LANGUAGE *Figurative language* is writing or speech not meant to be taken literally. Writers use figurative language to express ideas in vivid and imaginative ways.

FIGURE OF SPEECH A *figure of speech* is an expression or a word used imaginatively rather than literally.

FLASHBACK A *flashback* is a section of a literary work that interrupts the chronological presentation of events to relate an event from an earlier time. A writer may present a flashback as a character's memory or recollection, as part of an account or story told by a character, as a dream or a daydream, or simply by having the narrator switch to a time in the past.

FORESHADOWING *Foreshadowing* in a literary work is the use of clues to suggest events that have yet to occur.

FRAME STORY A *frame story* is a story that brackets—or frames—another story or group of stories. This device creates a story-within-a-story narrative structure.

FREE VERSE *Free verse* is poetry that lacks a regular rhythmical pattern, or meter. A writer of free verse is at liberty to use any rhythms that are appropriate to what he or she is saying.

GENRE A *genre* is a division, or type, of literature. Literature is commonly divided into three major genres: poetry, prose, and drama. Each major genre can in turn be divided into smaller genres. Poetry can be divided into lyric, concrete, dramatic, narrative, and epic poetry. Prose can be divided into fiction and nonfiction. Drama can be divided into serious drama, tragedy, comic drama, melodrama, and farce.

HUMOR *Humor*, used in an argument, can be an effective rhetorical device. Humorous language and details make characters and situations seem funny.

HYPERBOLE A *hyperbole* is a deliberate exaggeration or overstatement, often used for comic effect.

IDIOMATIC EXPRESSION *Idiomatic expressions* are figures of speech that cannot be understood literally. For example, a rainstorm might be described as "raining cats and dogs."

IN MEDIA RES *In media res*, which is Latin for "in the middle of things," is a plot device writers use to grab reader's attention.

IMAGE An *image* is a word or phrase that appeals to one or more of the five senses—sight, hearing, touch, taste, or smell.

IMAGERY *Imagery* is the descriptive or figurative language used in literature to create word pictures for the reader. These pictures, or images, are created by details of sight, sound, taste, touch, smell, or movement.

INCONGRUITY *Incongruity* is a technique writers use to create humor and occurs when two or more ideas relate to one another in a way that is contrary to the readers' expectations.

IRONY *Irony* is a contrast between what is stated and what is meant, or between what is expected to happen and what actually happens. In *verbal irony*, a word or a phrase is used to suggest the opposite of its usual meaning. In *dramatic irony*, there is a contradiction between what a character thinks and what the reader or audience knows. In *irony of situation*, an event occurs that contradicts the expectations of the characters, of the reader, or of the audience.

LETTER A *letter* is a written message or communication addressed to a reader or readers and is generally sent by mail. Letters may be *private* or *public*, depending on their intended audience. A public letter, also called a *literary letter* or *epistle*, is a work of literature written in the form of a personal letter but created for publication.

MEMOIR A *memoir* is a type of nonfiction autobiographical writing that tells about a person's own life, usually focusing on the writer's involvement in historically or culturally significant events—either as a participant or an eyewitness.

METAPHOR A *metaphor* is a figure of speech in which one thing is spoken of as though it were something else. The identification suggests a comparison between the two things that are identified, as in "death is a long sleep."

A *mixed metaphor* occurs when two metaphors are jumbled together. For example, thorns and rain are illogically mixed in "the thorns of life rained down on him." A *dead metaphor* is one that has been overused and has become a common expression, such as "the arm of the chair" or "nightfall."

MONOLOGUE A *monologue* is a speech delivered entirely by one person or character.

MOTIF A *motif* is a recurrent, or repeated, object or idea in a literary work.

NARRATION *Narration* is writing that tells a story. The act of telling a story is also called *narration*. The *narrative,* or story, is told by a storyteller called the *narrator.* A story is usually told chronologically, in the order in which events take place in time, though it may include flashbacks and foreshadowing. Narratives may be true or fictional. Narration is one of the forms of discourse and is used in novels, short stories, plays, narrative poems, anecdotes, autobiographies, biographies, and reports.

NARRATIVE A *narrative* is a story told in fiction, nonfiction, poetry, or drama. Narratives are often classified by their content or purpose. An *exploration narrative* is a firsthand account of an explorer's travels in a new land. "The Interesting Narrative of the Life of Olaudah Equiano" is a *slave narrative*, an account of the experiences of an enslaved person. A *historical narrative* is a narrative account of significant historical events.

A *personal narrative* is a first-person story about a real-life experience. In a *reflective narrative* the author describes describes his or her feelings about a scene, incident, memory, or event. A *nonlinear narrative* does not follow chronological order. It may contain flashbacks, dream sequences, or other devices that interrupt the chronological order of events.

NARRATOR A *narrator* is a speaker or character who tells a story. A story or novel may be narrated by a main character, by a minor character, or by someone uninvolved in the story. The narrator may speak in the first person or in the third person. An *omniscient narrator* is all-knowing, while a limited narrator knows only what one character does.

NONFICTION *Nonfiction* is prose writing that presents and explains ideas or that tells about real people, places, objects, or events. Two of the main types of literary nonfiction are historical writing and reflective writing. Essays, biographies, autobiographies, journals, and reports are all examples of nonfiction.

NOVEL A *novel* is a long work of fiction. A novel often has a complicated plot, many major and minor characters, a significant theme, and several varied settings. Novels can be classified in many ways, based on the historical periods in which they are written, the subjects and themes that they treat, the techniques that are used in them, and the literary movements that inspired them. A *novella* is not as long as a novel but is longer than a short story.

ONOMATOPOEIA *Onomatopoeia* is the use of words that imitate sounds. Examples of such words are *buzz, hiss, murmur,* and *rustle*.

ORATORY *Oratory* is public speaking that is formal, persuasive, and emotionally appealing. Patrick Henry's "Speech in the Virginia Convention" (p. 100) is an example of oratory.

OXYMORON An *oxymoron* is a figure of speech that combines two opposing or contradictory ideas. An oxymoron, such as "freezing fire," suggests a paradox in just a few words.

PACING *Pacing* is the speed or rhythm of writing. Writers use different paces to achieve different effects, such as suspense.

PARADOX A *paradox* is a statement that seems to be contradictory but that actually presents a truth.

PARALLELISM *Parallelism* is the presentation of similar ideas, in sequence, using the same grammatical structure.

PARALLEL STRUCTURE In a list, each item should use *parallel structure* in which the part of speech and grammatical phrasing is the same for all items.

PERSONIFICATION *Personification* is a form of figurative language in which a nonhuman subject is given human characteristics. Effective personification of things or ideas makes them seem vital and alive, as if they were human.

PHILOSOPHICAL ASSUMPTIONS Beliefs that are taken for granted are *philosophical assumptions*. Some assumptions are *explicit*, or directly stated. Other assumptions are *implicit*, meaning the reader must make inferences to understand.

PLOT *Plot* is the sequence of events in a literary work. In most fiction, the plot involves both characters and a central conflict. The plot usually begins with an *exposition* that introduces the setting, the characters, and the basic situation. This is followed by the *inciting incident*, which introduces the central conflict. The conflict then increases during the *development* until it reaches a high point of interest or suspense, the *climax*. The climax is followed by the end, or resolution, of the central conflict. Any events that occur after the *resolution* make up the *denouement*. The events that lead up to the climax make up the *rising action*. The events that follow the climax make up the *falling action*.

POETRY *Poetry* is one of the three major types of literature. In poetry, form and content are closely connected, like the two faces of a single coin. Poems are often divided into lines and stanzas and often employ regular rhythmical patterns, or meters. Most poems use highly concise, musical, and emotionally charged language. Many also make use of imagery, figurative language, and special devices such as rhyme.

POETIC STRUCTURE The basic structures of poetry are lines and stanzas. A *line* is a group of words arranged in a row. A line of poetry may break, or end, in different ways. Varied *line lengths* can create unpredictable rhythms.

An *end-stopped line* is one in which both the grammatical structure and sense are complete at the end of the line.

A *run-on, or enjambed*, line is one in which both the grammatical structure and sense continue past the end of the line.

POINT OF VIEW *Point of view* is the perspective, or vantage point, from which a story is told. Three commonly used points of view are first person, omniscient third person, and limited third person.

In the *first-person point of view*, the narrator is a character in the story and refers to himself or herself with the first-person pronoun "I."

The two kinds of third-person point of view, limited and omniscient, are called "third person" because the narrator uses third-person pronouns such as "he" and "she" to refer to the characters. There is no "I" telling the story.

In stories told from the omniscient third-person point of view, the narrator knows and tells about what each character feels and thinks.

In stories told from the *limited third-person point of view,* the narrator relates the inner thoughts and feelings of only one character, and everything is viewed from this character's perspective.

PREAMBLE A *preamble* is a statement that explains who is issuing the document and for what purpose.

PRIMARY SOURCE A *primary source* is one created by someone who directly participated in or observed the event being described.

PROSE *Prose* is the ordinary form of written language. Most writing that is not poetry, drama, or song is considered prose. Prose is one of the major genres of literature. It occurs in two forms: fiction and nonfiction.

PROTAGONIST The protagonist is the main character in a literary work.

REFRAIN A *refrain* is a repeated line or group of lines in a poem or song. Most refrains end stanzas. Although some refrains are nonsense lines, many increase suspense or emphasize character and theme.

REGIONALISM *Regionalism* in literature is the tendency among certain authors to write about specific geographical areas. Regional writers present the distinct culture of an area, including its speech, customs, beliefs, and history.

RHETORICAL DEVICES Rhetorical devices are special patterns of words and ideas that create emphasis and stir emotion, especially in speeches or other oral presentations. *Parallelism*, for example, is the repetition of a grammatical structure in order to create a rhythm and make words more memorable. Other common rhetorical devices include: *analogy, drawing comparisons between two unlike things; charged language,* words that appeal to the emotions; *concession*, an acknowledgement of the opposition's argument; *humor,* using language and details that make characters or situations funny; *paradox,* statements that seem to contradict but present a truth *restatement,* expressing the same idea in different words, *rhetorical questions,* questions with obvious answers, *tone, the author's attitude toward the audience*

RHYME *Rhyme* is the repetition of sounds at the ends of words. Rhyming words have identical vowel sounds in their final accented syllables. The consonants before the vowels may be different, but any consonants occurring after these vowels are the same, as in *frog* and *bog* or *willow* and *pillow*. **End rhyme** occurs when rhyming words are repeated at the ends of lines. *Internal rhyme* occurs when rhyming words fall within a line. *Approximate,* or *slant, rhyme* occurs when the rhyming sounds are similar, but not exact, as in *prove* and *glove*.

REPETITION *Repetition* of words and phrases is a literary device used in prose and poetry to emphasize important ideas.

RHYTHM *Rhythm* is the pattern of beats, or stresses, in spoken or written language. Prose and free verse are written in the irregular rhythmical patterns of everyday speech.

RHETORICAL QUESTIONS Rhetorical questions call attention to an issue by implying obvious answers.

ROMANTICISM *Romanticism* was a literary and artistic movement of the nineteenth century that arose in reaction to eighteenth-century Neoclassicism and placed a premium on imagination, emotion, nature, individuality, and exotica. Romanticism is particularly evident in the works of the Transcendentalists.

SECONDARY SOURCE A *secondary source* is one created by someone with indirect knowledge of the event being described. Secondary sources rely on *primary sources,* or firsthand descriptions.

SENSORY LANGUAGE *Sensory language* is writing or speech that appeals to one or more of the five senses.

SEQUENCE OF EVENTS Authors often use *sequence of events*, or the order in which things happened, to structure nonfiction pieces that describe historical events or explain a change over time. Authors frequently describe important events in *chronological order,* or time order.

SETTING The *setting* of a literary work is the time and place of the action. A setting may serve any of a number of functions. It may provide a background for the action. It may be a crucial element in the plot or central conflict. It may also create a certain emotional atmosphere, or mood.

SHORT STORY A *short story* is a brief work of fiction. The short story resembles the novel but generally has a simpler plot and setting. In addition, the short story tends to reveal character at a crucial moment rather than developing it through many incidents. For example, Thomas Wolfe's "The Far and the Near" concentrates on what happens to a train engineer when he visits people who had waved to him every day.

SERIAL COMMA A *serial comma* is a comma placed after each item in a list except for the final item.

SIMILE A *simile* is a figure of speech that makes a direct comparison between two subjects, using either *like* or *as*.

SLANT RHYME In *slant rhyme,* the final sounds in two lines of a poem are similar, but not identical.

SOCIAL COMMENTARY In works of *social commentary,* an author seeks to highlight, usually in a critical way, an aspect of society.

SPEAKER The *speaker* is the voice of a poem. Although the speaker is often the poet, the speaker may also be a fictional character or even an inanimate object or another type of nonhuman entity. Interpreting a poem often depends upon recognizing who the speaker is, whom the speaker is addressing, and what the speaker's attitude, or tone, is.

STANZA A *stanza* is a group of lines in a poem that are considered to be a unit. Many poems are divided into stanzas that are separated by spaces. Stanzas often function just like paragraphs in prose. Each stanza states and develops a single main idea.

Stanzas are commonly named according to the number of lines found in them, as follows:

1. Couplet: a two-line stanza
2. Tercet: a three-line stanza
3. Quatrain: a four-line stanza
4. Cinquain: a five-line stanza
5. Sestet: a six-line stanza
6. Heptastich: a seven-line stanza
7. Octave: an eight-line stanza

STREAM OF CONSCIOUSNESS *Stream of consciousness* is a narrative technique that presents thoughts as if they were coming directly from a character's mind. Instead of being arranged in chronological order, the events are presented from the character's point of view, mixed in with the character's thoughts just as they might spontaneously occur.

STYLE A writer's *style* includes word choice, tone, degree of formality, figurative language, rhythm, grammatical structure, sentence length, organization—in short, every feature of a writer's use of language.

SUSPENSE *Suspense* is a feeling of growing uncertainty about the outcome of events. Writers create suspense by raising questions in the minds of their readers. Suspense builds until the climax of the plot, at which point the suspense reaches its peak.

SYMBOL A *symbol* is anything that stands for or represents something else. A *conventional symbol* is one that is widely known and accepted, such as a voyage symbolizing life or a skull symbolizing death. A *personal* *symbol* is one developed for a particular work by a particular author.

SYMBOLISM *Symbolism* refers to an author's use of people, places, or objects to represent abstract qualities or ideas.

SYNTAX *Syntax* is the structure of sentences.

THEME A *theme* is a central message or insight into life revealed by a literary work. In most works of fiction, the theme is only indirectly stated: A story, poem, or play most often has an *implied theme*.

TONE The tone of a literary work is the writer's attitude toward his or her subject, characters, or audience. A writer's tone may be formal or informal, friendly or distant, personal or pompous. The tone of a work can also be described as technical, conversational, or colloquial.

TRANSCENDENTALISM *Transcendentalism* was an American literary and philosophical movement of the nineteenth century. The Transcendentalists, who were based in New England, believed that intuition and the individual conscience "transcend" experience and thus are better guides to truth than the senses and logical reason. Influenced by Romanticism, the Transcendentalists respected the individual spirit and the natural world, believing that divinity was present everywhere, in nature and in each person.

USAGE *Usage* is the way in which a word or phrase is used. The meaning, pronunciation, and spelling of some words have changed over time.

VOICE A writer's voice is the way in which the writer's personality is revealed in his or her writing. Elements that influence a writer's style are diction, the types of words used, syntax, the types of sentences used, and tone, the writer's attitude toward the topic or audience.

ALLEGORY / ALEGORÍA Una *alegoría* es un relato o cuento con dos niveles de significado: un nivel literal y uno o más niveles simbólicos. Los hechos, ambientación y personajes de una alegoría son símbolos de ideas o cualidades.

ALLUSION / ALUSIÓN Una *alusión* es una referencia a una persona, lugar, hecho, obra literaria u obra de arte muy conocida. Los escritores a menudo hacen alusiones a relatos de la Biblia, a los mitos griegos y romanos, a las obras de Shakespeare, a hechos políticos e históricos y a otros materiales con los que suponen que sus lectores estén familiarizados.

ANALOGY / ANALOGÍA Una *analogía* establece una comparación extensa de relaciones. Se basa en la idea de que la relación entre un par de cosas es como la relación entre otro par. A diferencia de la metáfora, una analogía requiere una comparación explícita, a menudo usando las palabras *como* o *semejante*.

ANAPHORA / ANÁFORA Una *anáfora* es un tipo de estructura paralela en la que una palabra o frase se repite al principio de cláusulas consecutivas para dar énfasis.

ANECDOTE / ANÉCDOTA Una *anécdota* es un relato breve sobre un hecho interesante, divertido o extraño, que se narra con el fin de entretener o decir algo importante.

APPEAL / APELACIÓN Una *apelación* es un recurso retórico que se usa en los escritos de argumentación para persuadir al público.

Una apelación a la ética (Ethos) muestra que un argumento es justo.

Una apelación a la lógica (Logos) muestra que un argumento está bien razonado.

Una apelación a la autoridad muestra que alguien importante respalda las ideas.

Una apelación a las emociones (Pathos) tiene como fin influenciar los sentimientos de los lectores.

ARGUMENT / ARGUMENTO Un *argumento* es un escrito o discurso que trata de convencer al lector para que siga una acción o adopte una opinión en particular. Un argumento es una manera lógica de presentar una creencia, una conclusión o una postura. Un buen argumento se respalda con razonamientos y pruebas.

AUTOBIOGRAPHY / AUTOBIOGRAFÍA Una *autobiografía* es una forma de no-ficción en la que una persona narra su propia vida. Las *memorias* son relatos en primera persona de hechos personal o históricamente significativos en los que el escritor participó o de los cuales fue testigo directo. Las memorias son una forma de escrito autobiográfico.

BIOGRAPHY / BIOGRAFÍA Una *biografía* es una forma de no-ficción en la que un escritor cuenta la vida de otra persona.

CATALOGUE / CATÁLOGO Un *catálogo* en poesía es una lista de gente, objetos o situaciones que se usan para evocar un abanico de experiencias o emociones.

CHARACTER / PERSONAJE Un *personaje* es una persona o animal que participa de la acción en una obra literaria. A continuación hay algunos términos que se usan para describir varios tipos de personajes:

El *protagonista*, o *personaje principal*, en una obra literaria es aquel en el que se centra la obra. Los *personajes importantes* en una obra literaria incluyen el personaje principal y otros personajes que tienen papeles significativos. Un *personaje menor* es aquel que no tiene un papel importante. Un *personaje complejo* es aquel que muestra muchos rasgos diferentes. Un *personaje plano* muestra solo un rasgo. Un *personaje dinámico* se desarrolla y crece en el curso del relato. Un *personaje estático* no cambia a lo largo de la obra.

CHARACTERIZATION / CARACTERIZACIÓN
La *caracterización* es el acto de crear y desarrollar un personaje. En una *caracterización directa*, el autor expresa explícitamente los rasgos de un personaje. En una *caracterización indirecta*, el personaje se revela a partir de una de estas maneras:

1. palabras, pensamientos o acciones del personaje
2. descripciones de la apariencia física del personaje o de su procedencia
3. lo que otros personajes dicen sobre el personaje
4. la forma en la que otros personajes reaccionan al personaje

CLAIM / AFIRMACIÓN Una *afirmación* es una opinión, conclusión o punto de vista determinado que el escritor presenta mediante un *argumento*.

CONCESSION / CONCESIÓN La *concesión* es un recurso retórico que reconoce los argumentos de la oposición.

CONFLICT / CONFLICTO Un *conflicto* es una lucha entre fuerzas opuestas. A veces la lucha es interna, o dentro de un personaje. Otras veces la lucha es externa, o entre un personaje y una fuerza exterior. El conflicto es uno de los elementos principales de la literatura narrativa porque la mayoría de tramas se desarrollan a partir de conflictos.

CONNOTATION / CONNOTACIÓN La *connotación* es la asociación que una palabra trae a la mente, además de su definición del diccionario. Muchas palabras que son similares en sus significados del diccionario, o denotaciones, son muy diferentes en sus connotaciones. Los poetas y otros escritores escogen sus palabras cuidadosamente para que las connotaciones de esas palabras sean apropiadas.

COUNTERCLAIM / CONTRAARGUMENTO

Un *contraargumento* es una objeción o desafío a la *afirmación*—u opinión, conclusión o punto de vista determinado—que el escritor presenta en un *argumento*. El escritor suele incluir contraargumentos para anticiparse a los desafíos.

DENOTATION / DENOTACIÓN

La *denotación* de una palabra es su significado objetivo, independientemente de otras asociaciones que esa palabra traiga a la mente.

DESCRIPTION / DESCRIPCIÓN

Una *descripción* es un retrato en palabras de algo que se puede percibir con los sentidos. Los escritores crean descripciones usando imágenes.

DIALECT / DIALECTO

El *dialecto* es la forma de un lenguaje hablado por la gente en una región o grupo particular. Los escritores a menudo usan dialecto para hacer que sus personajes parezcan más reales y para reflejar el habla de una zona determinada.

DIALOGUE / DIÁLOGO

Un *diálogo* es una conversación entre personajes. Los escritores usan el diálogo para revelar personajes, para presentar hechos, para añadir variedad a la narración o para despertar el interés de los lectores.

DICTION / DICCIÓN

La *dicción* comprende la elección de palabras que hace un autor o hablante. La dicción es parte del estilo de un escritor y se puede describir como formal o informal, sencilla u ornamentada, común o técnica, abstracta o concreta.

DRAMA / DRAMA

Un *drama* es una historia escrita para ser representada por actores. El guión de un drama proporciona el diálogo para que los personajes hablen, así como las *acotaciones* que dan información sobre el vestuario, la iluminación, la ambientación, los objetos y la manera en la que los personajes se mueven o hablan. Las convenciones dramáticas incluyen soliloquios, apartes, o el paso del tiempo entre actos o escenas. La *exposición dramática* es un ensayo breve o comentario en prosa del escritor y que tiene como objetivo que los lectores y productores entiendan a los personajes y sus conflictos. El *conocimiento previo* incluye información sobre el período en el cual tiene lugar la acción.

DRAMATIC MONOLOGUE / MONÓLOGO DRAMÁTICO

Un *monólogo dramático* es un poema o discurso en el que un personaje imaginario le habla a un oyente silencioso.

DRAMATIC POEM / POEMA DRAMÁTICO

Un *poema dramático* es aquel que usa las reglas del drama. Estos poemas pueden ser monólogos o diálogos o pueden presentar el parlamento de varios personajes. "The Death of the Hired Man" de Robert Frost es un ejemplo muy famoso de poema dramático.

Ver también *monólogo dramático*.

EPIC THEME / TEMA ÉPICO

Un *tema épico* es el mensaje subyacente de que todas las personas de todas las épocas están conectadas por experiencias compartidas.

EDITORIAL / EDITORIAL

Un *editorial* es una forma de escritura persuasiva o argumento. Los editoriales deben tener una postura clara, respaldarse con razonamientos e incluir una apelación a la ética, a la lógica, a la autoridad o a la emoción.

ELLIPTICAL PHRASING / FRASEO ELÍPTICO

El *fraseo elíptico* es un estilo de poesía en el que el poeta omite palabras que se espera que sean comprendidas por el lector.

ENUMERATION / ENUMERACIÓN

Una *enumeración* es un estilo de documento en el que las ideas principales se listan en orden numérico.

ESSAY / ENSAYO

Un *ensayo* es una obra breve de no-ficción sobre un tema en particular. Los ensayos pueden clasificarse como *formal* o *informal*, *personal* o *impersonal*. También se pueden clasificar de acuerdo a su propósito, como por ejemplo *de causa y efecto*, *satírico* o *reflexivo*. Otras maneras de clasificar ensayos es por el modo de discurso, como por ejemplo *expositivo*, *descriptivo*, *persuasivo* o *narrativo*.

EXPLANATORY ESSAY / ENSAYO EXPLICATIVO

Un *ensayo explicativo* describe y resume información sobre un concepto recogida a partir de varias fuentes.

FICTION / FICCIÓN

La *ficción* es un escrito en prosa que cuenta algo sobre personajes y hechos imaginarios. Los cuentos y las novelas son obras de ficción.

FIGURATIVE LANGUAGE / LENGUAJE FIGURADO

El *lenguaje figurado* es un escrito o discurso que no se debe interpretar literalmente. Los escritores usan lenguaje figurado para expresar ideas de forma vívida e imaginativa.

FIGURE OF SPEECH / FIGURA RETÓRICA

Una *figura retória* es una expresión o palabra usada de forma imaginativa en vez de literal.

FLASHBACK / FLASHBACK

Un *flashback* o *escena retrospectiva* es una sección de una obra literaria que interrumpe la presentación cronológica de los hechos para relatar un hecho de un tiempo anterior. Un escritor puede presentar un flashback como el recuerdo de un personaje, como parte de lo que cuenta un personaje, como un sueño o simplemente haciendo que el narrador cambie a un tiempo en el pasado.

FORESHADOWING / PREFIGURACIÓN

La *prefiguración* es el uso, en una obra literaria, de claves que sugieren hechos que van a suceder.

FRAME STORY / CUENTO DE ENMARQUE

Un *cuento de enmarque* es un relato dentro del cual se incluye otro relato o relatos. Este recurso permite crear una estructura narrativa del tipo "cuento dentro del cuento".

FREE VERSE / VERSO LIBRE

El *verso libre* es una forma poética en la que no se sigue un patrón regular de metro ni de rima. Un escritor de verso libre tiene la libertad de usar cualquier ritmo que sea apropiado a lo que está diciendo.

GENRE / GÉNERO

Un *género* es una categoría o tipo de literatura. La literatura se divide por lo general en tres géneros principales: poesía, prosa y drama. Cada uno de estos géneros principales se dividen a su vez en géneros más pequeños. La poesía se puede dividir en lírica, concreta, dramática, narrativa y épica. La prosa se puede dividir en ficción y no ficción. El drama se puede dividir en drama serio, tragedia, drama cómico, melodrama y farsa.

HUMOR / HUMOR El *humor*, usado en un argumento, puede ser un recurso retórico efectivo. El lenguaje y los detalles humorísticos pueden hacer que los personajes y las situaciones parezcan divertidos.

HYPERBOLE / HIPÉRBOLE Una *hipérbole* es una exageración o magnificación deliberada que a menudo se usa para producir un efecto cómico.

IDIOMATIC EXPRESSION / EXPRESIÓN IDIOMÁTICA Las *expresiones idiomáticas* son figuras retóricas que no se pueden entender literalmente. Por ejemplo, una tormenta se puede describir como "llover a cántaros".

IMAGE / IMAGEN Una *imagen* es una palabra o frase que apela a uno o más de los cinco sentidos: la vista, el oído, el tacto, el gusto o el olfato.

IMAGERY / IMÁGENES Las *imágenes* son el lenguaje figurado o descriptivo que se usa en la literatura para crear una descripción verbal para los lectores. Estas descripciones verbales, o imágenes, se crean incluyendo detalles visuales, auditivos, gustativos, táctiles, olfativos o de movimiento.

IN MEDIA RES / IN MEDIA RES *In media res*, que quiere decir "en el medio de las cosas" en latín, es un resurso que usan los escritores para captar la atención del lector.

INCONGRUITY / INCONGRUENCIA La *incongruencia* es una técnica que usan los escritores para crear humor y ocurre cuando dos o más ideas se relacionan entre sí de una manera que no es de la esperada por el lector.

IRONY / IRONÍA *Ironía* es un contraste entre lo que se dice y lo que se quiere decir, o entre lo que se espera que ocurra y lo que pasa en realidad. En una *ironía verbal*, las palabras se usan para sugerir lo opuesto a lo que se dice. En la *ironía dramática* hay una contradicción entre lo que el personaje piensa y lo que el lector o la audiencia sabe que es verdad. En una *ironía situacional*, ocurre un suceso que contradice directamente las expectativas de los personajes, del lector o de la audiencia.

LETTER / CARTA Una *carta* es un mensaje escrito dirigido a un lector o lectores y generalmente se envía por correo. Las cartas pueden ser *privadas* o *públicas*, dependiendo de la audiencia a la que van dirigidas. Una *carta pública*, también llamada *carta literaria* o *epístola*, es una obra literara escrita en forma de carta personal pero creada para ser publicada.

MEMOIR / MEMORIAS Unas *memorias* son un tipo de escrito de no ficción autobiográfica en el que el autor cuenta algo de su propia vida, generalmente centrándose

en la participación del autor en hechos significativos históricos o culturales, ya sea como participante directo o como testigo.

METAPHOR / METÁFORA Una *metáfora* es una figura literaria en la que algo se describe como si fuera otra cosa. La identificación sugiere una comparación entre las dos cosas que se identifican, como "la muerte es un largo sueño".

Una *metáfora mixta* ocurre cuando dos metáforas se unen. Por ejemplo, las espinas y la lluvia se mezclan ilógicamente en "le llovieron encima las espinas de la vida". Una *metáfora muerta* es aquella que se ha sobreutilizado mucho y se ha convertido en una expresión común, como "el brazo del sillón" o "la noche que cae".

MONOLOGUE / MONÓLOGO Un *monólogo* es un discurso narrado por completo por una sola persona o personaje.

MOTIF / MOTIVO El *motivo* es un objeto o idea que se repite de forma recurrente en una obra literaria.

NARRATION / NARRACIÓN Una *narración* es un escrito que cuenta una historia. El acto de contar una historia de forma oral también se llama *narración*. La *narrativa*, o relato, la cuenta el *narrador.* Un relato generalmente se cuenta en orden cronológico, en el orden en el que suceden los hechos, aunque puede incluir flashbacks y prefiguración. Las narrativas pueden ser verdaderas o inventadas. La narración es una de las muchas formas de discurso que existen y se usa en novelas, cuentos, obras de teatro, poemas narrativos, anécdotas, autobiografías, biografías e informes.

NARRATIVE / RELATO Se llama *relato* a la historia que se narra en una obra de ficción, de no-ficción, en un poema o en un drama. Los relatos a menudo se clasifican por su contenido o propósito. Un *relato de exploración* es una narración en primera persona de los viajes de un explorador en una tierra desconocida. "The Interesting Narrative of the Life of Olaudah Equiano" es un *relato de esclavos*, la narración de las experiencias de una persona esclavizada. Un *relato histórico* es la narración de hechos históricos significativos. Un *relato personal* es una narración en primera persona sobre una experiencia real. En un *relato de reflexión* el autor describe sus sentimientos sobre una escena, incidente, recuerdo o hecho. Un *relato no lineal* no sigue el orden cronológico. Puede contener flashbacks, secuencias de sueño u otros recursos que interrumpen el orden cronológico de los hechos.

NARRATOR / NARRADOR Un *narrador* es el hablante o el personaje que cuenta una historia. El cuento o novela lo puede narrar un personaje principal, un personaje menor o alguien que no está involucrado en la trama. El narrador puede hablar en primera persona o en tercera persona. Un *narrador omnisciente* lo sabe todo, mientras que un *narrador limitado* sólo sabe lo que hace un personaje.

NONFICTION / NO-FICCIÓN La *no-ficción* es un escrito en prosa que presenta y explica ideas o cuenta algo acerca de personas, lugares, ideas o hechos reales. Dos de los tipos principales de literatura de no-ficción son los escritos históricos y los escritos de reflexión. Los ensayos, las biografías, las autobiografías, los diarios y los reportajes son todos ejemplos de no-ficción.

NOVEL / NOVELA Una *novela* es una obra extensa de ficción. A menudo tiene una trama complicada, con personajes principales y secundarios, con un tema significativo y una ambientación variada. Las novelas pueden clasificarse de muchas maneras, basadas en los periodos históricos en los que se escribieron, en los temas que tratan, en las técnicas que se usan en ellas y en los movimientos literarios que las inspiraron. Una *novela corta* no es tan extensa como una novela, pero es más larga que un cuento.

ONOMATOPOEIA / ONOMATOPEYA La *onomatopeya* es el uso de palabras que imitan sonidos, tales como *zum, pío-pío, tic-tac* o *susurro*.

ORATORY / ORATORIA La *oratoria* es hablar en público de manera formal, persuasiva y emocionalmente atractiva. El "Discurso en la Convención de Virginia" es un ejemplo de oratoria.

OXYMORON / OXÍMORON Un *oxímoron* es una figura literaria que combina dos ideas opuestas o contradictorias. Un oxímoron, como "fuego helado", sugiere una paradoja en solo unas palabras.

PACING / RITMO LITERARIO El *ritmo literario* es la velocidad o el paso de la escritura. Los escritores usan diferentes ritmos literarios para lograr distintos efectos, como el suspenso.

PARADOX / PARADOJA Una *paradoja* es un enunciado que parece contradictorio pero que sin embargo presenta una verdad.

PARALLELISM / PARALELISMO El *paralelismo* es la presentación de ideas similares, en secuencia, usando la misma estructura gramatical.

PARALLEL STRUCTURE / ESTRUCTURA PARALELA En una lista, cada objeto listado debe usar *estructura paralela* en la cual la morfología y frase gramatical sea igual para todos los objetos.

PERSONIFICATION / PERSONIFICACIÓN La *personificación* es una forma de lenguaje figurado en la que se da rasgos y actitudes humanas a un sujeto no humano. La personificación efectiva de cosas o ideas hace que se vean llenas de vida, como si fueran humanas.

PHILOSOPHICAL ASSUMPTIONS / SUPOSICIONES FILOSÓFICAS Las creencias que se dan por sentadas son *suposiciones filosóficas*. Algunas suposiciones son *explícitas*, o enunciadas directamente. Otras suposiciones son *implícitas*, que quiere decir que el lector debe hacer inferencias para comprenderlas.

PLOT / TRAMA o ARGUMENTO La *trama* o *argumento* es la secuencia de los eventos que suceden en una obra literaria. En la mayoría de las obras de ficción, la trama implica tanto a los personajes como al conflicto central. La trama por lo general empieza con una *exposición* que introduce la ambientación, los personajes y la situación básica. A ello le sigue el *suceso desencadenante*, que introduce el conflicto central. Este conflicto aumenta durante el *desarrollo* hasta que alcanza el punto más alto de interés o suspenso, llamado *clímax*. Al clímax le sigue el final o resolución del conflicto central. Todos los hechos que ocurren después de la *resolución*, forman el *desenlace*. Todos los sucesos que conducen al clímax constituyen la *acción dramática creciente*. Los sucesos que siguen al clímax forman la *acción dramática decreciente*.

POETIC STRUCTURE / ESTRUCTURA POÉTICA Las *estructuras poéticas* básicas son los versos y las estrofas. Un *verso* es un grupo de palabras ordenadas en un mismo renglón. Un verso puede terminar, o cortarse, de distintas maneras. La variedad en la *extensión de los versos* crea ritmos inesperados.

En un *verso no encabalgado* la estructura gramatical y el sentido se completan al final de esa línea.

En un *verso encabalgado* tanto la estructura gramatical como el sentido de una línea continúa en el verso que sigue.

POETRY / POESÍA La *poesía* es uno de los tres géneros literarios más importantes. En poesía, la forma y el contenido están íntimamente relacionados, como dos caras de la misma moneda. Los poemas a menudo se dividen en versos y estrofas y emplean patrones rítmicos regulares, llamados metros. La mayoría de los poemas están escritos en un lenguaje altamente conciso, musical y emocionalmente rico. Muchos también hacen uso de imágenes, de figuras retóricas y de sonoros, tales como la rima.

POINT OF VIEW / PUNTO DE VISTA El *punto de vista* es la perspectiva desde la cual se narran o describen los hechos de un relato. Tres puntos de vista que se usan frecuentemente son: primera persona, tercera persona omnisciente y tercera persona limitada.

En el *punto de vista de primera persona*, el narrador es un personaje del relato y se refiere a sí mismo con el pronombre de primera persona "yo".

Los dos tipos de punto de vista de tercera persona, limitado y omnisciente, se llaman "tercera persona" porque el narrador usa pronombres de tercera persona como "él o "ella" para referirse a los personajes. No hay "yo" que narre la historia.

En los relatos contados desde el *punto de vista de tercera persona omnisciente*, el narrador conoce y cuenta cosas sobre lo que cada personaje piensa y siente.

En los relatos contados desde el *punto de vista de tercera persona limitada*, el narrador relata los pensamientos internos y sentimientos de sólo un personaje y todo se ve desde el punto de vista de ese personaje.

PREAMBLE / PREÁMBULO El *preámbulo* es un enunciado que explica quién expide un documento y con qué propósito.

PRIMARY SOURCE / FUENTE PRIMARIA Una *fuente primaria* es la que ha sido creada por alguien que participó u observó directamente el suceso que se describe.

PROSE / PROSA La *prosa* es la forma común del lenguaje escrito. La mayoría de los escritos que no son poesía, ni drama, ni canciones, se consideran prosa. La prosa es uno de los géneros literarios más importantes y puede ser de dos formas: de ficción y de no-ficción.

PROTAGONIST / PROTAGONISTA El o la *protagonista* es el personaje principal de una obra literaria.

REFRAIN / REFRÁN Un *refrán* es un verso o grupo de versos que se repite en un poema o canción. Muchos refranes terminan estrofas. Si bien es cierto que algunos refranes no tienen sentido, la mayoría sirve para aumentar el suspenso o para realzar un personaje o enfatizar un tema.

REGIONALISM / REGIONALISMO El *regionalismo* en literatura es la tendencia entre ciertos autores a escribir sobre áreas geográficas específicas. Los escritores regionales presentan la cultura específica de un área, incluyendo su dialecto, costumbres, creencias e historia.

REPETITION / REPETICIÓN La *repetición* de palabras y frases es un recurso literario que se usa en prosa y poesía para dar énfasis a ideas importantes.

RHETORICAL DEVICES / FIGURAS RETÓRICAS Las *figuras retóricas* son patrones especiales de palabras e ideas que dan énfasis y producen emoción, especialmente en discursos y otras presentaciones orales. El *paralelismo*, por ejemplo, es la repetición de una estructura gramatical con el propósito de crear un ritmo y hacer que las palabras resulten más memorables.

Otras figuras retóricas muy frecuentes son: la *analogía*, que establece una comparación entre dos cosas diferentes; el *lenguaje emocionalmente cargado*, en el que las palabras apelan a las emociones; la *concesión*, mediante la que se acepta el argumento del oponente; el *humor*, que usa el lenguaje y los detalles para hacer que los personajes o las situaciones resulten cómicas; la *paradoja*, enunciados que parecen contradecirse pero que presentan una verdad; la *reafirmación*, en la que se expresa la misma idea con distintas palabras; las *preguntas retóricas*, que son interrogaciones cuyas respuestas son obvias; el *tono*, la actitud del autor hacia la audiencia.

RHETORICAL QUESTIONS / PREGUNTAS RETÓRICAS Las *preguntas retóricas* llaman la atención a un hecho al insinuar respuestas obvias.

RIMA La *rima* es la repetición de los sonidos finales de las palabras. Las palabras que riman tienen sonidos vocálicos iguales en las sílabas finales acentuadas. Las consonantes que están antes de esas vocales acentuadas pueden ser diferentes, pero las consonantes que estén después de esas vocales deben ser iguales, como en *frog* y *bog* o en *willow* y *pillow*. La *rima de final de verso* tiene lugar cuando se repiten las palabras que riman al final de dos o más versos. La *rima interna* se produce cuando las palabras que riman están en el mismo verso. La *rima aproximada* tiene lugar cuando los sonidos son parecidos pero no exactos, como en *prove* y *glove*.

RITMO El *ritmo* es el patrón de cadencia o acentuación en la lengua hablada o escrita. La prosa y el verso libre se escriben en los patrones rítmicos irregulares del lenguaje hablado cotidiano.

ROMANTICISM / ROMANTICISMO El *romanticismo* fue un movimiento literario y artístico del siglo. XIX que surgió como reacción contra el neoclasicismo del siglo. XVII y que daba énfasis a la imaginación, la emoción, la naturaleza, la individualidad y lo extótico. El romanticismo es particularmente evidente en las obras de los transcendentalistas.

SECONDARY SOURCE / FUENTE SECUNDARIA Una *fuente secundaria* es la que ha sido creada por alguien con información indirecta del suceso que se describe. Las fuentes secundarias dependen de las *fuentes primarias*, o descripciones de primera mano.

SENSORY LANGUAGE / LENGUAJE SENSORIAL El *lenguaje sensorial* es un escrito o discurso que incluye detalles que apelan a uno o más de los sentidos.

SEQUENCE OF EVENTS / SECUENCIA DE SUCESOS Los autores a menudo usan la *secuencia de sucesos*, o el orden en que sucenden las cosas, para estructurar piezas de no ficción que describen hechos históricos o que explican cambios a lo largo del tiempo. Los autores frecuentemente describen hechos importantes en *orden cronológico*, u orden de tiempo.

SETTING / AMBIENTACIÓN La *ambientación* de una obra literaria es la época y el lugar en el que se desarrolla la acción. La ambientación puede servir varias funciones. Puede proporcionar el telón de fondo para la acción. Puede ser un elemento crucial en la trama o conflicto central. También puede crear una atmósfera emotiva.

SHORT STORY / CUENTO Un *cuento* es una obra breve de ficción. El cuento se parece a la novela, pero suele tener una trama y ambientación más sencillas. Además, el cuento tiende a revelar el carácter de los personajes en un momento particular en lugar de irlo desarrollando a lo largo de numerosos acontecimientos. Por ejemplo, el cuento "The Far and the Near" de Thomas Wolfe se centra en lo que le sucede a un maquinista cuando visita a la gente que lo ha saludado diariamente.

SERIAL COMMA / COMA EN SERIE En inglés, se pone una *coma en serie* después de cada objeto en una lista, excepto en el objeto final.

SIMILE / SÍMIL Un *símil* es una figura retórica en la que se usa la palabra *como* para establecer una comparación directa entre dos cosas.

SLANT RHYME / RIMA ASONANTE En una *rima asonante* los sonidos finales de dos versos del poema son similares, pero no idénticos.

SOCIAL COMMENTARY / COMENTARIO SOCIAL En obras de **comentario social,** el autor tiene como objetivo resaltar, de forma crítica, un aspecto de la sociedad.

SPEAKER / HABLANTE El *hablante* es la voz de un poema. Aunque a menudo el hablante es el poeta, el hablante puede ser también un personaje imaginario o incluso un objeto inanimado o cualquier otro tipo de sujeto no humano. Interpretar un poema a menudo depende de reconocer quién es el hablante, a quién se dirige el hablante y cuál es la actitud o tono del hablante.

STANZA / ESTROFA Una *estrofa* es un grupo de versos en un poema que se consideran una unidad. Muchos poemas se dividen en estrofas que están separadas por espacios. Las estrofas a menudo funcionan como los párrafos en la prosa. Cada estrofa enuncia y desarrolla una sola idea principal.

Las estrofas a menudo reciben su nombre del número de versos que las componen, como siguen:

1. Pareado o dístico: estrofa de dos versos
2. terceta: estrofa de tres versos
3. cuarteta: estrofa de cuatro versos
4. quintilla: estrofa de cinco versos
5. sextilla: estrofa de seis versos
6. septeto: estrofa de siete versos
7. octavilla: estrofa de ocho versos

STREAM OF CONSCIOUSNESS / MONÓLOGO INTERIOR El *monólogo interior* es una técnica narrativa que presenta los pensamientos como si vinieran directamente de la mente de un personaje. En vez de ordenarse cronológicamente, los hechos se presentan desde el punto de vista del personaje, mezclados con los pensamientos como si ocurrieran espontáneamente.

STYLE / ESTILO El *estilo* de un escritor incluye su dicción, tono, grado de formalidad, lenguaje figurado, ritmo, estructura gramatical, tamaño de las oraciones, organización, etc. En resumen, cada rasgo del uso del lenguaje de un escritor.

SUSPENSE / SUSPENSO El *suspenso* es la sensación creciente de incertidumbre sobre el resultado de los hechos.

Los escritores crean suspenso poniendo preguntas en la mente de sus lectores. El suspenso crece hasta el clímax de la trama, punto en el que alcanza su momento álgido.

SYMBOL / SÍMBOLO Un *símbolo* es algo que representa otra cosa. Un *símbolo convencional* es uno ampliamente conocido y aceptado, como un viaje como símbolo de la vida o una calavera como símbolo de la muerte. Un *símbolo personal* es el que desarrolla un autor en concreto para una obra en particular.

SYMBOLISM / SIMBOLISMO El *simbolismo* hace referencia al uso de personas, lugares u objetos que usa un autor para representar cualidades o ideas abstractas.

SYNTAX / SINTAXIS La *sintaxis* es la estructura de las oraciones.

THEME / TEMA Un *tema* es el mensaje central o la concepción de la vida que revela una obra literaria. El tema de un ensayo a menudo se menciona directamente en la tesis. En la mayoría de obras de ficción el tema se enuncia sólo indirectamente: un cuento, poema u obra de teatro a menudo tienen un *tema implícito*.

TONE / TONO El *tono* de una obra literaria es la actitud del escritor hacia su tema, sus personajes o su audiencia. El tono de un escritor puede ser formal o informal, amistoso o distante, personal o pretencioso. El tono de una obra también se puede describir como técnico, conversacional o coloquial.

TRANSCENDENTALISM /TRANSCENDENTALISMO El *transcendentalismo* fue un movimiento estadounidense literario y filosófico del siglo. XIX. Los transcendentalistas, que estaban radicados en Nueva Inglaterra, creían que la intuición y consciencia individual "transcendían" la experiencia y por tanto eran mejores guías a la verdad que los sentidos y la razón lógica. Influidos por el Romanticismo, los transcendentalistas respetaban el espíritu individual y el mundo natural, creyendo que lo divino estaba presente en todas partes, en la naturaleza y en cada persona.

USAGE / USO El *uso* es la manera en la que una palabra o frase se usa. El significado, pronunciación y ortografía de algunas de las palabras ha cambiado con el tiempo.

VOICE / VOZ La *voz* es el "sonido" distintivo de un escritor, o la manera en que "habla" en la página. Se relaciona a elementos tales como la dicción, los tipos de palabras, la sintaxis, el tipo de oraciones empleadas y el tono, que es la actitud del autor hacia el tema o la audiencia.

Every English word, depending on its meaning and its use in a sentence, can be identified as one of the eight parts of speech. These are nouns, pronouns, verbs, adjectives, adverbs, prepositions, conjunctions, and interjections. Understanding the parts of speech will help you learn the rules of English grammar and usage.

Nouns A **noun** names a person, place, or thing. A **common noun** names any one of a class of persons, places, or things. A **proper noun** names a specific person, place, or thing.

Common Noun	Proper Noun
writer, country, novel	Charles Dickens, Great Britain, *Hard Times*

Pronouns A **pronoun** is a word that stands for one or more nouns. The word to which a pronoun refers (whose place it takes) is the **antecedent** of the pronoun.

A **personal pronoun** refers to the person speaking (first person); the person spoken to (second person); or the person, place, or thing spoken about (third person).

	Singular	Plural
First Person	I, me, my, mine	we, us, our, ours
Second Person	you, your, yours	you, your, yours
Third Person	he, him, his, she, her, hers, it, its	they, them, their, theirs

A **reflexive pronoun** reflects the action of a verb back on its subject. It indicates that the person or thing performing the action also is receiving the action.

> I keep *myself* fit by taking a walk every day.

An **intensive pronoun** adds emphasis to a noun or pronoun.

> It took the work of the president *himself* to pass the law.

A **demonstrative** pronoun points out a specific person(s), place(s), or thing(s).

> this, that, these, those

A **relative pronoun** begins a subordinate clause and connects it to another idea in the sentence.

> that, which, who, whom, whose

An **interrogative pronoun** begins a question.

> what, which, who, whom, whose

An **indefinite pronoun** refers to a person, place, or thing that may or may not be specifically named.

> all, another, any, both, each, everyone, few, most, none, no one, somebody

Verbs A **verb** expresses action or the existence of a state or condition.

An **action verb** tells what action someone or something is performing.

> gather, read, work, jump, imagine, analyze, conclude

A **linking verb** connects the subject with another word that identifies or describes the subject. The most common linking verb is *be*.

> appear, be, become, feel, look, remain, seem, smell, sound, stay, taste

A **helping verb,** or **auxiliary verb,** is added to a main verb to make a verb phrase.

> be, do, have, should, can, could, may, might, must, will, would

Adjectives An **adjective** modifies a noun or pronoun by describing it or giving it a more specific meaning. An adjective answers the questions:

What kind?	*purple* hat, *happy* face, *loud* sound
Which one?	*this* bowl
How many?	*three* cars
How much?	*enough* food

The articles *the, a,* and *an* are adjectives.

A **proper adjective** is an adjective derived from a proper noun.

> French, Shakespearean

Adverbs An **adverb** modifies a verb, an adjective, or another adverb by telling *where, when, how,* or *to what extent*.

> will answer *soon, extremely* sad, calls *more* often

Prepositions A **preposition** relates a noun or pronoun that appears with it to another word in the sentence.

> Dad made a meal *for* us. We talked *till* dusk. Bo missed school *because of* his illness.

Conjunctions A **conjunction** connects words or groups of words. A **coordinating conjunction** joins words or groups of words of equal rank.

> bread *and* cheese, brief *but* powerful

Correlative conjunctions are used in pairs to connect words or groups of words of equal importance.

> *both* Luis *and* Rosa, *neither* you *nor* I

GLOSSARY: GRAMMAR HANDBOOK

Subordinating conjunctions indicate the connection between two ideas by placing one below the other in rank or importance. A subordinating conjunction introduces a subordinate, or dependent, clause.

> We will miss her *if* she leaves. Hank shrieked *when* he slipped on the ice.

Interjections An **interjection** expresses feeling or emotion. It is not related to other words in the sentence.

> ah, hey, ouch, well, yippee

PHRASES AND CLAUSES

Phrases A **phrase** is a group of words that does not have both a subject and a verb and that functions as one part of speech. A phrase expresses an idea but cannot stand alone.

Prepositional Phrases A **prepositional phrase** is a group of words that begins with a preposition and ends with a noun or pronoun that is the **object of the preposition.**

> before dawn   as a result of the rain

An **adjective phrase** is a prepositional phrase that modifies a noun or pronoun.

> Eliza appreciates the beauty **of a well-crafted poem.**

An **adverb phrase** is a prepositional phrase that modifies a verb, an adjective, or an adverb.

> She reads Spenser's sonnets **with great pleasure.**

Appositive Phrases An **appositive** is a noun or pronoun placed next to another noun or pronoun to add information about it. An **appositive phrase** consists of an appositive and its modifiers.

> Mr. Roth, **my music teacher,** is sick.

Verbal Phrases A **verbal** is a verb form that functions as a different part of speech (not as a verb) in a sentence. **Participles, gerunds,** and **infinitives** are verbals.

A **verbal phrase** includes a verbal and any modifiers or complements it may have. Verbal phrases may function as nouns, as adjectives, or as adverbs.

A **participle** is a verb form that can act as an adjective. Present participles end in *-ing;* past participles of regular verbs end in *-ed.*

A **participial phrase** consists of a participle and its modifiers or complements. The entire phrase acts as an adjective.

> Jenna's backpack, **loaded with equipment,** was heavy.
> **Barking incessantly,** the dogs chased the squirrels out of sight.

A **gerund** is a verb form that ends in *-ing* and is used as a noun.

A **gerund phrase** consists of a gerund with any modifiers or complements, all acting together as a noun.

> **Taking photographs of wildlife** is her main hobby. [acts as subject]
> We always enjoy **listening to live music.** [acts as object]

An **infinitive** is a verb form, usually preceded by *to,* that can act as a noun, an adjective, or an adverb.

An **infinitive phrase** consists of an infinitive and its modifiers or complements, and sometimes its subject, all acting together as a single part of speech.

> She tries **to get out into the wilderness often.** [acts as a noun; direct object of *tries*]
> The Tigers are the team **to beat.** [acts as an adjective; describes *team*]
> I drove twenty miles **to witness the event.** [acts as an adverb; tells why I drove]

Clauses A **clause** is a group of words with its own subject and verb.

Independent Clauses An independent clause can stand by itself as a complete sentence.

> George Orwell wrote with extraordinary insight.

Subordinate Clauses A subordinate clause, also called a dependent clause, cannot stand by itself as a complete sentence. Subordinate clauses always appear connected in some way with one or more independent clauses.

> George Orwell, **who wrote with extraordinary insight,** produced many politically relevant works.

An **adjective clause** is a subordinate clause that acts as an adjective. It modifies a noun or a pronoun by telling *what kind* or *which one.* Also called relative clauses, adjective clauses usually begin with a **relative pronoun:** *who, which, that, whom,* or *whose.*

> "The Lamb" is the poem **that I memorized for class.**

An **adverb clause** is a subordinate clause that, like an adverb, modifies a verb, an adjective, or an adverb. An adverb clause tells *where, when, in what way, to what extent, under what condition,* or *why.*

The students will read another poetry collection **if their schedule allows.**
When I recited the poem, Mr. Lopez was impressed.

A **noun clause** is a subordinate clause that acts as a noun.

William Blake survived on **whatever he made as an engraver.**

SENTENCE STRUCTURE

Subject and Predicate A **sentence** is a group of words that expresses a complete thought. A sentence has two main parts: a *subject* and a *predicate*.

A **fragment** is a group of words that does not express a complete thought. It lacks an independent clause.

The **subject** tells *whom* or *what* the sentence is about. The **predicate** tells what the subject of the sentence does or is.

A subject or a predicate can consist of a single word or of many words. All the words in the subject make up the **complete subject.** All the words in the predicate make up the **complete predicate.**

Complete Subject   Complete Predicate
Both of those girls | have already read *Macbeth.*

The **simple subject** is the essential noun, pronoun, or group of words acting as a noun that cannot be left out of the complete subject. The **simple predicate** is the essential verb or verb phrase that cannot be left out of the complete predicate.

Both of those girls | **have** already **read** *Macbeth.*
[Simple subject: *Both;* simple predicate: *have read*]

A **compound subject** is two or more subjects that have the same verb and are joined by a conjunction.

Neither the horse nor the driver looked tired.

A **compound predicate** is two or more verbs that have the same subject and are joined by a conjunction.

She **sneezed and coughed** throughout the trip.

Complements A **complement** is a word or word group that completes the meaning of the subject or verb in a sentence. There are four kinds of complements: *direct objects, indirect objects, objective complements,* and *subject complements.*

A **direct object** is a noun, a pronoun, or a group of words acting as a noun that receives the action of a transitive verb.

We watched the **liftoff.**
She drove **Zach** to the launch site.

An **indirect object** is a noun or pronoun that appears with a direct object and names the person or thing to which or for which something is done.

He sold the **family** a mirror. [The direct object is *mirror.*]

An **objective complement** is an adjective or noun that appears with a direct object and describes or renames it.

The decision made her **unhappy.**
[The direct object is *her.*]
Many consider Shakespeare the greatest **playwright.** [The direct object is *Shakespeare.*]

A **subject complement** follows a linking verb and tells something about the subject. There are two kinds: *predicate nominatives* and *predicate adjectives.*

A **predicate nominative** is a noun or pronoun that follows a linking verb and identifies or renames the subject.

"A Modest Proposal" is a **pamphlet.**

A **predicate adjective** is an adjective that follows a linking verb and describes the subject of the sentence.

"A Modest Proposal" is **satirical.**

Classifying Sentences by Structure

Sentences can be classified according to the kind and number of clauses they contain. The four basic sentence structures are *simple, compound, complex,* and *compound-complex.*

A **simple sentence** consists of one independent clause.

Terrence enjoys modern British literature.

A **compound sentence** consists of two or more independent clauses. The clauses are joined by a conjunction or a semicolon.

Terrence enjoys modern British literature, but his brother prefers the classics.

A **complex sentence** consists of one independent clause and one or more subordinate clauses.

Terrence, who reads voraciously, enjoys modern British literature.

A **compound-complex sentence** consists of two or more independent clauses and one or more subordinate clauses.

Terrence, who reads voraciously, enjoys modern British literature, but his brother prefers the classics.

Classifying Sentences by Function

Sentences can be classified according to their function or purpose. The four types are *declarative, interrogative, imperative,* and *exclamatory.*

A **declarative sentence** states an idea and ends with a period.

An **interrogative sentence** asks a question and ends with a question mark.

An **imperative sentence** gives an order or a direction and ends with either a period or an exclamation mark.

An **exclamatory sentence** conveys a strong emotion and ends with an exclamation mark.

PARAGRAPH STRUCTURE

An effective paragraph is organized around one **main idea,** which is often stated in a **topic sentence.** The other sentences support the main idea. To give the paragraph **unity,** make sure the connection between each sentence and the main idea is clear.

Unnecessary Shift in Person

Do not change needlessly from one grammatical person to another. Keep the person consistent in your sentences.

> **Max** went to the bakery, but **you** can't buy mints there. [shift from third person to second person]

> **Max** went to the bakery, but **he** can't buy mints there. [consistent]

Unnecessary Shift in Voice

Do not change needlessly from active voice to passive voice in your use of verbs.

> Elena and I **searched** the trail for evidence, but no clues **were found.** [shift from active voice to passive voice]
> Elena and I **searched** the trail for evidence, but we **found** no clues. [consistent]

AGREEMENT

Subject and Verb Agreement

A singular subject must have a singular verb. A plural subject must have a plural verb.

> **Dr. Boone uses** a telescope to view the night sky.
> The **students use** a telescope to view the night sky.

A verb always agrees with its subject, not its object.

> *Incorrect:* The best part of the show were the jugglers.
> *Correct:* The best part of the show was the jugglers.

A phrase or clause that comes between a subject and verb does not affect subject-verb agreement.

> His **theory,** as well as his claims, **lacks** support.

Two subjects joined by *and* usually take a plural verb.

> The **dog** and the **cat are** healthy.

Two singular subjects joined by *or* or *nor* take a singular verb.

> The **dog** or the **cat is** hiding.

Two plural subjects joined by *or* or *nor* take a plural verb.

> The **dogs** or the **cats are** coming home with us.

When a singular and a plural subject are joined by *or* or *nor,* the verb agrees with the closer subject.

> Either the **dogs** or the **cat is** behind the door.
> Either the **cat** or the **dogs are** behind the door.

Pronoun and Antecedent Agreement

Pronouns must agree with their antecedents in number and gender. Use singular pronouns with singular antecedents and plural pronouns with plural antecedents.

> **Doris Lessing** uses **her** writing to challenge ideas about women's roles.
> **Writers** often use **their** skills to promote social change.

Use a singular pronoun when the antecedent is a singular indefinite pronoun such as *anybody, each, either, everybody, neither, no one, one,* or *someone.*

> Judge **each** of the articles on **its** merits.

Use a plural pronoun when the antecedent is a plural indefinite pronoun such as *both, few, many,* or *several.*

> **Both** of the articles have **their** flaws.

The indefinite pronouns *all, any, more, most, none,* and *some* can be singular or plural depending on the number of the word to which they refer.

> **Most** of the *books* are in **their** proper places.
> **Most** of the *book* has been torn from **its** binding.

GLOSSARY: GRAMMAR HANDBOOK

Principal Parts of Regular and Irregular Verbs

A verb has four principal parts:

Present	Present Participle	Past	Past Participle
learn	learning	learned	learned
discuss	discussing	discussed	discussed
stand	standing	stood	stood
begin	beginning	began	begun

Regular verbs such as *learn* and *discuss* form the past and past participle by adding *-ed* to the present form. **Irregular verbs** such as *stand* and *begin* form the past and past participle in other ways. If you are in doubt about the principal parts of an irregular verb, check a dictionary.

The Tenses of Verbs

The different tenses of verbs indicate the time an action or condition occurs.

The **present tense** expresses an action that happens regularly or states a current condition or a general truth.

Tourists **flock** to the site yearly.

Daily exercise **is** good for your heallth.

The **past tense** expresses a completed action or a condition that is no longer true.

The squirrel **dropped** the nut and **ran** up the tree.
I **was** very tired last night by 9:00.

The **future tense** indicates an action that will happen in the future or a condition that will be true.

The Glazers **will visit** us tomorrow.
They **will be** glad to arrive from their long journey.

The **present perfect tense** expresses an action that happened at an indefinite time in the past or an action that began in the past and continues into the present.

Someone **has cleaned** the trash from the park.
The puppy **has been** under the bed all day.

The **past perfect tense** shows an action that was completed before another action in the past.

Gerard **had revised** his essay before he turned it in.

The **future perfect tense** indicates an action that will have been completed before another action takes place.

Mimi **will have painted** the kitchen by the time we finish the shutters.

Degrees of Comparison

Adjectives and adverbs take different forms to show the three degrees of comparison: the *positive*, the *comparative*, and the *superlative*.

Positive	Comparative	Superlative
fast	faster	fastest
crafty	craftier	craftiest
abruptly	more abruptly	most abruptly
badly	worse	worst

Using Comparative and Superlative Adjectives and Adverbs

Use comparative adjectives and adverbs to compare two things. Use superlative adjectives and adverbs to compare three or more things.

This season's weather was **drier** than last year's.
This season has been one of the **driest** on record.
Jake practices **more often** than Jamal.
Of everyone in the band, Jake practices **most often.**

Pronoun Case

The **case** of a pronoun is the form it takes to show its function in a sentence. There are three pronoun cases: *nominative*, *objective*, and *possessive*.

Nominative	Objective	Possessive
I, you, he, she, it, we, you, they	me, you, him, her, it, us, you, them	my, your, yours, his, her, hers, its, our, ours, their, theirs

Use the **nominative case** when a pronoun functions as a *subject* or as a *predicate nominative.*

They are going to the movies. [subject]
The biggest movie fan is **she.** [predicate nominative]

Use the **objective case** for a pronoun acting as a *direct object*, an *indirect object*, or the *object of a preposition.*

The ending of the play surprised **me.** [direct object]
Mary gave **us** two tickets to the play. [indirect object]
The audience cheered for **him.** [object of preposition]

Use the **possessive case** to show ownership.

The red suitcase is **hers.**

Diction The words you choose contribute to the overall effectiveness of your writing. **Diction** refers to word choice and to the clearness and correctness of those words. You can improve one aspect of your diction by choosing carefully between commonly confused words, such as the pairs listed below.

accept, except

Accept is a verb that means "to receive" or "to agree to." *Except* is a preposition that means "other than" or "leaving out."

> Please **accept** my offer to buy you lunch this weekend.

> He is busy every day **except** the weekends.

affect, effect

Affect is normally a verb meaning "to influence" or "to bring about a change in." *Effect* is usually a noun meaning "result."

> The distractions outside **affect** Steven's ability to concentrate.

> The teacher's remedies had a positive **effect** on Steven's ability to concentrate.

among, between

Among is usually used with three or more items, and it emphasizes collective relationships or indicates distribution. *Between* is generally used with only two items, but it can be used with more than two if the emphasis is on individual (one-to-one) relationships within the group.

> I had to choose a snack **among** the various vegetables.

> He handed out the booklets **among** the conference participants.

> Our school is **between** a park and an old barn.

> The tournament included matches **between** France, Spain, Mexico, and the United States.

amount, number

Amount refers to overall quantity and is mainly used with mass nouns (those that can't be counted). *Number* refers to individual items that can be counted.

> The **amount** of attention that great writers have paid to Shakespeare is remarkable.

> A **number** of important English writers have been fascinated by the legend of King Arthur.

assure, ensure, insure

Assure means "to convince [someone of something]; to guarantee." *Ensure* means "to make certain [that something happens]." *Insure* means "to arrange for payment in case of loss."

> The attorney **assured** us we'd win the case.

> The rules **ensure** that no one gets treated unfairly.

> Many professional musicians **insure** their valuable instruments.

bad, badly

Use the adjective *bad* before a noun or after linking verbs such as *feel, look,* and *seem.* Use *badly* whenever an adverb is required.

> The situation may seem **bad**, but it will improve over time.

> Though our team played **badly** today, we will focus on practicing for the next match.

beside, besides

Beside means "at the side of" or "close to." *Besides* means "in addition to."

> The stapler sits **beside** the pencil sharpener in our classroom.

> **Besides** being very clean, the classroom is also very organized.

can, may

The helping verb *can* generally refers to the ability to do something. The helping verb *may* generally refers to permission to do something.

> I **can** run one mile in six minutes.

> **May** we have a race during recess?

complement, compliment

The verb *complement* means "to enhance"; the verb *compliment* means "to praise."

> Online exercises **complement** the textbook lessons.

> Ms. Lewis **complimented** our team on our excellent debate.

compose, comprise

Compose means "to make up; constitute." *Comprise* means "to include or contain." Remember that the whole comprises its parts or is composed of its parts, and the parts compose the whole.

> The assignment **comprises** three different tasks.

> The assignment is **composed** of three different tasks.

> Three different tasks **compose** the assignment.

different from, different than

Different from is generally preferred over *different than*, but *different than* can be used before a clause. Always use *different from* before a noun or pronoun.

> Your point of view is so **different from** mine.

> His idea was so **different from** [or **different than**] what we had expected.

farther, further

Use *farther* to refer to distance. Use *further* to mean "to a greater degree or extent" or "additional."

> Chiang has traveled **farther** than anybody else in the class.

> If I want **further** details about his travels, I can read his blog.

fewer, less

Use *fewer* for things that can be counted. Use *less* for amounts or quantities that cannot be counted. *Fewer* must be followed by a plural noun.

Fewer students drive to school since the weather improved.

There is **less** noise outside in the mornings.

good, well

Use the adjective *good* before a noun or after a linking verb. Use *well* whenever an adverb is required, such as when modifying a verb.

I feel **good** after sleeping for eight hours.

I did **well** on my test, and my soccer team played **well** in that afternoon's game. It was a **good** day!

its, it's

The word *its* with no apostrophe is a possessive pronoun. The word *it's* is a contraction of "it is."

Angelica will try to fix the computer and **its** keyboard.

It's a difficult job, but she can do it.

lay, lie

Lay is a transitive verb meaning "to set or put something down." Its principal parts are *lay, laying, laid, laid. Lie* is an intransitive verb meaning "to recline" or "to exist in a certain place." Its principal parts are *lie, lying, lay, lain.*

Please **lay** that box down and help me with the sofa.

When we are done moving, I am going to **lie** down.

My hometown **lies** sixty miles north of here.

like, as

Like is a preposition that usually means "similar to" and precedes a noun or pronoun. The conjunction *as* means "in the way that" and usually precedes a clause.

Like the other students, I was prepared for a quiz.

As I said yesterday, we expect to finish before noon.

Use **such as,** not **like,** before a series of examples.

Foods **such as** apples, nuts, and pretzels make good snacks.

of, have

Do not use *of* in place of *have* after auxiliary verbs such as *would, could, should, may, might,* or *must.* The contraction of *have* is formed by adding *-ve* after these verbs.

I **would have** stayed after school today, but I had to help cook at home.

Mom **must've** called while I was still in the gym.

principal, principle

Principal can be an adjective meaning "main; most important." It can also be a noun meaning "chief officer of a school." *Principle* is a noun meaning "moral rule" or "fundamental truth."

His strange behavior was the **principal** reason for our concern.

Democratic **principles** form the basis of our country's laws.

raise, rise

Raise is a transitive verb that usually takes a direct object. *Rise* is intransitive and never takes a direct object.

Iliana and Josef **raise** the flag every morning.

They **rise** from their seats and volunteer immediately whenever help is needed.

than, then

The conjunction *than* is used to connect the two parts of a comparison. The adverb *then* usually refers to time.

My backpack is heavier **than** hers.

I will finish my homework and **then** meet my friends at the park.

that, which, who

Use the relative pronoun *that* to refer to things or people. Use *which* only for things and *who* only for people.

That introduces a restrictive phrase or clause, that is, one that is essential to the meaning of the sentence. *Which* introduces a nonrestrictive phrase or clause—one that adds information but could be deleted from the sentence—and is preceded by a comma.

Ben ran to the park **that** just reopened.

The park, **which** just reopened, has many attractions.

The man **who** built the park loves to see people smiling.

when, where, why

Do not use *when, where,* or *why* directly after a linking verb, such as *is.* Reword the sentence.

Incorrect: The morning is when he left for the beach.

Correct: He left for the beach in the morning.

who, whom

In formal writing, use *who* only as a subject in clauses and sentences. Use *whom* only as the object of a verb or of a preposition.

Who paid for the tickets?

Whom should I pay for the tickets?

I can't recall to **whom** I gave the money for the tickets.

your, you're

Your is a possessive pronoun expressing ownership. *You're* is the contraction of "you are."

Have you finished writing **your** informative essay?

You're supposed to turn it in tomorrow. If **you're** late, **your** grade will be affected.

Capitalization

First Words

Capitalize the first word of a sentence.

Stories about knights and their deeds interest me.

Capitalize the first word of direct speech.

Sharon asked, "Do you like stories about knights?"

Capitalize the first word of a quotation that is a complete sentence.

Einstein said, "Anyone who has never made a mistake has never tried anything new."

Proper Nouns and Proper Adjectives

Capitalize all proper nouns, including geographical names, historical events and periods, and names of organizations.

Thames River   John Keats   the Renaissance

United Nations   World War II   Sierra Nevada

Capitalize all proper adjectives.

Shakespearean play   British invaision

American citizen   Latin American literature

Academic Course Names

Capitalize course names only if they are language courses, are followed by a number, or are preceded by a proper noun or adjective.

Spanish   Honors Chemistry   History 101

geology   algebra   social studies

Titles

Capitalize personal titles when followed by the person's name.

Ms. Hughes   Dr. Perez   King George

Capitalize titles showing family relationships when they are followed by a specific person's name, unless they are preceded by a possessive noun or pronoun.

Uncle Oscar   Mangan's sister   his aunt Tessa

Capitalize the first word and all other key words in the titles of books, stories, songs, and other works of art.

Frankenstein   "Shooting an Elephant"

Punctuation

End Marks

Use a **period** to end a declarative sentence or an imperative sentence.

We are studying the structure of sonnets.

Read the biography of Mary Shelley.

Use periods with initials and abbreviations.

D. H. Lawrence   Mrs. Browning

Mt. Everest   Maple St.

Use a **question mark** to end an interrogative sentence.

What is Macbeth's fatal flaw?

Use an **exclamation mark** after an exclamatory sentence or a forceful imperative sentence.

That's a beautiful painting!   Let me go now!

Commas

Use a **comma** before a coordinating conjunction to separate two independent clauses in a compound sentence.

The game was very close, but we were victorious.

Use commas to separate three or more words, phrases, or clauses in a series.

William Blake was a writer, artist, and printer.

Use commas to separate coordinate adjectives.

It was a witty, amusing novel.

Use a comma after an introductory word, phrase, or clause.

When the novelist finished his book, he celebrated with his family.

Use commas to set off nonessential expressions.

Old English, of course, requires translation.

Use commas with places and dates.

Coventry, England   September 1, 1939

Semicolons

Use a **semicolon** to join closely related independent clauses that are not already joined by a conjunction.

Tanya likes to write poetry; Heather prefers prose.

Use semicolons to avoid confusion when items in a series contain commas.

They traveled to London, England; Madrid, Spain; and Rome, Italy.

Colons

Use a **colon** before a list of items following an independent clause.

Notable Victorian poets include the following: Tennyson, Arnold, Housman, and Hopkins.

Use a colon to introduce information that summarizes or explains the independent clause before it.

She just wanted to do one thing: rest.

Malcolm loves volunteering: He reads to sick children every Saturday afternoon.

Quotation Marks

Use **quotation marks** to enclose a direct quotation.

"Short stories," Ms. Hildebrand said, "should have rich, well-developed characters."

An **indirect quotation** does not require quotation marks.

Ms. Hildebrand said that short stories should have well-developed characters.

Use quotation marks around the titles of short written works, episodes in a series, songs, and works mentioned as parts of collections.

"The Lagoon"   "Boswell Meets Johnson"

Italics

Italicize the titles of long written works, movies, television and radio shows, lengthy works of music, paintings, and sculptures.

Howards End   *60 Minutes*   *Guernica*

For handwritten material, you can use underlining instead of italics.

The Princess Bride   Mona Lisa

Dashes

Use **dashes** to indicate an abrupt change of thought, a dramatic interrupting idea, or a summary statement.

I read the entire first act of *Macbeth*—you won't believe what happens next.

The director—what's her name again?—attended the movie premiere.

Hyphens

Use a **hyphen** with certain numbers, after certain prefixes, with two or more words used as one word, and with a compound modifier that comes before a noun.

seventy-two
self-esteem
president-elect
five-year contract

Parentheses

Use **parentheses** to set off asides and explanations when the material is not essential or when it consists of one or more sentences. When the sentence in parentheses interrupts the larger sentence, it does not have a capital letter or a period.

He listened intently (it was too dark to see who was speaking) to try to identify the voices.

When a sentence in parentheses falls between two other complete sentences, it should start with a capital letter and end with a period.

The quarterback threw three touchdown passes. (We knew he could do it.) Our team won the game by two points.

Apostrophes

Add an **apostrophe** and an *s* to show the possessive case of most singular nouns and of plural nouns that do not end in *-s* or *-es*.

Blake's poems   the mice's whiskers

Names ending in *s* form their possessives in the same way, except for classical and biblical names, which add only an apostrophe to form the possessive.

Dickens's   Hercules'

Add an apostrophe to show the possessive case of plural nouns ending in *-s* and *-es*.

the girls' songs   the Ortizes' car

Use an apostrophe in a contraction to indicate the position of the missing letter or letters.

She's never read a Coleridge poem she didn't like.

Brackets

Use **brackets** to enclose clarifying information inserted within a quotation.

Columbus's journal entry from October 21, 1492, begins as follows: "At 10 o'clock, we arrived at a cape of the island [San Salvador], and anchored, the other vessels in company."

Ellipses

Use three ellipsis points, also known as an **ellipsis,** to indicate where you have omitted words from quoted material.

Wollestonecraft wrote, "The education of women has of late been more attended to than formerly; yet they are still . . . ridiculed or pitied. . . ."

In the example above, the four dots at the end of the sentence are the three ellipsis points plus the period from the original sentence.

Use an ellipsis to indicate a pause or interruption in speech.

"When he told me the news," said the coach, "I was . . . I was shocked . . . completely shocked."

Spelling

Spelling Rules

Learning the rules of English spelling will help you make **generalizations** about how to spell words.

Word Parts

The three word parts that can combine to form a word are roots, prefixes, and suffixes. Many of these word parts come from the Greek, Latin, and Anglo-Saxon languages.

The **root word** carries a word's basic meaning.

Root and Origin	Meaning	Examples
-leg- (-log-) [Gr.]	to say, speak	*legal, logic*
-pon- (-pos-) [L.]	to put, place	*postpone, deposit*

A **prefix** is one or more syllables added to the beginning of a word that alter the meaning of the root.

Prefix and Origin	Meaning	Example
anti- [Gr.]	against	*antipathy*
inter- [L.]	between	*international*
mis- [A.S.]	wrong	*misplace*

A **suffix** is a letter or group of letters added to the end of a root word that changes the word's meaning or part of speech.

Suffix and Origin	Meaning and Example	Part of Speech
-ful [A.S.]	full of: *scornful*	adjective
-ity [L.]	state of being: *adversity*	noun
-ize (-ise) [Gr.]	to make: *idolize*	verb
-ly [A.S.]	in a manner: *calmly*	adverb

Rules for Adding Suffixes to Root Words

When adding a suffix to a root word ending in *y* preceded by a consonant, change *y* to *i* unless the suffix begins with *i*.

   ply + -able = pliable   happy + -ness = happiness

   defy + -ing = defying   cry + -ing = crying

For a root word ending in *e*, drop the *e* when adding a suffix beginning with a vowel.

   drive + -ing = driving   move + -able = movable

   SOME EXCEPTIONS: traceable, seeing, dyeing

For root words ending with a consonant + vowel + consonant in a stressed syllable, double the final consonant when adding a suffix that begins with a vowel.

   mud + -y = muddy   submit + -ed = submitted

   SOME EXCEPTIONS: mixing, fixed

Rules for Adding Prefixes to Root Words

When a prefix is added to a root word, the spelling of the root remains the same.

   un- + certain = uncertain   mis- + spell = misspell

With some prefixes, the spelling of the prefix changes when joined to the root to make the pronunciation easier.

   in- + mortal = immortal   ad- + vert = avert

Orthographic Patterns

Certain letter combinations in English make certain sounds. For instance, *ph* sounds like *f*, *eigh* usually makes a long *a* sound, and the *k* before an *n* is often silent.

   pharmacy   n**eigh**bor   **k**nowledge

Understanding **orthographic patterns** such as these can help you improve your spelling.

Forming Plurals

The plural form of most nouns is formed by adding -*s* to the singular.

   computer**s**   gadget**s**   Washington**s**

For words ending in *s, ss, x, z, sh,* or *ch,* add -*es.*

   circus**es**   tax**es**   wish**es**   bench**es**

For words ending in *y* or *o* preceded by a vowel, add -*s.*

   key**s**   patio**s**

For words ending in *y* preceded by a consonant, change the *y* to an *i* and add -*es.*

   cit**ies**   enem**ies**   troph**ies**

For most words ending in *o* preceded by a consonant, add -*es.*

   echo**es**   tomato**es**

Some words form the plural in irregular ways.

   women   oxen   children   teeth   deer

Foreign Words Used in English

Some words used in English are actually foreign words that have been adopted. Learning to spell these words requires memorization. When in doubt, check a dictionary.

   sushi   enchilada   au pair   fiancé

   laissez faire   croissant

Analyzing Text

Allegory, 681

Allusion, 46, 294, 344

American regional art, 472, 473

Analytical argument, 368

Analyze, 24, 34, 58, 165, 180, 414, 657, 680, 689, 802

  essential question, 79, 98, 114, 122, 210, 226, 234, 244, 258, 334, 343, 356, 367, 375, 469, 477, 488, 499, 507, 517, 527, 713, 734, 824, 839, 853

  media, 58, 89, 234, 349, 689

    essential question, 477, 719

    present and discuss, 477, 719

    review and synthesize, 477, 719

  prepare to compare, 856

  present and discuss, 79, 98, 114, 122, 210, 226, 234, 244, 258, 334, 343, 356, 367, 375, 469, 477, 488, 499, 507, 517, 527, 713, 734, 824, 839, 853

  review and clarify, 79, 98, 114, 122, 210, 226, 234, 244, 258, 334, 343, 356, 367, 375, 469, 488, 499, 517, 527, 713, 734, 824, 839, 853

  review and synthesize, 477, 507

Anecdotes, 415

Argument, 6

  analytical, 368

  claim, 295

  counterclaims, 295

  development of ideas, 211

  historical narrative as, 81

  persuasive appeals, 25

  rhetoric, 335

  structure, 295

Argumentative text, 548

Art and photography, 310, 472, 502

Assess, 189

Audience, 116

Audio, 186, 346, 686

Audio performance, 687

Author's style

  audience, 336

  author's choices, 659, 855

  author's point of view, 715

  diction, 336, 417

    colloquial language, 336, 417

    conversational tone, 417

    formal, 336

    technical language, 417

  enumeration, 37

  figurative language, 855

    metaphors, 855

    similes, 855

  formality, 27

  historical narrative as argument, 81

  irony, 358

    dramatic, 358

    situational, 358

    verbal, 358

  Irony, 659

    dramatic irony, 659

    verbal irony, 659

  mixed diction, 167

  onomatopoeia, 167

  parallelism, 49

  realism, 683

  rhetorical devices

    antithesis, 124

    parallelsim, 124

  syntax, 27

  tone, 417

  usage, 27, 336

  voice, 116

  word choice, 429

    dialect, 429

    idiomatic expressions, 429

  word pairing, 167

  words and phrases, 336

Autobiography, 93, 99, 481, 489, 704, 705

Biography, 72, 102, 107

Cite textual evidence, 24, 25, 34, 35, 46, 47, 58, 79, 80, 99, 114, 115, 122, 123, 164, 180, 181, 189, 210, 211, 226, 234, 244, 245, 258, 259, 294, 295, 304, 305, 334, 343, 344, 356, 357, 367, 368, 414, 415, 426, 427, 444, 445, 469, 470, 488, 499, 500, 507, 517, 518, 527, 528, 597, 598, 625, 626, 657, 658, 680, 681, 682, 689, 713, 714, 734, 735, 774, 775, 788, 789, 802, 803, 824, 825, 839, 840, 853, 854

Close read, 19, 20, 24, 31, 32, 34, 43, 46, 89, 157, 158, 160, 174, 176, 178, 290, 292, 302, 409, 411, 412, 421, 422, 424, 433, 434, 436, 439, 442, 564, 567, 570, 572, 575, 578, 582, 587, 588, 595, 597, 604, 606, 608, 613, 615, 619, 623, 625, 631, 635, 639, 643, 644, 648, 653, 655, 657,

662, 664, 667, 670, 672, 674, 677, 680, 765, 767, 768, 771, 772, 783, 784, 786, 795, 797, 798, 800

  annotate, 24, 34, 46, 79, 98, 114, 122, 164, 180, 210, 244, 258, 294, 304, 334, 343, 356, 367, 414, 426, 444, 469, 488, 559, 774, 788, 802, 824, 839, 853

  close-read guide, 131, 267, 385, 537, 743, 863

  conclude, 24, 34, 46, 79, 98, 114, 122, 164, 180, 210, 226, 244, 258, 294, 304, 343, 414, 426, 444, 469, 488, 499, 517, 527, 559, 713, 734, 774, 788, 802, 824, 839, 853

  notice, 517

  questions, 24, 34, 46, 79, 98, 114, 122, 164, 180, 210, 226, 244, 258, 294, 304, 334, 343, 356, 367, 375, 414, 426, 444, 469, 488, 499, 517, 527, 559, 713, 734, 774, 788, 802, 824, 839, 853

Close review, 58

  conclude, 58, 89, 189, 234, 316, 349, 477, 507, 689, 719

  questions, 58, 89, 189, 234, 316, 349, 477, 507, 689, 719

Compare and contrast, 58, 180, 774

Comparing texts, 72

  humor, 418

  legal opinion and magazine article, 360, 370, 378

  memoir and poems, 420, 510

  memoir and short story, 406

  narrative choices, 856

  short stories, 828, 842

Comparing text to media

  American regional art, 472

  artwork, 478

  audio performance of drama, 686, 690

  autobiography and video interview, 704

  fine art gallery, 462

  graphic adaptation, 82, 90

  interview, 716

  photographs, 502, 508

  podcast, 190

  podcast and public document, 338

  podcast and written text, 346, 350

  poem and radio episode, 186

  poems and photo gallery, 492

  video interview, 720

Concession, 47
Connect, 34, 46, 58, 165, 189, 304, 414, 597
Connections across time, 15, 151, 287, 405, 557, 763
Connect to style, 27, 37, 49, 183, 228, 297, 307, 345, 417, 429, 447, 471, 490, 519, 715, 736, 791, 805
Craft and structure
  allegory
    literal meaning, 681
    symbolic meaning, 681
    theme, 681
  allusions, 344
  analogy, 80
  analytical argument, 368
    claim, 368
    counterclaims, 368
    opinion, 368
  argumentation, 25
  argumentative structure, 295
  author's choices
    literary forms, 681
    narrative, 735
    narrative structure, 854
    rhetoric, 80, 123
    structure, 35, 840
  author's point of view, 227
    philosophical assumptions, 227
  author's purpose, 47, 415
    anecdotes, 415
    humorous descriptions, 415
    rhetoric, 47
  autobiography, 489
    dialect, 489
    dialogue, 489
    social context, 489
  Biblical allusions, 682
  characterization, 259, 658, 775
    dialogue, 658
    direct, 259, 658
    indirect, 259, 658
    motivation, 658
    themes, 775
  charged language, 25
  chronological structure, 305
  complex ideas, 714
    direct characterization, 714
    indirect characterization, 714
  conflict
    external, 626
    internal, 626
  development of ideas, 211
    argument, 211
    central ideas, 211, 470

    supporting details, 470
  diction, 123
  drama, 598, 626
    characterization, 658
    conflict, 626
    dialogue, 598
    dramatic exposition, 598
    rising action, 626
    stage directions, 598
  dramatic monologue, 245
    point of view, 245
    speaker, 245
  enumeration, 35
  figurative language, 500
    descriptive details, 518
    imagery, 518
  heading, 35
  hyperbole, 427
  imagery, 500
  incongruity, 427
  internal monologue, 357
  literary nonfiction, 99, 489, 528
    historical writing, 528
    reflective writing, 528
  monologue
    dramatic, 245
  narrative
    chronological order, 735
    flashback, 735
    foreshadowing, 735
    frame story, 789
    internal story, 789
    introductory story, 789
    in medias res, 735
    suspense, 803
  narrative structure, 854
    flashback, 854
    narrative point of view, 854
    stream of consciousness, 854
  personification, 500
    apostrophe, 500
  persuasive appeals, 25
    appeal to authority, 25
    appeal to emotion, 25
    appeal to logic, 25
  poetic devices, 500, 518
    figurative language, 518
    metaphor, 518
    personification, 518
    simile, 518
  poetic structure and style, 165, 181
    catalogues, 165
    elliptical phrasing, 181
    free verse, 165

    paradox, 181
    parallel structure, 165
    slant rhyme, 181
  point of view, 427
  preamble, 35
  primary sources, 115
  repetition, 500
  resolutions, 35
  rhetoric, 80, 335
    argument, 335
    effective, 335
    refrain, 335
  rhetorical devices, 47
  secondary sources, 115
  sequence of events, 825
    chronological order, 825
  structure, 840
    limited third-person point of view, 840
    omniscient point of view, 840
    stream of consciousness, 840
  suspense
    foreshadowing, 803
    pacing, 803
  textual details, 80
  thematic development
    imagery, 445
    symbolism, 445
  theme, 357
  transitional expressions, 470
Drama, 558, 560, 600, 601, 629, 660, 661
Dramatic monologue, 245
Draw conclusions, 46, 414, 426, 657, 802
Essay, 154, 211, 463
Essential question, 10, 46, 58, 128, 189, 200, 282, 349, 400, 414, 426, 444, 458, 534, 552, 680, 689, 700, 740, 758, 816, 860
Essential question connection, 24, 34, 164, 180, 294, 304, 774, 788, 802
Evaluate, 164, 165, 294, 414, 426, 444, 597, 625, 774, 788
Explanatory text, 396
Expository nonfiction, 73
Extended allusion, 344
Fiction, 248, 352, 418, 432, 722, 764, 780, 794, 828, 842
Fine art gallery, 473
First read, 72
  drama, 560, 600, 660
  fiction, 248, 352, 418, 432, 722, 764, 780, 794, 828, 842
  first-read guide, 130, 266, 384, 536, 742, 862

INDEX OF SKILLS

nonfiction, 16, 30, 72, 92, 102, 118, 152, 204, 214, 288, 300, 330, 338, 360, 406, 462, 480, 520, 704, 820

poetry, 152, 170, 236, 492, 510

speech, 40

First review media, 52

art and photography, 82, 310, 472, 502

audio, 186, 346, 686

public document, 230

video, 716

Foundational document, 18, 31

Frame story, 427

Generalize, 24

Graphic adaptation, 82, 90

Graphic novel, 82, 83

Historical narrative, 81

biography, 81

historical details, 81

numerical data, 81

quotations, 81

Historical perspective, 12, 34, 46, 58, 148, 164, 180, 189, 284, 294, 304, 402, 414, 426, 444, 554, 760, 774, 788

Humor, 418

Humorous descriptions, 415

Image gallery, 53, 311

Independent learning, 128, 264

close-read guide, 131, 267, 385, 537, 743, 863

first-read guide, 130, 266, 384, 536, 742, 862

share learning, 143, 268, 386, 538, 744, 864

strategies

create a schedule, 128, 264, 382, 534, 740, 860

practice what you have learned, 128, 264, 382, 534, 740, 860

take notes, 128, 264, 382, 534, 740, 860

Infer, 625

Informational text, 277, 278

Informative text

elements of, 318

model of, 318

Integration of knowledge and ideas, 149

causes and effects, 13

charts, 285

graphs, 403, 555, 761

table, 761

Interpret, 24, 46, 164, 165, 304, 444, 625, 657, 680, 689, 774, 788, 802

Interview, 716

Irony, 304, 358

Legal opinion, 360, 361, 370, 378

Letter, 102, 104

Literary criticism, 463

Literary history, 821

Literary nonfiction, 99, 489, 528

Literature and culture, 24, 802

Literature of the focus period, 15, 151, 287, 405, 557, 763

Magazine article, 360, 370, 371, 378

Make a judgment, 180

Make inferences, 24, 165, 180, 597, 657, 689, 774, 788

Media, 412

American regional art, 472

analyze, 58, 89, 234, 477

audio performance, 687

compare and contrast, 58

comparing text to, 82, 90, 186, 190, 338, 346, 350, 462, 472, 478, 492, 502, 508

connect, 58

essential question, 58, 89

fine art gallery, 473

graphic novel, 83

historical perspective, 58

image gallery, 53, 311

patents, 230

photo gallery, 492, 503

podcast, 346, 347

present and discuss, 89, 316

public document, 230, 231

radio broadcast, 187

review and synthesize, 316

storyboard, 733

synthesize, 89

technical drawings, 230, 231, 234

video, 717

video interview, 704

Memoir, 406, 408, 420, 510, 521

Narrative, 142, 735, 789, 803

fictional narrative, 754

historical narrative, 81

personal narrative, 141

slave narrative, 99

Nonfiction, 16, 30, 72, 92, 102, 118, 152, 204, 214, 288, 300, 330, 338, 360, 370, 406, 462, 480, 520, 704, 820

expository nonfiction, 73

literary nonfiction, 99, 489, 528

Novel excerpt, 723

Paradox, 47

Parallelism, 290

Paraphrase, 34, 180, 304

Personal narrative, 141

Philosophical writing, 205, 207, 215, 223

Photo gallery, 492, 503

Photographic journalism, 310

Photographs, 508

Podcast, 346, 347, 349

Poetry, 150, 152, 156, 160, 161, 162, 170, 172, 173, 174, 175, 176, 177, 178, 236, 238, 420, 492, 494, 496, 510, 512, 514

anaphora, 165

catalogues, 165

epic theme, 165

free verse, 165

poetic devices, 500

slant rhyme, 181

storyboard, 243

Political cartoons, 310

Predict, 597, 625

Public document, 230, 231, 338, 339

Purpose, 116

Radio broadcast, 186, 187

Realism

dialogue, 683

setting, 683

Relate, 180

Rhetorical devices

concession, 47

paradox, 47

rhetorical question, 47

Rhetorical questions, 47

Short story, 249, 353, 406, 419, 433, 765, 781, 795, 828, 829, 842, 843

Slave narrative, 99

Social commentary, 415

Speculate, 24

Speech, 40, 42, 47, 50, 120, 289, 301, 330, 331

Story element, 213

Summarize, 164

Support, 426, 788

Synthesize, 189, 444

Theme, 165, 180, 357, 681

Tone, 292

Video, 716

Video interview, 704

Visual propaganda, 52

Voice

diction, 116

syntax, 116

tone, 116

Assessment

Speaking and listening

oral presentation, 542

podcast, 390

speech, 748
storytelling, 272, 868
videorecorded commentary, 136
Writing to sources
argument, 134, 746
explanatory essay, 540
informational essay, 388
narrative, 866
personal narrative, 270

Language Conventions

Antecedents, 791
Blending information, 695
Clauses
independent clauses, 212, 345
subordinate (dependent) clauses, 212, 345
Conjunctions
coordinating, 369
subordinating, 377
Dialect, 777
Dialogue, 811
Eighteenth-century style, 100
mechanics, 100
sentence length, 100
usage, 100
Figurative language, 260, 529
hyperbole, 260, 490
idioms, 490
metaphors, 260
overstatement, 490
similes, 260
Formality, 27
Grammar, 28
Information from sources, 695
Motif, 805
symbol, 805
theme, 805
Noun phrases, 297
Nouns, compound, 246
closed, 246
hyphenated, 246
Parallelism, 49, 50
Phrases
noun, 297
prepositional phrase, 307
adjective phrase, 307
adverb phrase, 307
Poetic conventions
end-stopped lines, 519
enjambment, 519
repetition, 519
stanza breaks, 519
Poetic prose, 529
descriptive details, 529

figurative language, 529
imagery, 529
Poetic structures, 501
rhythm, 501
ellipses, 501
line lengths, 501
Pronouns
agreement, 736
antecedents, 697, 736, 791
indefinite pronouns, 697
personal pronouns, 599
first-person, 599
second-person, 599
third-person, 599
as subjects, 791
Punctuation
dashes, 471
for enumeration, 37, 38
hyphens, 471
introductory phrases and clauses, 455
Record information, 695
Regionalism, 777
Rhetoric, 49
Sentences
run-on sentences, 841
sentence fragments, 841
Sentence variety, 212, 448
complex sentences, 212
compound-complex sentences, 212
compound sentences, 212
declarative sentences, 447
exclamatory sentences, 447
imperative sentences, 447
interrogative sentences, 447
simple sentences, 212
subordinating conjunctions, 377
Sequence of tenses, 65
Style, 28, 66, 183
analogy, 228
brief anecdotes, 228
conversational, 228
dialogue, 811
diction, 228
direct address of the reader, 228
eighteenth-century, 100
figures of speech, 228
pithy statements, 228
precise words and phrases, 195
word choice, 228
Subjects, 791
Syntax, 27, 28, 37, 49
parallelism, 49
sentence patterns, 323
varying, 455
Tenses

consistency of, 65
future, 65
past, 65
past perfect, 65
present, 65
present perfect, 65
sequence of, 65
Usage, 27, 37
Verb phrases, 297
Voice
active voice, 826
passive voice, 826
Word choices, 28, 38

Research

Argument, 62
notes that make me rethink claim, 63
notes that oppose claim, 63
notes that support claim, 63
Assessing strengths and limitations, 320
Avoiding plagiarism, 320
Citations, 320
Conducting, 320
Evaluating sources for, 694
Evidence, 62
Field guide entry, 737
Map, 737
Paraphrasing, 320
Print and digital sources, 452
Quotations, 320
Research plan, 737
Research report, 125
analysis of the historical context, 125
analytical paper, 827
comparison-and-contrast presentation, 125
extended definition, 827
graph, 827
project plan, 125
review, 125
Research to clarify, 23, 33, 45, 88, 97, 113, 121, 163, 179, 209, 225, 233, 243, 257, 293, 303, 333, 348, 366, 413, 425, 443, 487, 498, 516, 596, 679, 712, 733, 773, 787, 801, 838, 852
Research to explore, 23, 45, 78, 88, 97, 121, 163, 179, 209, 225, 233, 243, 257, 293, 303, 333, 342, 355, 413, 425, 443, 468, 476, 487, 498, 516, 526, 624, 656, 679, 733, 773, 787, 823, 838, 852
Research used effectively, 452
Search engine, 62
Timeline, 737

Speaking and Listening

Argument, 738
  planning, 738
  present and evaluate, 739
  rehearsing, 739
Assessment
  oral presentation, 542
  podcast, 390
  speech, 748
  storytelling, 272, 868
  videorecorded commentary, 136
Class discussion
  discuss the questions, 29
  listen and evaluate, 29
  prepare your contribution, 29
  think about the question, 29
Compare-and-contrast chart, 59
Debate, 449
  establish rules, 449
  evaluate, 449
  explore and evaluate claims, 449
Dialogue, 793
  analyze characters, 793
  evaluate, 793
  plan, 793
  prepare delivery, 793
Discussion, 229
  defense, 229
  finding evidence, 229
  list, 229
  project plan, 229
  response, 229
Dramatic reading, 299
  choose examples, 299
  evaluate examples, 299
  listen to readings, 299
Explanatory talk, 532
  planning, 532
  present and evaluate, 533
  rehearsing, 533
Group discussion
  holding the discussion, 359
  preparation, 359
Image gallery, 317
  plan the project, 317
  prepare the script, 317
  present and discuss, 317
Media connection, 23, 44, 96
Multimedia presentation, 59
Narrative presentation, 858
  planning, 858
  rehearsing, 859
Note taking, 186, 346
Oral interpretation

analyze readings, 185
evaluate reading, 185
listen to readings, 185
Oral presentation, 117, 169
  analyze selection, 169
  choose a text, 169
  compare-and-contrast discussion, 491
  discussion plan, 491
  evaluate partner readings, 169
  informative talk, 491
  interview, 491
  presentation plan, 117
  public service announcement, 117
  Reader's Theater, 117
  rehearse presentation, 169
  research plan, 117
  role-play, 117
Oral response to literature, 807
Panel discussion, 380
  planning, 380
  presenting and evaluating, 381
  rehearsing, 381
Partner discussion, 779
Personal narrative
  gather evidence, 262
  plan with your group, 262
  present and evaluate, 263
  rehearse with your group, 263
Political infomercial, 59
Present an argument, 126
  plan with your group, 126
  present and evaluate, 127
  rehearse with your group, 127
Reading and discussion
  choose the passages, 309
  deliver reading and analysis, 309
  evaluation presentation, 309
  prepare delivery, 309
Small-group learning
  making a schedule, 71, 203, 329, 461, 703, 819
  strategies for, 68, 200
    clarify, 68, 200, 326, 458, 700, 816
    participate fully, 68, 200, 326, 458, 700, 816
    prepare, 68, 200, 326, 458, 700, 816
    support others, 68, 200, 326, 458, 700, 816
  working as a team, 70, 202, 460, 818
    apply the rules, 70, 202, 328, 460, 702, 818
    create a communication plan, 70, 202, 328, 460, 702, 818

    list your rules, 70, 202, 328, 460, 702, 818
    name your group, 70, 202, 328, 460, 702, 818
    roles for group projects, 71, 203, 329, 461, 703, 819
    take a position, 70, 202, 328, 460, 702, 818
Speeches, 39
  choose a position, 235
  deliver the speech, 39
  discussing the speech, 51
  evaluate the video, 51
  evaluate your presentation, 39
  plan your argument, 235
  practice and present, 51
  present and debate, 235
  tone, 299
  video recording of, 51
  write the speech, 39
Storytelling, 144
Thematic analysis, 685
Tone, 299
Videorecorded commentary, 136
Visual propaganda
  consider image choices, 59
  plan the project, 59
  prepare the script, 59
  present and discuss, 59
Whole-class discussion, 627
Whole-class learning strategies, 10
  clarify by asking questions, 10, 146, 282, 400, 552, 758
  interact and share ideas, 10, 146, 282, 400, 552, 758
  listen actively, 10, 146, 282, 400, 552, 758
  monitor understanding, 10, 146, 282, 400, 552, 758

Vocabulary

Academic vocabulary, 5
  analyze, 395, 450, 540
  assert, 547, 692, 746
  certify, 547, 692, 746
  colloquial, 753, 866
  confirm, 5, 60, 134
  conviction, 5, 60, 134
  deduction, 277, 388
  definitive, 547, 692, 746
  demonstrate, 5, 60, 134
  determine, 395, 450, 540
  epiphany, 753, 866
  establish, 5, 60, 134
  immutable, 547, 692, 746
  impact, 141, 192, 270

incident, 141, 192, 270
informational, 277, 388
inquire, 277
investigate, 388
literal, 395, 450, 540
protagonist, 753, 866
relevant, 547, 692, 746
resolution, 753, 866
sequence, 141, 192, 270
significant, 141, 192, 270
specific, 277, 388
subordinate, 395, 450, 540
supplement, 5, 60, 134
tension, 753, 866
trivialize, 395, 450, 540
unique, 141, 192, 270
verbatim, 277, 388
Concept vocabulary
abridging, 30, 32, 36, 38
acquiesce, 16, 21, 26, 28
adamant, 660, 667, 680, 684
ampler, 152, 166, 168
anticipation, 794, 796, 804, 806
ascendant, 820, 823, 824
assent, 16, 19, 26, 28
awkward, 764, 769, 776, 778
brawling, 492, 495, 499
brazenness, 48, 480, 482
breadth, 152, 166, 168
buttonholed, 418, 424, 428
cabana, 722, 725, 734
callously, 628, 641, 657
calumny, 560, 576, 597
cantina, 722, 725, 734
captivity, 170, 175, 182, 184
clammy, 842, 845, 853
collaborator, 704, 706, 713
conceded, 288, 291, 296, 298
conciliatory, 660, 666, 680, 684
conclave, 72, 73, 79
condemnation, 600, 603, 625
consecrate, 118, 120, 122
conspirators, 704, 707, 713
constrains, 16, 19, 26, 28
constricting, 794, 799, 804, 806
corrupted, 40, 43, 48, 50
cowering, 764, 769, 776, 778
cunning, 492, 495, 499
dedicate, 118, 120, 122
defamation, 560, 584, 597
deference, 828, 830, 839
degraded, 338, 340, 343
deicide, 520, 524, 527
dejected, 92, 94, 98

denounce, 288, 290, 296, 298
despotism, 40, 43, 48, 50
dictum, 828, 832, 839
digress, 236, 240, 244
dilatory, 432, 433, 446, 448
discern, 462, 465, 469
disparity, 288, 290, 296, 298
disposition, 360, 365, 367
disputation, 660, 669, 680, 684
dissented, 102, 109, 114
dyspepsia, 842, 851, 853
effrontery, 628, 640, 657
eminence, 406, 411, 416
eminent, 72, 74, 79
emperor, 170, 172, 182, 184
encroaching, 794, 795, 804, 806
equivocate, 288, 290, 296, 298
espionage, 704, 708, 713
etiquette, 828, 830, 839
exalted, 406, 411, 416
exasperating, 418, 419, 428
exercise, 30, 32, 36, 38
faultfinder, 214, 221, 226
fix, 330, 331, 334
foment, 102, 106, 114
forward, 48, 480, 482
furtive, 764, 767, 776, 778
garrulous, 418, 419, 428
gilded, 406, 410, 416
grade, 410
grandeur, 406, 416
hallow, 118, 120, 122
hangdog, 764, 772, 776, 778
heedless, 214, 219, 226
hermitage, 432, 436, 446, 448
hospitality, 432, 435, 446, 448
hypodermic, 842, 848, 853
imperial, 170, 173, 182, 184
imploring, 352, 354, 356
importunities, 352, 355, 356
indecisions, 236, 240, 244
infallibility, 40, 43, 48, 50
infringed, 30, 32, 36, 38
instantaneously, 794, 796, 804, 806
insurgent, 300, 302, 306, 308
integrity, 40, 44, 48, 50
interminable, 418, 420, 428
jurisdiction, 360, 362, 367
letterhead, 780, 782, 790, 792
loathsome, 92, 93, 98
loitered, 432, 434, 446, 448
machetes, 722, 729, 734
magistrates, 600, 603, 625
majority, 170, 172, 182, 184

malice, 300, 303, 306, 308
monotonous, 418, 420, 428
motifs, 248, 253, 258
multitudes, 152, 159, 166, 168
obdurate, 288, 289, 296, 298
obliged, 330, 332, 334
oppressed, 338, 340, 343
ornamented, 406, 410, 416
overcast, 780, 784, 790, 792
overture, 248, 253, 258
perish, 300, 302, 306, 308
perpetually, 794, 799, 804, 806
persistence, 352, 354, 356
petition, 30, 32, 36, 38
picturesquely, 406, 410, 416
plaintiffs, 360, 362, 367
populist, 72, 75, 79
prejudices, 40, 43, 48, 50
prelude, 248, 255, 258
prescribed, 30, 32, 36, 38
proceedings, 600, 606, 625
prolific, 152, 166, 168
quaint, 432, 436, 446, 448
racket, 330, 331, 334
rectitude, 16, 21, 26, 28
redeemers, 204, 208, 210
redress, 30, 32, 36, 38
remorseless, 628, 630, 657
renaissance, 820, 823, 824
rend, 300, 302, 306, 308
reverence, 520, 524, 527
rites, 520, 524, 527
salutary, 40, 44, 48, 50
sanctity, 204, 205, 210
scourge, 300, 302, 306, 308
self-assurance, 48, 480, 481
shotgun, 780, 784, 790, 792
shuffle, 764, 766, 776, 778
sidle, 764, 766, 776, 778
sinister, 510, 513, 517
sovereign, 170, 173, 182, 184
spatial, 462, 466, 469
squalor, 432, 436, 446, 448
stolid, 288, 289, 296, 298
strife, 510, 513, 517
subordinate, 338, 341, 343
superannuated, 794, 799, 804, 806
superfluous, 214, 218, 226
supplanted, 820, 822, 824
tedious, 236, 239, 244, 418, 428
teeming, 152, 166, 168
temporal, 462, 466, 469
transcendent, 204, 208, 210
treason, 170, 173, 182, 184

tyranny, 16, 19, 26, 28
unalienable, 16, 18, 26, 28
unrequited, 300, 302, 306, 308
vassals, 102, 104, 114
vast, 152, 166, 168
vigilant, 510, 514, 517
vindictive, 560, 571, 597
wanton, 492, 495, 499
waterfowl, 780, 782, 790, 792
wretched, 92, 94, 98
Media vocabulary
appeal, 52, 58
audio play, 686, 689
caption, 82, 89
caricature, 310, 316
commentary, 186, 189
composition, 310, 316
cross-section, 230, 234
depth of field, 502, 507
documentary, 716, 719
expression, 686, 689
eyewitness account, 716, 719
figure, 230
focal point, 502, 507
foreground and background, 502, 507
frame, 346, 349, 719
framing, 716
host, 186, 189
impressionism, 472, 477
inflection, 686, 689
interview, 186, 189
labeling and captions, 310, 316
layout, 82, 89
palette, 472, 477
perspective, 472, 477
propaganda, 52, 58
realism, 472, 477
romanticism, 472, 477
special elements, 346, 349
specifications, 230, 234
speech balloon, 82, 89
symbolism, 52, 58
tone, 346, 349
Technical vocabulary, 324
Word study skills
Anglo-Saxon suffix
-esque, 416
base words, 92, 480, 704
cognates, 375
connotations, 122, 356, 428, 657
context clues, 72, 102, 204, 236, 330, 338, 462, 492, 510, 520, 722, 820, 828
antonyms, 72

contrast of ideas and topics, 492
description as context clue, 102
restatement of idea, 492
synonyms, 72, 492
conversational use, 517
denotation, 122, 356, 428
endocentric compounds, 790
etymology, 517, 680, 734
exocentric compounds, 776
Greek prefix
dys-, 853
Latin combining form
multi-, 166
Latin prefix
di- / dis-, 244
ob-, 296
super-, 226
Latin root
-cid-, 527
-dei-, 527
-fama-, 597
-ject-, 98
-lig-, 334
-rect-, 26
-sanct-, 210
-scend-, 824
-strict-, 804
Latin root word
hospes, 446
Latin suffix
-al, 469
-ist, 79
-ity, 48
-or-, 713
-um, 839
multiple-meaning words, 36, 48
nuance, 306
present participle, 499
roots, 5
synonyms, 36, 306
technical words (jargon), 367, 625
word choice, 26, 36, 48, 79, 98, 114, 122, 166, 182, 210, 244, 258, 296, 306, 334, 343, 356, 367, 416, 428, 446, 448, 469, 499, 517, 527, 597, 625, 657, 680, 684, 713, 734, 776, 778, 790, 792, 804, 806, 824, 839, 853
word derivations, 182, 258
word families, 114
Word Network, 7, 143, 279, 397, 549, 755
word parts
familiar, 214, 248, 352, 360, 842
prefix, 118
root, 118

Writing, 190, 625
Active voice, 826
Adjective phrases, 307
Adverb phrases, 307
Advertisement, 101
Alternate ending, 756
Anecdote, 806
Anecdotes, 454
Argument, 5, 28, 60, 101, 134, 547, 684, 692
connect across texts, 61
develop a claim, 61
drafting, 64
elements of, 60
gather evidence, 61
historical narrative, 81
model argument, 60
notes that make me rethink claim, 63
notes that oppose claim, 63
notes that support claim, 63
prewriting/planning, 61
response to literature, 692
review evidence for, 745
revising, 66
rhetorical devices, 64
Argumentative essay, 684, 692
conventions, 695
deductive reasoning, 696
drafting, 696
editing, 699
indefinite pronouns, 697
inductive reasoning, 696
prewriting/planning, 693
proofreading, 699
publishing and presenting, 699
research, 694
revising, 698
Blog post, 184
Body, 64, 454
Clauses, 37, 345
Climax, 194
Colloquial language, 417
Compare, 90
Compare-and-contrast essay, 378, 720
drafting, 191, 351, 721
prewriting/planning, 190, 350, 378, 720
Conclusion, 64, 194, 198, 324, 454
Conflict, 194
Conjunction, coordinating, 369
Connect across texts, 61, 193, 319
Coordinating conjunctions, 369
Create cohesion, 65
Critical analysis, 448
Critical review, 690

drafting, 691
    prewriting/planning, 690
Define, 8
Definitions, 456
Description, 476, 506, 529
Dialect, 777
Dialogue, 841
Diction
    colloquial, 336
    formal, 336
Digital presentation, 247
    digital plan, 247
    filmed oral response, 247
    oral recitation and discussion, 247
    slide show, 247
Drafting, 64, 101, 191, 194, 351, 431,
    509, 531, 691, 721
    begin story memorably, 810
    end in satisfying way, 810
    establish point of view, 810
    evaluating draft, 66
    explanatory essay, 454
    first draft, 322, 696
    highlight the conflict, 810
    organizing text, 322
    outlining, 322
    present reasoning, 696
    sentence patterns, 323
Editing for conventions, 67, 199, 325,
    457, 699, 815
Editorial, 28
Enumeration, 37
Essay, 856
    argumentative essay, 684, 692, 693,
        694, 695, 696, 698, 699
    compare-and-contrast essay, 190,
        191, 378, 720
    drafting, 856
    explanatory essay, 450, 451, 452,
        454, 455, 456, 457
    how-to essay, 261
    informative essay, 318, 530
    interpretive essay, 478
    review and revise, 857
Evaluating sources, 321
Evidence Log, 9, 145, 281, 399, 451,
    539, 551, 757
Explain, 8
Explanatory essay, 450
    drafting, 454
    editing and proofreading, 457
    elements of, 450
    model of, 450
    prewriting/planning, 451
    publishing and presenting, 457
    researching, 452

revising, 456
    style, 455
Explanatory text, 430
    drafting, 431
    prewriting/planning, 430
Exposition, 194
Extended definition, 38, 779
Falling action, 194
Figurative language, 490
    hyperbole, 260
    metaphor, 260
    simile, 260
First person, 198
Focus statement, 280
Gather evidence, 61
Hyperbole, 427
Idioms, 429
Informative essay, 318, 530
    drafting, 91, 531
    identify key components, 531
    prewriting/planning, 90, 530
Informative eyewitness account, 308
Informative text
    biographical sketch, 337
    cause-and-effect article, 337
    extended definition, 337
    project plan, 337
Informative writing, 38
    misconceptions or disproven ideas,
        298
Interpretive essay
    drafting, 479
    prewriting/planning, 478
Introduction, 64, 454
Irony, 659
Letter, 101
Literary review, 101
Logical connections, 66
Metaphors, 855
Motif, 805
Multimedia presentation, 508
    drafting, 509
    prewriting/planning, 509
Narrative, 778
    fictional narrative, 808
        dialogue, 811
        drafting, 810
        editing and proofreading, 815
        prewriting/planning, 809
        publishing and presenting, 815
        revising, 814
        sensory language, 812
    first-person point of view, 715
    historical narrative, 81
    personal narrative, 192, 194, 195,

197, 198
    perspective, 715
    review notes for, 865
Narrative scene, 792
Note taking, 321
Noun phrases, 297
Nouns
    abstract, 183
    compound, 246
    concrete, 183
Onomatopoeic words, 168
Paragraph, 625
    active and passive voice, 826
    clauses, 345
    colloquial language, 417
    diction
        colloquial, 336
        formal, 336
    figurative language, 490
    idioms, 429
    metaphors, 855
    motif, 805
    pronoun antecedents, 736
    sentence variety in, 212, 447
    similes, 855
    situational irony, 358
Parallel structure, 37
Paraphrase, 61
Parts of speech, 183
    abstract noun, 183
    concrete noun, 183
    noun, 183
Passive voice, 826
Peer review, 67, 199, 325, 457, 699, 815
Personal narrative, 192
    conclusion, 194
    conflict, 194
    drafting, 194
    elements of, 192
    model for, 192
    precise words and phrases, 195, 197
    prewriting/planning, 192
    revising, 198
Phrases, 37
    adjective, 307
    adverb, 307
    noun, 297
    precise, 195, 197
    verb, 297
Poem, 501, 519
Precise words and phrases, 195
Prewriting/planning, 61, 190, 192, 319,
    350, 430, 451, 509, 530
    ask questions, 693
    compare and contrast, 319

connect across texts, 319, 809
create a story chart, 809
develop characters, 809
direct quotations, 319
evaluate evidence, 451
focus on a conflict, 809
gather evidence, 319, 451, 693
thesis statement, 451
working thesis, 319
Project plan, 101
Pronoun antecedents, 736
Proofreading for accuracy, 67, 199, 325, 457, 699, 815
Publishing and presenting, 67, 199, 325, 457, 699, 815
Punctuation
comma, 37, 49
dashes, 471
enumeration, 37
hyphens, 471
serial comma, 37
QuickWrite, 9, 131, 145, 267, 281, 385, 399, 537, 551, 743, 757, 863
Quotations
direct, 61
integrating, 321
Realism, 683
Reflect on writing, 28, 38, 50, 67, 168, 184, 199, 298, 308, 325, 448, 684, 699, 778, 792, 806, 815
Regionalism, 777
Research report, 261
comparison and contrast, 261
how-to essay, 261
problem-solution letter, 261
project plan, 261
working title, 261
Review, 228, 431, 531
Revising, 66, 198, 531
evaluating draft, 324, 698, 814
for evidence and elaboration, 66, 198, 324, 456
dialogue, 814
use of source material, 698
vocabulary and tone, 698
explanatory text, 431
for purpose and organization, 66, 198, 324, 456, 698
clarifying relationships, 698
conclusion, 814
sequence of events, 814
Rewrite, 27, 49, 100
dialogue, 599
unclear antecedents, 791

Rhetorical devices
antithesis, 124
Rhythm, 50
Rising action, 194
Sensory language, 168, 198, 812, 813
Sentences
adding clauses to, 345
adjective phrases, 307
adverb phrases, 307
with compound nouns, 246
coordinating conjunctions, 369
sentence variety, 212, 455
subordinating conjunctions, 377
Sentence variety, 212, 447, 455
Sequence verbs, 65
Similes, 855
Situational irony, 358
Sophisticated writing, 196
Storyboard, 113
Story element, 213
character, 213
dialogue, 213
plan for, 213
setting, 213
Style, 455
Subordinating conjunctions, 377
Summary, 8, 23, 33, 45, 78, 88, 113, 121, 144, 163, 179, 209, 225, 257, 280, 293, 303, 333, 342, 348, 366, 398, 413, 425, 443, 468, 487, 498, 516, 526, 550, 624, 656, 679, 712, 756, 773, 787, 823, 838, 852
Synonyms, 356
Technical vocabulary, 324
Timeline, 97, 355, 596, 801
Verb phrases, 297
Weaving research into test, 321
Word choice, 28, 38, 50, 66, 168, 184, 298, 308, 813
Word Network, 7
Word pairing, 167
Writing to compare, 190
compare-and-contrast essay, 350, 378, 720
drafting, 351, 721
prewriting/planning, 350, 720
compare interpretations, 190
conclude with evaluation, 191
critical review, 690
drafting, 691
prewriting/planning, 690
draw conclusions, 191
essay, 856
drafting, 856

review and revise, 857
explanatory text, 430
drafting, 431
prewriting/planning, 430
informative essay, 531
drafting, 531
identify key components, 531
prewriting/planning, 530
interpretive essay
drafting, 479
prewriting/planning, 478
multimedia presentation, 508
drafting, 509
prewriting/planning, 509
organize your ideas, 191
Writing to sources
anecdote, 806
argument, 101, 134, 684
argumentative essay, 684
assessment
argument, 134, 746
explanatory essay, 540
informational essay, 388
narrative, 866
personal narrative, 270
blog post, 184
critical analysis, 448
digital presentation, 247
digital plan, 247
filmed oral response, 247
oral recitation and discussion, 247
slide show, 247
editorial, 28
evaluation, 50
informative eyewitness account, 308
informative text
biographical sketch, 337
cause-and-effect article, 337
extended definition, 337
project plan, 337
informative writing, 38
misconceptions or disproven ideas, 298
narrative, 778
narrative scene, 792
research report, 261
comparison and contrast, 261
how-to essay, 261
problem-solution letter, 261
project plan, 261
working title, 261
sensory language, 168
story element, 213

INDEX OF AUTHORS AND TITLES

The following authors and titles appear in the print and online versions of *my*Perspectives.

A

Adams, Abigail, 103, 104
Ain't I a Woman?, 331
Alvarez, Julia, 722, 723
Amar, Akhil Reed, 72, 73
Ambush, 861
America, 162
America's Constitution: A Biography, from, 73
Antojos, 723

B

Baca, Jimmy Santiago, 511, 514
Balance Between Nature and Nurture, A, 383
Baldwin, James, 535
BBC Radio, 4, 187
Bears at Raspberry Time, 741
Bierce, Ambrose, 828, 829
Bill of Rights, 31
Birches, 535
Bishop, Elizabeth, 129
Blanco, Richard, 138
Blaustein, Arthur, 129
Books as Bombs, from, 383
Bradbury, Ray, 129
Brief History of the Short Story, A, 821
Brooks, Gwendolyn, 129
Browning, Sarah, 383
Brown v. Board of Education: Opinion of the Court, 361
Burns, Ken, 392
Busch, Akiko, 741

C

Carruth, Hayden, 741
Carver, Raymond, 780, 781
Cather, Willa, 248, 249
Chang, Lan Samantha, 861
Chicago, 494
Chopin, Kate, 352, 353
Civil Disobedience, from, 223
Cloudy Day, 514
Cofer, Judith Ortiz, 535
Common Sense, from, 129
Crucible, The
  Act I, 562, 687

  Act II, 601
  Act III, 629
  Act IV, 661

D

Daley, Jason, 741
Dear Abigail: The Intimate Lives and Revolutionary Ideas of Abigail Adams and Her Two Remarkable Sisters, 107
Declaration of Independence, 18
Declaration of Sentiments, 339
Dekanawidah, 129
Democracy Is Not a Spectator Sport, from, 129
Derricotte, Toi, 741
Dickinson, Emily, 171–178
Dillard, Annie, 535
Douglas, Frederick, 288, 289
Douglass, 383
Dunbar, Paul Laurence, 383
Dust Tracks on a Road, from, 481

E

Eliot, T. S., 237, 238
Emerson, Ralph Waldo, 204, 205, 207
Equiano, Olaudah, 92, 93
Erdrich, Louise, 794, 795
Espada, Martín, 383
Everyday Use, 765
Everything Stuck to Him, 781

F

Fame is a fickle food, 174
Farewell to Manzanar, from, 705
1-800-FEAR, 741
Fifth Fact, The, 383
Fish, The, 129
Fisher, Claude, 265
For Black Women Who Are Afraid, 741
Franklin, Benjamin, 41, 42
Frost, Robert, 535

G

Gallegos, Carmen, 278
Gettysburg Address, 120
Giving Women the Vote, 347

Gladding, Jody, 741
Great Lives: Emily Dickinson, from, 187

H

Hamadi, 265
Hawthorne, Nathaniel, 265
Hayden, Robert, 741
Hemingway, Ernest, 754
Hennessey, Jonathan, 82, 83
Housepainting, 861
Houston, James D., 704, 705
Houston, Jeanne Wakatsuki, 704, 705
Hughes, Langston, 383
Hurston, Zora Neale, 480, 481

I

I Hear America Singing, 160
I heard a Fly buzz—when I died, 177
I'm Nobody! Who are you?, 178
Interesting Narrative of the Life of Olaudah Equiano, The, from, 93
Interview With George Takei, 717
In the Longhouse, Oneida Museum, 512
Iroquois Constitution, from the, 129

J

Jacobs, Diane, 103, 107
Jefferson, Thomas, 17, 18
Jewett, Sarah Orne, 432, 433
Jilting of Granny Weatherall, The, 843

K

Kinnell, Galway, 265

L

L.A. Theatre Works, 687
Latin Deli: An Ars Poetica, The, 535
Leap, The, 795
Leaves of Grass, from Preface to the 1855 Edition of, 154
Letter to John Adams, 104
Lewis, Gwyneth, 186, 187
Life on the Mississippi, from, 408
Lincoln, Abraham, 119, 120, 300, 301
Literature of Place, A, 463
Lopez, Barry, 462, 463
Love Song of J. Alfred Prufrock, The, 238

M

Madison, James, 30, 31
Man to Send Rain Clouds, The, 861
Marshall, Thurgood, 129
Matatov, Helen, 129
McConnell, Aaron, 82, 83
McCourt, D. F. ("Duff"), 820, 821
Menand, Louis, 383
Miller, Arthur, 561, 562, 601, 629, 661
Momaday, Navarro Scott, 520, 521
Morris, Gouverneur, 30, 31

N

Nature, from, 205
Notorious Jumping Frog of Calaveras County, The, 419
Nye, Naomi Shihab, 265

O

O'Brien, Tim, 861
Occurrence at Owl Creek Bridge, An, 829
Old Man at the Bridge, 754
One Today, 138
On the Beach at Night Alone, 161

P

Paine, Thomas, 129
Parker, Arthur C., 129
Pedestrian, The, 129
Poe, Edgar Allan, 861
Poetry of Langston Hughes, The, 383
Porter, Katherine Anne, 842, 843
Preamble to the Constitution, 31

R

Reckless Genius, 265
Reflections on the Bicentennial of the United States Constitution, 129
Rockpile, The, 535
Runagate Runagate, 741

S

Sandburg, Carl, 493, 494, 496
Second Inaugural Address, 301
Secrets of Yellowstone National Park, 392
Self-Reliance, from, 207
Silko, Leslie Marmon, 861
Sleight-Brennan, Sandra, 346, 347
Song of Myself, from, 156
Soul selects her own Society—, The, 172
Soul unto itself, The, 173
Speech in the Convention, 42
Speech to the Young Speech to the Progress-Toward, 129
Stanton, Elizabeth Cady, 338, 339
Steinem, Gloria, 383
Story of an Hour, The, 353
Sweet Land of . . . Conformity?, 265

T

Takei, George, 716, 717
Tarbell, Ida, 383
Tell-Tale Heart, The, 861
There is a solitude of space, 176
They shut me up in Prose–, 175
Thoreau, Henry David, 214, 215, 223
Truth, Sojourner, 330, 331
Twain, Mark, 407, 408, 418, 419

U

United States Constitution: A Graphic Adaptation, The, 83
Untying the Knot, 535
Up From Slavery, from, 142

W

Wagner Matinée, A, 249
Walden, from, 215
Walker, Alica, 764, 765
Warmth of Other Suns, The, from, 383
Warren, Earl, 360, 361
Washington, Booker T., 142
Way to Rainy Mountain, The, from, 521
What a Factory Can Teach a Housewife, 383
What Are You So Afraid Of?, 741
What to the Slave is the Fourth of July?, from, 289
What You Don't Know Can Kill You, 741
White Heron, A, 433
Whitman, Walt, 153, 154, 156, 160–162
Whiteman, Roberta Hill, 511, 512
Who Burns for the Perfection of Paper, 383
Wilderness, 496
Wilkerson, Isabel, 383
Wood-Pile, The, 535

Y

Young Goodman Brown, 265

Z

Zigzag Road to Rights, The, 278

INDEX OF AUTHORS AND TITLES

The following authors and titles appear in the Online Literature Library.

A
Ambush

B
Balance Between Nature and Nurture, A
Baldwin, James
Bears at Raspberry Time
Birches
Bishop, Elizabeth
Blaustein, Arthur
Books as Bombs, from
Bradbury, Ray
Brooks, Gwendolyn
Browning, Sarah
Busch, Akiko

C
Carruth, Hayden
Chang, Lan Samantha
Cofer, Judith Ortiz
Common Sense, from

D
Daley, Jason
Democracy Is Not a Spectator Sport,
  from
Derricotte, Toi
Dillard, Annie
Douglass
Dunbar, Paul Laurence

E
Espada, Martín

F
1-800-FEAR
Fifth Fact, The
Fish, The

Fisher, Claude
For Black Women Who Are Afraid
Frost, Robert

G
Gladding, Jody

H
Hamadi
Hawthorne, Nathaniel
Hayden, Robert
Housepainting
Hughes, Langston

I
Iroquois Constitution, from the

K
Kinnell, Galway

L
Latin Deli: An Ars Poetica, The

M
Man to Send Rain Clouds, The
Marshall, Thurgood
Matatov, Helen
Menand, Louis

N
Nye, Naomi Shihab

O
O'Brien, Tim

P
Paine, Thomas
Parker, Arthur C.
Pedestrian, The

Poe, Edgar Allan
Poetry of Langston Hughes, The

R
Reckless Genius
*Reflections on the Bicentennial of the
  United States Constitution*
Rockpile, The
Runagate Runagate

S
Silko, Leslie Marmon
*Speech to the Young Speech to the
  Progress-Toward*
Steinem, Gloria
Sweet Land of . . . Conformity?

T
Tarbell, Ida
Tell-Tale Heart, The

U
Untying the Knot

W
Warmth of Other Suns, The, from
What a Factory Can Teach a Housewife
What Are You So Afraid Of?
What You Don't Know Can Kill You
Who Burns for the Perfection of Paper
Wilkerson, Isabel
Wood-Pile, The

Y
Young Goodman Brown

Acknowledgments

The following selections appear in Grade 11 of *my*Perspectives. Some selections appear online only.

Arte Publico Press. "The Latin Deli" from *America's Review* by Judith Ortiz Cofer (©1992 Arte Publico Press—University of Houston).

Audible Inc. "How to Tell a True War Story" from *The Things They Carried* by Tim O'Brien. Copyright ©1990 by Tim O'Brien.

BBC Worldwide Americas, Inc. Boston Tea Party ©BBC Worldwide Learning; The U. S. Constitution ©BBC Worldwide Learning; Great Lives: Emily Dickinson—BBC Worldwide Learning; Civil Rights Marches ©BBC Worldwide Learning; CBS Sunday Morning segment "Mark Twain and Tom Sawyer" ©BBC Worldwide Learning.

Bloomsbury Publishing Plc. "Antojos," Copyright ©1991 by Julia Alvarez. Later published in slightly different form in *How the Garcia Girls Lost Their Accents*. Used with permission of Bloomsbury Publishing Plc.

Brooks Permissions. "Speech to the Young, Speech to the Progress-Toward," reprinted By Consent of Brooks Permissions.

Browning, Sarah. "The Fifth Fact," from *Whisky in the Garden of Eden* (The Word Words, Washington, DC, 2007). Used with permission.

Chopin, Kate. "The Story of An Hour" by Kate Chopin, originally appeared in *Vogue*, 1894.

CNN. The Hollywood Blacklist: 1947–1960 ©CNN.

Contently. Why Do Stories Matter? That's Like Asking Why You Should Eat ©Contently 2015

Copper Canyon Press. Hayden Carruth, "Bears at Raspberry Time" from *Collected Shorter Poems* 1946–1991. Copyright ©1983 by Hayden Carruth. Reprinted with the permission of The Permissions Company, Inc., on behalf of Copper Canyon Press, www.coppercanyonpress.org.

Daily Signal. "Rugged Individualism Fades from National Character" by Marion Smith, from *Daily Signal*, June 11, 2012; http://dailysignal.com/print/?post_id=99695. Used with permission.

Don Congdon Associates. "The Pedestrian," reprinted by permission of Don Congdon Associates, Inc. Copyright ©1951 by the Fortnightly Publishing Company, renewed 1979 by Ray Bradbury.

Douglass, Frederick. "What to the Slave is the 4th of July?" by Frederick Douglass (1818–1895).

Dunbar, Paul Laurence. "Douglass" by Paul Laurence Dunbar (1872–1906).

Espada, Martin. "Who Burns for the Perfection of Paper," from *city of coughing and dead radiators* by Martin Espada. Copyright ©1993 by Martin Espada. Used by permission of the author.

Estate of Galway Kinnell. "Reckless Genius" by Galway Kinnell, from Salon.com. Used with permission of the Estate of Galway Kinnell.

Faber & Faber, Ltd. (UK). "The Love Song of J. Alfred Prufrock" from *Collected Poems*, 1909–1062 by T.S. Eliot. Reprinted by permission of the publisher, Faber and Faber, Ltd.

Farrar, Straus and Giroux. Jacket design and excerpts from *The United States Constitution: A Graphic Adaptation* by Jonathan Hennessey, artwork by Aaron McConnell. Text copyright ©2008 by Jonathan Hennessey. Artwork Copyright ©2008 by Aaron McConnell. Reprinted by permission of Hill and Wang, a division of Farrar, Straus and Giroux, LLC.; "The Fish" from *The Complete Poems* 1927–1979 by Elizabeth Bishop. Copyright ©1979, 1983 by Alice Helen Methfessel. Reprinted by permission of Farrar, Straus and Giroux, LLC.

Fischer, Claude. "Sweet Land of...Conformity?," *Boston Globe*, June 6, 2010, as adapted from the blog, Made in America.

Harold Ober Associates. "Dream Variations," reprinted by permission of Harold Ober Associates Incorporated. Copyright ©1994 by The Estate Of Langston Hughes; "I, Too," reprinted by permission of Harold Ober Associates Incorporated. Copyright ©1994 by The Estate Of Langston Hughes; "The Negro Speaks of Rivers," reprinted by permission of Harold Ober Associates Incorporated. Copyright ©1994 by The Estate Of Langston Hughes; "Refugee in America," reprinted by permission of Harold Ober Associates Incorporated. Copyright ©1994 by The Estate Of Langston Hughes.

Harper's Magazine. "The Leap," Copyright ©1990 Harper's Magazine. All rights reserved. Reproduced from the March issue by special permission.

HarperCollins Publishers. Pages 33–40 from *Dust Tracks on a Road* by Zora Neale Hurston. Copyright 1942 by Zora Neale Hurston; renewed ©1970 by John C. Hurston. Reprinted by permission of HarperCollins Publishers; "Untying the Knot" from *Pilgrim at Tinker Creek* by Annie Dillard. Copyright ©1974 by Annie Dillard. Reprinted by permission of HarperCollins Publishers.

HarperCollins Publishers Ltd. (UK). "Storyteller," "How to Tell a True War Story" from *The Things They Carried* by Tim O'Brien. Copyright ©1990 by Tim O'Brien. Reprinted by permission of HarperCollins Publishers Ltd.

Harvard Law Review. "Reflections on the Bicentennial of the United States Constitution," republished with permission of *Harvard Law Review*, from Harvard Law Review, 101, November 1987; permission conveyed through Copyright Clearance Center, Inc.

Harvard University Press. "They shut me up in Prose," *The Poems of Emily Dickinson: Reading Edition*, edited by Ralph W. Franklin, Cambridge, Mass.: The Belknap Press of Harvard University Press, Copyright ©1998, 1999 by the President and Fellows of Harvard College. Copyright ©1951, 1955 by the President and Fellows of Harvard College. Copyright © renewed 1979, 1983 by the President and Fellows of Harvard College. Copyright ©1914, 1918, 1919, 1924, 1929, 1930, 1932, 1935, 1937, 1942 by Martha Dickinson Bianchi. Copyright ©1952, 1957, 1958, 1963, 1965 by Mary L. Hampson; "I'm Nobody," *The Poems of Emily Dickinson*, edited by Thomas H. Johnson, Cambridge, Mass.: The Belknap Press of Harvard University Press, Copyright ©1951, 1955 by the President and Fellows of Harvard College. Copyright ©renewed 1979, 1983 by the President and Fellows of Harvard College. Copyright ©1914, 1918, 1919, 1924, 1929, 1930, 1932, 1935, 1937, 1942 by Martha Dickinson Bianchi. Copyright ©1952, 1957, 1958, 1963, 1965 by Mary L. Hampson.

Henry Holt & Co. "A Balance Between Nature and Nurture" by Gloria Steinem. Copyright ©2005 by Gloria Steinem. From the audio book collection THIS I BELIEVE: The Personal Philosophies of Remarkable Men and Women edited by Jay Allison and Dan Gedimen. Copyright ©2006 by This I Believe, Inc. Used by permission of Henry Holt and Company, LLC. All rights reserved; "A Balance Between

material, outside of this publication, is prohibited. Interested parties must apply directly to Penguin Random House LLC for permission; "Mother to Son," "Dream Variation," "I, Too," "The Negro Speaks of Rivers," and "Refugee in America" from *The Collected Poems of Langston Hughes* by Langston Hughes, edited by Arnold Rampersad with David Roessel, Associate Editor, copyright ©1994 by the Estate of Langston Hughes. Used by permission of Alfred A. Knopf, an imprint of the Knopf Doubleday Publishing Group, a division of Penguin Random House LLC. All rights reserved. Any third party use of this material, outside of this publication, is prohibited. Interested parties must apply directly to Penguin Random House LLC for permission.

Recorded Books, LLC. Excerpts from *Farewell to Manzanar* by Jeanne W. Houston and James D. Houston. Copyright ©1973 by James D. Houston, renewed 2001 by Jeanne Wakatsuki Houston and James D. Houston. Used with permission of Recorded Books.

Russell & Volkening, Inc. "Untying the Knot," reprinted by the permission of Russell & Volkening as agents for the author. Copyright ©1974 by Annie Dillard, renewed in 2002 by Annie Dillard.

Seymour Agency LLC. "A Brief History of the Short Story" by D. F. McCourt, from AE Sci Fi, http://aescifi.ca/index.php/non-fiction/37-editorials/792-a-brief-history-of-the-short-story?tmpl=component&print=1&layout=default&page=. Used with permission of the author and Seymour Agency.

Shihab Nye, Naomi. "Hamadi," by permission of the author, Naomi Shihab Nye, 2015. First appeared in *America Street*.

Simon & Schuster, Inc. "Old Man at the Bridge," reprinted with the permission of Scribner, a division of Simon & Schuster, Inc. from *The Short Stories of Earnest Hemingway* by Ernest Hemingway. Copyright ©1938 by Ernest Hemingway. Copyright renewed 1966 by Mary Hemingway. All rights reserved.

Skyhorse Publishing. Excerpted from *Democracy is Not a Spectator Sport* by Arthur Blaustein with the permission of Skyhorse Publishing, Inc.

Sleight Brennan, Sandra. Giving Women the Vote by Sandra Sleight-Brennan ©Sandra Sleight-Brennan.

Sterling Lord Literistic, Inc. "A Literature of Place," reprinted by permission of SLL/Sterling Lord Literistic, Inc. Copyright by Barry Holstun Lopez.

Susan Bergholz Literary Services. "Antojos," Copyright ©1991 by Julia Alvarez. Later published in slightly different form in *How the Garcia Girls Lost Their Accents* by Algonquin Books of Chapel Hill. By permission of Susan Bergholz Literary Services, New York, NY and Lamy, NM. All rights reserved.

Symphony Space. "Everyday Use" by Alice Walker, as performed by Carmen de Lavallade at Symphony Space on January 19, 1994. Courtesy of Symphony Space.

Syracuse University Press. *Arthur C. Parker on the Iroquois: Iroquois Uses of Maize and Other Food Plants, The Code of Handsome Lake; The Seneca Prophet, The Constitution of the Five Nations* by Arthur Parker. Copyright ©1981. Used with permission of Syracuse University Press.

Tarbell, Ida. "What a Factory Can Teach a Housewife" by Ida Tarbell, *The Association Monthly*, Volume X (February 1916–February 1917).

Television Academy Foundation. George Takei on the Japanese internment camps during WWII ©Television Academy Foundation.

The White House Photo Office. Richard Blanco reading 2013 inaugural poem courtesy of The White House.

U.S. Supreme Court. "Supreme Court Decision / Chief Justice Earl Warren's opinion, Brown v. Board of Education, 347 U.S. 483 (1954).

University of New Mexico Press (Rights). From *The Way to Rainy Mountain* by N. Scott Momaday. Copyright ©1969 University of New Mexico Press, 1969.

University of Pittsburgh Press. "For Black Women Who Are Afraid" from *Tender*, by Toi Derricotte, ©1997. Reprinted by permission of the University of Pittsburgh Press.

Venture Literary. From *The United States Constitution: A Graphic Adaptation* by Jonathan Hennessey, illustrated by Aaron McConnell. Copyright 2008. Used with permission of Venture Literary, Inc.

W. W. Norton & Co. "Who Burns for the Perfection of Paper," from *city of coughing and dead radiators* by Martin Espada. Copyright ©1993 by Martin Espada. Used by permission of W. W. Norton & Company, Inc.

Writers' Representatives, Inc. From *America's Constitution: A Biography* by Akhil Amar. Copyright ©2005. Used by permission of Akhil Amar c/o Writers Representatives LLC, New York, NY 10011. All rights reserved.

Wylie Agency. Excerpt from "Books as Bombs: Why the women's movement needed 'The Feminine Mystique'" by Louis Menand, originally published in *The New Yorker*. Copyright ©2011 by Louis Menand, used by permission of The Wylie Agency LLC.; *The Crucible* by Arthur Miller. Copyright ©1952, 1953, 1954 by Arthur Miller, copyright renewed © 1980, 1981, 1982 by Arthur Miller, used by permission of The Wylie Agency LLC.; "Everything Stuck to Him" by Raymond Carver, collected in *What We Talk About When We Talk About Love*. Copyright ©1974, 1976, 1977, 1978, 1980, 1981 by Raymond Carver; 1989 by Tess Gallagher, used by her permission; "The Man to Send Rain Clouds" from *Storyteller* by Leslie Marmon Silko. Copyright ©1981, 2012 by Leslie Marmon Silko, used by permission of The Wylie Agency LLC.; "Housepainting" by Lan Samantha Chang. Copyright ©1995 by Lan Samantha Chang, used by permission of The Wylie Agency LLC.

Yale University Press. From "Mary Chesnut's Civil War" by Mary Chesnut edited by C. Vann Woodward. Copyright © 1981 by C. Vann Woodward, Sally Bland Metts, Barbara G. Carpenter, Sally Bland Johnson, and Katherine W. Herbert. All rights reserved. Used by permission of the publisher, Yale University Press.

Copyright © SAVVAS Learning Company LLC. All Rights Reserved.

Credits